Acclaim for Men at Work by George F. Will

"*Men at Work* goes up on my sho ⬜ P9-CRL-493 ...t...
hit—a triple off the center-field wall, perhaps ... ...uch for
me to do here except join the standing O. . . . Will is a talented listener,
but the best voice in this book is his own. . . . Baseball rewards the stayer,
and I am delighted to have stayed around long enough to receive this fresh
gift from the game."   —Roger Angell, *The New Yorker*

"**There is something to learn on every page. The sweep and range is
without precedent**. Will himself is a craftsman of considerable magnitude,
an angel at the typewriter."   —*Chicago Tribune*

"**Will has well honored this fragile, elegant, rough, exacting sport**.
[The players and managers] talked with full and fine intelligence about
their artful labors to a man who knew what questions to ask."
      —*New York Times Book Review*

"**Gets my vote as this season's baseball book of choice.**"
      —Frederick C. Klein, *Wall Street Journal*

"**Terrific**. . . . [Will got] himself invited to sessions that a mere sportswriter wouldn't have been allowed near. And clearly he did a lot of
interviewing, extracting information that even the best-informed baseball
fan will find illuminating."   —Joseph Nocera, *New Republic*

"**Will defends the game as eloquently as anyone who ever collected
a bubblegum card or caught a foul ball**. *Men at Work* is not an ivory
tower book. Will crisscrossed America's locker rooms in search of baseball's secrets."   —*Los Angeles Times*

"**Hardcore baseball presented in a fluent style**. Sure to instill in readers
a greater appreciation of what is required to master the sport at the major
league level, therefore providing a deeper understanding of the foundation
of the game."   —*Library Journal*

"**An amazing book**. . .[with] a quantity of detailed knowledge that is
absolutely astounding. One wonders when George Will has the time to pay
attention to politics."   —*National Review*

"**Endlessly fascinating and revealing**. . . . Will tells you much about
each of these men that you are unlikely to have read in the daily sports
pages, even if you are an avid fan who reads a good sports section
every day."   —*Los Angeles Times Book Review*

"An intelligent book by one of America's most intelligent writers. Will's love for baseball shines through in this witty, insightful look at four of the game's skilled artisans. . . . Will is terrific at getting inside the heads of his subjects and taking the reader there."
— *Cleveland Plain Dealer*

"Absorbing. . . . [Will] combines an incisive writing style with his great love of baseball to offer a gritty look at the skills involved and a greater perspective on the game."   — *San Francisco Chronicle*

"A delight. Will has done his homework and even well-informed fans can gain things from him."   — *Boston Globe*

"A fascinating book which should challenge the most avid fan."
— *Los Angeles Daily News*

"*Men at Work* might stand among the best books written on the mechanics of the game. Will has done a masterful job of reporting, not just in speaking with living masters of the game but in probing the musty depths of baseball history."   — *Richmond Times-Dispatch*

"A rock solid look at the game. Will accomplishes what he no doubt has wanted to do for a long time: write a baseball book with style and authority. He definitely succeeds."   — *Booklist*

"A fascinating book about the serious business of baseball. [Will's] got the intelligence to ask the right questions and the patience to really listen to the answers. . . . A fine piece of work that doesn't take anything for granted."   — *Trenton Times*

"Impressive. . . . Even the most sophisticated of baseball fans is likely to find something new in here. Will has patiently and skillfully plumbed the minds and hearts of his four principal subjects and dozens of others, exacting insights the sources themselves may not have even realized."
— *Christian Science Monitor*

"*Men at Work* has all the sweep of the outfield at the old Polo Grounds. Will's subjects talk shop the way a stonecutter talks marble. Will sees a statue where others see a slab. . . . Like the game itself, Will's book is a team effort and he has managed extremely well."
— *San Diego Tribune*

"Will shows himself to be a master at enticing players into particularly enlightening discussions. The reader is left with a vivid understanding of how the game is played and the extraordinary talent and dedication required."   — *Publishers Weekly*

MEN AT WORK

MEN AT WORK

MEN AT WORK

―――◆―――

The Craft of Baseball

GEORGE F. WILL

HarperPerennial

A Division of HarperCollins*Publishers*

Grateful acknowledgment is made for permission to reprint excerpts from the following:

The Crack-Up by F. Scott Fitzgerald. Copyright 1945 by New Directions Publishing Corporation. Reprinted by permission of New Directions Publishing Corporation.

"The Sporting Scene—Hard Times (The Movie)" by Roger Angell from *The New Yorker*. Copyright © 1988. Reprinted by special permission. All rights reserved.

"Hub Fans Bid Kid Adieu" from *Assorted Prose* by John Updike. Reprinted by permission of Alfred A. Knopf, a division of Random House, Inc.

The Bill James Historical Baseball Abstract by Bill James. Reprinted by permission of Villard Books, a division of Random House, Inc.

"Seven and a Half Cents" from *The Pajama Game*. Reprinted by permission of Richard Adler Music and J. and J. Roth Company. Administered by the Songwriters Guild of America.

The *Bull Durham* screenplay by Ron Shelton. Reprinted courtesy of Orion Pictures Corporation.

A hardcover edition of this book was originally published in 1990 by Macmillan Publishing Company. It is reprinted here by arrangement with Macmillan Publishing Company.

MEN AT WORK. Copyright © 1990 by George F. Will. All rights reserved. Printed in the United States of America. No part of this book may be used or reproduced in any manner whatsoever without written permission except in the case of brief quotations embodied in critical articles and reviews. For information address HarperCollins Publishers, 10 East 53rd Street, New York, NY 10022.

First HarperPerennial edition published 1991.

Library of Congress Cataloging-in-Publication Data

Will, George F.
   Men at work : the craft of baseball / George F. Will. — 1st HarperPerennial ed.
    p. cm.
   Originally published: New York : Macmillan : London : Collier Macmillan, c1990.
   Includes index.
   ISBN 0-06-097372-2 (pbk.)
   1. Baseball—United States—History   I. Title.
GV863.A1W53   1991b
796.357'0973—dc20   90-55518
ISBN 0-06-097372-2

94 95 RRD 10 9 8 7 6 5 4 3 2

To GEOFFREY MARION WILL

". . . and here's the pitch. There's a sharply hit ground
ball to second . . . Geoffrey Will's got it . . ."

"There's a lot of stuff goes on."
—TONY LA RUSSA

CONTENTS

———◆———

INTRODUCTION

———◆———

The Hard Blue Glow

A few years ago, in the Speaker's Dining Room in the U.S. Capitol, a balding, hawk-nosed Oklahoma cattleman rose from the luncheon table and addressed his host, Tip O'Neill. The man who rose was Warren Spahn, the winningest left-hander in the history of baseball. Spahn was one of a group of former All-Stars who were in Washington to play in an old-timers' game. Spahn said: "Mr. Speaker, baseball is a game of failure. Even the best batters fail about 65 percent of the time. The two Hall of Fame pitchers here today [Spahn, 363 wins, 245 losses; Bob Gibson, 251 wins, 174 losses] lost more games than a team plays in a full season. I just hope you fellows in Congress have more success than baseball players have."

The fellows in Congress don't, and they know it. There are no .400 hitters in Washington. And players in the game of government are spared the sort of remorselessly objective measurement of their performance that ball players see in box scores every day. But Washington does have lots of baseball fans. In October, 1973, Potter Stewart, Associate Justice of the Supreme Court and avid Cincinnati Reds fan, was scheduled to hear oral arguments at the time of the Reds-Mets play-off game. He asked his clerks to pass him batter-by-batter bulletins. One read: "Kranepool flies to right. Agnew resigns." (Baseball also holds the attention of people at the other end of the system of justice. When Richard T. Cooper, a murderer, was on the threshold of California's death chamber, his final remarks included: "I'm very unhappy about the Giants.")

Because baseball is a game of failure, and hence a constantly

1

humbling experience, it is good that the national government is well stocked with students of the national pastime. There also is a civic interest served by having the population at large leavened by millions of fans. They are spectators of a game that rewards, and thus elicits, a remarkable level of intelligence from those who compete. To be an intelligent fan is to participate in something. It is an activity, a form of appreciating that is good for the individual's soul, and hence for society.

Proof of the genius of ancient Greece is that it understood baseball's future importance. Greek philosophers considered sport a religious and civic—in a word, moral—undertaking. Sport, they said, is morally serious because mankind's noblest aim is the loving contemplation of worthy things, such as beauty and courage. By witnessing physical grace, the soul comes to understand and love beauty. Seeing people compete courageously and fairly helps emancipate the individual by educating his passions.

Being a serious baseball fan, meaning an informed and attentive and observant fan, is more like carving than whittling. It is doing something that makes demands on the mind of the doer. Is there any other sport in which the fans say they "take in" a game? As in, "Let's take in a game tomorrow night." I think not. That is a baseball locution because there is a lot to ingest and there is time—although by no means too much time—to take it in.

Of all the silly and sentimental things said about baseball, none is sillier than the description of the game as "unhurried" or "leisurely." Or (this from folks at the serious quarterlies) that baseball has "the pace of America's pastoral past." This is nonsense on stilts. Any late-twentieth-century academic who thinks that a nineteenth-century farmer's day was a leisurely, unhurried stroll from sunup to sundown needs a reality transplant. And the reality of baseball is that the action involves blazing speeds and fractions of seconds. Furthermore, baseball is as much a mental contest as a physical one. The pace of the action is relentless: There is barely enough time between pitches for all the thinking that is required, and that the best players do, in processing the changing information about the crucial variables.

In a sense, sports are not complicated. Even the infield fly rule can be mastered, in time, without a master's degree from MIT. The object of a sport can be put simply. You put a ball in an end zone or through a hoop, or you put a puck in a net, and prevent the other fellows from doing so. Sports are not complicated in their objectives, but in execution they have layers of complexities and nuances. There is a lot of thought involved, however much many players deny or disguise that fact. When Dizzy Dean heard, before the 1934 World Series, that the Tigers' manager, Mickey Cochrane, was conducting a series of team meetings, Dean said, "If them guys are thinking, they're as good as licked right now." (The Cardinals beat the Tigers in seven games.) But even in his era Dean was one of baseball's cartoon characters, a caricature sent up from central casting, a Ring Lardner creation come to life. And certainly Dean bore no resemblance to most of the men who rise to the top of today's baseball and stay there for a while.

It has been said that the problem with many modern athletes is that they take themselves seriously and their sport lightly. That can not be said of the men discussed in this book. This book treats the elements of the game by examining four men in terms of functions dictated by the order of the game. A manager assembles a team, trains it, devises a lineup for a particular game and controls his team's conduct during the game. A pitcher throws the ball, a batter hits it, a fielder handles it. During the time I was writing this book I attended games and conducted interviews in 11 major league cities, from Canada to Southern California. I liken the experience to being guided through an art gallery by a group of patient docents who were fine painters and critics. Such tutors teach the skill of seeing. To see, to really *see* what a painter has put on canvas requires learning to think the way the painter thought. My baseball guides have been players, managers, coaches, front office personnel, writers, broadcasters and others of the small community of baseball.

Many players do not practice what they preach. They preach a simplicity sharply at odds with their real attention to the fine points. A pitcher will say, "I just try to move the ball around and throw strikes." A hitter will describe himself as of the "see ball, hit ball" school. But when players are prompted to talk about what they do, the complexity emerges. Baseball is an exacting profession with a technical vocabulary and a distinctive mode of reasoning. It involves constant attention to the law of cumulation, which is: A lot of little things add up, through 162 games, 1,458 innings, to big differences. A 162-game season is, like life, an exercise in cumulation.

It was an architect who said that God is in the details. It could have been a professional athlete, particularly a baseball player, most likely a catcher. Catchers, who have the game arrayed in front of them and are in on every pitch, not only work harder than other everyday players, they are required to think more. Ten of the 26 major league managers on Opening Day, 1989, had done some catching in their playing careers. It was, naturally, a catcher (Wes Westrum of the New York Giants) who said that baseball is like church: "Many attend but few understand."

Rick Dempsey, a catcher, is the sort of player whose natural skills were never such that he looked like a candidate for longevity in the major leagues. Yet 1989 was his twenty-first season. He is the sort of player often called a journeyman, and he certainly has journeyed, from Minnesota to the Yankees to the Orioles to the Indians, and in the spring of 1988 he talked his way into a tryout with the Dodgers. In the autumn he was in the World Series. It was his third Series. He played in all seven games of the Orioles' loss to the Pirates in 1979 and was the MVP of the 1983 Series in which the Orioles beat the Phillies in five games. Talking to Roger Angell of *The New Yorker* at the 1988 Series, Dempsey made clear the mental makeup that makes for survival in baseball:

> You have to play this game right. You have to think right. You're not trying to pull the ball all the time. You're not thinking, Hey, we're going to kill them tomorrow—because that may not happen. You're not looking to do something all on your own. You've got to take it one game at a time, one hitter at a time. You've got to go on doing the things you've talked about and agreed about beforehand. You can't get three outs at a time or five runs at a time. You've got to concentrate on each play, each hitter, each pitch. All this makes the game much slower and much clearer. It breaks it down to its smallest part. If you take the game like that—one pitch, one hitter, one inning at a time, and then one *game* at a time—the next thing you know, you look up and you've won.

———◆———

Winning is not everything. Baseball—its beauty, its craftsmanship, its exactingness—is an *activity* to be loved, as much as ballet or fishing or politics, and loving it is a form of participation. But this book is not about romance. Indeed, it is an antiromantic look at a game that brings out the romantic in the best of its fans.

A. Bartlett Giamatti was to the Commissioner's office what Sandy

Koufax was to the pitcher's mound: Giamatti's career had the highest ratio of excellence to longevity. If his heart had been as healthy as his soul—if his heart had been as strong as it was warm—Giamatti would one day have been ranked among commissioners the way Walter Johnson is ranked (by correct thinkers) among pitchers: as the best, period. Baseball's seventh commissioner, who was the first to have taught Renaissance literature at Yale, was fond of noting the etymological fact that the root of the word "paradise" is an ancient Persian word meaning "enclosed park or green." Ballparks exist, he said, because there is in humanity "a vestigial memory of an enclosed green space as a place of freedom or play." Perhaps. Certainly ballparks are pleasant places for the multitudes. But for the men who work there, ballparks are for hard, sometimes dangerous, invariably exacting business. Physically strong and fiercely competitive men make their living in those arenas. Most of these men have achieved, at least intermittently, the happy condition of the fusion of work and play. They get physical pleasure and emotional release and fulfillment from their vocation. However, Roy Campanella's celebrated aphorism—that there has to be a lot of little boy in a man who plays baseball—needs a corollary. There has to be a lot of hardness in a man who plays—who works at—this boys' game.

Success in life has been described as the maintained ecstasy of burning with a hard, gemlike flame. The image recurs. In his famous essay on Ted Williams's final game, "Hub Fans Bid Kid Adieu," John Updike wrote of Williams radiating "the hard blue glow of high purpose." Updike said, "For me, Williams is the classic ballplayer of the game on a hot August weekday before a small crowd, when the only thing at stake is the tissue-thin difference between a thing done well and a thing done ill." Baseball, played on a field thinly populated with men rhythmically shifting from languor to tension, is, to Updike's eyes, an essentially lonely game. The cool mathematics of individual performances are the pigments coloring the long season of averaging out. Baseball heroism comes not from flashes of brilliance but rather, Updike says, from "the players who always *care*," about themselves and their craft.

The connection between character and achievement is one of the fundamental fascinations of sport. Some say that sport builds character. Others say that sport reveals character. But baseball at its best puts good character on display in a context of cheerfulness. Willie Stargell, the heart of the order during the Pirates' salad days in the

1970s, insisted that baseball is, or at any rate ought to be, fun. Walking wearily through the Montreal airport after a night game, he said, "I ain't complaining. I asked to be a ball player." Indeed, it is likely that a higher percentage of ball players than of plumbers or lawyers or dentists or almost any other group are doing what they passionately enjoy doing. On another occasion Stargell said, "The umpire says 'Play ball,' not 'Work ball.' " (Actually, the rule book requires the umpire to call out only the word "play.") But professional baseball is work.

Happiness has been called "the sweet exaltation of work." What follows are the stories of four men who are happy in their work. From an appreciation of that work, many millions of people derive a happiness worth pursuing. This book is intended to help that pursuit. It also is a deep bow, not just to the particular players about whom I have written, but to all the baseball people who transmit the game, remarkably intact, through the whirl of American change. This book is a thank-you note. There is a book with the wonderful title *Baseball, I Gave You the Best Years of My Life.* What do we spectators give baseball besides the price of a seat and the respect implicit in paying attention? Baseball's best practitioners give in return the gift of virtues made vivid. This gift is a thing of beauty and joy forever, or at least until the next game, which is much the same thing as forever because the seasons stretch into forever. Yes, I know, I know. Even the continents drift. Nothing lasts. But baseball does renew itself constantly as youth comes knocking at the door, and in renewal it becomes better. To see why this is so, come along and see some baseball men at work.

1

THE MANAGER

———◆———

Tony La Russa, On Edge

On August 13, 1910, there was a baseball game of perfect symmetry. The Pirates and Dodgers played to an 8–8 tie. Each team had 38 at bats. Each had 13 hits. Each had 12 assists. Each had 5 strikeouts, 3 walks, 2 errors, 1 hit batsman and 1 passed ball.

Still, dissect any game, even that one, deeply enough and you will reveal layers of asymmetries. In most games these asymmetries cancel each other out. In most games victory is within reach of each team in the middle innings. Most games are won by small things executed in a professional manner.

It is a manager's job to prepare his team to play in such a manner. He is responsible for wringing the last drop of advantage from the situations that will occur in each game. To do this he must know the abilities his players have revealed in their past performances and he must have similar knowledge of the players in the opposite dugout. Every player has a past that reveals his skills, limitations, tendencies. You can look it up, especially if you have been disciplined about writing it down. And teams, too, have tendencies.

Ray Miller, whom we shall meet again, is the Pittsburgh Pirates' pitching coach. He is also a philosopher and scientist, or philosophical scientist. He says that baseball managers today are "very tendency-prone." Right, Ray. The most important and recurring word in the language of thoughtful baseball people is "tendency." In the sport of the long season, of thousands of innings and scores of thousands of pitches, tendencies tell. There is ample scope for the useful calculation of probabilities. As Bill James, the baseball writer from

Winchester, Kansas, notes, you don't see anyone keeping score at a football game. Baseball fans filling out a scorecard are not really noting the score. Rather, they are recording everything that produces or fails to produce a score. They can do this because, as James says, baseball is the game in which the players take turns. The action stops as players pause at particular points. This is the exacting orderliness that makes possible baseball's rich, thick statistical data base. And the data base must be constantly kept up to date by contemporary observation. Many years ago a baseball writer, puzzled by the positioning of a Mets infielder when Henry Aaron was at bat, asked Mets manager Wes Westrum, "Doesn't Aaron hit to right and right-center?" Westrum tersely replied, "Not this year."

At 1:30 in the afternoon on a muggy Monday in Boston the Oakland Athletics are working on their data base. Tony La Russa and three aides are working in the small, spartan, dull beige office used by the visiting team's manager, just off the larger but still cramped room where the team dresses. There will be a game tonight at Fenway Park and the pulse of the park is quickening. For the men in La Russa's office the atmosphere is like that inside a cramped bunker during a day of desultory shelling at Verdun. The booming cannons echoing in the concrete cubicle are actually beer kegs being unloaded, none too gently, off trucks and onto Fenway's concrete floors on the other side of the cubicle's wall. The only soft sound is the splat of tobacco juice into paper cups. (Red Man and Skoal Bandits are the preferred "smokeless tobaccos." David sunflower seeds and Bazooka bubble gum—not at the same time, please—are preferred by the younger generation.)

That is not a sound often heard in the management suites of major corporations. However, it is important to remember that a baseball manager is management. True, he also is in the ranks with the players—labor, if you will—in the sense that he is an active participant in a competition for two to three hours on game days. But all day, every day, in season or out, he is management. If a baseball club were to develop the corporate culture comparable to that of, say, IBM—and the Athletics are the most likely to do that—it would, in the best business school manner, draw up a job description for the office of manager. It would find in that function five component parts.

First, the manager participates in the formation of the 24-man roster (usually 10 pitchers and 14 players) and the farm system that develops talent, and the scouting and drafting of young players for that system. The club's general manager and his associates can not do this without close consultation with the manager. They must consider his preferred style of play. And the manager must, in turn, be prepared to modify his preferences to fit available personnel.

The manager's second function is to prepare the 24 players to play. That involves giving them the relevant information about opponents. It also involves taking care that all 24 players are used often enough to maintain high morale and to have role players ready to replace injured regulars. Third, the manager must provide himself and his coaches with data useful for decisions during the game. Fourth, the manager must manage the players in game situations. The fifth function is far more important than it was even just a few years ago. It is to represent the team to the public, in countless press and broadcast interviews before each game and in a general debriefing and assessment immediately after each game. These interviews, which require equal and huge amounts of patience and delicacy, do much to define the team to its public. And they reverberate back into the clubhouse and affect morale.

This day, in Boston, the manager is seated at a metal desk dreary enough to be government-issue. He is wearing socks but no shoes, jeans but no shirt and a frown of concentration. On the desk is *The Elias Baseball Analyst*. With La Russa are Lach, Dunc and Schu. Frenchy will filter in and out.

Rene Lachemann, former manager of the Mariners and Brewers, is the 1988 Athletics' first-base coach. He is halfway dressed in his uniform—pants and undershirt—and on his feet are shower clogs. He chews tobacco and swears constantly, almost musically, using the strongest language to express or embellish even the mildest thoughts and feelings. Dave Duncan, a former catcher, is the Athletics' pitching coach. Tall, quiet and reserved, he speaks almost always in a tone high school teachers use to sedate unruly classes. Duncan has the demeanor of a deacon. He is in full uniform. So is Ron Schueler, whose official title is Special Assistant to the Vice President, Baseball Operations. Schueler is a jack of many trades and a master of one of baseball's modern trades, that of advance scout. He has been in Boston watching the Boston Red Sox play the Mariners. Jim Lefebvre, a.k.a. Frenchy, is the third-base coach and hitting instructor. He was National League Rookie of the Year in 1965 with the Dodgers, and was named to the National League All-Star team in 1966. By 1973 he was playing in Japan. He is a man of overflowing ebullience. It sometimes seems that he can not negotiate a sentence without laughing somewhere in the course of it. Of course that is subject to change because during the 1988–89 off-season he was sentenced to serve as manager of the Seattle Mariners.

As the beer kegs bounce and rumble on the other side of the wall, the sound in the room is the soft murmur of men swapping information. Duncan does most of the talking. La Russa listens, occasionally questioning or commenting, constantly writing notes in a tiny, meticulous shorthand. This meeting amounts to panning for gold, sifting mountains of mere gravel, one panful at a time, looking for glittering flakes. And finding them. "We threw him 20 first-pitch strikes last year and he swung at one of them," says Duncan about one Red Sox hitter. "I have him with one ground ball to the left side and that was right down the third-base line." "The three fastball hits he got last year were all up, two up in the middle, one on the inside part. He got one, two, three, four, five, six, seven, eight outs on fastballs." "Bankhead [a Seattle Mariners pitcher] struck him out yesterday with curves." "He's a good middle-breaking-pitch hitter—that's his bat speed." "Last year he was trying to go the other way—inside out—with runners on base." "In for effect, out away." "Mac's [Red Sox manager John McNamara] been pitching out." "In sacrifice situations, they tell me, bunt the ball to Dewey [Red Sox first baseman Dwight Evans] because he can't make that throw [back to first base]." "He's showed bunt but doesn't bunt." "In any kind of RBI situation, first pitch he's hacking." The Athletics think they have the sign second baseman Marty Barrett uses to put on a pickoff play. "And [catcher Rick] Cerone and [third baseman Wade] Boggs have a [pickoff] play. They just throw a fastball away and Cerone comes up throwing. They got a guy at third the other day." "He was trying to hit Bankhead to right-center." "Book him." (That means, pitch him "by The Book," which is high and in with fastballs and low and away with breaking balls.)

The meeting is relaxed, quiet, low-key and with little nonsense. It is a steady compilation of small decisions about defensive positioning (". . . second base two strikes to pull . . . shortstop in the hole . . . right fielder toward the line . . . third baseman straight . . .") that will be dispensed to the team in a meeting on defense in about three hours. This is what that meeting sounded like:

DUNCAN: "Walter [Weiss]. The Hriniak approach to hitting. You see consistencies in that, right? The guys that practice his method of hitting, basically, are looking down and out over the plate. Most of those guys are vulnerable to down and in, more so than guys with a conventional approach to hitting.* Another thing about this club is that they are aggressive, swinging early in the count."

LACHEMANN: "With the exception of Boggs."

DUNCAN: "A lot of their young guys are up there hacking, so make quality pitches early in the count. If you make good pitches early in the count you can get them out without throwing a lot of pitches to them and getting them to hit your pitches. Burks. He's a bad breaking-ball hitter. He's a dead high fastball hitter. You can jam him, get in on him good with fastballs, you can go down and away with fastballs. Keep it down, throw him a lot of off-speed pitches."

RON HASSEY, formerly of the White Sox, who is the Athletics' catcher tonight: "I remember him going deep [hitting a home run] when I was with Chicago, with a fastball."

DUNCAN: "The fastball to him is basically a purpose pitch [that is, not meant to be hit but rather to set up another pitch]."

On and on and on it goes. Barrett, says Duncan, is a "guess hitter" so change the pattern of pitches. Lachemann warns Hassey, "Don't let him peek on you," meaning that Lachemann thinks Barrett likes to sneak looks back at the catcher giving the signs, or at least location. Lachemann says, "Schu says he's hot." So jam him inside, but the only pitch he can hit off The Wall (the Green Monster, Fenway Park's left-field wall) is an inside pitch that misses a bit out over the plate. Hassey says, yes, when Barrett closes his stance it means he wants to shoot the ball the other way. But Barrett knows teams are pitching him inside so he's opening up and hitting down the left-field line. With Boggs, take it for granted until late in the game or an RBI situation that he will take the first strike. So get the first strike with a fastball down the middle. Evans is a Hriniak protégé, looking for thigh-high out and away. Go by The Book: hard stuff up and in, keep the breaking stuff down and use them early in the count. On

---

*In 1988 Walt Hriniak was the Red Sox batting coach. In 1989 he became the White Sox batting coach. The "Hriniak approach," which will be discussed later, has a pedigree that traces to the late Charlie Lau. Lau's name will crop up several times in these pages, as it continually does in baseball conversations. When La Russa managed the White Sox he hired Lau as a coach. La Russa has enormous respect for Hriniak as a teacher and he believes that the Lau-Hriniak style of hitting makes batters less vulnerable to pitchers' wiles than any other style. It produces the best coverage of the plate by the bat. Also, it leaves pitchers with only a few ways to attack the batter, and those ways are difficult to execute.

Greenwell, anything you do inside has got to be off the plate or it is going to be out of the park. Hassey says, let's get the first strike with a breaking ball, then use the fork ball and mix the fastball in and out. When he starts diving for the outside pitch, bust him inside. Cerone is hot, swinging at a lot of first pitches. But his bat speed right now is slow, so he might not be able to get around on fastballs.

Jim Lefebvre, talking to the hitters about Red Sox pitchers, says Jeff Sellers has not pitched for ten days and has been erratic even when pitching regularly. He will give up walks "so be a professional hitter—make him throw strikes." Lefebvre asks Don Baylor, formerly with the Red Sox, if he can add anything. He can: "He's [Sellers] 3-and-2 on every hitter who goes up there. One night he was 3-and-2 on nine hitters. His fastball sails, almost like a cutter. He doesn't know why, whether he's holding the ball cross-seams or whatever." (A cut fastball is not, as the name might seem to suggest, a scuffed ball. Rather, it is a semi-slider, a fastball that runs because the pitcher "cuts" his delivery, turning his wrist a bit to pull down through the ball when releasing it.) And, Baylor adds, reliever Dennis Lamp's slider is not quite up to the name. It is a "slurve." He is throwing a lot of four-seam fastballs. (A four-seamer is gripped in such a way that it comes out of the hand rotating so that four seams instead of just two are spinning into the air that piles up in front of the ball. This gives maximum motion to the ball.) Baylor continues on Lamp. "He's been called for four balks. Run on him."

Lefebvre mentions that Red Sox reliever Bob Stanley is still living down the wild pitch he threw in the sixth game of the 1986 World Series. "He faced one hitter yesterday and 33,000 people booed him." Anyone know pitcher John Trautwein? Walt Weiss says he faced him last year in Triple-A ball. Watch his backdoor slider (that is a slider that starts outside and slices in over the outside corner of the plate). Lefebvre warns the team to be "alive when on third. Cerone has a new pickoff move with Boggs." Duncan reminds his relief pitchers that Brady Anderson, like most Hriniak-influenced hitters, likes to dive out for the down-and-away pitch, so he is vulnerable to the down-and-in pitch. Barrett flashes the pitch signs—fastball or breaking ball—to the Red Sox outfielders and it is possible for someone in the Athletics' bull pen to read Barrett's signs and relay them—by, say, crossing or uncrossing his arms—to the bench or batter.

There is more, much more, but you get the picture. It is a pointillist painting, lots of dots of information resulting in a filled canvas, a portrait of the Red Sox. The proper way to view a pointillist painting is to stand back far enough to permit your eyes to see the points of color blend into forms with sharp lines and clear shades and shadings. Standing back is what the manager and his coaches do before they step onto the field.

Usually the Athletics' bus leaves the hotel heading for the park at 5:00 P.M., but this is the first game of the first series of the season with the Red Sox, so the middle infielders and center fielders have come to the park early for a series of meetings. The first meeting is about what La Russa considers the first order of business: "How to get guys out." Does that mean how to pitch to them? Not really. It means, primarily, defensive positioning. (As we shall see when it is Cal Ripken's turn to speak, pitching and defensive positioning are parts of a single piece of music written as a duet. No soloist can play baseball properly.) With players seated on a tatty couch, folding chairs and the floor, Duncan calls the meeting to order.

DUNCAN: "Burks. Right-handed hitter. Third base, we play him straight. Shortstop, we play him to pull. Second baseman will be up the middle until there's two strikes on him and then we'll move back to straightaway. [With two strikes, Burks will be more tentative, more defensive, less free-swinging, with a more compact stroke.] First base will be slightly off the line. Shortstop, stay in the hole with two strikes. Left field, we play him straight. Center field, we play him to the left-field side, right fielder plays him straight."

LEFEBVRE INTERRUPTS: "He's a stolen base threat."

A PLAYER: "Does he steal third?" The answer is yes. ANOTHER PLAYER ASKS: "Will he bunt?" The consensus is "both ways," meaning first- and third-base lines.

DUNCAN: "Barrett, straight at third. Shortstop is going to play Barrett a couple of steps up the middle. Second base is going to play him straight. First base about a step off the line."

LACHEMANN INTERRUPTS: "Second base be alive with a runner on first base and less than two outs."

DUNCAN ELABORATES: "He'll try to shoot the ball that way. Be ready to go into the hole."

A PLAYER: "Doesn't he hit most of the balls in the air that way?"

DUNCAN: "He does. Outfield. We're going to shade the left fielder toward left-center. Center fielder is going to be on the right-field side of straightaway. The right fielder is going to be straight."

LA RUSSA: "He's a hit-and-run threat but you have a tough call playing second because of Burks and the stolen base threat. Who is covering and how quickly do you leave?" (Barrett is a right-hander, and normally in a stealing situation with a right-hander up the second baseman would cover. But Barrett likes to "shoot the ball" through the hole between second and first with the first baseman holding the runner on, so the second baseman should not leave his station too soon.)

DUNCAN: "Boggs: Third base is off the line. Shortstop and second base both, we're going to pinch the middle [that is, move the short-stop to his left and the second baseman to his right, each closer to the imaginary line that bisects the diamond]. First baseman straight. In the outfield, left fielder straight, center fielder to the left-field side. Right fielder is going to play slightly toward center field. Evans: Straight all the way around the infield. Straight in left. Center, barely off straightaway to the left-field side. The right fielder will shade just a little to right-center. Greenwell: Left-handed hitter. Straight at third. To the middle strong at shortstop on Greenwell. Not a shift but a strong to the middle. Second base play him a step to pull. First base is going to be straight on him. So Walter [Weiss, shortstop], you just have to get strong to the middle on him. And a slight pull at second base. Horn: Left-handed hitter. All right, we're going to shift on him. Third base off the line. Walter, you get directly behind second base. Second base will be playing normal pull. First base straight pull."

A PLAYER: "What position does he play?"

LACHEMANN: "He's a fucking DH. He don't have no fucking position. Big guy."

DUNCAN: "In the outfield we're going to give him the left-field line. The center fielder is going to be about five steps over into right-center. And the right fielder will play a straight pull. Is that right, Hendu? [Dave Henderson, who played with the Red Sox for several seasons, nods.] Rice: We're off the line at third and first. And we're straightaway at the middle infield positions. We're just kind of crimping the hole a little bit on him. Anderson: Left-handed hitter. Third baseman is going to play off the line, just a little bit, even with the bag. Shortstop will play a step up the middle, second base straight, first baseman straight. In the outfield we're straight, on the right-field side."

A PLAYER: "Will he bunt?"

ANOTHER PLAYER: "Yeah. He was their leadoff man when Burks was down."

A THIRD PLAYER: "Who do they like to hit-and-run with?"

LACHEMANN: "Last year I got Barrett on tape—I don't know if he's still doing the same thing—put on his own hit-and-run. He'd rub the end of the bat, that tells the runner on first."

HENDERSON: "That's what I had with him."

A PLAYER: "He won't count on you [Henderson] remembering." (General laughter.)

DUNCAN: "Benzinger: Switch-hitter, hitting left-handed. Off the line at third. How strong in the middle do you think we ought to play him? Fairly strong up the middle?"

HENDERSON: "Up the middle to pull. Not like a Greenwell."

DUNCAN: "Two or three steps to the middle. Slight pull at second base. Straight at first. Bunch the outfield and play him on the right-field side. Play him just the opposite of hitting right-handed."

LACHEMANN: "You guys out there in center field, you gotta be backing up hits off the fucking Wall all the fucking time. If you go back to the fucking Wall, the other guy's gotta come over and help you."

HENDERSON: "You've got to make a decision early. If you're going for the ball, go for it so the other guy can tail off [that is, play a carom off The Wall if the ball is not caught]."

Some bits of information tossed about in these meetings this day concerned how the Red Sox played the previous few days against the Mariners. These bits came from Ron Schueler. As the team's advance scout, he sees the team that the Athletics will play next, or a team the Athletics will play soon. An advance scout reports back to the manager by telephone or in writing or, as in this case, in person. His subject is the upcoming opponent's tendencies. Advance scouts are paid to be tendency-prone. Such a scout is a sort of spy, but he is quite open about it. In fact, there is a nice camaraderie among such intelligence agents as they sit behind the screen behind home plate in every major league park. They are armed with stopwatches to time pitchers' and catchers' release times (we shall deal with this shortly) and batters' times running to first base. They also have charts and, sometimes, radar guns to time the velocity of pitches. The lap-top computer, the fax machine and Federal Express might all have been invented for advance scouts. All these modern marvels are used by them.

Sitting in Montreal, later in the summer, thinking about the Giants' next series, against Houston in San Francisco, Roger Craig, the Giants' manager, said he was most interested in what his advance scout could tell him about the other team's manager. "When we get home we'll have a report by Federal Express. I'll look at whether Astros manager Hal Lanier runs Gerald Young on the first pitch a lot, or if he'll hit-and-run Bill Doran with the count 2–1, or if he'll put Billy Hatcher on his own to run even when he's at second base." This interest in the other manager is related to the fact that Craig calls more pitchouts than any other major league manager. This use that Craig makes of advance scouts illustrates why the Athletics scout themselves, in this sense: They keep track of what they tend to do in particular situations. For example, runner on third, no one out. How many times has the situation occurred recently? What did the Athletics do? What worked? Tracking such situations is La Russa's way of scouting La Russa. He detects his own tendencies before he becomes so predictable that other managers notice and adjust. "If I always hit-and-run on 1–0, they are going to pitch out on 1–0."

Tony Kubek, the shortstop-turned-broadcaster, credits Casey Stengel with inventing the advance scout. Stengel introduced the pioneer in a Baltimore hotel meeting room. The Yankees were going to face Connie Johnson, a black pitcher. Stengel had sent to Baltimore, in advance of the team, Rudy York, the former slugger for the Tigers. York was famous for his ability to read pitchers. "I'll try," says Kubek with becoming embarrassment, "to make it seem not as racist as it was right then. We had only two black players, Elston Howard and Suitcase Simpson, and Mickey [Mantle] and Whitey [Ford] made it all seem funny. Anyway, York says that when Johnson throws his breaking ball, when he goes above his head with his glove, you see a lot of white. 'You know how those Negroes'—he used another term—'are. They have those white palms.' "

From such a humble beginning (if it really was the beginning; let's assume it was, because baseball likes to nail down details about origins) the advance scout has grown into an important institution. Indeed, after the 1988 World Series we had, briefly, a remarkable phenomenon, the Advance Scout Superstar. A story made the rounds that Kirk Gibson had been able to hit his ninth-inning game-winning home run in game one off Dennis Eckersley because the Dodgers' advance scout had reported this: With a 3–2 count on a left-handed hitter Eckersley always throws backdoor sliders. (Again, that is a slider that looks as though it will be outside but at the last instant bends in over the outside corner.) Gibson is left-handed, the count was 3–2.

Kubek scoffs at this story. Suppose, he says, that in 1988 the advance scout saw Eckersley pitch 15 games, which is probably a lot more than he actually did see. Even in 15 games, how many times did he see Eckersley go 3–2 on a left-handed hitter? (Eckersley's strength in 1988 was throwing strikes, and not getting behind in the count. He walked only 11 batters all season in 72⅔ innings. In 1989 he did even better, giving up just three walks in 57⅔ innings.) Eckersley probably didn't have three occasions all year to throw a 3–2 backdoor slider to a left-hander. Maybe the advance scout saw one of those? Kubek said something like this to that scout during Spring Training, 1989, and the response he got was something between a shrug and a wink.

Kubek, who is a liberal and therefore is as warmhearted as all get out, thinks advance scouts have a right to do a bit of bragging because they are a neglected underclass. They do important work in baseball's shadows. La Russa is understandably less disposed toward sentimentalism about that advance scout or anything else related to Gibson's hit. Speaking even more tersely than usual, La Russa says simply, "Gibson had two strikes on him and was in his emergency stance, shortened up. The only pitch he could hit for power would be something off-speed. Shouldn't have thrown a slider."

That was then. This is now. This is Boston. It is time to be prepared for gathering a different kind of intelligence. In military parlance it is "real time" intelligence, meaning information that can quickly affect the course of an ongoing action. This night one of La Russa's coaches, Bob Watson, will be watching Bill Fischer, the Red Sox pitching coach, who, Watson thinks, handles pitchout signs for the Red Sox.

In 1988 Bob Watson watched the manager or whoever else in the opposing team's dugout was giving the throw-over and pitchout signs. So Rene Lachemann, coaching at first with a runner on first, stood in a position to watch Watson and La Russa in the dugout and warn the runner if a throw-over or pitchout was coming. On the day before this game in Boston, the Athletics had played the Orioles in Baltimore and Watson's watchfulness had been rewarded. Frank

Robinson, the Orioles' manager, had called two pitchouts on consecutive pitches, and Watson had decided he had deciphered Robinson's pitchout sign. That may have saved the game by preventing the Athletics from putting on a hit-and-run play and running into an out on a pitchout.

In the eighth inning, with Carney Lansford the runner on first, and an 0–1 count on batter Stan Javier, La Russa put on a hit-and-run play. Javier, getting the sign from the third-base coach, stepped out of the batter's box and asked (by staring down toward third) the coach to give the sign again. That was a dead giveaway to the Orioles that the Athletics were putting on some sort of play. At that point La Russa and Watson saw Robinson make the sign that Watson was now sure was the Orioles' pitchout sign. So La Russa waved across from the first-base dugout to get the attention of his third-base coach, Lefebvre. La Russa took off the hit-and-run and put on the bunt sign. (La Russa has, on occasion, given a hit-and-run sign to his third-base coach, then called time and conspicuously swept a hand across his chest, as though sweeping off the sign, and then given a second sign to disregard the "takeoff" sign and leave the original play on.) The Orioles did not, in fact, pitch out on the next pitch, probably because Robinson saw La Russa waving and assumed La Russa had broken the code. Javier bunted the runner to second, Canseco drove the run in with a home run. So much for subtlety. But if Lansford had been thrown out by a pitchout on a hit-and-run play, and Javier had made an out, the game might have gone another way.

All that started because Javier was not casual enough while picking up a sign. Some players have a terrible time mastering the art of acting nonchalant when getting a sign to do something demanding—to steal or participate in a hit-and-run play. A few days earlier, in Montreal, Roger Craig had had the same problem with a player. With a Giants runner on third and the pitcher coming to the plate, Craig put on a squeeze play. But the batter, seeing the sign from the third-base coach, did such a double take that Expos manager Buck Rodgers must have known that the Giants were plotting some knavish trick. And Rodgers knows Craig well enough to suspect a squeeze play. So Craig jumped up and made a highly theatrical charade of changing signs—and at the end of that process he put the squeeze play back on.

The Yankees had a nonchalance problem with the young Yogi Berra who, when on first base, was as talkative as a magpie. At least he was talkative until he got the sign that a hit-and-run play was on. Then he would clam up and concentrate. Before long the Yankees noticed that Berra was being thrown out on pitchouts. Opposing teams had noticed his pattern. The Yankees told Yogi to keep quiet all the time when on base. Then the Yankees, realizing the absurdity of that idea, told him to keep talking even after he had had a sign.

"Here is something that has just started," La Russa says, his voice taking on the energy that comes to him when he is describing a new miniwrinkle on an old wrinkle. "The first person I saw use it was Roger Craig against us in Spring Training last year. The second time I saw it was from Tommy Lasorda in the World Series. I don't think anybody in the American League does it, so the A's are going to be the first ones. The third-base coach puts on a sign. Or he doesn't. In any case, he goes through a series of stuff. The hitter reads it. Now the pitcher looks in for the sign from the catcher. The catcher looks in to his manager in the dugout. The manager signals 'throw-over.' The pitcher comes set, throws over. Now, every time you throw over or step off, Roger Craig starts having his third-base coach go through another set of signs. Slows the game down a bit, but it puts an element of doubt in the other manager's mind. Suppose the runner tipped off that he was going and you were in a throw-over or a step-off move. Now the manager who called the throw-over or step-off move says, 'Sonofagun, he's going.' And that manager wants to pitch out. But the other manager has just put on another set of signs. So now the pitcher's manager thinks, 'He [the other manager] saw his runner tip off that he's going. He thinks, maybe I'll pitch out. Did he take it [the runner going] off? Or put it on?' Another element of doubt. Anytime you can get the other side uncertain in its thinking . . ."

In the third-base coach's box in Boston this night Lefebvre will be thinking, when the Athletics have runners on base, about the positioning of the other team's second baseman, first baseman and right fielder. If the right fielder is lined up directly between those two infielders, Lefebvre knows that any ball hit hard enough to get between them is going straight at the right fielder. But if the right fielder is shifted, he would field a hard-hit ball while running at an angle that would make it difficult for him to make a hard, accurate throw to third or home. Therefore it would be a good gamble going for an extra base.

"In baseball," says Lefebvre, "you take nothing for granted. You look after all the little details, or suddenly this game will kick you right in the butt." He remembers the eighth inning of a tied game against the Yankees, when the Athletics had large, lumbering Dave Parker on second with no one out and the right-handed Mark McGwire at bat. The Yankees' right fielder, Dave Winfield, was shaded toward center, playing McGwire deep and to pull. From La Russa came the signal for McGwire to try to hit to the right side. If McGwire put the ball in play to the right he would either move Parker to third on an infield out and Parker could then be scored on a hit or a sacrifice fly, or McGwire could drive the ball through for a hit, in which case the ball would be behind Parker, who would be watching Lefebvre for a sign. Lefebvre, coaching third, would have a decision to make. Parker would be watching Lefebvre for a sign to hold up at third or to try to score. "Now," says Lefebvre, "when McGwire hits to the right side, it's not just a nice little ground ball. It's a line shot." In that game, McGwire drove the ball into right field. Lefebvre weighed Winfield's strong arm against Winfield's difficult task of fielding the ball running back to his left, toward the right-field line, then throwing accurately to the plate. Lefebvre waved Parker around third. Parker scored what turned out to be the winning run.

When coaching third Lefebvre watches the depth of the opposing team's outfielders and watches the opposing team's dugout, looking for the "no doubles" sign, which often is a hand on the back of the coach's head and means the outfielders should play especially deep. He also tries to spot the other team's sign telling the outfielders to throw in to second on any single. That sign means a guaranteed run in a situation like this: One night in Texas the Rangers were leading, 3–2, the Athletics had a runner on second and two outs. Lefebvre saw the throw-to-second sign, so he knew to wave in the runner on any single. The Rangers were acting sensibly: The hitter was the potential lead run. If the Rangers tried and failed to throw out the runner heading home from second, the game would be tied and the lead run would have gone to second on the unavailing throw home.

Generally half an hour before a game, Duncan takes his two catchers, Ron Hassey and Terry Steinbach, into La Russa's office to chat about this and that. In one such meeting in Oakland, Hassey noted that in an at bat the previous night Dwight Evans adjusted well to a particular pitch. Remember, Duncan said, every hitter has a distinctive stance but teams heavily influenced by the theories of the late Charlie Lau almost have a team stance, or at least a team tendency. So there is a general truth about pitching to them: Pitch inside for effect, and away to get them out—that is, inside to discourage them from diving across the plate. A television set overhead was showing a Mets-Padres game in which Benito Santiago, the Padres' cannon-armed catcher, yet again threw from his knees and nailed a runner trying to steal second. "I can't get the ball to third from my knees," said Steinbach with the severe self-judgment that seems to come easily to most athletes at the highest level of this sport.

When Duncan goes to his office he brings a lot of paperwork. His office is the dugout. The paperwork La Russa takes to the dugout is simply a card noting the record of each Red Sox batter against each of the Athletics' relief pitchers. Duncan's paperwork, on the other hand, is in thick three-ring binders that contain his charts.

Duncan's charts on a hitter show what kind of pitches he has hit, where they have been thrown (for example, "mh"—middle of the plate, high), what the counts were, and where the balls were put in play. If a pitch was not put in play the notation might be "kc" (strikeout, called) and where that third strike was ("mi"—middle of the strike zone, inside). A rectangular box represents the strike zone for pitches that have been thrown for strikes and not put into play. These charts record pitches that seem to make the particular hitter uncomfortable; that is probably why the particular hitters have let a lot of these pitches go by.

Duncan also gathers data on "first-pitch tendencies." For example, he has noted that out of 15 first-pitch strikes thrown to one American League outfielder, he swung at 10 of them, and that any pitch on the outside part of the plate is the best way to throw a first-pitch strike to him without him getting a hit. Another chart reveals a player with a strong tendency to take a first pitch if it is a breaking ball, so any curve in the strike zone is apt to start an Athletics pitcher off ahead of this hitter. Duncan's charts are so complete that in Spring Training he can tell his pitchers that the previous season they threw, say, 62 percent of all their first pitches for strikes (he considers 60 to 65 percent good) and he can tell them what percentage of those first-pitch strikes were put into play.

With these charts handy in the dugout, Duncan can, at a glance, see, for example, that a hitter got eight hits off the Athletics last season, seven of them fastballs, all of them in the middle of the plate or inside. On the chart that displays pitches this player has put into play for outs or swung at for strikeouts, Duncan sees a cluster of fastballs and one breaking ball, all down and in, and another smaller cluster of four fastballs and two sliders on the outside corner, belt-high. When he looks at these two charts together he sees that most of the balls this batter is putting into play are down and in, and three out of ten are for hits. If he is a .300 hitter on down and in pitches, pitch him elsewhere. He is putting the ball in play on high and outside pitches, but a low percentage are for hits. Duncan prepares two such sets of charts on each hitter, one for the hitter against left-handers, one against right-handers.

Duncan starts the season with charts on the last 40 at bats of opposing players against the Athletics in the previous season. These charts are slowly retired as the new season generates sufficient fresh data. The charts are produced in a two-step process. A sort of first rough draft of the batter's profile is done during each game by someone sitting in the stands behind home plate. This person measures velocity with a radar gun and notes the location of each pitch. After the game, Duncan fine-tunes this record by watching a tape of the game. He can whiz through a taped game quickly because he is looking only at the other team batting, and he is interested only in pitches that are strikes or that are swung at whether or not they are in the strike zone. In the dugout during the game, when someone gets a hit off the Athletics, Duncan makes a pencil mark on the chart of the playing field, noting where the ball went, and noting also his guess of the kind of pitch (fastball, breaking ball, change-up) and location. These are guesses because the dugout does not provide the best vantage point. The next day, after using tapes of the game to confirm or modify his impressions, Duncan puts the information on the chart in ink.

Duncan has charts for all balls put in play by particular players off Athletics pitching, a chart for those balls put in play to the infield, a chart for those to the outfield. The charts show the kinds of pitches hit and the locations—where they were in the strike zone. Duncan's charts of the strike zone are the clearest possible proof that the *de facto* strike zone no longer bears much resemblance to the *de jure* strike zone spelled out in such precise irrelevance in the rule book. Duncan's chart of the strike zone is divided into three segments.

The top of the top segment is at the hitter's belt. A pitch referred to as "up in the strike zone" is a pitch mid-thigh to belt-high.

Duncan's charts are especially accurate at identifying a hitter in decline. A chart on such a hitter will show that most of the pitches he hits safely are pitches thrown in the middle of the plate. That is, he is hitting only the pitchers' mistakes.

"I don't trust my memory," Duncan says. "That is the main reason I started doing all this. When I was trusting my memory, what I was doing, primarily, was remembering the hits that hurt us. The guy gets a double to right-center field to beat you and it sticks out in your mind. But you forget about those ten balls that he made outs on to left-center field. I wanted to make sure I had in front of me *every* ball he'd hit, not just the ones I remember."

Lefebvre, too, is an ardent believer in La Russa's information-intensive approach to each series in the season. "The aim," he says, "is to make our hitters a little more calculating. Not to tell them how to hit, but to get them thinking about particular pitchers."

Aggressiveness by batters can be devastating for a pitcher whose preferred pattern is to get ahead in the count and then nibble at the strike zone. A team that comes to the plate hacking on first pitches will prevent him from getting comfortable. He will have to start nibbling with the first pitch; he will fall behind in a lot of counts. And suddenly the batting average of the Athletics will be, in effect, 50 points higher. Roger Craig, a former pitcher and now manager of the San Francisco Giants, puts Lefebvre's point this way: "The most important pitch in baseball is strike one. If you're hitting .350 and I get a strike on you, now you've become a .250 hitter if I do my job."

Lefebvre wants to know the sort of information an advance scout can provide. How does a particular pitcher start off particular kinds of hitters? If he misses with his first pitch, is there a pattern to his next pitches? "A lot of pitchers," Lefebvre says, "are what we call 'two-lane' pitchers—sinker in, slider away." One chart on Boggs shows that he took 38 consecutive first pitches from right-handed pitchers. So two things are certain. One is that the pitcher should lay the first pitch to Boggs in, not bothering to nibble or be fancy. The other is that doing so will help only a bit with the best two-strike hitter in baseball. But every little bit helps with a Boggs.

Lefebvre remembers a little nugget of information that was unearthed in a hitters' meeting on a day the Athletics were to face the slow, nibbling "junk" thrown by the Yankees' Tommy John.

"Tommy John did not make his living throwing strikes. He threw mostly borderline pitches and balls. He pitched most guys low-and-away, low-and-away, so for years we told everybody to move up on him. But he only moved his pitches a little farther away. However, Don Baylor had some success by backing up. It forced John to adapt to Baylor, pitch more up, partly because it changed the umpire's perspective of where the ball is [relative to Baylor's strike zone]." The day Baylor told this to the hitters' meeting the Athletics pounded John.

La Russa and Lefebvre say there are six ways a pitcher becomes vulnerable. Three of them are at specific points in the game. The first is when he is facing the first batter in the first inning. The pitcher has felt sharp in the pregame warm-up in the bull pen, but there he faced no batter, no pressure, no umpire. Also, he is not as loose as he was in the pregame warm-ups—not as sure which pitches will be working—and he is working from a different mound. So you want to make the first inning particularly tough, beginning with the leadoff man. He should plant doubts in the pitcher's mind by working the count. If he makes an out he should at least hit the ball hard. That will get the pitcher thinking that he doesn't have all the stuff he thought he had. When La Russa managed the 1989 American League All-Star team, he decided, at the suggestion of Dave Duncan, to bat Bo Jackson in the leadoff spot. La Russa's aim was to make the National League's starting pitcher, Rick Reuschel, as "uncomfortable" as possible as quickly as possible. Jackson hit the second pitch of the game 450 feet for a home run.

The second specific point in the game when the pitcher is vulnerable is whenever he gets two quick outs in an inning and then lets up. "We always think about a 'closer' as someone who finishes a game," says Lefebvre. "A good starting pitcher closes nine times— once an inning." The third time a pitcher is vulnerable is in the fifth inning. "That's decision time," says Lefebvre. "He knows that if he can get through the fifth he can get a decision because he has a bull pen to save him. You see guys start to aim the ball, their velocity goes down, their breaking ball is not as sharp, they get out of that groove."

The fourth and fifth vulnerabilities of pitchers concern unpreparedness, physical and mental. A pitcher who is not in good condition is susceptible to a sudden loss of mastery—a decline in the velocity of his pitches and an inability to control their location. And a pitcher is vulnerable who has not looked at the kind of charts that Duncan keeps. "A guy comes out of the bull pen and sees a batter standing up there and he doesn't know who he is and then throws him a fastball and he hits it nine miles," Lefebvre says. "The pitcher goes into the dugout and says, 'By the way, what does that guy hit?' and the pitching coach tells him, 'The pitch you just threw.' "

The sixth point of vulnerability is, Lefebvre says (somewhat murkily), "when adversity goes against you." Adversity has a way of doing that. He explains what he means: "Bases loaded. Count is 2-and-2. Boom! He throws his best pitch. Umpire says 'ball.' Or the pitcher makes the hitter hit a double-play ball and an infielder boots it. The pitcher loses his concentration. We talk about these things in meetings. We say, 'Stay close to this guy because if something goes wrong, he falls apart.' There are several guys in this league—I mean *stars*—who have their routines. As soon as you break their routines, they get uncomfortable. So we try to figure ways to do that. For example, we get a runner on first base and get very edgy and aggressive."

Of course there are other pitchers you go out of your way not to annoy. Several times during the research for this volume Lefebvre expressed a keen interest in not saying anything that might make Roger Clemens angry. In their pursuit of an edge, teams can overreach. La Russa is a lot like Clemens—short fuse, large charge—and he knows not to make matters worse by making a competitor like Clemens cross. Even smart managers can do foolish things, and that is one.

◆

Managers can do memorable things. On the day in 1944 when the Cubs' Bill Nicholson hit four home runs in a doubleheader against the Giants, Mel Ott, the Giants' manager, ordered Nicholson walked intentionally—with the bases loaded and two outs. Paul Richards (White Sox, 1951–54, 1976; Baltimore, 1955–61) occasionally ordered the pitcher intentionally walked with two outs so the leadoff man would not begin the next inning. But most of the things that managers do that matter do not involve anything particularly noticeable, let alone exotic. For example, writer Leonard Koppett, author of *A Thinking Man's Guide to Baseball*, remembers a routine game in 1965 when, with the score tied with two outs in the bottom of the ninth, the Yankees had a runner on first and the

Yankee batter had a 3–1 count. The pitcher had to get the next pitch over the plate, yet Yankee manager Johnny Keane ordered the batter—to his consternation—to take the pitch. It was, not surprisingly, a strike, producing a full count. However, a full count was exactly what Keane wanted. On a full count with two outs, the runner on first would be running with the pitch, so he would be sure to score on a double. And that is exactly what happened. Had the same hit occurred on a 3–1 count, the runner would not have scored. Besides, the pitcher still wanted to get the 3–2 pitch in the strike zone because a walk would have moved the runner into position to score the winning run on a single.

Obviously managers matter. What is not obvious is how much. It is sometimes said that because players' talents are so thoroughly revealed and rewarded over the course of the long season, managers do not win games other than by assembling the team. But that is a *non sequitur.* Talent is the ability to do some things, not all things. So the right player must be in the right place in the right situation. That is very much the result of good managing.

La Russa played professional baseball until he was 32. He says he should have quit when he was 24 because he kept getting worse. He is exaggerating, but not a lot. He was a mediocre player. A lot of excellent managers were marginal players. Which is to say, they made playing careers out of the margin that mind could give them. There have, of course, been great players who were successful managers, even player-managers. Lou Boudreau was one, Joe Cronin another. In 1926 Rogers Hornsby, Ty Cobb, Tris Speaker, Eddie Collins and George Sisler, all future Hall of Famers, were player-managers. But in modern times, mediocre playing careers have been the preludes to some of the most distinguished managerial careers.

Earl Weaver, who won 1,480 games and had a .583 winning percentage through 17 seasons, never made it to the major leagues as a player. Sparky Anderson, the only manager to win 800 games in each league (863 with the Reds and 895 with the Tigers through the 1989 season), was a .218 hitter in his only year in the major leagues (1959, with the Phillies).

Whitey ("Baseball has been good to me since I quit trying to play it") Herzog, the Cardinals' manager, is now regarded as the National League's Spinoza. In his playing career he drifted through four teams in eight years, compiling a batting average of .257. Gene

Mauch managed 3,941 games (the fourth-highest total in major league history) after playing for six teams in nine years and batting .239.

La Russa was born and raised in Tampa. What the Chesapeake Bay is to crabs, Tampa is to baseball talent: a rich breeding ground, known for both quantity and quality. Wade Boggs and Dwight Gooden are just two who were boys in Tampa and now are prospering in the major leagues. La Russa's mother, though born in Tampa, was of Spanish descent, and his father spoke Spanish. La Russa spoke Spanish before he spoke English. Being bilingual is a considerable advantage for a manager in an era when nearly 20 percent of all the players under contract in professional baseball are from Latin America. Managing was far from La Russa's mind when, the night he graduated from high school in 1962, he signed with the Athletics. The team was then in Kansas City and was the toy of Charlie Finley. La Russa got $50,000 for a signing bonus. He was 17 and the world was his oyster. The next year he was in the major leagues for 34 games, 44 at bats, 11 hits. He did not know it at the time, but when the season ended he had already appeared in a quarter of all the major league games of his playing career.

Back in Tampa after the 1963 season, he arrived late for a slow-pitch softball game with some friends from high school. Youth is impetuous; even La Russa was then. At that softball game he went straight to shortstop without warming up. It was filthy luck that in the first inning a ball was hit in the hole. He fielded it, fired to first and tore a tendon in his arm near the shoulder. He played with a sore arm for 15 more years. Along the way he collected two shoulder separations, a knee injury and chips in his elbow (probably from throwing awkwardly with a sore arm). In 16 years as a professional player, he had a total of 176 at bats in 132 major league games for the Athletics, Braves and Cubs. His career batting average was .199. He never hit a home run.

His best season convinced him that his best was not going to be good enough. In 1972 he hit .308 for the Braves' Triple-A Richmond club, but he was not called up to the parent team. Convinced that his playing career had a low ceiling, he turned toward another career. After five off-seasons at Florida State University Law School he had a degree. He was admitted to the bar in 1979. However, by then he was headed for managing.

It is said that the study of law sharpens the mind by narrowing it.

But, then, the study of anything narrows the mind in the sense of concentrating attention and excluding much from the field of focus. Besides, a sharp mind, like a straight razor, becomes sharper by being stropped. Tony La Russa is the fifth major league manager to possess a law degree. The four other lawyer-managers (Branch Rickey, Miller Huggins, Hughie Jennings, Monte Ward) are in the Hall of Fame.

La Russa was 34 when, with 54 games remaining in the 1979 season, he became manager of the White Sox. There have been younger managers. Roger Peckinpaugh became the Yankees' manager at 23, and in 1942 the Indians' shortstop, Lou Boudreau, then 24, became the youngest manager to start a season. But by 1989 La Russa was managing in his eleventh season, three more than the 8 Peckinpaugh managed and just 5 behind Boudreau's 16. If La Russa stays in a major league dugout—and he can if he wants to—until he is 65, he will have managed 31 seasons, more than Walter Alston (23), more than Leo Durocher and Joe McCarthy (24), more than Casey Stengel and Bill McKechnie (25), Gene Mauch (26) and Bucky Harris (29): in fact, more than any other manager except John McGraw (33) and Connie Mack (53).

The rearing elephant sewn on the sleeve of the Oakland Athletics' uniforms has a pedigree involving two of baseball's larger-than-life managers. John McGraw was manager of the Baltimore Orioles in 1901, the American League's first year. McGraw, whose dislikes were many and fierce, disliked the league's president, Ban Johnson, and objected to the admission to the league of the Philadelphia Athletics, a franchise owned and managed by Cornelius McGili-cuddy—Connie Mack. McGraw derided the Athletics as the "white elephants" and Mack, to taunt McGraw, adopted the white elephant as his team's symbol. The Athletics promptly won the pennant in 1902, the year McGraw jumped to the New York Giants. The elephant logo came and went several times during the fluctuating fortunes of the Athletics' franchise. It returned in 1988 for the first time since the Athletics' 13-year sojourn in Kansas City. And in 1989 the two franchises of McGraw and Mack, having followed the course of empire westward, were back at each other, in the World Series.

Connie Mack was born the year after Fort Sumter was fired upon and died the year before Sputnik was launched. He holds one of baseball's most secure records: most seasons as a manager. Mack also holds an unenviable record: most consecutive seasons managing in the same league without a championship (19). Between Mack and La Russa no one managed the Athletics for more than three consecutive years. Longevity isn't as long as it once was.

Today, and in the future, long managerial careers may not occur as easily as they once did. Until relatively recently there was a side of baseball that was not very meritocratic. Baseball served as a haven for some managers and coaches who were not particularly good. This haven existed because baseball people were kind to their pals.

To the familiar classifications of social systems, now add a new category to cover the peculiar governance of baseball. To aristocracy, plutocracy and democracy add baseball's contribution to government: "palocracy," government by old pals. Baseball has traditionally been run by men whose lives have been intersecting and entwined for decades. They have known one another from the rocky playing fields and spartan offices of the low minor leagues all the way up to the manicured playing fields and well-appointed suites of the major leagues. You do not talk long with a baseball person before you hear the phrase "baseball person." Often it is accompanied by a negative: So-and-so is "not a baseball person." No adjective is required, thank you very much. A baseball person is a good baseball person. A palocracy can make for kinder, gentler governance, but it also can make the world safe for mediocrity. (The prince of managerial mediocrity was Wilbert Robinson. Uncle Robbie of the Dodgers managed for 19 years and produced this record: 1,397 wins, 1,395 losses. It is a shame one of those wins was not a loss.)

Closed systems, such as tenured university faculties or diplomatic corps or military services, are vulnerable to systemic mediocrity. People who have gone to the same schools, climbed the same career ladders, absorbed the same values and assumptions and expectations, become intellectually insular and professionally self-protective. They forgive one another their mistakes, and mediocrity becomes cozy.

As baseball becomes more meritocratic in every aspect it does not need to become bland and (in a gray-flannel sense) managerial. Colorfulness is not incompatible with quality. The most vivid image of a manager in modern times is that of Casey Stengel, who said things like, "What about the shortstop Rizzuto who got nothing but daughters but throws out the left-handed batters in the double play?" Dumb, right? Stengel was dumb like a fox. Few managers are intellectuals but all managers talk a lot. Managing, like politics, is mostly talk, and some smart managers say strange things. Detroit's Sparky Anderson says that Jose Canseco has the body of a "Greek goddess," but you know what Sparky means. Some of the brightest managers—Leo Durocher for one, Earl Weaver for another—had tempers that sometimes made them seem less intelligent than they were. (Weaver was once ejected from a game during the exchange of lineup cards.) Youth is hot and when La Russa became manager at age 34 he had a temper that was too easily detonated. But the best balm is a steady diet of winning. He had only three losing seasons in his first 11 seasons (1979–89) as a major league manager.

La Russa was just 41 when he had the fundamental experience of managing: He was fired. The White Sox fired him in 1986. The Chicago experience "toughened me up pretty well." He certainly is tough enough now. Once when Jose Canseco was a rookie and did not hustle on a play, he returned to the dugout to find La Russa furious. La Russa told him, "Do that again, I'll knock you on your ass."

La Russa never became one of the hard-core unemployed. On July 1, 1986, less than a month after being fired, he was hired by Oakland. The Athletics were in last place, 21 games below .500, which is not easy to be before the All-Star break. The rest of the year they were 45–34. In 1987 they played only .500 ball but in the American League West that was good enough for third place. The 1988 Athletics were the first American League West team to lead the league in wins since the 1983 White Sox, who were managed by La Russa. In 1987 and 1988 the Athletics were 105–63 against the American League East—a thumping 57–27 in 1988.

———◆———

Situations are shaped in innumerable ways by managers, by what they do to prepare for a game and what they do during the game. La Russa says, with a fine sense of semantic tidiness, that what are called baseball "instincts" really involve much more than instinctual behavior. These "instincts" are actually the result of "an accumulation of baseball information. They are uses of that information as the basis of decision-making as game situations develop. Your instincts may say 'pitch out now' and later you may say, 'Why did I do that?' When you trust your gut you are trusting a lot of stuff that is there from the past." "A manager's job," said Earl Weaver, "is to select the best players for what he wants done. They're not all great players, but they can all do something." The style of managing must be suited to the kind of team you have. But a team does not fall unbidden from the sky. It is built. And to some extent—limited by the nature of the talent rising from the farm system and the talent available from trades—you build a team suited to the style of managing you prefer.

You also build a team to suit where you will play—and not just your home field. In 1968 there were only two fields with artificial turf. In 1989 there were ten. Because each team now plays a good number of games on artificial turf—on a plastic carpet put down on concrete—speed is more essential than it used to be. Or, to be more precise, speed is more widely recognized as valuable than it used to be. Artificial turf has reminded some people of how valuable speed always has been in baseball, anywhere, at any time. For example, a slow runner on first often allows the defense to "play soft," not holding the runner on. This allows the pitcher to throw off-speed pitches to left-handed hitters who may get around on those pitches and pull them but will not have a huge hole in the right side to pull them through. This is true on a natural or artificial field.

Today's increased emphasis on speed is one reason why many fans feel as Bill James does. "I do not like artificial turf," writes James. "I like the game that artificial turf creates." It is a game in which in 1987, the year the Cardinals won the pennant, Vince Coleman, the Cardinals' speedster, scored 23 percent of his 121 runs with no hit coming from his teammates after he reached base. A runner is neither undignified nor unaesthetic when he gobbles up 270 feet by, for example, stealing second, going to third on an infield grounder to the right side and scoring on a sacrifice fly. If you are fast, the sacrifice fly does not even need to be very deep. Things get exciting.

Runs that come one at a time matter. Most runs come that way. By concentrating more baseball minds on the myriad ways of moving 90 feet, and on how to score one run at a time, artificial turf has had the partially—I say partially—redeeming effect of restoring balance to baseball. The balance was lost when home runs became too important to too many teams and fans.

After the 1916 season, in which the National League's home-run leader had 12, the league was alarmed about the degradation of baseball by this epidemic of vulgar power. So the league ruled that all outfield fences had to be at least 270 feet from home plate.

(Actually, only two parks were affected, the Polo Grounds in New York and what would come to be called Baker Bowl in Philadelphia.) At that time sports pages listed stolen bases and sacrifices in addition to batting averages, but did not list home runs.

The future, however, was in the process of being born in Boston. In 1915 a Red Sox pitcher in his first full season had 4 home runs. These 4 by Babe Ruth were almost a third of the Red Sox total of 14. In September, 1919, when Ruth was about to set the single-season home-run record with 29, Edward G. Barrow, Ruth's manager on the Red Sox, said:

> After Babe has satisfied himself by hanging up a record for home runs that will never be touched, he will become a .400 hitter. He wants to establish a record of 30 or 35 home runs this year, and when he has done that he will start getting a lot of base hits that will win us more games than his home runs. He will just meet the ball and hit it to left field as well as Ty Cobb. He will not be trying to knock the ball out of the lot after this season. He will be content with his record because it will be far and away out of the reach of any other player the game is likely to develop.

Ruth was a wonder, but he was more a harbinger than an aberration. The home run was here to stay, which was fine. What was not fine was that home runs began to drive out other forms of offense. When home runs became the center of baseball's mental universe, the emphasis shifted away from advancing runners. The new emphasis was on just getting runners on base to wait for lightning to strike. The major league teams of the 1950s were like American automobiles of the 1950s: There was not much variety or subtlety. In the era of automotive megachrome and tail fins baseball was played (I am exaggerating slightly) like a board game: Move here, then wait; move there, then wait again. The stolen base was like the foreign car: It was considered cute and fun and not quite serious, and was not often seen. In the first seven years of that decade no *team* stole 100 bases in a season. Think about that. Not a single one of the 16 teams stole as many bases as Maury Wills was to steal in 1962 (104).

The 1959 World Series between the Dodgers and the White Sox foreshadowed the transformation of baseball back to a game emphasizing speed. The "Go-Go Sox" attack, if such it could be called, consisted largely of Luis Aparicio and Nellie Fox, two small middle infielders who could hit-and-run and steal. And the 1959 Dodgers were a far cry from the last Dodgers team that had appeared in a Series, the 1956 slugging team of Duke Snider, Gil Hodges, Roy Campanella and Carl Furillo. The 1959 Dodgers led the league in fielding, strikeouts, bull pen saves and stolen bases. Those sufficed.

The wonder is that baseball took such a wrong turn into the cul-de-sac of the 1950s. Yes, that was a conservative decade. The Eisenhower years have been characterized as "the bland leading the bland." Bland was fine in politics, especially after the overstimulation of the Depression and the Second World War. But baseball is entertainment and bland entertainment is not fun. True, the decade of Mantle, Mays and Snider—one city's center fielders—can not really be called dull. But when baseball became monochrome, it was not as entertaining as it should have been, even though some color came from home runs. It was insufficiently entertaining because it was not sufficiently intelligent.

Furthermore, a lot of teams—those with power shortages relative to the big bruising teams—were at more of a competitive disadvantage in the 1950s than they needed to be. They would have done better if, instead of swinging from their heels, they had got up on their toes and run. Again, I concede the point that baseball boomed in the 1950s. But it did not boom as it was to do in the 1980s.

The 1947 season had provided what should have been sobering evidence of the competitive weakness of counting on home runs to power a team to a pennant, and the evidence would accumulate over the next two decades. The first team to hit more than 200 home runs in a season was the 1947 Giants. They hit 221. They finished fourth. Of the 22 teams that have hit 200 or more home runs in a season, only 5 won pennants: the 1953 and 1955 Brooklyn Dodgers, the 1961 New York Yankees, the 1962 San Francisco Giants and the 1982 Milwaukee Brewers. Only 2 of those 5 (the 1955 Dodgers and the 1961 Yankees) also won the World Series.

The Cubs of 1971 had three players with 300 or more career home runs (Ernie Banks, Billy Williams, Ron Santo) and finished in a tie for third place with a record of 83–79. The 1987 Cubs hit 209 home runs, more than any National League team in a decade, and they gave up just 159, but they were outscored by 81 runs, 801 to 720, and crashed into the cellar. Only 70 other teams had hit at least 50 more home runs than their opponents and only one of those 70 had been outscored. The 1987 Cubs' opponents had 179 more men reach base by hits, walks and hit batters. The 1986 Mets won the National League East by 21½ games, the largest margin in the history of divisional play and second in major league history to the 27½-game margin of the 1902 Pirates. The Mets managed their feat with the relatively modest total of 148 home runs.

The 1987 Orioles became the twenty-second team in history to hit 200 or more home runs in a season, and the first team in history to give up 200 home runs while hitting 200. They were next to last in runs scored. Nearly half (45.6 percent) of their runs were scored by batters who had hit home runs or by runners who were on base when home runs were hit. For the Orioles it was feast or famine, and the home-run feasts, although unusually frequent, were not frequent enough. The 1987 Orioles got fewer runners into scoring position than any other team and they finished sixth. The 1988 Athletics hit only 156 home runs but finished first.

Because baseball is a game of normal human proportions and abnormally small margins, people tend to make too much of sheer bulk when a lot of it is assembled on one team. Before the 1927 World Series, in which the Yankees were to sweep the Pirates, the Pirates' Lloyd "Little Poison" Waner (150 pounds) watched Ruth, Lou Gehrig, Bob Meusel and the rest take batting practice, then he turned to his brother Paul and said, "Jesus, they're big." They were indeed. And one of baseball's durable myths is that the Yankees' batting practice that day so demoralized the Pirates that they rolled over and died. Actually, although the Yankees swept the Pirates in four games, the Yankees won games one and four by one run and got only three more extra-base hits than the Pirates (ten to seven). But bigness can be mesmerizing in baseball.

It was perhaps inevitable, given the physical bulk of the middle of their lineup, that the 1988 Athletics would be a much misunderstood team. They were, to the end, underestimated. Fans did not appreciate their versatility, which was illustrated when Jose Canseco stole second base for his fortieth stolen base. He had reached first base on a bunt. That was his only bunt hit of the season, but he and other Athletics sluggers had, as players say, "showed bunt" occasionally during the season. That is, they had shortened up on the bat as if preparing to bunt. By doing this they had achieved some hits because the opposing third basemen had been drawn in a step or two or three, thereby making it easier to get a sharply hit ball past them. Otherwise, third basemen against the powerful Athletics would have played unusually deep. It is hazardous enough playing third base in the big leagues; it is doubly so against the Athletics' right-handed power hitters like Canseco and McGwire. But it becomes especially worrisome when these line-drive hitters can credibly shorten up and threaten to drop a bunt down the third-base line for a hit. A line drive reaches a third baseman faster than the fastest pitch travels to the plate. By "showing bunt" the Athletics' batters pull their opponents' third basemen in, make them nervous and add a few points to the Athletics' team batting average. "Watch where the third baseman plays against us," says La Russa. "Even to the bag, a step beyond it or a couple of steps in. Do you know what that means? There are balls in the hole and balls down the line that he doesn't get to. Why would you want to let the third baseman play all the way back on the grass and take away all those hits, without showing the bunt and drawing him in?"

The 1988 Athletics had plenty of power:

	HR	RBI
Jose Canseco	42	124
Mark McGwire	32	99
Dave Henderson	24	94
Dave Parker	12	55
Terry Steinbach	9	51
TOTAL	119	423

However, the 1987 Athletics had more power:

	HR	RBI
Mark McGwire	49	118
Jose Canseco	31	113
Mike Davis	22	72
Carney Lansford	19	76
Terry Steinbach	16	56
TOTAL	137	435

But not even the 1987 Athletics measured up to the 1961 or 1927 Yankees:

1961 YANKEES

	HR	RBI
Roger Maris	61	142
Mickey Mantle	54	128
Bill Skowron	28	89
Elston Howard	21	77
Yogi Berra	22	61
TOTAL	186	497

1927 YANKEES

	HR	RBI
Lou Gehrig	47	175
Babe Ruth	60	164
Bob Meusel	8	103
Tony Lazzeri	18	102
Earl Combs	6	64
TOTAL	139	608

The 1988 Athletics won 18 of 19 in late April and early May and had only one minislump after that. When it occurred, cutting their lead to three in mid-July, they reeled off 22 wins in the next 28 games. They wound up with winning records against all clubs but the Royals (5–8), had the best record in the major leagues on the road (50–31) and demolished the once haughty American League East (57–27). They were 30–16 in one-run games, 14–5 in extra innings and won 24 games in their last at bat. They were a moderately dominating team, but only moderately. Consider a comparison.

The 1986 Mets outscored their opponents by 205 runs. Mildly impressive, but only mildly. It was the best differential since the 224 of the 1976 Big Red Machine. But since 1900, 65 teams have done better than the Mets' 205. The run differential has narrowed over time as the differences in the capabilities of the teams have narrowed. This narrowing has occurred for the same reason the .400 hitter has disappeared. As baseball knowledge has become deeper and more broadly disseminated, wide disparities in individual and team performances have become rarer. To put all this in perspective, the 1927 Yankees had a run differential of 376, and even that is not the record. It is not close to the 1939 Yankees' record of 411. The 1988 Athletics' run differential of 180 was just 44 percent of 411.

The 1988 Athletics had a per-game margin over opponents of 1.3 runs. Note well, even a very good team like the 1988 Athletics has only a slim advantage. But it has it often.

To get that edge often, a manager must fret constantly. On a sunny May morning in Baltimore, La Russa is breakfasting abstemiously, as is his wont, on fruit and cereal and nothing else. He is thinking—worrying, naturally; for him, the distinction between thinking and worrying is a distinction without a difference—aloud.

"Parker is struggling. I'm going to hit him second against Boddicker tonight." Parker is a large, slow slugger who is past his prime. He is hardly the prototype of a number-two hitter. But he is in a slump and is swinging at a lot of bad pitches. Boddicker is an off-speed finesse pitcher. The key to La Russa's thinking is his leadoff hitter, Carney Lansford, who always has hit Boddicker well and who, at the moment, is white hot, hitting everyone. If Parker comes up with no one on base, Boddicker will tantalize him to the point of distraction, frustration and futility. Parker will chase everything. "But suppose Lansford, a legitimate base-stealing threat, is on first. The pitcher is caught. The catcher is caught. You have to go one way or the other, but you can't have it both ways. One way is to try to pitch to Parker with off-speed, off-the-plate junk. But that way you give up second base to a Lansford steal. Or you try to take away the steal by coming at Parker with a pitch he might hit for extra bases. That is why if I have a legitimate stolen-base guy, I don't like to have a little slap-type hitter hitting next. A power hitter puts the pitcher in the problem."

In 1988 the Athletics ranked sixth in the American League in sacrifice bunts. (The Chicago White Sox led with 67 sacrifice bunts; the A's had a total of 54.) If a leadoff man singles in the first inning, will La Russa ever bunt? "Very rarely." Even if the number-two batter has almost no chance to get a hit, La Russa prefers to try something more aggressive than a bunt, such as a hit-and-run to get the ball in play. This is a consideration when deciding whether to bunch or scatter the best hitters through the lineup. La Russa is often a scatterer. "Suppose you don't have much thump in your lineup. You try to space out your hitters a bit. If you have four good hitters, bat one first, one third, one fourth, one seventh. If you bunch them all together you are grouping your best shot to score in just three innings. The other six you're going out with no firepower. Instead, take one of your guys who may not be an outstanding hitter but who can handle the bat, and bat him second because if the first guy gets on base, you can do something with the batter to advance the runner." Something like hit-and-run. Hitting-and-running is safer than bunting if your batter is someone who almost always makes contact. Bunting is a difficult art. It is devilishly easy to bunt the ball foul twice and then have to swing away defensively because you are behind in the count. And especially on artificial turf it is devilishly hard not to bunt the ball so far that a fielder can pounce on it and throw the runner out at second. Also, when the runner is breaking for second with the pitch and the bunt is popped up, the runner can be doubled off first. If the batter is a good contact hitter he probably will not swing and miss and leave the runner exposed to being thrown out at second. So in a hit-and-run situation the only risk would be a line drive to an infielder that gets the breaking runner doubled up at first.

In both cases, bunting or hitting-and-running, you start the runner, so he is at risk. Granted, if the batter hits a line drive at an infielder, the runner who started with the pitch probably will be doubled up. But if the ball is hit on the ground, the runner probably can not be forced at second. And if the ball goes through the infield—ideally, through the hole opened by the movement of the shortstop or second baseman toward second as the runner breaks from first—the runner winds up at third.

It is an old baseball joke that big-inning baseball is affirmed in the Bible, in Genesis: "In the big inning, God created. . . ." La Russa knows the key to creating big innings. "First and third, nobody out. You're talking about a big inning. To me, the secret of scoring a lot of runs is, as many times as you can get a guy into scoring position, do it." But when considering a hit-and-run, there are three variables. They are the pitcher's control, the batter's ability to make contact and the runner's speed. La Russa wants to have at least two in his favor. "Suppose the other team has a guy on the mound who throws real hard and is wild. Suppose you have a real free swinger at the plate and a slow runner on first. That's about as bad a situation as you could pick for a hit-and-run, no matter what the score or game situation is. You want to hit-and-run when you know the pitch is going to be close enough to the strike zone that the batter can put it in play. Your free swinger may swing through even a good pitch, and the slow runner breaking from first base will be dead."

Again and again and again La Russa returns to baseball's fundamental trade-off, the purchase of opportunity by the coin of risk. The crucial concept in baseball is the creation of opportunities. That means putting people on base. Fans are fascinated by each hitter's average with runners in scoring position. But the difference between an average of .275 and .250 is of little importance compared with the more important matter of how many runners the team gets into scoring position. Consider a team loaded with power hitters but short on hitters with high on-base averages. Such a team may have more trouble scoring runs in bunches than does a team short on power hitters but capable of getting lots of men to first base and willing to take risks by running.

Thinking aloud about the risks in this game that has risks on every hand, La Russa plays Ping-Pong in his mind with alternatives. Ping: "If the pitcher against us is Frank Viola, someone we hardly ever hit, or Dave Stieb, well, push it. Why sit back and get beat? So what if you have a play that has a poor chance of being successful? Your chances that day are poor anyway. So, for example, if you have a slow runner on first, a power hitter at the plate and a 2–0 count, it is a good time to start the runner because the other side will be surprised." Pong: "But it may also be a bad time because the power hitter may not be reliable about putting the ball in play to prevent the slow runner from being thrown out at second."

La Russa believes in taking risks precisely because baseball, the game of failure, is all risks, the odds being what they are: against. Against almost anything you try. "If we get a man to second with no one out, we may have three guys coming up who can hit home runs, but why stand around and wait for that? Let's have the next guy get the runner to third and pick up one run. It's not correct to sit and wait for extra-base hits."

La Russa does not tailor the Athletics' game to the park they are playing in on a given day. "The game tells you what to do," he says, "not the park." A good pitcher can turn a bandbox park into the Grand Canyon. La Russa is more apt to play for one run at a time, with a lot of hitting and running, when, as in a League Championship Series and World Series, television dictates a starting time around 5:30 P.M. Pacific Time. Pitchers have an enormous advantage throwing through slanting sunlight and twilight. And the

weather—the temperature, the humidity, the winds—can also influence La Russa's approach to a game. "If it's hot and the ball is
carrying, maybe you don't bunt, don't play for one run." But
meteorology has precious little to do with managing. What will
prevail is the manager's fundamental style, which is another name
for tendency.

"We wanted to establish an A's style of play," says La Russa, "a lot
of effort and playing with an idea." La Russa's idea is to find a way
to find an edge in every situation. Earl Weaver's credo was: Make
all your outs at home plate, not on the bases. That is not La Russa's
style. As soon as some managers fall behind by even a run they
become less aggressive about starting runners or otherwise risking
outs on a steal or a hit-and-run. La Russa thinks such restraint is often
unreasonable. Suppose, he says, you are down by three runs going
into your at bat in the third inning. Suppose your eighth-place hitter
gets on first with one out, your ninth-place hitter is, to begin with,
a ninth-place hitter and he is struggling. Assume, for good measure,
that he is facing a sinker-ball pitcher, so a ground ball is probable.
La Russa says: Start the runner. The ninth-place hitter probably will
not get a hit, but if he grounds out you will have a man at second
and two outs and your leadoff man up. The fact that you are behind
does not make it more likely that the ninth-place hitter will score
the runner by getting an extra-base hit.

Even with a home-run hitter like Canseco in the middle of his
order, La Russa says, "You've got your best chance to win when
you've got good sharp line drives all over the park. Canseco stays in
control, with discipline, trying to just hit the ball hard. He can hit
.290, even in the .300s, he's got that good a stroke. And he's so strong
that every once in a while, there goes one." Even in a year when
there are 40 or more every-once-in-a-whiles from Canseco, he gets
a lot more singles than home runs—more singles than extra-base
hits. What is true of Canseco is true of baseball generally. In 1988
there were more than twice as many doubles (6,386) as home runs
(3,180), but there were 25,838 singles. Baseball is still what it always
has been and always will be, basically a 90-feet-at-a-time game.

Baseball people love numbers, but there are limits to what can be
quantified, even in baseball. Part of baseball's charm is the illusion
it offers that all aspects of it can be completely reduced to numerical
expressions and printed in agate type in the sports section. La Russa,
who when younger was considered the archetype of the numbers-
crunching modern manager, has no such illusions. He constantly

recurs to one intangible: intensity. One way to build it is to keep pushing for small achievements. Remember the law of cumulation: The result of many little things is not little. Playing "little ball," scrambling to manufacture runs—"looking for just 90 feet, every once in a while," La Russa calls it—energizes a team. It puts a team up on the balls of its feet, ready to run. And the intensity carries over into defense.

"When a team comes in to play the A's, their dugout should not be comfortable. They should be thinking, 'Uh oh, they steal third, they hit-and-run, they bunt for a base hit, they try to hit the hole, they knock the pivot man down.' I remember when I was playing second base against a team like that, you're worn out when the day is over. A station-to-station club is easy to play against because you just play the ball." A station-to-station team, meaning a team that puts runners on base and waits for *the batter alone* to make something happen, simply has fewer ways to score runs. You do not often string together three singles in an inning. True, if you take risks you can run yourself out of a big inning, and as La Russa says, "You don't want to shoot down your chance for a crooked number [more than one run]." But if you are aggressive in ways other than by blasting extra-base hits, you can put together big innings that are built in part out of the other team's anxieties. La Russa wants the other team to look out from its dugout "and get real bad vibes" about his team's physical and mental aggressiveness. He wants them to be saying, or at least thinking, "Oh, man, do you see those A's, with all that talent, they're not just out here letting the numbers fall into place. Did you see that slide into second base? He just knocked our pivot man into left field. Did you see the way Jose handled that two-strike situation, the way he spread it out, put the ball in play? See what Mc-Gwire did? They're down by three runs so he took the 2-and-0 pitch. See McGwire take the ball to right field with a runner on second base?" La Russa says, "That's what happened last year [1988]. I had managers tell me, 'I hate to say it, but your club is fun to watch.' "

The Athletics' aggressiveness was not fun for the Toronto Blue Jays to watch in the sixth inning of the first game of the American League Championship Series of 1989. With the score tied 3–3, the Athletics had the bases loaded with one out. Carney Lansford hit what could have been an inning-ending double-play ball to the Blue Jays' shortstop, Tony Fernandez. He fielded the ball a tad too casually and tossed the ball so that it arrived a fraction of a tenth of a

second later than it should have in the glove of second baseman
Nelson Liriano. Unfortunately for Liriano, the runner arriving from
first was fast and was not feeling friendly. It was Rickey Henderson,
who had reached first base by being hit on the wrist by a pitch. He
hit Liriano, whose throw went down the right-field line allowing two
runs, including the winning run, to score. "Rickey," said La Russa
later, "had just been hit by a pitch and he's out there with a lot of
adrenaline pumping. You see that pivot man pay the price. That's
our style."

Many fans think that the maximum aggression in baseball is the
big swing that drives the ball 400 feet. However, leaving aside the
fact that a lot of balls driven 400 feet are just loud outs, there is also
the fact that a 30-foot bunt can be more aggressive. "The most
aggressive thing in baseball," says La Russa, "is guys on base running
around and sliding, raising dust." In 1988 only 3 percent of all batted
balls put in play in the major leagues were bunts. But that is hardly
the whole story of the role of bunting. Again, the ability to bunt, and
the threat to do it, pulls in the infield and creates better angles
through which to hit the ball for singles. Get enough of those 90-foot
advances, you win.

The foremost recent practitioner of "little ball" was Gene Mauch,
who managed for 26 years for the Phillies, Expos, Twins and Angels.
He retired shortly before Opening Day, 1988. The fact that Mauch
never managed a team to the World Series and won only two divisional titles is cited as evidence that "little ball" leads to little glory.
Well, now. Leave aside the fact that Mauch's Angels came within
one strike of getting past the Red Sox and into the 1986 World
Series. Note instead how hard it is to prove that "little ball" tactics
actually mean a low-scoring team. The Elias Bureau, which special-
izes in slaying theories with facts, calculates that in the three seasons
1985, 1986 and 1987 Mauch's Angels executed 260 sacrifice bunts,
more than twice the average of the rest of the league (128). But
these bunt-crazed Angels also scored approximately the same number of runs as the rest of the league's teams averaged. In fact, slightly
more: 2,288 to 2,276. One-run innings accounted for 29.9 percent
of the Angels' scoring, 29.7 percent of the rest of the league's. And
the Angels had more three-run innings than the other teams averaged (162 to 141).

Besides, the difference between "little ball" and big-inning baseball is not usually as big as you might think. "Little ball" may mean

a lot of one-run innings, but even "big bang" teams will have more one-run innings than innings with "crooked numbers." And most of their big innings (more than two runs) will be three-run innings. Four-run innings will be much rarer. An Elias study of a recent season found that even in the American League, where the DH increases the number of big innings, only one half inning in every 110 produced five or more runs. It was one in every 135 in the National League.

Whitey Herzog's Cardinals of the 1980s have been track teams built to scamper across the carpet of cavernous Busch Stadium. They are rightly considered the archetype of teams built to avoid reliance on the long ball. In the 1982 World Series the Cardinals, who had hit 67 home runs during the season, met—and beat—the Milwaukee Brewers, who had hit 216. And in 1987 the Cardinals scored four or more runs in 16 consecutive games. That was the longest such streak since 1950.

Advocates of big-inning baseball have an axiom by which they dismiss one-run-at-a-time baseball. The axiom is: If you play for one you get one—only one. But to that axiom the appropriate response is: Perhaps, but you get that one. And it matters. The 1986 *Elias Analyst* reported that scoring the first run gave the typical American League team, in 1985, a 2-to-1 edge on its opponents. In addition, the worst team in the league, after scoring first, had a better record than the best team in the league when its opponents scored first. The Elias study of the 1986 season showed that 65 percent of all American League games were won by the teams that scored the first runs. And in 84 percent of those wins the team that scored first never fell behind. In the National League, where the parks are generally larger and there is no DH, scoring is a bit lower and the value of early runs is a bit higher. In 1986 National League teams scoring first won 67 percent of the time, never trailing in 86 percent of those wins. This is a reason why La Russa toils so hard at getting the Athletics ready to play from the instant of the first pitch.

Compare conditions in baseball with those in another emblematic American industry. In the automobile industry from the 1920s through the 1950s competition was not nearly as fierce as (thanks to industrious foreigners—and I do mean *thanks*) it has become. Back then, if the door seal let the rain in, or a door handle fell off, the industry just shrugged. Those were little things, common to all brands, and were not taken very seriously. But in recent decades increased competition has raised standards. Something similar has happened in baseball.

The man who feels the increased pressure most is the manager. His players prepare for a game by doing what they have done all their lives—throwing, fielding, swinging a bat. The manager must prepare for his several roles, and he must also superintend all the roles of all the players. He must not take it for granted that his players will be properly motivated day in and day out. La Russa motivates by giving everyone work. He uses role players enough to make them feel needed and appreciated—and to make the regulars feel some bracing competition from the bench. Over the course of a 162-game season, a group of young men, some of them quite young—younger than major leaguers used to be—are going to be together a lot. They are going to be away from home half the time, spending hours hanging around hotels and playing cards in clubhouses. Over the course of such a season, intensity and concentration must be constantly cultivated. "Every player on our club, without exception, is so much better off [financially] than he was two years ago," La Russa says. "So now there is not the survival motivation."

When you play every day, 162 times, it becomes difficult to be ready to play with proper intensity from the first pitch of the first inning. Most teams start most games at less than full energy. But 162 first innings are one-ninth of a season, or the equivalent of 18 games. And La Russa believes they are even more important than that. "The best two ways to win are to play real well early or real well late. The middle innings take care of themselves. The first inning may be the only inning in which your leadoff man leads off. And every year the same statistic comes out showing that clubs that score first, their winning percentage in those games is anywhere from .550 to .650."

Earl Weaver was a strong proponent of baseball megatonnage. A manager's best friend, he said, is the three-run home run. He considered it irrational to bunt a runner over from second to third with no outs, counting on a sacrifice fly to drive him in. Weaver reasoned that a successful sacrifice bunt is by no means a lead-pipe cinch, and that a sacrifice fly is harder to come by than people think. So leave the runner at second and hope for a single to bring him in rather than counting on two contingencies (the bunt, the sacrifice fly). La Russa disagrees.

"Advancing guys in run-scoring situations is the key to consistent offense. A man leads off with a double. If we don't score with a runner on second and no one out, the other side is going to get a lift. It is difficult to get a sacrifice fly, but it is not easy to get a base hit either. You get more fly balls than singles. So you look at who you have at bat. Hopefully, you have someone who can hit the ball hard to the right side, so you don't have to give up the out automatically with the bunt. One of our best at that is McGwire. We keep those stats, a running month-by-month total of about six, seven, eight situations. One of them is runner on second, no outs. How many times you need to get the runner over, to hit it or bunt it. McGwire has been asked to do it six times this season [1988]. Five times he has gone to the right side *for hits.*"

La Russa offers the following scenario. The Athletics' leadoff man, Carney Lansford, doubles in the first inning. The second batter is Stan Javier, a switch-hitter who does not pull often and who this day is batting left-handed against a pitcher throwing fastballs on the outside edge of the plate. Javier can not pull him, can not hit the ground ball to the right side, so he is going to bunt. That way, Lansford will be at third when the third hitter, Jose Canseco, comes up. On the other hand, suppose you have someone like Don Baylor, a right-hander, at the plate. He is a dead pull hitter and not a good bunter. With a runner on second and no one out, you are not going to ask him to push the ball to the first-base side or to bunt. Just let him swing. "I always want at least to get the guy to third. Because there is another statistic. When we score first, our winning percentage is very high.

"Here is another fact Jim Lefebvre pulled out, something I had never seen before. He took last year's club [the 1987 Athletics], a pretty good offensive club, and looked for the stat of how many innings were scoring innings in a game. It didn't matter how many runs we scored. When we scored at least three different times in a game, our winning percentage was at least .600, even if the scoring was just a one and a one and a one. This year around the All-Star break Jim did that stat for this year's team. When we scored four times we were something like 15–1."

There is, he says, a psychological advantage in getting the lead and then increasing it. That builds an expectation of defeat in the other team, especially if you have a bull pen that can hold leads. So La Russa thinks scoring runs one at a time is important because scoring frequently is important. This is so despite the fact, frequently cited by proponents of big-inning baseball, that in 75 percent of all games the winning team scores more runs in one inning than the losing team scores in the whole game. It is generally true that the more scoring there is, the more the cream among baseball's teams will rise to the top. The ideal of "may the best team win" is most apt to be fulfilled in lopsided games. The better of two teams is most apt to win blowouts because close games are more apt to turn on luck— bad bounces, broken-bat singles, line shots—rockets—hit right at some fielder.

But, again, reliance on extra-base hits is not the only, or even the most reliable, way to score runs in bunches. One of baseball's few recent dynasties, the Athletics of 1972–74, won three consecutive world championships with a team batting average below that of the league over the three seasons. The Athletics did get a lot of long hits. And a lot of those long hits were preceded by walks. Furthermore, the Athletics had a high level of successful steals and (partly for that reason) a high rate of success at avoiding hitting into double plays.

One problem with building a team that relies heavily on home runs is that the number of home runs can vary considerably from one season to the next. In 1987 both leagues and nine teams (six American League, three National League) set records for most home runs in a season. This was the continuation of a trend. The American League had set a home-run record in 1986. The trend ended, as trends tend to do, but not before the scandal known as Rawlingsgate or (depending on your point of view; I tend to skepticism) the great sound and fury about next to nothing. Here is what happened.

In 1984, the last year of Commissioner Bowie Kuhn's reign, there were 3,258 home runs. In 1987 there were 37 percent more than that, 4,458. That led—especially among pitchers, who are prone to dark suspicions—to dark suspicions. Had the ball been "juiced" to pump up offense and gate receipts?

Certainly the ball has changed over time. The earliest balls were leaden—literally. They were homemade, using little lumps of lead wrapped with twine and covered with animal hide, sometimes chamois or sheepskin. When rubber replaced the lead at the core, some balls weighed as little as 3 ounces. But since 1876 the ball has had a constant size (9 to 9¼ inches in circumference) and weight (5 to 5¼ ounces). The only certain change in the ball in more than half a century was the 1975 change of covering from horsehide to cowhide.

The crucial matter is "co-efficient of restitution," which is what folks in the bleachers mean by the propensity of the ball to get to the bleachers—"liveliness." The COR is measured by firing balls from an air cannon at a velocity of 85 feet per second directly at a slab of wood 8 feet away. Major league baseball requires a rebound rate of 54.6 percent of the original velocity, with a permitted deviation of no more than plus or minus 3.2 percent.

COR is not the whole story. Smoothness could be as important as liveliness, according to Tony Kubek. He believes the seams on the ball were flatter in 1987 than in 1988. The smoother surface of the ball flattened out many breaking balls and caused the ball, once hit, to have less wind resistance and thus travel farther. Okay, you say, but why were the seams flatter? I am glad you asked. One explanation is the "Happy Haitian Theory." The balls are made by Rawlings in Haiti. Perhaps the thread in the seams was pulled tighter, and the seams were flatter, because Haitians were full of pep and vim after the overthrow of the dictator "Baby Doc" Duvalier. Maybe the yarn inside was wound tighter for the same reason, making the balls both livelier and smoother.

In any case, in 1988 home runs dropped by 1,278, or 29 percent below the 1987 level. But there was a continuation in the upward trend in the production of theories. The Elias authors noted that after August 6, 1987, when the bat of the Mets' Howard Johnson was seized on the suspicion that it had been "corked," home-run production went down. The authors suggested that the bats, not the balls, were juiced, and the illegal bats were quickly taken out of service. (Drilling out the end of a bat and filling the core with cork makes the bat lighter and increases "bat speed." Think of it as a way of giving Tony Gwynn's wrists to a normal hitter.) The problem with this explanation of the home-run barrage is that the only evidence is an inference, and one that probably was an example of the *post hoc ergo propter hoc* fallacy. (The rooster crows and then the sun rises, so the crowing caused the sunrise.) Did the deterrent effect of one seized bat cause a lot of cheaters to mend their ways? Not likely. Besides, there may not be a lot of cheats. Johnson's bat turned out to be perfectly legal.

In 1989 home runs were down 30.8 percent below the 1987 total. The two-year decline coincided with bad times in Haiti, but almost everything always coincides with bad times there. The truth about the great 1987 home-run surge may never be known. Life is like that. And life goes on. But baseball managers can derive from this episode a lesson for sensible living: Always remember that the home run is a fickle servant.

What is true from season to season is even more true from day to day. Frank Robinson can hardly be accused of disdain for home runs. He hit 586 of them, more than all but three other players (Aaron, Ruth, Mays). The speed he combined with power enabled him to steal 204 bases. Robinson is now a manager, and he has to manage players a lot less talented than he was. He says, "Speed comes to the park every day. The three-run home run doesn't. Speed is the most consistent thing you have."

The Athletics' 1988 season ended with a power outage. In the World Series, Canseco and McGwire hit .053 and .059, respectively. Each had one hit, a dramatic home run. Perhaps too dramatic. Canseco's was a grand slam that bounced off the center-field television camera in Dodger Stadium in the first game. McGwire's was a ninth-inning game winner in Oakland in the third game. It was only the eighth game-ending home run in Series history, the seventh having come off Kirk Gibson's bat two games earlier. La Russa believes the Athletics began losing the 1988 World Series six innings before Gibson hit that game-winning home run. They began losing when Canseco erased a 2–0 Dodgers lead with his grand-slam home run. Any team, says La Russa, plays better when "edgy." After Canseco's slam, La Russa could sense in the dugout the confidence that whatever they might need they would get. It seemed too certain, too easy.

"Playing the game right, pitching the game right. We want to be an aggressive, come-after-you club, throw strike one, make them put the ball in play, know how to finish a hitter off if you're ahead of him. There's a lot of ways to play this game right. That's how the Dodgers beat the A's in the World Series. They played the game right. That is one of the beauties of baseball. I don't care how much talent you have or don't have. If you play the game intelligently, if you execute the fundamentals, you can win."

In game four, which the Dodgers won, 4–3, they got two of the four runs by the perfect execution of what La Russa calls "pushing." With runners on first and third and one out, the runner on first stole second, thereby eliminating the double-play possibility. The next Dodgers batter hit what would have been a double-play grounder to second. The Athletics threw out the runner at first while the runner on third scored. The second time there was one out, a runner on third and Steve Sax was on first. Sax was running when a ground ball was hit. If he had not been running, the Athletics would have gotten a double play and been out of the inning. Instead they had to settle for one out and the (it turned out) winning run came home from third.

"Technically," says La Russa, "a successful hit-and-run is one where you just put the ball in play and advance the runner to second base. But if you get a base hit on the play, that's golden. The Dodgers got base hits on 11 of their 15 hit-and-runs. *Nobody's* success rate is 11 of 15, not even close to that. I give Tommy Lasorda a ton of credit."

In the 1950s Lasorda was a pitcher with a lousy arm and a record to prove it: He had a major league career of 58⅓ innings, no wins, 4 losses. So Lasorda learned to use his head. La Russa likes that.

———◆———

La Russa's mantra comes from Bill Rigney, one of baseball's sages. Today Rigney is a sort of utility infielder of baseball's executive suites, working in the Athletics' front office. He is a former infielder for the Giants and former manager of the Giants, Angels and Twins. He played in the 1951 play-off game when Bobby Thomson hit the home run that broke Brooklyn's heart. He has seen a lot and talks enchantingly about it. Rigney's baseball talk is nonstop, inexhaustibly interesting and laced with lovely anachronisms, such as his references to teams as "the Baltimores" or "the Houstons." His distilled wisdom, and La Russa's mantra, is that the four important things in baseball, in order of importance, are: play hard, win, make money and have fun. The problems start when the third and fourth take precedence over the first and second.

"Baseball," says Tom Trebelhorn, manager of the Milwaukee Brewers, "has got to be fun, because if it is not fun, it's a long time to be in agony." La Russa agrees but adds: Time flies when you are having fun and what is fun is winning. So back to the first point: play hard. The manager sets the tone and the example. A manager is a player in the sense that his attention and what he does during the game helps to determine the outcome. What he does most is purposeful watching.

When La Russa is concentrating on the action his lips are thin and straight as a mail slot. He looks like an angry man, but he is not. He

is, however, serious—about everything. His two young daughters—
budding ballerinas—are being educated at home so they can see
more of their father and can experience some educational travel
during the off-season. A wit once said that it was not true that
Gladstone lacked a sense of humor—Gladstone just was not often in
a mood to be amused. La Russa is no stranger to laughter, but he
does not often laugh when he is within a fly ball's distance of a
ballpark. With his ample dark hair and thick eyebrows, and the bill
of his cap pulled low, keeping his eyes in perpetual shadow, his
watchfulness has an aspect of brooding. He spends the hours of each
game giving signs in response to what he sees on the field in front
of him, and in response to what he sees—or thinks he sees, or thinks
he would be seeing if he could decipher the evidence—in the dugout across the field.

As a voracious gatherer of information, he begins looking for an
edge even when away from the ballpark. He thumbs through other
teams' media guides to find out if, say, Team A is having more
success getting out a particular batter on Team B than Oakland is.
If so, he may call a friend with Team A—if he has one—to solicit
information. He is more likely to do this if Team A is in the American
League East. At the ballpark his watchfulness begins long before the
game does. La Russa watches the other teams' batting practice as
often as possible to see what particular hitters are working on. In
Boston in May, 1988, when Jim Rice was off to a slow start, La Russa
watched intently to see whether Rice was trying to pull the ball. (He
was.)

"I think the manager has to keep control of every piece of the
game, including the running game." He means the baserunning by,
and against, the Athletics. He has never given a player a season-long
"green light"—permission to run whenever he wants to. When Canseco became the first 40-40 man, hitting 42 home runs and stealing
40 bases, he had, La Russa estimates, a green light to run at his
discretion on, at most, 27 of those steals. One player who has a green
light, unless La Russa takes it off, is Carney Lansford. Canseco is a
lot faster; Lansford is a lot more experienced. In most other cases,
if the Athletics' first-base coach tells the runner nothing, the runner
has a red light. He can not go unless he gets a sign to steal. Or the
coach may tell him he has a green light in this inning or this game.
Otherwise they go "pitch to pitch," using a flash sign that may come
from the bench or the third-base coach or the first-base coach. The

sign is never "go." It is "you may go." It means everything is in favor of trying to go, so if you get anything from a decent to a good jump, go.

La Russa assigns to himself the lion's share of responsibility for slowing down the other team's running game. "The single most important thing the pitcher and catcher can do is make the right pitch, so they should concentrate on that. Let me handle the running game. I keep the records, I pay attention to the opposing manager, and I've watched the runner more closely than they can." So whoever is catching for the Athletics is constantly in danger of getting a crick in his neck. Catching is hazardous enough, but a sore neck is an occupational hazard for the Athletics' catcher who, when runners are on base, is constantly looking over to La Russa.

La Russa has four signs he can give when his catcher looks over to him in the dugout: throw over to first base, hold the ball, pitch out and make "a bad-ball pitchout." The last is used when you are fairly sure you have decided on the other team's signs and are reasonably sure the runner has been given the steal sign. A simple pitchout would cause the other side to wonder, did they guess right or do they have our signs? The Athletics' pitchers are taught to throw the bad-ball pitchout head high but not far outside. The catcher rising to receive the pitch is in a good position to throw to second. The bad-ball pitchout is not a bad enough pitch that it can be used in a hit-and-run situation because a good contact hitter might be able to put it in play.

Dave Duncan is right: We remember best the things that hurt us. So La Russa will long remember the pitchout he did not call during the 1988 World Series.

"In game two, Hershiser got three hits. The second hit he got, there was one out, a runner, Alfredo Griffin, on first. Hershiser tried to bunt once and fouled it off. Then they let him swing and he fouled it off. Then a ball. A 1–2 count. You could tell by the runner's lead that it looked like he was going. And the Dodgers put some signs on. A lot of times with a two-strike count you don't bother about signs. So I said, 'I think something is on. They wouldn't hit-and-run on a 1–2 count with the pitcher up.' If I had trusted what I was *seeing* I would have put on a pitchout. It was screaming at me to pitch out. But I didn't. We threw a ball down and away, Hershiser threw the bat at it and punched a little hit down the right-field line, *with the runner going.* They knew he could put the ball in play." Griffin would have made it to third in any case. However, right fielder Canseco missed the cutoff man throwing back to the infield and Griffin scored. "It was great baseball," says La Russa.

Most good managers are as watchful as La Russa. Although Roger Craig sometimes delegates to a coach the duty of watching one or more of the key people on the other side of the field, he generally wants to watch the opposing team's manager, third- and first-base coaches and base runner before every pitch. He uses pitchouts and hit-and-runs more than most managers. (Evidence of the latter: The Giants start so many runners the team hits into fewer double plays than might be expected.) Many managers delegate to coaches various decisions that La Russa himself makes—whether to play the infield in or back, whether to throw through or hold the ball on a first-and-third steal situation, when to pitch out.

The king of pitchouts was Nick Altrock, who pitched in the dead-ball era. He had such a deadly pickoff move that he was said to have walked some batters because he thought picking them off first was the most expeditious way of getting them out. "A pitchout," says La Russa, "is an important part of defense. If I go against a team that doesn't pitch out on us, it's just like getting a free pass—run anytime you want. If you run two games in a row on a 2–0 count, in the third game we will pitch out on you." To avoid the cost of a pitchout (a setback in the count), pitchers try to inhibit the other teams' running game with convincing pickoff moves. But throwing over to first base also has a cost, drawn against the pitcher's stamina. "The best shot—really airing it out—takes a lot out of a pitcher. So we have a play in which instead of putting a sign on twice, we throw over twice, the first one is your average throw, the next is your killer."

Baseball is a game of quick episodes; it is also a game of anticipation. Therefore, advance information can be invaluable. That is why so much attention is given to stealing signs. "At least three clubs in our league—Milwaukee, Cleveland, Toronto—work hard to steal signs when they have a runner on second base. And that really irritates me. Okay, if it's an edge and the other team lets you take it, you go ahead. But if I were a pitcher, and I had to deal with all the changes of signs that the other team makes necessary by stealing signs, I would not put up with the disruption of my concentration. I'd do what Clemens did last year. He was going against Cleveland or some other team notorious for stealing signs. They give the batter location, in or away"—La Russa shows how, standing like a base runner, bent over at the waist, legs apart, patting one thigh or the other—"or they'll actually signal the pitch. As Clemens came to the stretch, he looked back and saw that the runner at second was giving the location. Clemens stepped off the mound, walked back there and said to the runner, 'If I ever see that again from you or anybody on your team I'm going to bury the guy at the plate.' " La Russa says the runner at second gave Clemens some back chat so Clemens returned to the mound and on the next pitch sent the batter sprawling.

Another way of combating such communication is to give the communicator at second base a credibility problem. "I was talking with Whitey Herzog about that," La Russa says. "He said that if he were a pitcher and saw a guy giving signs from second base, he'd call for the ball away and hit the guy in the ribs. The guy got a signal [from the runner on second] saying away. Pretty soon they don't talk."

The ancient practice of stealing catchers' signs from second base has been made easier by the satellite dish. This has vastly expanded access to telecasts of other teams. Center-field cameras give perfect pictures of catchers giving signs, so when runners get to second base they often do not need to decode the other teams' signs. A coach has done that already by watching tapes before the game. The runner may even know the "switch" sign, the one the catcher uses to switch the real sign from the first to, say, the third one given. Some teams have started relying less on advance scouts and more on people whose jobs are to tape games off satellites and cull information from the tapes, including the other teams' signs.

Jim Frey, who is in his fifth decade in organized baseball, has managed the Royals to a pennant and the Cubs to their first moment of postwar glory, the 1984 division title. Frey, now the Cubs' executive vice president for baseball operations, says the 1984 Cubs stole signs by television. When the Cubs were playing at Wrigley Field, Frey would send right fielder Keith Moreland or catcher Jody Davis into the clubhouse in the bottom of innings when they were not due to hit. These two veteran players were skillful at deciphering the opposing catcher's signs, which could be seen on the clubhouse television because the center-field camera was covering home plate on each pitch. Of course even when such deciphering occurs, the use of the intelligence depends on having runners get to second base—and having players who, when they get there, can concentrate on communicating to the batter what the catcher is signaling. You also need hitters who want to use the information.

One way to avoid having a catcher's signs stolen is to have the catcher stop giving signs. When Whitey Ford thought his catcher's signs were being stolen, he called the pitches himself, shaking his head specified times for particular pitches while his catcher ran through meaningless signs. Similarly, during the 1988 World Series, as catchers Terry Steinbach and Ron Hassey were constantly turning toward La Russa in the dugout, a television camera was frequently focusing on La Russa as he gave a variety of pitchout or throw-over or similar signs by touching various parts of his face and head. Except he was not giving any signs. They were being given by someone sitting next to him. Billy Martin used to give steal signs before some batters reached first base. When a count reached 3–0 on a batter who, if walked, Martin wanted to steal, Martin would flash the steal sign to his third-base coach. If the man walked and the other team turned its attention to Martin, looking for him to reveal his intentions, it was too late to steal the sign.

(At this point there was to have been a paragraph giving a particularly fascinating detail about La Russa's use of another kind of pilfered information. However, as a condition of being given access to team meetings—a reasonable condition—and in order to allow La Russa to speak without inhibition in our many meetings, I had agreed to excise any detail that he might decide he did not want to see published. There were very few of these. But on the morning of October 27, 1989, the day the World Series resumed in San Francisco, he asked that I remove the paragraph that had been here. Because the detail being removed was such a telling illustration of his meticulousness, I put up a small, brief argument for keeping it in. It was a feeble argument and, considering the man I was trying to persuade, it was singularly dumb. "That detail makes you look good," I said foolishly. He replied frostily, "The way a manager looks good is by winning games. That detail might cost me a run." Case closed, as lawyers like La Russa say.)

It is best that managers not expect too much precision in a high-energy game with layers-within-layers of complexity. Tom Trebelhorn remembers learning the limits of managing when he was managing Rickey Henderson in Boise, Idaho. "I had Rickey when he was 17 years old. Of course I had him running on his own. All I had was a 'stop' sign for when I didn't want him to go. But Rickey wanted the signs like everyone else. I said, 'Rickey, that's silly. We've worked on breaks and leads. What if you get on first and you want to run and I don't give you the steal sign. What are you going to do?' He said, 'I'll probably run.' I said, 'Well, okay, what if you get on first and I give you the steal sign and you don't think it's right and you don't want to run, what's that going to do? You probably won't get a good jump and you'll probably get thrown out and you should *never* be thrown out. I want you to feel it, I want you to taste it, smell it, get a good lead, get a good break, relax and go.' But Rickey said no, everyone else gets on base, they get the signs, I think it's neat, I want signs, too. I said okay, so we go over the signs: We've got take, bunt, hit-and-run, steal. And we've got a 'takeoff' sign, the one that erases—takes off—all signs. So Rickey gets on first, he looks over, I go through some signs, I finish with the takeoff. He steals second. Looks over for another sign. I go through most of the signs again, I don't even come close to the steal sign. I finish by wiping everything off with the takeoff sign. He steals third. Later I say, 'Rickey, this is ridiculous. You want the signs but you don't know them.' He says, 'I know the signs. You gave me the takeoff sign and I took off to second and I took off to third.'"

Trebelhorn, who will be 42 on Opening Day, 1990, is a manager like La Russa. A former high school teacher, he had a professional career batting average of .241 in five seasons, all in the minor leagues in places like Bend, Oregon; Walla Walla, Washington; Burlington, Iowa; Birmingham, Alabama; Lewiston, Idaho. He is an advocate of edgy baseball. "I'll tell you what I like," says Trebelhorn. "A Paul Molitor bunting for a base hit. A steal of second. A Jimmy Gantner take-it-with-you [a drag bunt for a base hit] to the right side getting Molitor over to third. A Robin Yount hard ground ball to the backhand side of the second baseman whose only play is to first, Paulie scores. I love that." So, he says, do the fans. "Our fans have changed." In 1982 the pennant-winning Brewers of Harvey Kuenn were called "Harvey's Wall-bangers," pounding out home runs, and fans flocked to see them. Today, Trebelhorn says, the fans write asking him to bunt more.

"Every club is a lot more active in trying to take the extra 90 feet," Trebelhorn says. "Not necessarily by bunting but by good flow on the bases—being able to go first to third, second to home, with runners on base being able to read a pitch in the dirt." Trebelhorn says that one of his slower players, Joey Meyer, "clogs up" the base paths. "One hundred and eighty feet, please—at least. If he hits a lot of singles and gets a lot of walks, he can't be our DH because that causes problems. What do you do if he leads off the seventh inning of a tight game with a single? You've got to run for him. So you tie up the game and you've got his spot coming up again in the tenth. It sure would be nice to have a possible home run, but I've had to run for him."

When Trebelhorn was managing in the minor leagues, even when his team was far behind he would have his team running, to create learning opportunities. And that policy won games. "If we were way behind and they played behind our runners, we ran. If you don't want us to run, then hold us on. And we're still going to run. In Fresno [California], when I was managing Modesto, we were behind 9–3 and they didn't hold us on first. We stole second. They didn't hold us close at second, we stole third. Hit a sacrifice fly, it's 9–4. We get another guy on, they hold him on, we still steal second. Now the catcher is fuming. We steal third, he throws the ball into left field, it's 9–5. We lose 9–5. After the game, the catcher says, 'That's really horseshit.' I said, 'If you're catching tomorrow night, I'm going to show you what horseshit really is.' The next night we went 15 for 15 stealing. Rickey Henderson stole 7 bases in the game. And we barely won the game, 11–9."

In 1988 National League teams attempted an average of 2.49 steals per game. American League teams averaged 2.10 steals per game. National League teams averaged 1.85 steals, American League teams averaged 1.34. American League runners had a slightly higher success rate, 68 percent to 67.2 percent. In 1989 National League teams attempted 2.31, American League teams 2.04. National League teams stole 1.57, American League teams 1.40. Again the American League success rate was slightly better, 68.6 to 68.1. These numbers give only negligible support to the standard knock against the American League, which is that the league plays stand-around baseball—stand around and wait for big things to happen, things like three-run home runs. National League teams, so the argument goes, try harder to make things happen by hitting and running, stealing and generally using their legs. National League partisans insist that a team that uses its legs is also using its head. So-called "little-ball," playing for one run at a time, and hence 90 feet at a time, requires a higher ratio of mind to muscle.

Ray Miller, who has coached in both leagues, says he has been at Wrigley Field when the wind was blowing out and the balls were flying out, and he has been there when the wind was blowing in and the balls that batters crushed died before reaching the wall. But in the American League there is Seattle's Kingdome, Minnesota's Metrodome, Fenway Park, Tiger Stadium, Arlington Stadium. "They're all Wrigley Fields," says Miller. He believes the bigger ballparks make for better baseball because there is less emphasis on "getting Godzilla to the plate" to hit a home run. There is, accordingly, more emphasis on getting one run at a time. Rick Dempsey, who now has caught in both leagues, believes that National League teams are more inclined to play for one run at a time. This is either a cause or an effect, or both, of there being more base-stealing talent in the National League. And that has something to do with there being more fields with artificial turf. "You can get a better jump and run faster on that stuff," says Dempsey, the word "stuff" expressing his distaste for the stuff. And he believes National League catchers will, when facing a running situation, call for more fastballs than they otherwise would call.

One reason people think this is so about the National League is that they think it ought to be so. Six of 12 National League fields have artificial turf and only 4 of 14 American League fields do. Another reason why many people think there are pronounced differences between the brand of baseball played in the two leagues is that there used to be such differences. There were when Maury Wills and other Dodgers in the early and mid-1960s were winning by manufacturing a few runs and counting on Drysdale and Koufax to make do with a few. A third reason why the leagues are thought to have different personalities is that this disparages the American League as the dumb league. National League partisans say the American League asked for disparagement when it adopted the designated hitter rule, which allegedly diminishes the strategic decisions a manager can make.

La Russa has managed only in the American League and therefore only with the DH. He does not feel it cramps his style or denies him scope for his talents. He is right.

The reason the American League has the DH can be stated simply. By 1972 American League attendance had fallen to 74 percent of National League attendance. Fans like offense. In 1973 the American League adopted the DH. One reason for retaining the DH is that it contributes to the public stock of harmless pleasure in the form of constant controversy.

I have tried to think through the DH controversy in the light of political philosophy, the queen of moral disciplines and the profoundest guide to the right way to live. I have gotten nowhere. Or to be more precise, I have gotten two places—to opposite conclusions. Let us at least try to bring orderliness to this controversy that is so disordered by passion. Let us begin by setting a scene that puts it in context. Consider the case of the laughing umpire.

The DH almost always bats for a pitcher. Because the National League did not adopt the rule, the designated hitter was permitted in the World Series only every other year. In 1986 Peter Ueberroth, baseball's commissioner, made a Solomonic decision. The DH would be permitted in games played in the American League team's park. The first game of the 1986 Series was played in the National League team's park, Shea Stadium, so the Red Sox pitcher, Bruce Hurst, had to bat. It was his first at bat in eons. The spectacle was so ludicrous that the umpire laughed.

Think about that. Umpires are carved from granite and stuffed with microchips. They are supposed to be dispassionate dispensers of Pure Justice, icy islands of emotionless calculation. In short, umpires should be natural Republicans—dead to human feelings. Hurst struck out his first two trips to the plate. On his way to his third strikeout, Hurst said defiantly: "I'm serious!" And the umpire cracked up. Can something that causes such a collapse of decorum be in the national interest?

The three arguments against the DH are: Tradition opposes it, logic forbids it, and it is anti-intellectual because it diminishes strategy. All three arguments fail.

Tradition? The National League, which fancies itself too highfalutinly traditionalist for the DH, plays an awful lot of pinball "baseball" on plastic rugs spread on concrete in cavernous antiseptic new stadiums in Houston, Cincinnati, Philadelphia, Pittsburgh, Montreal and St. Louis. Besides, by now the DH has a lengthening tradition. If longevity sanctifies, the DH is semi-sanctified.

The logic-chopping argument against the DH is given by Dwight Gooden, pitcher and logician: "The DH is a tenth player. Softball has ten players. Baseball has nine players." This attempt to win the argument by semantic fiat fails because . . . well, if the Constitution is what the Supreme Court says it is, baseball is whatever the rules say it is. This argument makes me queasy, so I will tiptoe off the thin ice and go back to the accusation that the DH diminishes strategy.

The theory that the DH is a war against intellect, and makes baseball safe for slow-witted managers, is a weak reed on which to lean for support. The theory is that when pitchers must bat, managers must be Aristotles, deciding when to remove pitchers for pinch hitters or when to have pitchers bunt. But it is disproportionate to preserve such choices, which are usually obvious, at the cost of having pitchers—one-ninth of the batting order—cause umpires to laugh.

National League chauvinists make much of the fact that in their league, if the fifth hitter gets on base, the sixth hitter must move him over so the seventh hitter will have a chance to drive him in. Otherwise the opposing team will pitch around the eighth hitter to get to the pitcher. So there is more emphasis on scoring one run at a time. But in fact, National League baseball may be more uniform and routinized because the so-called strategy regarding when to pinch-hit for the pitcher, or have him bunt, is so banal. More nonpitchers bunt in the American League than in the National League. And American League teams differ more than National League teams in their use of sacrifices. In some ways the DH makes managing more difficult. Again, most pinch-hitting situations are obvious. What often is far from obvious is when to remove pitchers who never need to be removed to increase offense. That is an American League manager's problem.

To the argument that the DH takes a lot of strategy out of managing, La Russa responds brusquely, "It definitely does not. The National League is a great propaganda league. 'We're the hard-throwing, running, let's-go-get-'em league and the American League is . . .' It's not true." Warming to his defense of the DH, he says that handling a pitching staff—perhaps a manager's most important task—is tougher in the American League. "Every decision you make in the American League regarding your pitching staff is based solely on who you think should pitch to the next hitter, or in the next inning. In the National League you get certain times when the decision is taken right out of your hands."

The best case *for* the DH is this: It represents that rarest of things, the triumph of evidence over ideology. The anti-DH ideology is that there should be no specialization in baseball, no division of labor: Everyone should play "the whole game." That theory is obliterated by this fact: Specialization is a fact with or without the DH. Most pitchers only go through the motions at bat.

Bruce Hurst may be baseball's worst batter, but few pitchers are even adequate batters and many are, strictly speaking, laughable. So without the DH, every ninth batter is unserious. A pitcher hitting is like a shortstop pitching. Baseball does not expect an unserious pitcher—say, the shortstop—to pitch to one of every nine batters on the opposing team.

National League managers occasionally put a pitcher at another position—right field, for example—for an out or two to enable that pitcher to stay in the game while another pitcher copes with a few batters. And a National League manager can dazzle us with a "double switch." That is a lineup shuffle usually used late in a game with the pitcher due up in the next inning. The manager changes the pitcher and a position player at the same time. He puts the position player in the pitcher's spot in the batting order so that player can bat in the next inning, and he puts the new pitcher in the batting order in the spot occupied by the player who has been replaced by the new position player.

The "double switch" is nifty, but it is not frequently used. And it is not sufficiently nifty to be a powerful argument against the DH. As Tom Boswell says, "Watching pitchers hit 50 times a week for the sake of two moments of strategy *isn't enough fun.*" The obvious solution to the DH conundrum is to expunge pitchers from the batting order but not replace them with a DH. Just have an eight-man batting order. A compromise solution would include what can be called the Carman Codicil. When Phillies pitcher Don Carman got his second major league hit after about 80 at bats, he was promptly picked off second. "I had never been to second," he said by way of extenuation. The compromise: Only witty pitchers should bat.

——◆——

At precisely 8:00 A.M. on Wednesday, August 31, 1988, Tony La Russa strides into the coffee shop of a motel hard by the Oakland–Alameda County Coliseum. That is where the Athletics play and where La Russa spent the night. Nine hours earlier his team had beaten the Boston Red Sox and they will do so again in four hours. La Russa is wearing running shoes, blue sweat pants and a T-shirt the distinctive orange of a Wheaties cereal box. The front of the shirt is emblazoned with the Wheaties logo. When a fan who recognizes him compliments him on the shirt, La Russa replies, tersely, "Read the back." The back says: "Commitment to Excellence."

Last night the mighty Athletics, who play "bashball" and after hitting home runs bump forearms rather than merely swap high fives, beat the Red Sox, 1–0. The Red Sox pitcher was Roger Clemens, who struck out 9 in 6⅓ innings. When you are facing Clemens, you come to the park knowing you are going to scratch for runs. The Athletics scratched. The runner who scored, Carney Lansford, reached first on a single to left, stole second and went to third on a wild pitch. He scored on a ball that traveled 30 feet. It was a suicide squeeze bunt laid down by Glenn Hubbard, who stands 5 feet 7. Funny business, baseball. Why is La Russa not laughing?

Laughing? He is not even eating. All he has ordered is a wedge of melon, and he is barely picking at it. His stomach is, he says, not exactly upset, but he is still too tense, too drained to eat. The squeeze was only the third attempted by the Athletics that season. It was the first that had worked. Going into the ninth, Dave Stewart had thrown 120 pitches. He struck out Ellis Burks on three pitches. He did the same to Todd Benzinger. He got an 0–2 count on Jim Rice, then missed with a borderline ball. Rice fouled off two, then struck out. It was, La Russa says, one of the most draining games of his career.

Today's game starts at noon. No one will have had enough sleep. It is the last day in August. Tomorrow begins the month when, for the best baseball teams, life is real, life is earnest. Emotions are high, as are the stakes. Nerves are often raw and tempers are short. Last night one player on each team was hit by a pitch. It is time to think about the ethical and prudential problems of batters being thrown at, and of retaliating when it happens to your batters. La Russa's policy is the result of much reflection. He has thought often and hard about his reputation as a man with a hard side.

"If a guy is hitting well against our club, I have never, *ever* told a pitcher, 'Let's go ahead and hit him.' Some guys do that." In 1987, when McGwire was setting a record for rookies with 49 home runs, he hit 2 home runs on a Saturday against the Red Sox and got hit on Sunday. Hit on the head. La Russa's normally muted tone changes as disgust fills his voice when he speaks about the practice some teams have of saying, "This guy's wearing us out—knock him on his ass." Gary Gaetti, the Twins' third baseman, embodies everything La Russa likes in a player—intelligence, intensity, hustle. Once when an Athletics pitcher deliberately hit Gaetti, at a time when Gaetti was blistering Athletics pitching, La Russa called the pitcher on the carpet and told him, "You'll never pitch for me again if you do that again." La Russa explains, "We can make him [a hot hitter] uncomfortable pitching in on his hands. But that is it."

Regarding retaliation, La Russa has a doctrine of measured response. "It's a 2–1 game and your big guy gets bopped in the bottom of the eighth inning. Now you've got to go out in the top of the ninth with a one-run lead and you need three outs. Who should make the decision whether you retaliate? It's got to be the manager. Sometimes you walk up to your player who got hit and say, 'I really believe this guy took a shot at you. We'll get somebody in the first inning tomorrow.' " La Russa is a stickler for proportionality in punishment. "You try to match, as best you can. If they take a shot at your big producer, then you take a shot at their big producer. If they've just cold-cocked McGwire and their first batter in the inning is their light-hitting second baseman, that's not the guy. If someone takes a shot at Walter Weiss, then you look for their promising rookie or their second-year player who is a big star."

In game three of the 1983 American League Championship Series between La Russa's White Sox and the Orioles, the Orioles' pitcher, Mike Flanagan, hit Ron Kittle with a slider. A slider is a good pitch to hit someone with because it is two to three miles per hour slower than a fastball and it is more apt to look like an accident. La Russa knew that Kittle was Flanagan's biggest problem. So in the next inning someone comparable to Kittle—a young power hitter named Cal Ripken—got hit. "We will never, ever retaliate above the shoulder. So the guy will get stung but he will play again," La Russa stresses.

"Once you establish that you'll protect your players, that is a part of the game you shouldn't have to worry about. Then the only things left are those natural, unavoidable confrontations between two competitive teams trying to beat each other. If someone throws a fastball outside and Jose hits a home run to right field, they may try to throw a fastball inside to get him out. If they miss they might hit him. You'll never avoid those. We are a very aggressive, pitching inside-off-the-plate club."

Two changes, one in equipment and one in teaching, have complicated the problem of deciding what is and what is not fair in the war between pitchers and batters for control of the inside and outside edges of the strike zone. Batting helmets, which were not made mandatory until 1971, increased batters' aggressiveness by decreasing fear. And the batting style taught by the late Charlie Lau has made many hitters seem (to pitchers) excessively, provocatively aggressive. Lau, whose most famous work of art is George Brett, was the White Sox batting instructor when La Russa was the White Sox manager.

The gospel according to Lau is: Shift your weight to your back foot as the pitcher winds up, then stride in toward the plate, shifting your weight to provide the power at the moment of contact. Striding in is dangerous to the hitter—and to the pitcher's career if he lets it occur without any resistance. It gives the batter too much control of the outside corner.

"You want to hit?" La Russa asks. "First you have to see the ball, and you have to stay on it. Second, you need a positive move toward the pitcher. You can't wait to see whether the ball is coming at you. You can't be on your heels. If you are, you flinch when a guy throws a breaking ball, you take too many pitches because you're a little leery. If you have a whole club like that, you can't hit. They won't step into the ball and take their chances. If you don't protect yourself, it's just one of those edges that people will take away. It's a little bit scary to go up there and face that ball being thrown hard. If you know your club isn't going to protect you, you're going to lose a big edge at the plate. Everyone is going to go up there a little timid, a little farther from the plate.

"Some umpires get a little ticked off when somebody takes a cheap shot, messes with their game. They'll hold off on a warning until you retaliate. But sometimes the minute your guy gets hit, they'll put the warning in and tie your hands. Then you tell the umpires between innings—I've never lied to them about this—'I understand the warning. We've got six innings to play and we're not going to take a shot at anybody. But our basic pitching philosophy against this club is that they crowd the plate. I don't want to lose this game because our pitchers stayed out over the plate. So I'm telling you we're going to be pitching inside to get guys out. If at any time in this game or this series I want to take a shot, I'll come and tell you it's coming.' Otherwise an umpire puts in a warning, and your pitcher is afraid to throw inside. He might get thrown out of the game. So he moves out over the plate and starts getting creamed."

All this theorizing at the breakfast table will become intensely practical on the field in a few hours. The Red Sox pitcher, Mike Smithson, will get hit hard right from the start. He will get exasperated and will throw at the Athletics' third baseman, Carney Lansford, who has done some of this early damage to Smithson. Lansford will duck the pitch, but the fact that Smithson deliberately threw at him was obvious to everyone, including the person who mattered most, the home plate umpire, Richie Garcia. His response illustrated one of the nuances of governance inside the game.

Garcia came to umpiring from the Marine Corps, which is good training for a vocation that an umpire once summed up in seven words: "Call 'em fast and walk away tough." Toughness is not enough, but it is necessary. Once when Babe Pinelli called Babe Ruth out on strikes, Ruth made a populist argument. Ruth reasoned fallaciously (as populists do) from raw numbers to moral weight: "There's 40,000 people here who know that last one was a ball, tomato head." Pinelli replied with the measured stateliness of John Marshall: "Maybe so, but mine is the only opinion that counts." Or, as Garcia tells young umpires (and every parent should tell every child): "Just because they are yelling at you doesn't mean you are wrong." Long ago the ethic of umpiring was expressed with great dignity by Bill Guthrie: "Der ain't no close plays, me lad. Dey is either dis or dat." That is true, *de jure*. De fact is, however, that, *de facto*, things are different.

When Smithson threw at Lansford, Garcia took off his mask, looked out to the mound and for a moment seemed about to issue a warning. That would have required both teams to behave. Anyone henceforth convicted (by the home plate umpire's instant and of course unappealable judgment) of throwing at anyone would be ejected. Garcia's brief pregnant pause ended not with a warning but with a brisk brushing off of home plate with his whisk broom. His message was muted but clear: The Athletics would get to retaliate. They did, in strict accordance with La Russa's principle of proportionality. In the next inning Lansford's counterpart, Wade Boggs, the Red Sox third baseman, got thrown at. He was not hit but he had to bail out of the batter's box. The game continued. The Athletics won.

They had played 134 games and were in first place by nine. Their manager was, in his fashion, almost content as he looked ahead to a trip to Texas.

————◆————

A few days later, La Russa is not pleased. A plate of pasta, his preferred postgame fare, is cooling on the desk in the visiting manager's office in Arlington, Texas. La Russa is pleased enough with the pasta. The man who runs the visiting team clubhouse at Arlington Stadium has a four-star rating among players. But La Russa is cooling off from a particularly grating loss to the Rangers on September 6, 1988.

The Athletics came close, but came up short. In the ninth they got the potential tieing runs to third and second with a power hitter at the plate. La Russa worked all the pedals on the organ, even putting a pinch runner in for a pinch runner. To no avail. The Athletics lost, 3–1.

The near-miss in the ninth inning was the final frustration in an evening that La Russa had gloomily expected to be frustrating. The Rangers were pitching Charlie Hough, who had already beaten the Athletics five consecutive times. Hough, 40, looks like Lyndon Johnson with a secret sorrow. His meandering, maddening knuckleball comes to the plate slower than the throws he makes to first to hold runners close. This night La Russa tried a midget—well, sort of; these things are relative—in place of muscle. He pulled mighty Mark McGwire from the starting lineup because sometimes the torment of trying to hit Hough has sent McGwire into two- or three-game minislumps. And this night La Russa put Mike Gallego in the lineup at second base. He's just 5 feet 8. Confronted with that small strike zone, Hough might have to abandon his knuckleball and throw Gallego his fastball, such as it is, which is not much.

Before the game Lefebvre took Canseco aside for a slight stroke alteration, using a batting tee. Generally Lefebvre had three jobs with Athletics hitters. The first was physical: getting them ready to swing. As anyone knows who has greeted the spring with too much enthusiastic swinging of a bat, swinging uses a lot of muscles in a special symphony. For the untrained, 15 minutes of hitting fungoes can make it hard to get out of bed the next morning. Lefebvre's second job concerned mechanics: getting the hitters' hands, hips, heads and other parts working together. The third task concerned the mental part of hitting: deciding how to handle particular pitchers. This, he says, is 90 percent of hitting.

In 1988 Lefebvre had a batting coach's dream. It was Jose Canseco having what players call a "career year," meaning a year as good as the particular player can expect to have. Of the 42 home runs Canseco hit in the regular season, 16 came with 2 strikes on him. He hit 3 more in the League Championship Series and a grand slam in the World Series. Of his 46, 31 either tied a game or gave the Athletics the lead. Lefebvre jokes that coaching a talent like Jose

Canseco is simple: "My number-one chore was to see that his bats weren't cracked. 'They all right? Okay, then go up and hit.' " But Lefebvre was not doing himself justice. Before the game against Hough, Lefebvre took Canseco to a batting tee in front of the backstop to practice swinging up through the ball a bit more than normal. Hough's knuckler was going to come bobbing and weaving toward the plate and Lefebvre thought Canseco, who normally swings up slightly, would do best if he increased that a bit, with the bat coming up as the ball fluttered down. For about 15 minutes Lefebvre, facing Canseco, traced a rising arc with his extended arm while Canseco ripped balls off the tee into the net. In the game Canseco would get three hits.

Fat lot of good they did. Hough bewildered the Athletics for the sixth consecutive time. But he needed help in the ninth inning.

In the ninth, with the Athletics down by two runs, with two outs and a runner on first, McGwire pinch-hit and singled. Now there were runners on first and third and the plot suddenly thickened. Tony Phillips was put in the game as a pinch runner for McGwire on first. But before the batter after McGwire, Dave Henderson, stepped into the batter's box, Hough was pulled from the game, replaced by Cecilio Guante. If Hough had stayed in the game, with his deceptive little semi-balk move to first, the Athletics would not have contemplated getting the potential tieing run into scoring position by stealing second. But with Guante in, the running game was given back to La Russa. Luis Polonia is a better base stealer than Tony Phillips so Polonia was sent in as a pinch runner for pinch runner Phillips.

Any pitcher who has a release time of 1.4 seconds is, La Russa says, "runnable." Polonia running on a pitcher who is 1.4 to the plate is going to be safe almost every time. Guante, when he is not worried about a stolen base, has a big delivery and a time of 1.6. "So," La Russa says, "what he does instead of the big delivery is this. Instead of lifting his front leg toward the plate, he simply slides his leg toward the plate. Now he has a time of 1.2." La Russa knew Guante could do this, but La Russa felt that by putting Polonia on first base he had Guante "between a rock and a hard place." If Guante stayed with his big delivery, Polonia would get to second. If Guante went to the slide step, Henderson at the plate would be a happy fellow.

"You try to get more leverage with the pitcher," La Russa explains. "Dave Henderson is a three-run home run standing at the plate. Does the pitcher want to throw Henderson a short [lacking some velocity] fastball? The slide step costs Guante velocity. It's a tough time for a pitcher to go to a slide step because you're going to lose a little of your stuff and the guy at the plate may go for extra bases." So Polonia helped the Athletics' offense just by being at first. And he did not have to stay there. He could steal if La Russa could anticipate when Guante would, and when he would not, use the slide step with Henderson at the plate. "It's a guessing game," La Russa says. "I know he's not going to slide step Henderson five pitches. It's just too risky for him." Guante did not slide step in his first pitch, but neither did he use his big, slow delivery. He split the difference. The pitch was a ball. "I didn't think he'd slide step 1–0." La Russa ordered a steal. He guessed wrong but got away with it. Guante used the slide step but Polonia beat the throw to second. Now the tieing run could score on a single. But the Athletics were down to their last out and with Polonia at second, with no one on first, Guante went back to his big delivery and got back the foot he had lost off his fastball. The tricky stuff was over. Now it was the pitcher against the hitter. The pitcher won. Henderson hit a fly caught by the left fielder. Texas won.

As the pasta congealed, La Russa took out his briefcase and started poring over paperwork, looking ahead to Kansas City. The Royals are 6–0 against the Athletics. Four games on Kansas City's artificial turf mean that some players need to be rested. He must decide which ones. Good. He has something to worry about.

◆

On a cold rainy February day in 1989 in Oakland, where February is concentrated grayness, the Athletics' offices in the Oakland–Alameda County Coliseum are a warm swarm of green and gold and anticipation. A truck is being loaded with bats and balls bound for Phoenix. The manager is thinking of Spring Training, and beyond, to Opening Day, and beyond that deep into April, to a series with the White Sox. Rummaging through his briefcase, La Russa extracts one of the tools of his trade, a three-by-five index card. Over the course of a season he fills hundreds of these with notations in his small, precise print. The card he has just fished from the briefcase lists every playing date in April from Opening Day, April 3, on. Next to each day there is a number—1 or 2 or 3 or 4 or 5—for the starting pitchers and where they rank in the rotation. Opening Day is still

53 days away but La Russa has his starting pitchers selected for every game up to May 1. Because of an open date, his number-one starter, Dave Stewart, would be rested enough to pitch in place of the fifth starter in the third game of a three-game series in Chicago at the end of the second week of April, but La Russa's charts show that the fifth starter, Mike Moore, eats up the White Sox. Stewart will be saved.

Now, as the rain falls and his spirits rise, La Russa, semi-formal in blue jeans and a tan sport jacket, begins to talk about "situation baseball," particularly the double-steal possibilities with runners on first and third. The double steal is difficult to execute. La Russa estimates that anytime you try a trick play against major league talent, the odds are 40–60 or 30–70 against. "But, if you have a guy at the plate who is not a very good RBI man, who doesn't have a good chance of driving them in, well, go ahead and take a shot."

Because baseball skills are so difficult, and because the difference between success and failure is usually so slight, aggressive managing often involves putting one's batters and runners in harm's way. Aggressive managing means making moves that will fail if the other team executes its response perfectly. But if the running team is going to force an imperfect response, it must be perfect in executing its own aggressive move. Over the course of a season, the best teams will, more often than not, force failure—which is anything less than perfection—from opponents.

La Russa talks the way he manages and the way he wants his team to play, controlled but intense. The pace of his conversation is brisk, the words crisp, the sentences clipped at the end so as to leave no loose ends. His is a style, a personality, of carefully moderated but constantly maintained edginess. Those are qualities needed for plays in the first-and-third situation—eight of such plays. There is a straight steal in which the runner at third bluffs a dash toward home as the runner on first tries to steal second. The hope is that the bluff by the runner on third will cause a hesitation on the part of the catcher of a sufficient fraction of a second to make the steal of second successful. And there are seven other permutations of the first-and-third situation.

One is the regular double steal. The runner on first breaks for second. If the catcher comes up to throw through to second, then the instant the catcher's arm starts forward the runner on third breaks for home. The second play is especially suited for first-and-third with two outs. The man on first breaks toward second, then stops. If the catcher throws through to second, the runner on third breaks for home the instant the catcher's arm starts forward.

The third play is a delayed double steal. As soon as the pitcher is committed to deliver the ball to the plate, the runner on first takes, La Russa says, "about three hops toward second. Slower runners do this in a way that suggests getting ready to run on a hit, not to steal. The second baseman or shortstop—whoever is supposed to cover second—sees this runner stop and relaxes regarding a steal. But on the third hop, just as the ball gets to the plate and while everyone's attention is focused there, he takes off for second. He probably will be out if the infielders are paying attention and cover second. But the infielder may be late in breaking for the bag and the catcher may therefore hesitate before throwing. Now, the advantage of doing this with a runner on third is that the infielder is normally late in getting to second to cover a delayed steal. He takes the throw on the run, then he has to adjust himself and throw the ball back to the plate. In 1984, early in the season, we [the White Sox] were playing in Yankee Stadium. We were losing, 1–0, in the seventh or eighth inning. Greg Luzinski ["The Bull," who was as large and slow as a tank] was on third with two outs and a runner on first. We put on the delayed double steal. The runner on first took off. The catcher hesitated, then fired to second. The moment he threw, Luzinski broke for the plate. Willie Randolph [the Yankees' second baseman] was playing back to cut off a base hit. He caught the throw on the dead run, made a great off-balance throw, made it a close play at home. Safe."

The fourth play is used against a left-handed pitcher. As soon as the pitcher comes to a set position, the runner on third initiates the play by breaking for home. The instant he takes off, the runner on first, who is watching him, breaks for second. The left-handed pitcher is facing the runner on first. The runner racing for second may draw a throw. If he does, even if he is out, the runner on third will score. Or a split second of indecision on the part of the pitcher may allow the runner from first to reach second and the runner from third to score.

"Now," says La Russa, mentally moving to the defensive team's dugout, "here is how to defeat it. If, when the pitcher sees the guy breaking for second, he steps off [the rubber] and checks the runner on third, he just throws home and the runner is out." If the runner has not broken from third and the pitcher throws to second, that runner should get in a rundown and the runner on third may score. But if the pitcher raises his arm and takes even one step toward the runner going to second, and only then throws home, it will be too late.

The fifth play is a version of the fourth, but against a right-handed pitcher. The runner on first breaks for second. The runner on third, with the pitcher facing him, edges down the line toward home and breaks for the plate when the pitcher turns and commits to throw to second. If the pitcher does his job right, he hears his infielders shout that the runner behind him is going for second, he steps off the rubber, freezes the runner on third and throws to second.

The sixth play is the "stumble start." It is a tactic for freezing the catcher. The runner on first takes a few quick steps toward second and then pretends to fall. (La Russa demonstrates, sprawling on the carpet. His conversation could spoil the creases in his jeans if they had creases.) The catcher sees this stumble out of the corner of his eye. As soon as the catcher commits to throw to first to nail the floundering runner, the man on third, who has a long lead, breaks for home.

The seventh play was a favorite of Billy Martin. It is used against a left-handed pitcher who has a slow move to first base. The runner on third takes a long lead. The runner on first takes enough of a lead to tempt the pitcher, who is facing him, to try to pick him off. As soon as the pitcher starts his pickoff, the runner on third breaks for home. If the runner on third has misread the pitcher's intention and the ball goes to the plate, the runner usually can get back to third.

The eighth play depends on getting the runner on first picked off and hung up with the ball in the first baseman's hand. The runner heads for second and the instant the first baseman throws to second, the runner on third breaks for home.

Other than as the front end of a double steal, the steal of home is a vanishing thrill. It never was common. Ty Cobb stole home more than anyone else, 46 times, but that was over a span of 24 seasons. Yet in olden times, even big men did it. Lou Gehrig stole home 15 times, Babe Ruth 10 times. In the postwar era, things have been different. Lou Brock, the all-time base-stealing leader (until Rickey Henderson breaks his record), stole 938 bases but never stole home. Through 1988 Henderson had stolen home only four times, and never since 1982. The man who may have helped kill the thrill was one of its most artful practitioners, Rod Carew. He holds the single-season record with seven steals of home. He was one reason why more pitchers began pitching from a stretch instead of a windup with runners on third.

The increased willingness of even popular hitters to "show bunt" has caused third basemen to play closer to the bag, limiting the lead a runner can get. Furthermore, in this age of long careers and large salaries, runners do not relish the risks involved in slamming full tilt into catchers, who tend to be on the large side.

Still, the first-and-third double-steal possibilities are so sweet that they once were a reason for stealing first base. In 1908 Germany Schaefer of the Tigers found himself on second with a teammate on third. To set up the double steal, the inventive Schaefer ran back to first, making it safely to the base, perhaps because of the element of surprise. On the next pitch he broke for second. The catcher threw to second. On the throw, the runner on third scored. Oh, yes: Schaefer was safe at second.

Second base is the base most stolen. La Russa thinks that stealing third base is a neglected offensive weapon. "I get criticized for stealing third 'meaninglessly.' Usually that means there are two outs. But it can be a high-percentage steal. And I guarantee that if you do that 15 times over the course of a season, you will score 3 or 4 extra times." One of the iron axioms in "The Book" (that unwritten code of baseball tenets that "everyone knows" are true) is that you never want to make the third out at third base. That axiom means, in practice, conservatism on the base paths with two outs. It means not trying to stretch a double into a triple, not trying to steal third. The theory is that second base is scoring position and third is not much better. The theory is wrong.

If you get to third with less then two outs you have many more ways to score than you had at second: soft outfield single, infield hit, sacrifice fly, infield out, safety squeeze, suicide squeeze, error, balk, wild pitch, passed ball, steal of home. And you score on most of those with two outs. Furthermore, just the knowledge that your team sometimes steals third—that knowledge, plus convincing behavior by runners on second—improves your hitting. "Watch clubs play the A's. You know what their shortstops and second basemen do? Jockey, jockey, jockey. Because they know we steal third. With our powerful hitters most infielders want to play back. But what we want to do as an offensive team is not let them have it both ways.

If they worry about us stealing third and jockey to hold us on second, it's going to cost them some range.

"We were playing somebody—I forget who—and their pitcher was slow to the plate, so our guys started saying 'We can go, we can steal third, can't we, skipper?' I said, remember there are two things necessary for a steal. One is the pitcher being slow to the plate. The other is the infielders forgetting the runner. In that game the shortstop came over, we couldn't steal third because he was right behind our runner, so he's not able to take a lead big enough to take advantage of the pitcher's slow delivery. Later in the game, one of our slower runners, someone like [catcher Terry] Steinbach, was on second. They were so conscious of their pitcher being vulnerable to stealing and of us likely to steal third, that while they were busy bluffing him back to second, a little grounder, about a 15-foot hopper, was hit in the vacated hole between short and third and Steinbach scored a big run."

Stealing third can be, and usually should be, easier than stealing second. It is, of course, true that the catcher's throw is shorter to third. (The throw from home to second is 127 feet 3⅜ inches, or more than 37 feet longer than the throw to third.) However, the runner's lead off second should be longer than his lead off first. The two important variables are the pitcher's release time and the infielders' awareness. "If these are going for you," La Russa says, "then your slowest runner can steal third. Greg Luzinski could steal third."

La Russa managed Luzinski on the White Sox and explains how to make a Luzinski into, if not Mercury, or Maury Wills, at least a legitimate threat to steal third. Second is too hard. A left-handed pitcher is facing a runner on first base. Even a right-hander can, with reasonable peripheral vision, keep an eye on a runner at first longer than a pitcher can watch a runner on second. At some point a pitcher has to be done looking at second base and must look in the opposite direction, toward the plate. Most pitchers will have a pattern. They will look toward second once, or twice. In any case, it is generally possible to know when a particular pitcher is done looking. Regarding infielders' awareness, usually either the shortstop or second baseman has responsibility for primary coverage of second base, keeping the runner close to the bag. If the hitter at the plate is right-handed, the second baseman will generally be keeping the runner close; if the hitter is left-handed, the shortstop is responsible.

Now, says La Russa, suppose the batter is right-handed. That is the best situation for stealing third because the catcher will have to throw past the batter to get the ball to third. Suppose Luzinski is on second and Carlton Fisk, the Sox catcher, is up. Fisk is a powerful right-handed hitter. The shortstop will want to play over in the hole. He is not going to pay attention to Luzinski. The second baseman is supposed to, but he wants to play as deep as possible against the big, powerful and slow Fisk. Now, suppose the pitcher is a "one-looker." Luzinski can start with a ten-step lead. Stealing third is easier than stealing second even if you have only one of the two variables (pitcher's release, infielders' awareness) on your side. Of course, a third variable is the ability to pick the right pitch to run on. By learning opposing pitchers' patterns, you can guess, with reasonable confidence, a breaking ball or change-up.

There are techniques that can be called semi-steals that can get a runner from third to home or from second to third. In one play, there is a runner at third. The batter lays down a base-hit bunt—that is, a bunt not anticipated and not intended as a sacrifice—toward third. The third baseman fields the bunt with the runner on third creeping in right behind him. If the third baseman tries to throw the runner out at first, the runner can stroll the rest of the way home from third. If the third baseman stops to drive the runner back toward third, the bunter will get a base hit out of it. The only danger to the team at bat is a rare one—a shortstop who can instantly diagnose the play and sprint to third in time to trap the runner from getting back to the base.

The second variation begins with a runner at second and the batter faking a base-hit bunt. As soon as he shortens up on the bat, the third baseman charges in and the runner breaks toward third, which is momentarily unprotected. The batter takes the pitch and proceeds with his at bat with the runner 90 feet closer to home. "We've done that—accidentally," La Russa remembers. The runner on second decided to steal, the batter decided to bunt, the batter shortened up on the bat to do so but did not like the pitch, and everyone marveled at the serendipitous result—a runner on third.

Baseball history has many examples of what can be done by combining foresight, guile, brass and speed. Back at the beginning of the 1980s, when Billy Martin brought "Billyball" to Oakland as the Athletics' manager, he used a play in which Rickey Henderson, as a runner on first, would set out to steal second while Dwayne Murphy, a left-handed hitter, would drop a base-hit bunt toward third.

When Henderson broke toward second, the shortstop would race to cover second and the third baseman would charge the bunt. Henderson would turn second at full throttle and wind up at the unprotected third base. Murphy would either get a hit or, if he was out, his bunt was, in effect, a two-base sacrifice.

That play is a cousin of one that Ty Cobb and his teammate Sam Crawford occasionally used when Cobb was on third and Crawford walked. Crawford would stroll toward first and then suddenly sprint around the base and tear toward second as Cobb was creeping down the line from third. If the startled team in the field threw to second, Cobb scored easily. Otherwise Crawford arrived at second with a two-base walk.

What all such plays have in common is the constant push for a very slight edge. That push makes for edginess in both dugouts. La Russa's base runners are taught to develop "antsy leads." Most teams, when the other team has a runner on first, have a pitcher step off the rubber and hold the ball or throw over—all to give whoever is responsible, the manager or the coach, time to watch the runner to see if he tips off whether he is going. The "antsy lead" is a way of convincing the pitcher's team that you are, indeed, going. The point of convincing them is to "work the count" by drawing a pitchout. If you draw it, you gain in the count and you may take the pitchout weapon away from the other team, at least for that runner. "But it's important to take an antsy lead all the time, even if you are stealing," says La Russa. "If you don't, those guys [in the other dugout] will see the difference and say 'He's not trying to decoy us—he's going.' They're smart over there." He leans back in his chair, sighs contentedly and says, "There's a lot of stuff goes on."

It will be going on again soon, come spring. Come on, spring.

————◆————

Spring Training is delightful everywhere but it is best in Arizona. The aridness of the region gives the green of the grass a particularly blazing brilliance. Some players complain that they can not sweat in Arizona's dry climate but they are mistaken. They are sweating but the evaporation is virtually instantaneous. Others complain that because there is no humidity, the air is so thin that breaking balls do not have enough movement. There is a grain of truth to that complaint. However, aesthetics have their claim and the yellow cast of the sandy soil and the gleaming green make Cactus League baseball as pleasing to the eye as the Athletics' green and gold uniforms.

Mornings at the Athletics' Spring Training camp begin with the team assembled in right field under the direction of a lean, limber man who places a boom box on the ground and fills the air with music. Under his guidance the team bends and stretches and generally works on baseball's most recent fetish—flexibility. It is a sensible fetish. Baseball is a game of torque on the body's trunk—swinging a bat, throwing, reaching to pick up the ground balls.

This, then, is how to begin again, by getting the body ready for baseball's suddenness. Baseball is not, like basketball or hockey or soccer, a game of steady flows. Rather, it is an episodic game of explosive exertions. They take a toll on muscles and can tear them and tendons and ligaments that are not patiently prepared for the ordeal. Hence this languorous 10:00 A.M. spring session with music, men slowly preparing for thousands of bursts of effort in the hard, hot summer.

What La Russa has liked most about his recent Athletics teams was their "daily pushing, grinding." Now it is March and the Athletics are tied with the Seattle Mariners and everyone else in the American League West. It begins again. Grinding can have different effects on different materials. It can dull some material by grinding it down; it can give other material a sharp edge.

"Baseball," says La Russa, "is the all-time humbler."

2

THE PITCHER

Orel Hershiser,
In the Future Perfect Tense

Minutes after Orel Hershiser won the fifth and final game of the 1988 World Series, Tony La Russa was asked to explain the defeat of his Athletics. In five games the Dodgers' pitchers had held the Athletics to 2 home runs, 5 extra-base hits, 11 runs and a team batting average of .177. La Russa answered: "It's been going on in baseball for 100 years. When pitchers make quality pitches, batters do not make good contact." Not far from where La Russa spoke an Oakland fan spotted Hershiser walking through the bowels of the stadium. The fan shouted: "You were lucky, Hershiser." Hershiser, without breaking stride, replied: "Oh, yeah? Grab a bat, kid." Then, after a pause, he smiled.

Hershiser had a lot of luck in 1988. One reason he had it is that he paid for it. He bought it with finely focused intelligence. "During the second game of the World Series," La Russa recalls, "I was standing next to Dunc [Dave Duncan]. It was the first time I had been against Hershiser. About the fourth or fifth inning I said to Dunc, 'We've got a problem. This guy reminds me of someone we both know. Watch him.' Dunc said, 'I think I know who you're talking about.' Just the way he was going about his business, competing, paying attention, his sense of what the situation was. He reminded me of Tom Seaver, the smartest pitcher I have ever been around." When Hershiser entered professional baseball he began hearing a refrain from older baseball people. It was: "I wish I knew what I know now back when I could still do it." He decided to know it in time. For six weeks at the end of the 1988 season he seemed to know everything. The six weeks began immediately after August 24. And he knew a lot that night, too.

On the evening of August 24 he lost a 2–1 decision to the Mets in Los Angeles. That was all the losing he would do for the rest of 1988. Midway through his next start, in Montreal, he would begin one of the most remarkable pitching performances in major league history. And he might have won on August 24 if the Mets' Mookie Wilson had hit a home run rather than just a triple. Funny business, baseball. Sometimes less is more.

With the Dodgers leading 1–0, Wilson hit a towering drive to the right-field fence, about two feet short of a home run. The Dodgers' right fielder, Mike Marshall, got to the ball but could not catch it. Should have, but didn't. He wrestled it to the ground and Wilson stood on third. If it had been a home run the score would have been tied but the Mets would not have had a rally going. The bases would have been empty; the pitching and defensive dynamics—they are interlocked—would have been different.

In the clubhouse after the game Hershiser, his elbow in a tub of ice, told a cluster of writers and broadcasters, "If that ball is caught they probably don't score any runs. I probably don't walk [the next batter, Wally] Backman—I was pitching carefully to him to save the run. Then Hernandez hits a three-hopper to first, through the hole because we're holding Backman on." With Wilson on third, Hershiser walked Backman on a 3–2 pitch, a fastball away. Then Keith Hernandez hit a 1–0 slider, dribbling a dinky grounder past the first baseman, Tracy Woodson, who was holding Backman on. Even so, Woodson would have got to the ball if he had not slipped when moving for it to his right. If he had got to the ball he could have thrown the runner out at home or started a 3–6–3 double play.

But "could haves" do not count. After the hit by Hernandez it was first-and-third again, still no outs. Hershiser struck out Darryl Strawberry. The next batter, Kevin McReynolds, hit the first pitch, a fastball, to center for a sacrifice fly. The score was 2–1, and it would remain so.

The next morning a United Airlines charter lifts out of LAX, through the smog clogging the Los Angeles basin. The flight is carrying the Dodgers to Philadelphia to begin a road trip the next night.

Hershiser is wearing glasses and carrying a briefcase. He jokes that when he retires he may "bulk up" and become a professional wrestler using the name "The Mad Librarian." He settles in for the five-hour flight and some morning-after reflections.

Aside from the fact that he lost, it was a typical night for him. He pitched well. He had to. The Dodgers' hitters are in a dry spell. In fact, it has been an arid season. Last night's game was the seventh 2–1 loss for the Dodgers so far in a season in which they would lose ten 2–1 games. So Hershiser had to scratch for every edge he could find. For example, in the first inning, after the first Mets batter grounded out to second baseman Steve Sax, Hershiser walked over to first baseman Woodson and said something. When asked what he said, Hershiser laughs, pauses to weigh candor against the politeness owed a teammate and says: "Oh, boy. I know exactly what I said but I don't know if I should say it in public." Candor wins: "Woodson doesn't play first for us very often. I said, 'Just remember, with Sax throwing you don't stretch too early.' " Meaning what? "Saxy has some errant throws at times"—that was the understatement of the 1988 season—"and if you stretch too early you won't be able to catch the ball. If you stretch straight at him early and the throw is to one side, you can't move, you're stuck."

The previous night the Mets got their first hit in the fourth inning, a single to center. The ball came back to the infield, was thrown to Hershiser, and he promptly threw it to the umpire to have it replaced, which it was. Why did he want that? "The particular ball I had was okay for throwing fastballs but it wasn't a very good ball for throwing curves." The 108 stitches sewn on every baseball by Haitian hands are not quite as uniform as they would be if machines did the work. "The ball that I throw for a curve, I look for a high seam on the ball to pull on. If the ball doesn't have a high seam, if it has just two equal seams, or seams that are a little bit on the large size, it's okay for my sinker because I really don't need a high seam for my sinker. Even though I like a high seam for it, I can throw it without a high seam and I don't go out of my way to find the perfect ball every time. But in a key situation like last night, after they got a hit and they have a chance to score a run or start a big inning, I make sure I have the right ball in my hand. I change balls a lot out there and I think the umpires know that, and I don't want them to get tired of me throwing the balls in." He has had the experience that Jim Palmer, another notorious perfectionist, occasionally had.

The intensity of Palmer's attention to detail was about equal to Hershiser's intensity cubed. Palmer would throw a ball to the umpire, who would throw Palmer a new ball but would put the one Palmer rejected back into the pouch on his belt. Later in the game the umpire would throw it back to Palmer, to see if Palmer would notice. Usually Palmer rejected it again.

In a later inning of the Mets' game, with the Mets' pitcher up and a runner on second—a clear bunt situation—the Dodgers' shortstop broke over toward the runner on second just as Hershiser went into his motion. The shortstop looked badly out of position, but appearances can be deceiving, especially when they are supposed to deceive. That was a play the Dodgers put on in just that sort of situation. "We break the shortstop to the bag," Hershiser explains, "which makes the runner think we're throwing to second, so he's going back to the bag. I throw home and throw a strike to *get* the guy to bunt. If he does, the runner on second has got a terrible jump." And that substantially increases the chances of throwing the runner out at third. Because this maneuver opens such a huge hole at short, it can not be used when the batter is skillful enough to abandon the bunt and try to shoot the ball through the yawning hole on the left side, into left field. "We can only do that with a pitcher who can't swing the bat. He doesn't have good bat control, so we'll give him the hole. And even with a good bunt we might throw out the guy at third."

But it is usually wise to have the third baseman charging on a bunt, which he can not do if the shortstop has been jockeying far to his left. "The third baseman is more used to handling the ball [than a pitcher] and we're charging at three areas instead of two. With only one charging the third base–pitcher's mound area, the only bunt we're going to get a double play on is the one directly to me. If two of us charge, there are more bunts we can get two on."

The Dodgers, like all teams, have a play in which the shortstop sprints to third ahead of the runner coming from second on a bunt. But going for the lead runner is risky and in the game with the Mets the Dodgers wanted to be sure to get one out. Better to have a runner on third with one out than to risk having first-and-third and no outs and a big inning brewing. Furthermore, with the Mets' pitcher having just bunted, the top of the Mets' order was coming up. Hershiser got past that patch of trouble. He had only one bad time, beginning with Mookie Wilson's triple, but it was bad enough to beat him.

Asked how many pitches he threw last night, he guesses 115 to 120 and calls up to pitching coach Ron Perranoski sitting a few rows ahead. Perranoski knows: 127. Hershiser's recall of components of last night's game is complete. He knows, for example, that he threw nine pitches to the first batter in the game, Mookie Wilson. "I threw five pitches to get to 3–2, he fouled three off, I finally got him out. The next guy was out on two pitches, and Hernandez was out on three. So the first inning I threw 14 pitches."

In Hershiser's next start, against the Montreal Expos, he will face the Expos' first baseman, Andres Galarraga, who is having a wonderful year. How good does Hershiser think he is? "He's *very* good. He's patient. He waits for your mistake." How many mistakes does Hershiser make in a game? "A mistake is a pitch I didn't execute well, one I left in an area where they could hit it. You don't call a ball a mistake because you miss the strike zone. That's not a mistake. A mistake, to me, is a ball I leave in the middle of the plate. I probably threw about five of those last night." Five mistakes out of 127 pitches. And not all of those were hit safely. Not all were even put into play. He struck out Strawberry on a mistake. "The count was 1–2 and I threw a curveball in the strike zone that he swung at and missed. Bad pitch. One-and-2, I've got three pitches to get him out. I might throw him three balls that are close to the plate. He'll probably chase one of them. But on my very first pitch at 1–2, I threw a curveball for a strike. It was an unbelievable curveball—don't get me wrong. It was a hard, hard breaking curveball—star wars—but it was still in the hitting area." Hershiser also got away with a mistake to Dave Magadan. "When I got Magadan to line out to third and got out of the inning, I was mad at myself because I had made a stupid pitch. But I was fortunate. It was a ball right in the area he likes to hit. It was up and away, and my strength is low and away. And I threw the ball too hard, so the ball straightened out. I allowed the intensity of the situation to overcome what is best for my ability, which is to be a little more relaxed."

Relaxation is, paradoxically, a form of baseball concentration. Relaxation must be *willed.* It is the necessary unclenching of the mind. It is a form of discipline. The Dodgers were flying into the final leg of a pennant race that would allow neither time nor energy for might-have-beens. They can drive players 'round the bend at any time.

A case in point: In the bottom of the seventh, right before the Mets went ahead, 2–1, the Dodgers got two hits and runners on first and third, no one out. The next batter, Dave Anderson, bounced the ball back to the pitcher and the runner on third, Tracy Woodson, was thrown out trying to score. After Woodson was thrown out, Hershiser was up. He bunted the runners over to second and third but made the second out. Steve Sax was up next. He popped out to end the inning. Woodson might have made a mistake in heading home as soon as the ball was hit. The reason for breaking from third is to prevent a double play, and if there had been one out there would be no questioning the decision to head for home. But in this case the runner might better have waited until the pitcher turned and threw to second, and then headed home. If he had made it, the Dodgers would have led, 2–0. Anderson had swung at the first pitch. If he had not swung and if the pitch had been a ball, Lasorda might have put on a squeeze play because, with the count 1–0, the pitcher probably would have put a buntable pitch in the strike zone.

But let the dead past bury its dead. "You get into close games, you've got to execute. Suppose you lose a game, 4–2, and they beat you on a two-run home run in the ninth after it had been 2–2 the whole way. You say, 'Oh, if the guy hadn't hit that home run, we would've won.' But you go back to the first inning when you couldn't bunt the guy over. Maybe in the fifth inning there was a man on third with less than two outs and you didn't get him in. Another inning you were first-and-third, no outs, and you didn't score."

Hershiser believes he did his duty last night. "After I threw the three perfect innings I said, all right, just two more sets like that. Last night the first set we were tied. The second set I won, 1–0. The third set they won, 2–0. They won, 2–1. If I can just go two sets I've done my job as a starting pitcher. That third set is all above and beyond the call of duty." He adds, "If I can go out and throw nine innings and give up two runs for the rest of my career, I'm going to pitch a long time and make a lot of money and get a lot of wins."

In the first-class section of the plane sit the manager, coaches and other dignitaries. They include a broadcaster who once was a pitcher and now is in the Hall of Fame, partly because of a record that will, during the next six weeks, be broken by the pitcher sitting about 15 rows to the rear.

◆

The plane landed in Philadelphia. Five nights later, in Montreal, Hershiser took off. The Expos scored two runs off him in the fifth inning. That was it for the National League against him in 1988. Beginning in the sixth inning he pitched 59 consecutive scoreless innings, eclipsing along the way the achievements of four Hall of Famers: Carl Hubbell (45⅓), Bob Gibson (47), Walter Johnson (55⅔) and Don Drysdale (58⅔), the broadcaster who had been seated in first class. And the streak was just part of Hershiser's achievement. In his last nine starts of 1988 he racked up a record of 7–0 with seven shutouts. As icing on the cake there was a twelfth-inning relief appearance to nail down victory in the fourth game of the play-off against the Mets. And all that was before he beat the Athletics twice and became World Series MVP. He became the first pitcher to achieve shutouts in both the League Championship Series and World Series in the same season. Between September 5 and the last game of the World Series Hershiser pitched eight shutouts. He yielded 5 earned runs in 101⅔ innings, and one of those scored after he had left the game. Counting (as the official record does not) the first game of the play-offs, he pitched 67 consecutive scoreless innings. He figures that even a very good pitcher who is pitching well should expect to give up an average of a hit an inning. In his final 13 appearances he gave up hits at about half that rate, 55 in 101⅔ innings.

In his last 101⅔ innings in 1988 his ERA was 0.44. That was bettered only by Bob Gibson's 0.19 over 96⅔ innings. However, Gibson did that in 1968, which, as will be demonstrated, was a peculiar season that brought about some changes that make Hershiser's achievement even more impressive. In the game in San Diego in which he broke Drysdale's record, Tony Gwynn, the hitter Hershiser most respects, grounded four times to the second baseman. As we shall see, Gwynn should never hit four consecutive balls to the right side of the infield.

Suppose Hershiser had shut out the Mets on August 24. (If Mike Marshall had caught Mookie Wilson's fly ball, a shutout could easily have been the result.) That would have been Hershiser's second shutout in a row. Now, suppose he had not been scored on in the middle of that next game, in Montreal, when he began his record-breaking shutout streak. The streak would have been more than 82 scoreless innings in the regular season, and 90⅓ counting the first 8⅓ innings of game one of the play-offs.

On the other hand, suppose there had been a single run some-where in the middle of Hershiser's streak. That would not have diminished the quality of his season. A run, earned or unearned, could have scored on a bloop hit off a great pitch, on a bad bounce of what should have been an easily fielded ball, or on an error. Happens all the time. But it did not happen for 59 innings.

If Dave Stieb of the Blue Jays had not given up a bad-hop single with two out in the ninth of one game in September, 1988, and had not given up a broken-bat single with two out in the ninth in the next game, Hershiser would have had to share the headlines with Stieb's back-to-back no-hitters for the Blue Jays. (Stieb was only the sixth pitcher in history to pitch two consecutive one-hitters. In his second start in 1989 he pitched another one-hitter, becoming the first pitcher to throw three one-hitters in four starts and coming tantalizingly close to the dizzying achievement of three no-hitters in four starts.)

Was Hershiser lucky? Obviously. So what? Some sports achievements are all luck. Usually these are single instances, such as Don Liddle's good luck in having baseball's greatest center fielder playing behind him one day in October, 1954.

With the score tied in the first game of the 1954 World Series between the New York Giants and the Cleveland Indians, the Giants brought in Don Liddle to pitch to Vic Wertz with two runners on. The Indians' batter crushed a Liddle pitch 460 feet to the deepest part of the deepest center field in baseball, where only Superman could catch it. Superman did. Willie Mays made his famous over-the-shoulder catch and, even more remarkably, threw to hold the runner on third base. Liddle was immediately yanked. He strode into the dugout, put down his glove and said, "Well, I got my man." Liddle was lucky. Hershiser was more than lucky. You have to be good, very good, to get 177 men out without anyone scoring.

Some of baseball's most memorable achievements were helped along by repeated instances of luck. In Don Larsen's perfect game for the Yankees against the Dodgers in the 1956 World Series, the Dodgers' Sandy Amoros missed a home run by about a foot; Mickey Mantle made a sparkling running catch at his knees of a sinking line drive off the bat of Gil Hodges; and Jackie Robinson ripped a line drive off Andy Carey, the Yankees' third baseman, but the ball bounced straight to shortstop Gil McDougald, who threw out Robinson. (After the game, manager Casey Stengel was asked the dumbest question in the history of journalism: Was that the best game he had ever seen Larsen pitch? Stengel said: "So far.") Some of the hits that kept Joe DiMaggio's 56-game streak going in 1941 were lucky. Twice DiMaggio benefited from close calls by official scorers on hits that could have been called errors. Twice he got dinky hits—a catchable fly ball fell untouched, and a full swing produced a slow roller that dribbled into an infield that was pulled back.

However, Professor Stephen Jay Gould of Harvard—paleontologist, polymath and serious student of baseball—argues that long streaks necessarily are products of, are compounds of, skill and luck. Great athletes have a higher probability of success than normal athletes have in any instance—any at bat, any inning pitched. A streak is a series of discrete events occurring with the probability that is characteristic for a particular player at a particular point in his career. Frederick the Great, when asked what kind of generals he preferred, answered: "Lucky ones." He was, as was his wont, being serious. His point was that luck is unpredictable but talent takes advantage of it. Thus the talented have, in effect, more of it. It magnifies the tendencies of the talented. In the future, just over the horizon, in the next game, the next inning, the next at bat, there lurks something that can never be wholly subdued by talent or eliminated by training and preparation. That recurring thing is luck. Baseball, with its long, leveling season, is the severest meritocracy in sports. There is ample time for talent to tell. The ratio of talent to luck is high. But luck is part of the equation.

How good was Hershiser's season? Very. In 1988 the league batted .213 against him, but right-handers did not do much worse (.206). His record (23–8, 2.26 ERA, 178 strikeouts in 267 innings) fell short of Ron Guidry's 1978 season (25–3, 1.74 ERA, 248 strikeouts in 273⅔ innings). A streak, a season. How good has Hershiser's career been? Very good. That is all, but that is a lot. Few people appreciate how hard it is to be a consistently successful pitcher. Ted Williams was, of course, right. Hitting a baseball is the hardest task in sport. But baseball would be unbalanced and uninteresting if it were not almost as hard consistently to pitch baseballs so skillfully that they can not be hit safely often enough to score runs constantly.

Only one pitcher in either league—Dave Stewart of the Athletics—won 20 games in 1987 and 1988 and 1989. Jack Morris of the Detroit Tigers was the only major league pitcher with at least 15 wins in each of the seven years from 1982 through 1988. His streak ended in 1989. Only two pitchers, Morris and John Tudor, had winning seasons every year of the 1980s, through 1988. Their streaks ended in 1989. In 1988 Frank Viola won the Cy Young Award with a 24–7 season for the Twins. In 1989 with the Twins and Mets, he was 13–17. Of the 56 Cy Young winners through 1988, 19—slightly more than a third—had losing records the year after they won the award. Why is it so rare that individuals have high levels of performance over more than a few seasons? Because pitching is hard. A difference of a few miles per hour in the delivery, or a few inches in the location, of a few pitches thrown to major league hitters can make a decisive difference in wins and losses. Through 1989 Hershiser had winning records in three of his first six seasons (not counting 1983 when he pitched just eight innings). If losing as many as he wins makes a pitcher rank as mediocre, for two consecutive seasons, 1986 (14–14) and 1987 (16–16), Hershiser was mediocre.

That is a big "if" because won-lost records are not very revealing, as 1989 showed. In 1989 Hershiser was 15–15. He only climbed to .500 by winning his last start, 3–1. It was a twelve-inning game. He pitched eleven innings. His ERA was 2.31, comparable to his 2.26 in 1988. He pitched approximately the same number of innings (256⅔ to 267) and got exactly the same number of strikeouts (178). In 1988 his ratio of hits plus walks to innings pitched was a sparkling 1.052. In 1989 it was 1.181, a difference of about 1 hit or walk every 8 innings. In 1989 he lost four times, 1–0, and in four other losses the Dodgers did not score while he was in the game. In his last nine starts the Dodgers drove in just 7 runs. At one point he found himself in the midst of another kind of scoreless innings streak: The Dodgers went 34 consecutive innings without scoring while he was pitching. In his 15 losses the Dodgers scored a total of 17 runs. He allowed only 41 runs in those 15 losses. If the Dodgers had scored just 19 more runs for him in his last eight losses, his record would have been 23–7. In 1988, 23–8 won him the Cy Young Award and a contract that for the next three seasons would pay him about $600 per pitch.

The 1984 season was the first full season for both Hershiser and Dwight Gooden of the New York Mets. Through 1989 their records were: Gooden, 100–39; Hershiser, 98–64. Over that span Frank Viola won more games than either (106–73). During those six seasons Hershiser had three more victories than Jack Morris (95–68) and Roger Clemens (95–45) and just eight more victories than the fifth winningest pitcher, Charlie Hough (90–82). Hough is hardly a byword for glamour, or even a household word, even in the homes of baseball fans.

The famous "Class of '84" included these seven rookie pitchers: Dwight Gooden, Roger Clemens, Mark Langston, Jimmy Key, Mark Gubicza, Ron Darling and Hershiser. Gooden is the class of that class, so far. In 1984 the 19-year-old Gooden set a National League record with a total of 32 strikeouts in two consecutive games. In those 17 innings he walked none and in one game he did not go to three balls on any batter. In that game he threw only 28 balls in 120 pitches. In 1985 Gooden became the youngest pitcher ever to win 20 games, the youngest to win the Cy Young Award, and the first since Sandy Koufax in 1965 and 1966 and Steve Carlton in 1972 to win the pitcher's triple crown, leading the league in wins, strikeouts and ERA. In fact, Gooden, like Koufax in 1965 and 1966, led the major leagues in those three categories. At the end of the 1989 season he was in the select circle of starting pitchers with a winning percentage of .700 or better over six seasons.

On June 19, 1989, when Gooden won his one-hundredth game at age 24 years and 7 months, he was the third-youngest pitcher (behind Bob Feller, who was 22 in 1941, and Frank "Noodles" Hahn, who was 24 years and 2 months in 1903) to win 100 games. Gooden's record was 100–37, a .730 percentage. On that day Hershiser, then 30, had a record of 91–55, .623. However, Hershiser is doing something that neither Gooden nor Roger Clemens is certain to do. It is something that one can not assume that any young pitcher will go on to do. Hershiser is pitching with steady success in his thirties. He may be one of those pitchers who are markedly better after 30. This is more an achievement of mind than of muscle. Or, more precisely, it testifies to the use of mind to conserve muscle.

Anyway, a .623 winning percentage is very good, particularly for a man who began life as a spina bifida baby. "Clark Kent at least had a good body," Hershiser says. "I'm Jimmy Olsen." Not true. When Nature designed Hershiser, it had a pitcher in mind. Hershiser has a pitcher's body and mind. He may look slight; when he is standing next to Kirk Gibson, the Dodgers' unshaven and untamed former football player, he may even look frail. But at 6 feet 3 and 192 pounds Hershiser is very much the modern player. Long ago pitchers used to be the biggest, strongest men on the field. They were intimidators. And pitchers have not been getting smaller. (In 1988 Nolan Ryan, at 6 feet 2 and 210 pounds, was only the fifth-largest Astros' pitcher.) But other players have been getting bigger faster. So there is a sense in which Tom Boswell is right when he says "hitters are mesomorphs, pitchers are ectomorphs." Rendering that thought into the vulgate, Boswell says that in the locker room pitchers look like the guys the other players beat up. Indeed, the most dominating pitcher over a full season in the Seventies and Eighties weighed about 160 pounds. That was Ron Guidry's weight in 1977.

Actually, Hershiser is one of baseball's best all-around athletes. "I'm an everyday player in the guise of a pitcher." He was a terrific schoolboy hockey player, but he always had his eye on the ball, not a puck. When he was eight years old the Personna razor blade company sponsored a nationwide throw, hit and run contest. Hershiser finished third in the nation and got to go to Yankee Stadium for the finals. "But," he says, "from there my career went downhill." His coaches at Cherry Hill High School in New Jersey and at Bowling Green State University in Ohio must have been surprised when he went on to serious success. He was cut from his high school varsity team in his freshman and sophomore years. He was cut from his college team in his freshman and sophomore years even though he was on a baseball scholarship. His 6–2 record as a junior was just good enough to get him drafted by the Dodgers in the seventeenth round, "more as a suspect than a prospect," he says.

There is no shame in being selected deep in the draft. Baseball is so difficult, and its particular skills require so much honing, and the honing requires so much character, that the baseball draft is a highly unscientific, uncertain plunge. Other players picked in late rounds who turned out to be good investments include Andre Dawson (11th round), Roger Clemens (12), Jack Clark (13), Dave Parker (14), Jose Canseco (15), Mark Langston (15), Frank Viola (16), Kent Hrbek (17), Bret Saberhagen (19), Don Mattingly (19), Ryne Sandberg (20), Bob Boone (20), Paul Molitor (28) and Keith Hernandez (42).

"Ever since I was eight years old I wanted to come back to a big-league stadium, and I never doubted that I would." Almost never. He says that once when playing Double-A ball in San Antonio he gave up 23 earned runs in three appearances and began to wonder whether he would get "back to" a big-league stadium. Ever since he was eight he had felt as though he had been there.

Born in September, Hershiser's parents had a choice about when he would start school. They took the early option, so he grew up competing with boys a bit older. He thinks it helped him. "I was always battling uphill. It gave me good work habits, made me work hard." Hershiser is a German name. It descends from one of the Hessian mercenaries that George Washington routed at Trenton after he crossed the Delaware—which he did after pitching a dollar (a sinker?) across the river, or so 'tis said. Hershiser got his nickname, "Bulldog," from that fountain of folk wisdom and applied philosophy, his manager, Tommy Lasorda. Early in Hershiser's career, when he was struggling, Lasorda called him into his office for a pep talk. Lasorda is nothing if not long on pep. In the course of what you may be sure was a soliloquy, Lasorda said he was going to start calling Hershiser "Bulldog." Why? asked the pitcher. Lasorda explained: "Suppose the game is tied in the ninth against Atlanta, the bases are loaded, Dale Murphy is up and I bring you in to pitch. If the public address announcer says someone called Orel Hershiser is coming in, Murphy is eager. But if the announcer announces Bulldog Hershiser, Murphy may be worried."

Or as Ron Perranoski puts it, with the pith one would expect of a former relief pitcher, "We nicknamed him Bulldog for the very aggressive face he doesn't have." Perranoski remembers Hershiser from Single-A ball in Clinton, Iowa, and before that in the Arizona instructional league. "The first impression of him is of a librarian. But when he was in the instructional league I knew he liked to play golf and I wanted to test what kind of competitor he was, how aggressive he was. We had a little wager." Pause. "He showed me he was a great competitor."

Two kinds of people are particularly important to a pitcher, those who catch him, and his pitching coaches. Perranoski, the Dodgers' pitching coach, was in the 1960s one of the developers of the specialty of relief pitching. It is a vocation for the professionally aggressive. He pitched for 4 teams over 13 seasons, compiling 179 saves and a 2.79 career ERA. Because he made his living primarily by putting out fires other people had lit, and preventing late-inning disasters, he is a connoisseur of pressure. He has iron-gray hair—one understands why—and a solid, stolid mien.

When warming up starting pitchers in the bull pen before games, Perranoski has them work on their various "release points"—the different arm positions at which the fastballs, breaking balls and change-ups are released. When Hershiser is pitching, Perranoski's job is to watch for mechanical problems, particularly a tendency for Hershiser to "open up" his shoulder—to turn it too much toward third base—which causes his fastball to come up in the strike zone. Perranoski's experience is that "you lose the snap on your curveball before you lose the velocity on your fastball. Then the curveball, instead of snapping, it just sort of rolls."

Perranoski recalls that when Hershiser first came up to the major leagues, "I really had to calm him down a little bit as far as his actions on the field were concerned. If he was going good, striking batters out, he had a little bit of hot dog in him. He might get the ball back from the catcher and snap it with his glove. He wasn't trying to show anyone up but they might not understand that. I'd say, 'Don't wake up a sleeping dog over there.' " Rick Dempsey understands that, but adds, "How a pitcher conducts himself on the mound is very important to the rest of the guys out there." Dempsey is convinced that the confidence of a Hershiser or a Roger Clemens is contagious. When they take the mound confident they can handle the other team, their own team relaxes. Their teammates are apt to score more than they would if they were pressing because they were worried about needing to get runs in bunches. "It's funny," says Dempsey. "When you think you aren't going to have to score a lot of runs, you are apt to score a lot. And when a new young pitcher comes up the team is apt to think, 'We've got to bear down and score some runs for this guy,' and they wind up not getting many." If relaxation is something that can be willed, a pitcher—central to his team's emotional as well as physical geometry—can will it for his team.

One evening in August, 1988, Dempsey was relaxing in the dugout in Philadelphia's Veterans Stadium. It was the beginning of the road trip that would take them next to Montreal, where Hershiser's scoreless innings streak would begin. Hershiser, said Dempsey that evening, is like Jim Palmer, who was easy to catch precisely because he was so opinionated about pitching. A trace of wonder still comes into Dempsey's voice when he remembers Palmer's extraordinary recall of crucial experiences. Standing on the mound, Palmer could inform Dempsey that he was not going to throw a particular pitch to a particular batter in a particular situation because the batter had hit such a pitch hard in a similar situation two years earlier. "I called a game for Palmer once against the White Sox when I *never* dropped down two fingers. He never threw anything but fastballs. He changed speeds a lot, but never threw any other pitch. Every batter was waiting for him to throw his curve. Everyone was baffled. And he beat them, 5–1."

Hershiser, like Palmer, has a confidence easily mistaken for arrogance. But confidence is necessary, especially in the National League. In that league a pitcher who lacks confidence may be constantly tempted to try to tailor his style to the team he is facing or the park he is in. For example, says Dempsey, some pitchers make the mistake of making fundamental changes in their approach when they are facing the Cardinals, a team some players think of as a track team that has been taught to play baseball. Some pitchers want to throw the Cardinals more fastballs than they normally would throw. "But if you do that you are falling right into their hands as far as hitting-and-running goes." If a running team can be confident of an unusually high ratio of fastballs, it can be more confident of hitters making contact, and hitting-and-running becomes safer. Dempsey says an opponent's running game is not a big factor "if your team is hitting the ball well. If you're not and you're playing a lot of one- and two-run games, you've really got to slow the other team's running game down a bit." On the other hand. . . . There is always another hand. "In the case of the Cardinals, who don't have a lot of power, and are counting on getting a lot of singles, you can call a lot of fastballs." Because few are going to be hit into the seats.

Dempsey, who has caught in both leagues, believes there are more "low-ball umpires" in the National League, umpires who call as strikes some pitches that in the American League would generally be called low balls. The higher strike zone in the American League could be a lingering effect of the umpires' equipment. Until 1980 American League umpires behind the plate did not wear, as they now do, the sort of chest protectors that National League umpires have long worn, the small wraparound kind under their shirts or jackets. They wore "mattress"-style protectors over their clothing. These cumbersome protectors made it difficult for them to bend over and look along the catcher's sight line. As a result, while National League umpires crouched low, on the inside corner, American League umpires called pitches from directly behind the plate, over the catcher's head. And National League umpires saw more low strikes, or so it is said.

According to Mike Scioscia, who has caught most of Hershiser's games, Hershiser's four-seam fastball (a ball held across, rather than with, the four seams) "gives the illusion of rising but all it does is probably stay a little straighter than the sinker." When Scioscia is catching Hershiser he has two signs for location (inside and outside) and four for pitches (sinker, breaking ball, change-up, four-seam fastball). If Scioscia wants the ball up in the strike zone, it is such an odd call for a sinker-ball pitcher that he usually goes to the mound to ask for it. Hershiser's sinker requires Scioscia to resist temptation and exercise diplomacy, lest he have trouble with the man in blue standing behind him. Scioscia says a lot of catchers try to "steal" strikes for their pitchers by not turning their mitts palm-upward on a low pitch. This, they think, will not make the pitch seem so low. But catching a low pitch with the fingers up requires the catcher to, in Scioscia's words, "jerk the pitch." Once the umpire sees that, he assumes the pitch was low.

One way Scioscia can be helpful to Hershiser is by being watchful, and thoughtful. Talking to *Sports Illustrated*'s Peter Gammons about the 1988 World Series, Scioscia said, "I watched the A's hit in batting practice before the first two games to look for little tendencies. For instance, when I heard the hitter ask the batting practice pitcher for a curveball, I watched to see if the hitter made any adjustment with his feet. If he did he would probably move his feet similarly in a game, and that would indicate to me that he was sitting on [waiting to pounce on] the breaking ball." (Mike Flanagan of the Blue Jays says "stance-reading" has attained such subtlety that some batters try to mislead those doing the reading: "Chet Lemon will move way up in the box like he was looking for a curve so that you'll throw him a fastball.")

A pitcher sets his own pace but the catcher calls the game, so he can influence the pace. Scioscia says, "You pace a pitcher with pitch selection. It's not cutting down on the number of fastballs you call because actually it takes more effort to throw a curveball. The key is the number of pitches you'll waste in a game. You're not going to pitch around as many hitters as you might earlier in the game." By "pitch around" he does not mean giving the hitter first base by not throwing strikes. Rather, he means trying to get an undisciplined free swinger out on pitches that are not strikes. "Pitching around" a batter requires more pitches than otherwise might be thrown. It is a defensive weapon that may have to be used late in a game. In every election, American democracy gives the government essentially the same instructions: Maintain our services, cut the deficit and do not raise taxes. Pitchers, too, are forever being given unhelpful directives: "Don't give this guy anything good to hit—but don't walk him." That is what is meant by pitching around a batter.

With a runner on first when Hershiser is pitching against a team managed by someone who likes to bunt, Hershiser, according to Scioscia, does a few unorthodox things. First, he's not afraid to throw breaking balls, thereby breaking the rule that in such a situation you throw high fastballs because they are hard to bunt. Hershiser's theory is that a bunter is like any other hitter, so the first priority is to upset his timing. However, Scioscia says, Hershiser's approach is the luxury of someone who knows he can throw his breaking pitches for strikes.

Sometimes the best thing a pitcher can do about a runner on first is to forget about him. Mike Scott of the Astros is a severe realist. He is not the only National League pitcher who believes that the only way to cope with Vince Coleman as a base runner is to prevent him from becoming one. Scott's approach is: If you can't keep him off first, at least keep him off your mind. He can outrun the ball, so there is no point in fretting. You only make matters worse by losing your concentration on the next hitter. Scioscia says he has been taught not to change pitch selection to subsequent batters just because a base-stealing threat, even the likes of Coleman, has reached first. "If you change your pitch selection you're apt to get a hit and have first-and-third or, worse, a double with a run in. What I've got to do is first check the runner's lead and then control his jump. You control it by varying your timing to home plate, throwing over to first, stepping off the mound. Don't let him time your movement. Now, once you start you've got to keep a short leg kick, which Orel has, to give the catcher a chance to get the runner if he goes."

Hershiser has reacted to the likes of Coleman (and Tim Raines and Gerald Young) by adopting a new delivery from the stretch position. He used to come to a set position with his feet close together. This allowed him to get power behind his pitches from a full stride. Now he begins his motion from a set position with his "plant leg"—his left leg, which he plants as he comes forward toward the plate—almost as far toward the plate as it will be when he plants it and follows through. This costs him velocity—about three miles per hour off his fastball—but he thinks the sacrifice is well worth it because "no matter how good a jump the runner gets, it's almost impossible for him to steal." Scioscia says, "Orel has a quick release but, more important, he has good stuff with men on base. Some pitchers will sacrifice their good stuff to try to hold a runner on first. It's not just that they may go too much to fastballs. It's that if you call a curveball you might get one that will roll a little bit because a guy is so wrapped up in his quick delivery to the plate that he is not making his best pitches. Orel has the ability to give me a quick release and still give me his best stuff. It all has to do with pressure and command out there. Orel knows that if he takes a long time throwing the ball to the plate, then any walk he gives up is going to be a double."

Hershiser rarely shakes off Scioscia's signs more than a couple of times an inning. "Let's say he throws me a bad curveball. I'm thinking we'd better go to a sinker because if he gets that sloppy curve in the strike zone the batter is going to hit it. But Orel is out there thinking, 'I threw a sloppy curveball but I know what I have to do to throw a good one.'" In the seventh inning of the second game of the 1988 World Series, Hershiser, facing Carney Lansford, shook off Scioscia's sign twice just to get Lansford, a thoughtful veteran, thinking too much. (Not all shake-offs of signs involve such cunning. The young Lefty Gomez, facing a scary slugger, once shook off his catcher so many times that the catcher came to the mound for an explanation. "Let's wait a while," explained Gomez. "Maybe he'll get a phone call.") Pitchers work in different and constantly changing contexts. What they try to do depends on the score, the risk of a run scoring immediately and the stage of the game. (The importance of two runners on base in the second inning may not be the same as the importance of two runners on in the ninth.) And the controlling conditions include the condition of the pitcher himself: How does he feel?

"The season takes a big toll on you," says Scioscia, who makes a living squatting, being hit by batted balls and colliding with base runners. "I think a pitcher probably has his really good stuff 60, 70 percent of the time. You are usually going to be a little short on your fastball or some other pitch." Sometimes a pitcher will not have a clue as to how he is going to do until he does it—or fails to. Mike Scott remembers the night in St. Louis when he felt the best he has ever felt when warming up. He felt as though he was throwing 100 miles per hour to the exact spots he wanted to throw to. "I thought, 'There's no way they can hit me.' I didn't get out of the first inning. The first guy—Brock or Templeton—got a hit. Then I walked somebody. Then Hernandez hit a home run. Then Ted Simmons hit a line drive by my ear that was caught against the center-field wall for an out. Then someone hit a home run off the stadium restaurant and I was out of the game."

Scioscia knows how baseball goes when things are not going smoothly. He once was knocked cold by Jack Clark in a collision at the plate, but he held on to the ball and made the putout. Pitching, he says, requires making do when you can't make the ball do what it does on your best days. "Anyone can win when they're pitching well. But guys like Orel and Fernando [Valenzuela] can win when they don't have great stuff. They know that you don't have to throw strikes to get a guy out." A pitcher once said: "Control without stuff is far better than stuff without control. Whenever you hear it said that such and such a pitcher didn't have a thing, you can bet he had control if he didn't have anything else." (That was said by Yankees pitcher Carl Mays the year before he threw the only pitch to kill a batter.) Scioscia says that if he had to select the most valuable of the three virtues—velocity, movement, location—that pitchers culti-vate, "I'd pick location because of the 'holes' in every batter's swing. Willie Mays had holes, they were just smaller than anyone else's." That is Scioscia's answer to the perennial question about who is easier to pitch to, a power hitter or a contact hitter. Scioscia says it is easier to pitch to a hitter with a lot of "holes" in his swing, and that is usually a power hitter. But if you make a mistake with a power hitter, it hurts a lot more than a mistake to a contact, singles hitter. So Scioscia says that Hershiser, who has good control, matches up well against a power hitter with more "holes" to pitch to. Hershiser agrees but still does not enjoy it. When asked for an example of a hitter who bothers him, Hershiser says, "Any power hitter. I don't want to see [Atlanta's Dale] Murphy coming up with the score tied or a one-run game." What makes Murphy so tough? "You make a mistake, he hits it." What is enough of a mistake? "A curveball in the middle and a little high, compared with a curveball low and away." What is the difference in inches? "Six inches each way."

———◆———

Baseball is indeed a game of inches and the most important 17 of them form the width of the five-sided slab of rubber called home plate. The last really good news for pitchers came nine decades ago, in 1900, when the plate was changed from a 12-inch square to a five-sided object 17 inches wide. But that did not settle things. Life is a battle and baseball life is an endless series of skirmishes about who will control the periphery of the plate, batters or pitchers. The stakes are high. A 90-mile-per-hour fastball in on the fists is hard to hit and nearly impossible to hit with power. If that fastball is 6 horizontal inches farther out over the plate, all the 90-mile-per-hour speed is doing is generating energy for the impact with the bat. "You throw the ball on the outside corner," Hershiser says, "you have a perfect pitch and you have either an out or a strike. You make a mistake, you miss for a ball, you get four of those. You pitch inside, you can have a strike on the inside corner, but if you miss over the middle of the plate, you don't have either a strike or a ball, you have a double or a home run. So you pitch away. But you have to come inside to protect the outside of the plate." That is, if you do not pitch inside the hitter will crowd the plate, even dive across it, and suddenly the outside corner will be, in effect, the middle of the plate and there will be nowhere to throw the ball.

Ron Perranoski says, "If you have 8 inches inside and 4 inches outside, you have quite a lot of area that they [batters] have to adjust to." To be precise, 29 inches for the pitcher to work in rather than just the 17-inch plate. However, says Hershiser, just as it is risky not to pitch inside, it is also risky to pitch there. "You can't make a living pitching in all the time because your mistake either hits the batter or gets hit hard. So the odds are better away."

Still, the pitcher's principal problem today is to get away with pitching inside as often as he needs to. There is too much litigiousness by batters who, like all other Americans, are very sensitive about their rights, real and imagined. Tim McCarver grudgingly credits hitters (McCarver was a catcher and is on the pitchers' side) with "successful lobbying efforts to push the ball out over the plate." This lobbying has consisted of aggressive responses to brushback pitches, responses ranging from baleful glares to bench-clearing brawls. Scioscia agrees that umpires have, for whatever reason, become less tolerant of pitches that come inside. "Let's say a fastball is called inside and the count is 0–2. A pitcher who has pitched long enough, and has been in our meetings and knows what we are trying to do, knows that in that situation he's got to throw the ball off the plate between the hitter and the plate, maybe 8 inches inside. Now, let's say the pitch gets away and comes up and in. Here is where we're running into trouble with umpires saying you're throwing at a guy. But actually you're not going to hit a guy or knock him down or even take a chance of hitting him when you're 0–2."

During the 1988 League Championship Series, Hershiser says, "The Mets crowded the plate, trying to take my sinker away from me. They knew I like to throw it low and away. I adjusted back, throwing a lot of fastballs in." Such an adjustment is not optional if the pitcher wants to make his living in the major leagues. "You can't let the outside part of the plate become the middle or the inside. That's when you have to pitch in to get them off the plate. You have to pitch in often enough that the outside corner is still the outside corner. You have to keep the definition: 'That's the outside corner, fellas.' " Mike Scott is equally emphatic: "There isn't a successful pitcher who just throws on the plate and away, on the plate and away. Because if you do that, they'll just sit there and drill you. You've got to make them uncomfortable. You've got to put a little fear in there."

Fear can be instilled unintentionally, or at least by wildness that seems unintentional. Six times Nolan Ryan has led his league in both strikeouts and walks. Bob Feller did that four times. Wildness makes hitters nervous and nervousness makes them vulnerable. Wildness makes it easier to make them flinch.

Aluminum bats (a bane we shall deal with in the next chapter) have taken away one of the educational processes essential for pitchers, the process of learning to pitch inside. "You can't do that in high school or college," Hershiser says, "because you can't break any bats." When a pitcher jams a batter who is using an aluminum bat, the batter is often able to fight off the pitch and dump a hit over the infield. So until pitchers enter professional baseball, they tend to pitch away, away, away. As a result, they do not get practice pitching in, and when they start pitching in they hit batters unintentionally.

Intentionally throwing at batters is a punitive measure justified, Hershiser indicates, by, among other things, naughty behavior by batters, such as peeking. The catcher can help prevent peeking back at the catcher by moving at the last instant. Hershiser has begun to come forward in his delivery before Scioscia shifts toward the zone where the ball is coming. And every once in a while, especially with a runner on second, Hershiser will throw inside without even telling his catcher the pitch is coming there. He will let the catcher set up outside, then throw inside, just to make sure the batter is not peeking at the catcher's location and to convince the other team that he is a little wild. "My strength is location, not blowing people away with high gas." If the batter peeks, or if the runner on second signals pitch locations, that makes Hershiser a book easy for batters to read. If the runner signals to the batter that the pitch will be inside, that tells the batter the kind of pitch, too. It is almost certainly a fastball. If the runner signals a pitch away, the batter moves up on the plate and takes away the outside corner, where Hershiser's sinker is effective.

Hershiser remembers the way Willie Stargell of the Pirates used to stand in the batter's box cranking the bat around rapidly in a big circle until the pitcher was in motion. Hershiser suspects that Stargell did that partly to disguise his head movements that enabled him to peek and see where the catcher was setting up. Remember the way Joe Morgan of the Reds used to flap his left elbow while at bat, just before each pitch, darting his eyes back at his elbow? Hershiser suspects that Morgan was peeking. Notice, says Hershiser, the way Keith Hernandez of the Mets wiggles his fingers on the bat handle. "Hernandez is always looking at his fingers? He's not looking at his fingers."

Hershiser watches to see that his catcher does not move into position too soon during day games because the catcher's shadow is so easy for the batter to see. But there are shadows at night, too. When the Padres came from behind to beat the Cubs in the final game of the 1984 League Championship Series, their comeback was capped by hits by Tony Gwynn and Steve Garvey. Gwynn got his hit because he glanced down and saw the shadow cast by the Cubs' catcher, Jody Davis, who had moved to take an outside pitch. When told of this episode, Hershiser laughs his boyish laugh but speaks words from the man's world in which he works: "When a pitcher sees that, or a catcher suspects that, you can guarantee that the batter is going down—in a hurry. He's stealing meal money." In 1987 Hershiser hit nine batters (one every 29 innings), which suggests he is not nice beyond the point of prudence.

Drysdale hit a batter every 22.2 innings. Koufax hit a batter every 129 innings. In 1966 Koufax pitched 323 innings and hit no one. The difference between Drysdale and Koufax was not control, it was a matter of temperament. Pitchers like Don Drysdale and Early Wynn (who said he would throw at his grandmother "only if she was digging in") could not pitch today the way they did 25 years ago. Neither could Sal "The Barber" Maglie, who once said this about throwing at batters: "It's not the first one. It's the second one that makes the hitter know I meant the first one." The last of the no-damned-nonsense-about-niceness pitchers may have been Bob Gibson. Never mind in games, you were not safe during batting practice. One day when Gibson was the Atlanta Braves' pitching coach he was pitching batting practice and called to a young hitter waiting near the cage, "Eddie, you're in there." The young hitter did not like to be called Eddie and replied, in a less than respectful tone, "The name is Ed." Gibson quietly said, "All right, *Ed*, get in there." Then with the first pitch he drilled Ed in the ribs.

In Eric Rolfe Greenberg's *The Celebrant,* one of the best baseball novels, the protagonist muses, "To be a pitcher! I thought. A pitcher standing at the axis of event." That is indeed where the pitcher works, at the point from which all action begins. But the protagonist does not understand everything. He adds, "And to live in a world without grays, where all decisions were final: ball or strike. . . ." Wrong. There is much gray in a pitcher's world. Pitching inside, moving batters off the plate, punishing their bad manners (if that is what peeking is), retaliating for teammates who have been hit—these are aspects of baseball's gray area. Cheating is different. It is a matter of black and white.

Once when Earl Weaver visited Ross Grimsley on the mound in a crisis Weaver said, "If you know how to cheat, start now." Hershiser figures that 15 to 20 percent of all National League pitchers scuff balls or throw spitballs or otherwise cheat. A scuffed ball is an otherwise pristine ball with a small, strategically placed nick or scratch. In the hands of a pitcher who knows how to hold and throw it, such a ball has just enough aerodynamic irregularities to have extremely effective movement. Hershiser says he will not scuff a ball but has thrown scuffed balls that were waiting for him on the mound when he returned after the Dodgers had batted. He says it is hard to overestimate the potency of a skillfully scuffed ball as a weapon. The scuffed balls he has thrown have either produced strikeouts or, if the batters made contact, balls that stayed in the infield. "It is unbelievable. I have such a natural sinker already and I can double the break with a scuffed ball."

Cheating is, of course, nothing new. Whitey Ford has written about his rich repertoire of techniques for cheating. He had a ring with a sharpened edge for scuffing. When the ring was banned, his cooperative catcher, Elston Howard, would scuff the ball on a sharpened rivet on his shin guards. Ford used spit, sometimes applied by, or helpfully wiped away by, his infielders as the ball was whipped around the infield after an out. Ford even caused a rule to be written. At the 1957 World Series between the Yankees and the Milwaukee Braves the guild loyalty of pitchers took precedence over mere team considerations: Braves pitchers Lew Burdette and Warren Spahn showed Ford how to throw a mudball. That is—was—a pitch with an exaggerated break because of a bit of dirt stuck to one side of the ball. Ford would wet the ball with saliva located in the pocket of his glove, then hold the ball with the wet spot down and reach for the resin bag with the ball in his hand, brushing the wet spot in the dirt. Unfortunately for Ford, baseball's crime-busters soon made it a criminal offense for a pitcher to pick up the resin bag with a hand in which he is holding a ball.

Gaylord Perry, pitcher and author *(Me and the Spitter)*, won 314 games and probably would be in the Hall of Fame by now (he will be eventually) were it not for the fact that, as he more or less cheerfully admits, he cheated. The "foreign substances" he applied to the ball included saliva, Vaseline, K-Y jelly and fishing line wax. (A Cubs pitcher accused of applying foreign substances to the ball hotly protested that everything he applied "was made in the good ol' USA.") Dave Duncan was Perry's catcher on the 1974 Indians when Perry had a 21–13 record. According to Duncan, Perry threw only one spitball all year. Duncan says Perry adopted odd, furtive mannerisms on the mound to make batters wary and angry. They concentrated on finding him out rather than knocking him out of the game.

An axiom sometimes spoken and often thought is: An amateur who cheats to win is a cheat; a professional who cheats to feed his family is a competitor. The axiom is pernicious, permissive and plain wrong because it suggests that something done for money is, for that reason, legitimized. That is obviously untrue. A deceitful action is especially contemptible when done in cold premeditation, and sneakily. Which brings us to the distinction that Bart Giamatti had occasion to draw between two kinds of violations of rules.

Giamatti was the designated metaphysician of American sport. In 1987, when he was president of the National League, he flexed his mental muscles regarding disciplinary action against a pitcher who was caught using sandpaper to scuff balls. Giamatti noted that most disciplinary cases involve impulsive violence, which is less morally grave than cheating. Such acts of violence, although intolerable, spring from the nature of physical contests between aggressive competitors. Such violence is a reprehensible extension of the physical exertion that is integral to the contest. Rules try to contain, not expunge, violent effort. But cheating derives not from excessive, impulsive zeal in the heat of competition. Rather, it is a cold, covert attempt to alter conditions of competition. As Giamatti put it, cheating has no organic origin in the act of playing and devalues any contest designed to declare a winner among participants playing under identical rules and conditions. Toward cheating, the proper policy is zero tolerance.

Fear of the wrath of a stern commissioner may suffice to deter some pitchers from cheating. Hershiser invokes a yet higher authority. "I feel that if I would scuff the ball or cheat, God would not honor my ability and my trying and all of a sudden my record would start going down. He would punish my witness. I don't know if God is like that. I read in the Bible that He will correct us. I know I could be better, better at a human level, but I don't know if, at the spiritual level, I could live with myself. I just can't do it." He pauses, thinking. "Maybe when I'm forty and I gotta do it to do it, I'll see it differently. Spiritually, I'll figure out a way. 'Lord, let me make this money and I'll give it to the church.'" And he laughs the carefree laugh of someone for whom 40 is still only a rumor.

Later Hershiser returns, unbidden, to the subject of cheating. "The guys that do it are actually stealing money out of the honest guys' pockets." His suspicion is that the scuffers who are successful draw fans to the ballparks, make money for everyone and so are left alone. Baseball's enforcers might come down on a scuffer who is the tenth man on a pitching staff, but he is probably not effective and is probably being hit hard or he would not be the tenth man, so why bother? "I don't know. If they make it an unwritten rule that you can do it, if they are not going to go after guys, I think I will spiritually say it's okay. Just like a shortstop or second baseman says I don't need to actually touch second base when turning a double play."

In late July, 1989, when Mike Scott of the Astros drove the Dodgers deeper into fifth place with his sixteenth win, Hershiser dropped his diplomatic reticence: "[Scott] cheats up a storm. It's not too much fun to sit there and watch him cheat. It's unbelievable. It's not just speculation. It's fact. I know guys that have played with him. [Astros first-base coach] Phil Garner played with us, he said [Scott] did it. Other guys have, too. Even umpires say he does it. But they say the league won't back them up after Don Sutton tried to sue Doug Harvey for charging him with scuffing." Scott replied that no pitcher is more closely watched (because more constantly accused) than he is. He has, he said, been checked and rechecked and not found guilty. Scott also said he did not care what Hershiser thinks and added, "I would be ticked, too, if I was 15 games out of first place."

———◆———

Pitchers tend to be conspiracy theorists. Pitchers tend to be correct. Pitchers believe that owners, pandering to the unwashed mob that does not appreciate the artistry of pitching, are constantly plotting to handicap pitchers and increase offense. The pitchers are mistaken only in thinking this is a conspiracy. A conspiracy is supposed to be secret. The plot against pitchers is about as secret as a steam calliope. However that may be, Hershiser, like most pitchers, believes baseball is forever finding ways to be beastly to pitchers. "There never," he states categorically, "has been a rule change favorable to the pitcher." He exaggerates, but only a bit. The last time pitchers benefitted much from a rules change was more than a century ago. (What will some people want to change next, to the detriment of pitchers? The bats, as we shall see in the next chapter.)

It is hard to say where, back in the mists of history, the origins of baseball are. However, it is reasonable to say that baseball as we know it began in the 1880s. Pitching is the heart of the game and by 1887 the rules had been changed enough to allow pitching as we know it. In their exhaustive treatise, *The Pitcher,* John Thorn and John B. Holway note that baseball's first codified rules, written in 1846 by Alexander Cartwright, said this: "The ball must be pitched, not thrown, for the bat." Note the preposition "for." The distinction between pitching and throwing was that a pitch must be delivered underhand and with a stiff wrist. A pitcher was an unglamorous functionary obligated to help the batter put the ball in play. Until 1887 the batter was even allowed to tell the menial pitcher to serve up the ball high or low.

Law follows culture and mores and in 1872 baseball's rules surrendered to the fact that by then most pitchers were snapping their wrists as they released the ball, although they still had to release it from below the waist. In 1872 the rules changed to legalize this and pitchers became what Cartwright had called, disapprovingly, throwers. In 1887 another failed prohibition ended and pitchers were allowed to throw overhand. Today the distinction in baseball talk between pitching and throwing is reversed. It's the distinction between artifice and mere power. Pitching is the science of systematically confusing batters. Throwing is reliance on raw strength. A pitcher is what a thrower becomes when he gets serious (or older, which is much the same thing).

When restrictions were removed from the pitcher's use of his own arm and wrist, the anti-pitching forces fell back to fight on another front. In 1879 the rules stipulated nine balls before a walk was awarded. Then the plotting against pitchers got into high gear. The number of balls for a walk was lowered to eight, then seven, then six, back up to seven for one season, then five, then four in 1889. (For one season, 1887, a strikeout required four strikes, but this was going too far even for dedicated persecutors of pitchers.)

While the rules were becoming less permissive about how many times a pitcher could miss the strike zone, pitchers were developing ways of making the ball behave oddly en route to, and while passing through, the strike zone. The patron saint of modern pitchers might be William Arthur "Candy" Cummings, a 120-pound lad who, in the summer of 1863, while other young men were crossing the wheat field at Gettysburg and completing the siege of Vicksburg, was tossing clamshells, making them "turn now to the right, now to the left." The first curveball was a clamshell. By 1867 Cummings was curving balls around Harvard's bats for the New York Excelsior Club. Batters have not really been happy since then. But batters have been having most of the rules changes go their way. The pitcher's location has changed from a boxlike area (hence the phrase "knocked out of the box") to a slab of rubber on an elevation. At one point early on, the pitcher was allowed a run-up in the area of the box, like a bowler in cricket, before uncorking a pitch. But the pitcher's mound was moved from 45 feet away from home to 50 feet in 1881, and in 1893 it was moved to its current distance of 60 feet 6 inches. The arrival of Wilt Chamberlain and other dominant centers caused changes in the rules of basketball concerning the dimensions of the lane in front of the basket. Similarly, the final change in the location of the pitcher's mound was provoked (or so it is said) by the fastball of Amos Wilson "The Hoosier Thunderbolt" Rusie. Connie Mack, who saw every great pitcher from Cy Young to Bob Feller, said Rusie threw hardest. His fastball must have been a scorcher if it drove the pitcher's rubber back 10 feet. In any case, the change did not bother Rusie, who was 29–18 in 1893. However, the major league batting average soared from .245 to .280. That is not surprising, considering that putting the pitcher farther away increased the time the batter had to see the pitch, and had the effect of taking 10 miles per hour off a fastball.

It is bad enough (from the pitcher's point of view; let's take that point of view because no one else does) that the place pitchers throw from has been shoved so far back. But look, too, at what they are throwing at, and what they are throwing. Consider what has happened to the strike zone and the ball.

Baseball knows on which side its bread is buttered—the side of offense. That is the people's choice. As soon as snap-wrist and overhand pitching were permitted, hitting declined. So, in the fullness of time (and not much time was wasted), the ball was "juiced." By 1894 the league ERA was a giddy 5.32. But the ball was still not very lively, and not many balls were used in any game, so they lost a lot of life along the way to the ninth inning.

In 1872 the rules stipulated that in even innings a team captain could request replacement of an "injured" ball. Until 1886 a ball lost was not considered really lost until after players had used an allotted five minutes to try to find it, if the umpire so ordered. By 1897 a new moralism was abroad in baseball and a $5 fine could be levied on any player guilty of injuring a ball. But normal play did plenty of injuring. It was not unusual for a game to be played with one or two or three balls. By the end of the game the ball was as resilient as a dumpling. Or a tomato. "We often played five or six innings with one ball," Napoleon Lajoie recalled. "And after two or three innings you thought you were hitting a rotten tomato." There is a certain amount of hitters' self-pity in that account. Compassion should be tempered by the knowledge that Lajoie hit the tomato for .422 in 1901 and .339 over 21 seasons. Some offense was possible.

As recently as June 29, 1929, the Cubs and Reds played a full nine-inning game and used just one ball. That was an oddity. In 1919, the season that ended with the White Sox–Reds World Series, the National League used 22,095 baseballs. Then the "Black Sox" scandal broke. Just five seasons later, baseball had revived. The revival was related to the fact that, in 1925, the National League used 54,030 baseballs. More balls were being hit over fences, in part because more dirty gray balls were being taken out of play and replaced by clean white ones. Not until 1934 were both leagues required to use the same ball. However, the crucial change had occurred in 1920 when both leagues began using balls made with the same kind of yarn, from Australia. It does not seem proper, this foreign yarn inside the great American artifact, but we must not flinch from the truth. The Australian yarn was stronger than American yarn and could be wound tighter, giving the balls more bounce. During World War II the ball was not exactly dead, but it was deader than it had been immediately before or has been since. This was because war shortages forced manufacturers to use an inferior wool for the yarn wrapped around the cork center. Luckily, all wars end, and the ball bounced back. Peace was hell, for pitchers.

However, nothing lasts, not even hell. Two decades after the end of World War II the batters were again losing their 100-year war with pitchers. It is an old axiom that "good pitching will stop good hitting—and vice versa." What good pitching does is produce a year like 1968, which in turn produces countermeasures by the people who write the rules. (The real powers behind the rule book are the people who balance baseball's financial books.)

In 1968 the major league batting average was .237, the lowest ever. The 1968 Yankees batted .214, far worse than the .240 of the 120-loss Mets of 1962. Carl Yastrzemski led the American League with .301. The average number of runs per game (6.84) fell almost to the record low (6.77) set in 1908, when the ball was dead. Willie McCovey led the National League in RBIs with 105 and was the only man in the league to top 100. Twenty-one percent of all games were shutouts. Denny McLain became the first pitcher since Dizzy Dean in 1934 to win 30 games (McLain was 31–6). He pitched 28 complete games and had a 1.96 ERA, but he did not have the best year among major league pitchers. Neither did Juan Marichal, although he was 26–9 and pitched 30 complete games. Don Drysdale set what was wrongly thought to be one of baseball's unassailable records by pitching 58⅔ consecutive scoreless innings, but not even that was the most remarkable performance by a pitcher in 1968.

The most remarkable pitcher was Bob Gibson. He set a National League record with a 1.12 ERA. Gibson's Cy Young and MVP award-winning season probably was the greatest season any pitcher ever had. The astonishing thing about his 22–9 record is that he managed to lose nine times. He says he should have been 30–1, and he would have been if the Cardinals had scored even four runs in each of his starts. In those nine losses he allowed just 27 runs. He lost 1–0 twice and 2–0 once. In his 34 starts he pitched 28 complete games, including 13 shutouts. In nine other games he allowed opponents just one run. In his 34 starts he was removed six times for pinch hitters. He was never removed during an inning, from the mound—never knocked out of the box.

Numbers like these proved that something had to be done. Something was done, and it worked, immediately. In 1968 there had been six .300 hitters in all of baseball. In 1969 there were three times that many. The number of 100 RBI men rose from 3 to 14, the number of 40 or more home-run hitters rose from 1 to 7. (Frank Howard's total of 44 in 1968 is one of baseball's great aberrations.) What resuscitated offense was some creative fiddling with the game.

Casting about for ways to pump more pop back into offense, the owners, being good Americans, thought of a technological fix. So in 1969, during Spring Training, they experimented with a new ball. The results included ludicrously long home runs hit by pitchers and other people who had no business hitting for power, and line drives dangerous to the physical well-being of pitchers. That ball was quickly thrown away.

More seriously, after 1968 five teams moved their fences in. Center field in Philadelphia's Connie Mack Stadium came in from 447 to 410 feet. The most serious attack on pitching supremacy, however, lay in the rule book. The 1969 solution (if such there can ever be) to the problem (if such it is) of the dominance of pitching involved shaving the mound and shrinking the strike zone. The mound was lowered by one-third, from 15 inches to 10 inches. And the strike zone became the subject of a remarkably futile episode of rule writing.

In the momentous year of 1887 (the centennial of the Constitutional Convention and the year when throwing overhand became an inalienable right of pitchers) the strike zone was defined as extending from the top of the batter's shoulders to the bottom of his knees. That was good enough to get this great land of ours through two world wars, but in 1950 the rule makers succumbed to the fidgets and said: Henceforth the strike zone shall be from the armpits to the top of the knees. In 1963 it was redefined yet again, back to the 1887 dimensions. Then after the trauma of 1968, the "armpits to the top of the knees" strike zone was restored. Bart Giamatti said people look to games for "stable artifice," an island of clear rules, of predictable governance in a world of flux. If that is what fans are looking for, they should not look too closely at the strike zone.

Or at the rule book. All those words on paper are fine, but the game is not played on paper, and out on the field the strike zone has wandered south. It is bad enough that the zone has been redefined promiscuously. Much more important is the fact that, as we saw in Dave Duncan's charts, the *de jure* zone bears no resemblance to the *de facto* zone—the one the umpires are enforcing. Again, if the Constitution is what the Supreme Court says it is, then the strike zone is what the umpires say it is, and the strike zone today runs from the belt down to as far below the knees as the particular umpire behind the plate likes to call strikes.

Before the 1988 season the rule makers, with their touching faith in the magic of words to control the men in blue, tried to restore the sovereignty of written law. They tried to do this with a small surrender. They tried to expand the strike zone by shrinking it. They redefined the top of the zone as being at the letters on the uniforms. (They blushed and fainted dead away at the thought of desecrating the sacred rule book with the scarlet word "nipples.") Their theory, or hope, was that umpires would bring up the top of the strike zone at least slightly if the official top of the zone was defined down, a little more to their liking. The change made not a particle of difference in umpires' behavior.

Thorn and Holway say "the steady onslaught" of pitching is so powerful that unless it is periodically countered it will produce the extinction of the .300 hitter. The reasons, they say, are that pitchers are becoming bigger and stronger and they are replaced more often by big, strong relief pitchers. Meanwhile, hitting proficiency is limited by the human limits of reaction time and hand-eye coordination. However, bear in mind the fact that baseball has not yet suffered a really traumatic imbalance, one that could not be corrected by minor modifications of the terms of competition.

Perhaps—we shall never know—baseball came close to such a trauma in the 1950s. It had a glimpse of what could have been a really discombobulating force. In the 1950s the Orioles had a pitching prospect who became a baseball legend without ever becoming a big leaguer. Steve Dalkowski came out of a Connecticut high school with throwing mechanics that were terrible and, it turned out, impervious to all attempts to improve them. But in spite of his flaws he probably threw harder than anyone who ever pitched in the major leagues. Harder and wilder. He was never properly timed under suitable conditions. There was no mound at the U.S. Army's Aberdeen Proving Ground where he was timed by a radar gun. But the consensus was that he threw approximately 115 miles per hour. Two of the hardest throwers of modern times, Nolan Ryan and Goose Gossage, were timed at 103 miles per hour at the 1985 All-Star Game in Minneapolis. A Dalkowski fastball once hit an umpire in the mask, breaking the mask and putting the umpire in the hospital for three days. Dalkowski with even adequate control might have been intolerable for baseball. He might have been the almost unhittable pitcher. If so, he would have been boring.

A few years ago George Plimpton wrote a whimsical novel that made a point both serious and lovely. *The Curious Case of Sidd*

Finch was the story of a mystic whose Buddhist discipline, learned in Tibet, enabled him, when his concentration was undisturbed, to throw a ball 160 miles per hour with perfect control. The Mets prepared a catcher by having him catch balls dropped from the Goodyear blimp. (A ball dropped from 1,000 feet reaches the ground traveling 170 miles per hour.) Plimpton's novel is a playful exploration of this truth: All sport, but especially baseball, depends on a fragile equilibrium. The equilibrium depends on both a high level of performance by many participants and on the maintenance of imperfection. Plimpton has Davey Johnson, Finch's manager on the Mets, say, "What he does doesn't really belong in baseball." True. Anything like it would ruin the game.

There is no danger of that. The tension between pitcher and batter will maintain baseball's most fundamental equipoise. What pitchers continue to do in self-defense against the Forces of Darkness (offense) is to use their heads about how they use the great freedom they received for their arms in the Emancipation Proclamation of 1887. Mankind has moved a far piece from Cummings and his curving clamshells but mankind has not exhausted novelty. There always seem to be new ways to make a thrown and revolving sphere deviate in deceptive ways from a straight path.

One winter early in this decade Roger Craig, a former pitcher and at the time the Detroit Tigers' pitching coach, was working with youngsters at the San Diego School of Baseball. He was interested in finding a breaking pitch that young boys could throw without jeopardizing their undeveloped arms and shoulders. It had to be a pitch that did not depend on the torque of a snapped wrist. Unlike a fastball, which has a natural backward rotation, a curveball is given an unnatural spin by twisting the arm or wrist or both. (A curveball is harder on the arm than a fastball because the pitcher spins the ball while generating high arm speed.) Craig tinkered with the grip used by the few pitchers who threw a fork ball. The result of Craig's experimenting was, within a few years, something like a revolution. Rarely, if ever, has a pitching innovation had so much impact so quickly.

The split-finger is a fastball with a difference. The difference is not in the arm speed, or in the motion with which it is thrown, but in the action of the ball as a result of the way the pitcher grips it. He grips the ball with his first two fingers spread wide along the seams. Pitchers speak of the ball "tumbling" out from between their fingers. This has the effect of slowing the ball's velocity without altering the pitcher's fastball arm speed or motion, the two factors by which most batters orient their calculations. The ball tumbles out of the pitcher's hand with a fastball rotation but less speed. When it works well, the pitch plunges as it reaches the plate. Pitchers say the pitch is like sex: When it is good it is terrific and when it is bad it is still pretty good. Meaning: When it works it sinks fast, often falling out of the strike zone, resulting in missed swings or ground balls. And even when it does not sink as it is supposed to, its reduced velocity makes it a useful change-up. At its best it behaves somewhat like a spitball—another pitch without backspin.

Some baseball curmudgeons insist that there is nothing new under the sun and that the split-finger is just a fork ball with a fancy name. Do not try to tell that to hitters. Or to Mike Scott. As late as 1984 Scott was a marginal (5–11, 4.68 ERA) pitcher. Then he learned the split-finger and in 1986 was the Cy Young winner who won the division-clinching game for the Astros with a no-hitter. Scott says it took him less than a week to learn the split-finger. What did he stop throwing when he started throwing it? "Everything else." He explains: "A year or so later I still had a sign for a slider because I had been a fastball-change-slider pitcher. One day [Astros catcher Alan] Ashby comes out to the mound and I said, 'Why do we even have a three [three fingers down as a sign for a slider]? There's no situation in which I'd rather throw the slider than a split-finger.' " Scott says that only about 30 percent of the split-finger fastballs he throws "really dive." "If it's 0–2 and there is no one on base, I'll throw it really hard. It may bounce. It's either going to be a great pitch or a ball."

Before the arrival of the split-finger the slider was the most recent significant addition to the pitcher's arsenal. Some baseball people think the slider, like the split-finger, is yet another sign of national decadence. They say it was made necessary because of the decline of a fundamentally important American skill, the ability to throw a serious curveball. Roger Craig, of course, does not subscribe to the decadence theory of the slider or split-finger, but he does admit, "You don't see the big curveball like you used to with Erskine, Podres, Koufax. Today's pitchers have shortened it up into a slider. But Hershiser has the big curve." The big curve, which Hershiser has and Craig had, is indeed seen less now than in the 1950s. There is more reliance on the slider because it is easier to control and throw for strikes, and you can throw it almost as hard as a fastball. Craig says that a big curve that a catcher is going to catch low and away is going to go almost through the middle of the strike zone. "A slider," says Roger Craig, "is easier to control, you can throw it harder. A good pitcher can throw it almost as hard as a fastball, and it is easier than a curve to throw for a strike." Craig, who talks slowly and does not smile promiscuously, has the demeanor of a man who has had some searing experiences. For sure he did in those two seasons (1962 and 1963) pitching for the Mets when his record was 15–46. In 11 of those losses the Mets were shut out, so his manager, Casey Stengel, was, as usual, talking scrambled sense when he said, "You've gotta be good to lose that many." Still, he did lose them, so if he does not like batters, he should be forgiven. Whether they will forgive him for the fork ball is another matter.

Craig is one of the Thomas Edisons of the pitching profession. He is more inventive than most people, but necessity is the mother of pitching inventiveness. As Hershiser says, the batters keep learning. So pitchers keep improvising. Pitching is a vocation with multiplying variations. And as one team looks at another, pitching is a multiple problem. A batter thinks not just of facing a particular pitcher but of coping with a pitching staff—different starters in a series and several pitchers in a game. To a batter, a pitching staff is a monster with 10 or 11 pitching arms. The composition of a staff can cause problems for opponents. The 1989 Texas Rangers could send heat-throwing Nolan Ryan to the mound one night and knuckleballer Charlie Hough the next night (or the other way around). The Rangers' opponents had difficult adjustments to make.

Because pitching is such a many-faceted profession, let us leave Orel Hershiser for a moment and consider two other members of the pitchers' guild, Greg Swindell and Jim Gott. For a while they worked not far from one another, about 120 miles apart, in Cleveland and Pittsburgh.

◆

Long ago, when mankind was young and wit was fresh, if someone in an audience called out, "Say something funny," Mort Sahl, the comic, would say: "John Foster Dulles." Today's last-gasp laugh-getter for desperate comics is some reference to Cleveland. Cleveland has indeed had all the problems of an old industrial city. And yes, the Cuyahoga River did catch fire once. But such problems do not obscure the city's fascinating dimension, which may be what some of Cleveland's detractors despise: The city embodies the American middle—Midwestern middle-class civilization. Ohioans were, in a sense, the first thoroughly American Americans. Ohio's northern part was once "New Connecticut"; the southern part was the Virginia Military District. "Ohio," said a nineteenth-century writer, "is at once North and South; it is also—by the grace of its longitude and its social temper—both East and West. It has boxed the American compass." Ohio was the first defined wilderness area made into a state, and the names of its communities include London, Dublin, Berlin, Geneva, Moscow, Holland, Poland, Smyrna, Cadiz, Lisbon, Antwerp, New Paris and New Vienna. One historian suggests that Ohio has produced eight presidents because an Ohio candidate could not seem alien to any other part of the nation. In 1784 George Washington examined a map of the wilderness and predicted that "where the Cuyahoga River flows into Lake Erie shall arise a community of vast commercial importance." A century later, a Clevelander explained his city to an Easterner whose eyes were irritated by the air: "Smoke means business, and business means money and money is the principal thing." Ohio's largest city has always been bound up with America's basic commodities. Edison was born 60 miles west of Cleveland, which became the first city in the world with electric lighting in a public place, and the first to unite electricity and steel in transportation (in streetcars). One of Cleveland's thoroughfares, Superior Street, is a reminder of the link between Cleveland and Lake Superior, which is surrounded by iron ore deposits. For years those deposits were shipped to Cleveland's mills and turned into rails and locomotives. Oil was needed before transportation could move from steel wheels to rubber tires (tires are a giant industry in the state bisected by the National Pike, U.S. 40). The world's first producing oil well was 100 miles east of Cleveland, and oil's potential was first understood by a product of Cleveland's Central High School, John Davison Rockefeller. Cleveland is the only major American city where the original city center is still the city's hub. Public Square is the site of the Soldiers' and Sailors' Memorial, which a guidebook gently describes as an example of "the literalness of Victorian art." It is a stupendous pile, a granite-and-bronze clutter of guns and warriors. But an even more stupendous pile is a five-minute walk away. It is the Mistake on the Lake, Memorial Stadium, home of the Cleveland Indians.

Spring comes late to the shores of Lake Erie and it comes last to the cavernous stadium. Greg Swindell thinks that is swell. He thinks Cleveland's spring climate, which often is like March well into May, is an advantage to him. As a pitcher he is either moving around throwing the ball and keeping warm or he is bundled up on the bench. And hitters, who hate to be pitched inside in the best of times, especially hate it in cold weather because making contact down on the handle produces painful stinging in cold hands.

Cleveland has generally been on the receiving end of baseball pain. The Cleveland Spiders of 1899, then in the National League, set a major league record for the most regular-season losses and worst percentage: 20–134, .130. They finished eighth, 84 games out of first and 35 games out of seventh. Of the first 88 American League pennants, the Yankees, among the original eight franchises, have won the most (33). The Indians have won the least (3). Entering 1990 the Indians had gone 29 seasons (not counting strike-shortened 1981) without finishing within 10 games of a division or league title. If the pain ends soon, Swindell's left arm will be one reason for the relief. But it is never wise to make predictions about pitchers.

In 1988, after Swindell had started the season with a spectacular 10–1 streak, a reporter asked him what he expected for the rest of the year. No way, said Swindell, I'm not going to make a prediction. Why, I could go out and lose eight in a row. Which he promptly did. From May 30 to July 19 his record went from 10–1 to 10–9. Still, he finished 18–14. It is a rare pitcher who wins 18 in his first full season. Paul Hoynes, who covers the Indians for the *Cleveland Plain Dealer,* made this list of the top left-handers in the American League in the late 1980s and the number of games each won in his first full season: Frank Viola (7), Jimmy Key (4, and 10 saves), Ted Higuera (15), Mark Langston (17), Charlie Leibrandt (10), Frank Tanana (14).

Looking at tapes of Swindell's losing streak, Mark Wiley, the Indians' pitching coach, found the flaw. It was perfection. Swindell was finishing his delivery too well. That is, he was too well positioned, too perfectly poised facing the batter. He was letting up at the end of his motion, not driving through toward the plate with the driving force from his thick lower body. When he is pitching best, that force causes him to fall away a bit toward the third-base side.

However, there is a problem with that. It can be dangerous, leaving the pitcher unprepared to defend himself against line drives. Swindell says that does not worry him: "I don't think you think about it." But then indicates that he thinks about it. "It has to worry you, but we're pretty good athletes. Canseco has hit one right at me knee-high and I jumped over it. I'd rather give him a single than get hurt." People do get hurt in baseball, by the ball. By the ball coming in from the mound and by the ball going out toward the mound. Cleveland knows. The most serious injury in the history of baseball involved a batter hit by a pitch, and one of the most serious injuries happened to a pitcher hit by a batted ball. In both cases the victims were Indians. On August 16, 1920, Carl Mays, pitching for the Yankees, hit Ray Chapman, Cleveland's shortstop, in the head. Chapman died the next day. Chapman was the best-hitting shortstop in the American League at the time. Bill James believes he probably was destined for the Hall of Fame. He was the first and, so far, only fatality in major league baseball. Clevelanders wore black crepe and 24 priests presided at Chapman's funeral. The death had a consequence. It was generally believed that Mays was not trying to hit Chapman, that a pitch—perhaps a spitball—got away from Mays. And it was believed that Chapman had trouble picking up the flight of the pitch because the ball was dark with dirt and grass stains— among other things. Baseball officials decided that henceforth more of an effort would be made to keep a clean ball in play. That is why today, in the glamorous world of the big leagues, you usually can find in the bowels of the ballpark, 90 minutes before game time, a middle-aged man sitting in long underwear, his hands covered with mud from the Delaware River. The man with the mud will be umpiring home plate that day. Before every game 60 baseballs are rubbed with mud—only the Delaware stuff will do—to remove the ball's slickness. (The long underwear spares umpires the discomfort of itchy dust and the inelegance of sweat-stained trousers. Umpires understand, as Charles de Gaulle did, that dignity sustains authority.)

In the 1930s Lena "Slats" Blackburne, a coach for the Philadelphia Athletics, was bothered by the fact that when umpires rubbed new balls with dirt from the playing field to remove the slickness from the (at that time) horsehide, the ball became scratched. There must, he thought in the American way, be a better way. He found some nearby mud, from a river in southern New Jersey, and in 1938 helped found the Lena Blackburne Rubbing Mud Company. To be strictly accurate, the river is *rumored* to be the Delaware. The actual location is a secret as closely held as the recipe for Coca-Cola. The rubbing is baseball's way of remembering Ray Chapman.

Another of baseball's serious injuries occurred 37 years later in Cleveland, again in an Indians-Yankees game. On the night of May 8, 1957, Herb Score, then 23, was on the mound for the Indians, throwing what was then probably the best fastball in baseball. Gil McDougald, the Yankees' shortstop, ripped a screaming line drive through the middle. It struck Score in the face, breaking his nose and nearly blinding him in his right eye. He never really recovered as a pitcher. In 1955, his first year, he had been 16–10 with a 2.85 ERA and a league-leading 245 strikeouts in just 227⅓ innings pitched. In 1956 he was 20–9, 2.53, and again led the league with 263 strikeouts in 249⅓ innings. After the accident, he pitched for the Indians and White Sox for five more years but won only 17 more games. Was he destined for the Hall of Fame? Perhaps. Pitchers are subject to burnout, so it is hard to say where he would have wound up. Where he did wind up is in the broadcasting booth, where in 1989 he spent his twenty-sixth season doing radio and television.

Score insists that the problem after 1957 was with his arm, not his psyche, and had nothing to do with the accident. "I came back and pitched as well as I ever did the next year but I tore a tendon in my elbow that year." And he recalls that getting hit by batted balls was nothing new to him. "I got hit a lot, on the shins. I didn't see half the pitches. I had to look at the scoreboard to see if they were balls or strikes. When I was a young pitcher, in my first or second year here, I didn't cover first base on a ground ball that the first baseman fielded. I didn't see where the ball went. [Manager] Al Lopez chewed me out and made me take extra fielding practice. I couldn't tell him that I didn't see the ball. It would have seemed like I was making excuses."

In 1988 Doc Edwards, then the Indians' manager, was glad to see Swindell falling away toward third again. But he thinks that the flaw in Swindell's follow-through was a weak excuse for losing those eight in a row. The real reason, says Edwards, was simpler and more serious. Edwards, a man of exemplary concision, says: "He quit pitching." He means Swindell went back to being a mere thrower. "Instead of mixing pitches, he reverted to the style that gets big strong boys through Little League, high school and even college. They just rear back and throw hard and set three guys down and go over and sit on the bench. You can't do that up here. We had to convince Swindell that he's not this overpowering pitcher that everybody was writing about."

Power pitching has been a Cleveland tradition since the arrival in 1936 of a 17-year-old prodigy from Van Meter, Iowa—Bob Feller. The 1954 Indians' staff, which won a record 111 games, included Bob Lemon (23–7), Early Wynn (23–11), Mike Garcia (19–8) and Feller (13–3). The 1968 Indians' pitching staff, which included "Sudden Sam" McDowell and Luis Tiant, became the only staff in major league history to have more strikeouts than hits allowed. Swindell rocketed up to the major leagues from Texas in the wake of, and wearing the same number as, The Rocket Man, Roger Clemens. On May 10, 1987, Swindell struck out 15 Royals, becoming the first Indian since McDowell to fan 15 in a game. That solidified the misunderstanding about Swindell. He was portrayed as a power pitcher pumping out what Hershiser calls "high gas." He was supposed to pile up impressive numbers of strikeouts.

Swindell knew better. He knows that high velocity is nice but it is no substitute for *pitching*. High velocity is especially necessary if you are not a real pitcher, because you can get away with a lot more mistakes when the ball is going 94 miles per hour than you can when it's going 84 miles per hour. And high velocity can propel you into the record books, even all the way to Cooperstown.

In 1973, the first year of the DH, Nolan Ryan, then with the Angels, struck out 383. That is the major league record. It could have been much higher. If pitchers had still been batting, Ryan might easily have run up 425 strikeouts. (The National League record is Koufax's 382 in 1965.) In 1987, at age 40, Nolan Ryan, then with the Astros, set a major league record by striking out 11.48 batters for every nine innings pitched. His average was more than three-quarters of a strikeout per game higher than all but one pitcher's season record in baseball history (Dwight Gooden's 11.39 in 1984). The Elias Bureau calculated that Ryan's record was "the statistical equivalent of batting nearly .400 in today's environment, or of hitting 65 home runs." In 1988 Ryan, then with the Astros, was 41 and for the second time since turning 40 he had a league-leading number of strikeouts. In 1989 Ryan, at age 42, led the league in strikeouts again. He had 11.319 strikeouts for every nine innings pitched, the third-best season record of all time. But at the major league level, throwing hard is not enough. "If it was," says Ray Miller, pitching coach and logician, "Nolan Ryan would be 500 and 2. Nobody in the history of the game has thrown longer or harder than he has and he's only about 20 games over 500." (At the end of the 1989 season Ryan's career record was 289–263.) Miller notes that no Orioles pitching staff, not even in the salad days of Cy Young awards and 20-game winners, has ever led the league in strikeouts.

Every power pitcher should have burned into his memory the date September 15, 1969. That night Steve Carlton broke the Cardinal team record of 17 strikeouts, set by Dizzy Dean. And he broke the then major league record of 18 held by Bob Feller, Sandy Koufax and Don Wilson. Carlton struck out 19, which is still the National League record, jointly held with Tom Seaver, who fanned 19 in 1970. But Carlton lost the game, 4–3. He threw 152 pitches but two of them were hit for two-run home runs by Ron Swoboda (who also struck out twice). Even Carlton, who should be elected to the Hall of Fame in his first year of eligibility, had days when it would have been better for him to throw fewer pitches, get fewer strikeouts, settle for banal ground balls and get the win. Piling up strikeouts is not smart. Dwight Gooden is smart. The following are Gooden's year-by-year totals of games in which he recorded 10 or more strikeouts:

1984	15
1985	11
1986	5
1987	5
1988	1

By the All-Star break in 1989 he had had two such games. (And he had a sore arm that sidelined him for most of the rest of the season.) The decline in the number of games in which Gooden was overpowering was said, by some people, to show that he, at age 24, was in decline. But not so fast. It might also show that he is wise beyond his years, that he understands what Sandy Koufax came to understand. Koufax said he became a good pitcher when he quit trying to keep batters from hitting the ball and started making them hit the pitches he wanted them to hit. Actually, try as he might to get them to hit it, poor Koufax kept striking them out. It must have been frustrating for him.

Swindell is, in baseball parlance, "not afraid of the bat." He is less determined than Hershiser is to get batters to swing at pitches out of the strike zone. Doc Edwards, a former catcher, says, "All the good pitchers I ever caught"—they were as different as the elegant Whitey Ford and the intimidating Sudden Sam McDowell—"were not afraid of coming into the strike zone. The ones who were not good major league pitchers had that fear of coming into the strike zone, so they were always 1–0, 2–0, 2–1, 3–1, 3–2 and they eventually got to the point where they had to throw it over the middle of the plate."

"When Greg throws a good game," says Mark Wiley, pitching coach, "there will be at least three or four bullets—*bullets*—hit right at [center fielder Joe] Carter." Just as Swindell is not afraid of the bat, he is not afraid to use the large park in which he plays half his games. The configuration of a park matters. So do winds and other factors.

The most important changes in parks have been in the National League. Most of that league's parks are relatively new. (Other than Wrigley Field, which opened in 1914, the oldest National League park is San Francisco's Candlestick Park, which did not open until the Giants' third season on the San Andreas fault, 1960.) And most of the new ones are relatively big. That is good for pitchers, and for the teams that play there. (Question: When you hear the phrase "hitters' park," which parks—one in each league—come to mind? Right. Wrigley Field and Fenway Park. Question: Which two teams have not won a World Series since 1908 and 1918, respectively? Right again. Moral: It is bad to play in a park that is beastly to your pitchers.) In the 13 seasons from 1977 through 1989, there were only five 1–0 games at Atlanta's Fulton County Stadium. From 1977 through 1989 there were forty-six 1–0 games in the Astrodome. If Swindell were pitching in his hometown, Houston, he could have a lot of eight-pitch innings, letting batters launch long outs into the large Astrodome outfield.

Some pitchers adjust to parks, but only up to a point. Because Hershiser is a sinker-ball pitcher who forces batters to hit a lot of ground balls, he (and his infielders) have a harder time on artificial turf: The balls get through so fast. Pitching in St. Louis against what he calls "the rabbits"—the running Redbirds whose speed takes advantage of a large park with artificial turf—Hershiser adjusts by pitching higher. He is content to let the Cardinals hit fly balls into Busch Stadium's capacious outfields. But a pitcher's mechanics are different when pitching up, so by doing that a pitcher risks upsetting his rhythm. It can take several starts to get it back.

The danger of allowing the conditions in a particular park to control your thinking about how to pitch is, according to Mike Scott, apparent at Wrigley Field. "You get to where you say, 'I can't give this guy a fat pitch.' So it's ball one. Now he's looking fastball so you go breaking ball and miss and it's ball two. Now you're at his mercy. So you just have to attack them, and if they get seven runs, you get eight." Scott says that if the wind is blowing out at Wrigley Field, he will not watch batting practice. It is too demoralizing. But when the wind is blowing in, Wrigley, with its high infield grass, is a pitcher's park. If the wind is blowing strongly straight out at Wrigley Field, Scott holds his fingers a little closer together when throwing the split-finger. This means the ball has a little less than the usual movement, but when thrown into the wind the normal split-finger can have too much movement and be hard to throw for strikes. A knuckleball pitcher throwing into the wind often can not control his pitches well enough to throw strikes.

Baseball people, with cheerful indifference to the facts of physics, talk about pitchers in puzzling ways. They say things like "his fastball takes off as it reaches the plate," or "it gets a final burst." Both things are said about Swindell. (Cliff Gustafson, Swindell's coach at the University of Texas, says that two of Swindell's strengths are that he "hides" the ball well in his delivery and his fastball "explodes" or "jumps" in the last six or eight feet.) Both are probably nutty, but there is a kernel of truth inside the nuttiness. Tom House, pitching coach of the Rangers, says, "We made a motion study of pitchers who are considered sneaky-fast, and we found that they gained their extra 'speed' by delaying the hitters' recognition of the release point, often by throwing up their front elbows as they came forward. Or you can change the delivery—come up top once, then three-quarters, sidearm, all over the place." Many hitters "overswing" on Swindell because they think he is throwing harder than he is. Edwards explains, "He has great deception because he hides the ball well." Deception can be, and with Swindell is, partly in the throwing motion, particularly a motion that brings the ball across the body so that the ball is coming out of the white of the uniform. Some pitchers, and Swindell is one, toss their heads before releasing the ball and some batters focus on the pitcher's head when gauging the rhythm of the pitcher's delivery.

Many things that seem like handicaps can help pitchers. Mordecai Centennial "Three Finger" Brown (he was born in 1876) found that his handicap wasn't—a handicap, that is. His terrific curveball was the result of the odd way he was forced to grip the ball. Ewell "The Whip" Blackwell, the sidearming Cincinnati right-hander, was said to look less like a pitcher than like a man falling out of a tree. The Giants' Juan Marichal, he of the extraordinary high kick, looked to Roger Angell "like some enormous and highly dangerous farm implement." Doc Edwards remembers Stu Miller, the soft-throwing journeyman with a 16-season record of 105–103. "He would fling his glove at you, flop his head, and you'd swing, and then in would come the rabbit [Miller's hippity-hopping knuckleball]. You had to swing at the third thing thrown at you. But with the ball coming out of all that deception, you couldn't pick up the ball." Some baseball people believe that a left-hander who throws 87 miles per hour is as effective as a right-hander who throws 92 miles per hour. Mark Wiley explains the 5-mile-per-hour advantage this way: "A right-handed hitter has longer to see a left-handed pitcher. Greg throws his slider so hard and at such a low trajectory that the batter gets a good long look at it and says, 'Fastball.' Then just when he starts his swing, it buries itself out of the strike zone toward the hitter's back knee. Not many hitters can stop their swings in time."

Andy Allanson is the Indians' catcher who has received most of Swindell's pitches. Like a lot of catchers, Allanson talks as though he pitches as well as catches. ("I've had some success against Mattingly. He's had some 0-for-4s and 0-for-5s with me.") In a sense, he does. He is part of the thinking and rhythm of the pitcher's game. "The secret of this game," says Allanson, "is to get hitters 'in between'—a little bit ahead of the curve, a little bit behind the fastball." Allanson uses throw-overs to first base to make the base runner a disadvantage to the hitter. "It takes rhythm to hit. When the pitcher throws over, it breaks the hitter's concentration and focus." The same is true with pitchers shaking off signs. Allanson sometimes gives the pitcher a sign to shake his head as though he is shaking off the sign.

A perennial argument among pitchers and their coaches is: What matters most in a pitch—velocity, movement or location? Obviously the ideal is to have them all, to be able to put a breaking ball, or a fastball with a hop, where you want it. Allanson has no doubts about what matters most. "I rank location first. It tells the hitter you have command. Then movement. Only third comes velocity." Allanson says Swindell has command of two pitches, his fastball and curve. That, Allanson says, is one more than most pitchers have. By "command" he means the ability to throw the pitch for a strike to get ahead in the count or keep from walking someone. Allanson estimates that 60 percent of American League pitchers do not throw breaking balls for strikes more than 60 percent of the time. (The Mets' Davey Johnson, a severe mathematician who does not grade on the curve, has a lower opinion of National League pitchers. Johnson believes that those who are real pitchers, rather than mere throwers, are those who can make a hitter hit a particular pitch thrown to a particular place. He thinks that at any given time real pitchers are about 5 to 7 percent of the people employed as pitchers.)

Swindell is one of the best in the business at the most important ingredient in pitching—throwing strikes. In 1988 he produced this pretty number: just 45 walks in 242 innings. It was, therefore, newsworthy when, in late April, 1989, Swindell walked two Rangers in a row. It was just the second time in 442 major league innings that he had walked two consecutive batters. Those bases on balls will kill you. Not always, of course. In 1941 the Yankees' Lefty Gomez shut out the Browns, 9–0, in spite of the fact that he gave up 11 walks. But, then, Lefty was a lefty, so strange events were bound to follow him around. Doc Edwards, marveling at Swindell's control, says, "That's an oddity in a young left-hander." Asked why a left-hander should be different, Edwards says cheerfully, "I don't know."

Swindell works the top, and just over the top, of the strike zone as it is actually called by umpires—a bit above the belt. He gets a lot of outs on pitches that would not be called strikes. ("You have to have the prestige of a Jim Palmer," says Edwards, "to get that borderline high pitch called a strike.") But they are pitches that a lot of batters can not lay off. The problem with getting people out with pitches mid-thigh to belt-high is that you get a lot of foul balls, so you can get a lot of eight-, nine- and ten-pitch outs. Swindell prefers to face power hitters rather than contact hitters like Wade Boggs. The latter kind foul off too many pitches, which is tiresome. Besides, Swindell can not be blamed for suffering from a bad case of Boggsophobia. In one outing in Boston in 1987, Boggs, leading off, hit a Swindell fastball for a double off The Wall. The second time up he ripped a slider and Cleveland's left fielder had to make a spectacular diving catch. The third time up he hit a change-up for a double. The fourth time he hit a line drive that hit the outside of Swindell's glove and broke his middle finger.

For Swindell and Allanson, not being afraid of the bat is a matter of simple thrift, economizing the supply of pitches in Swindell's left arm. Against an aggressive team that comes to the plate eager to hack, Allanson tries to have a lot of 11-pitch innings, and few 8- and 7- and even 6-pitch innings, and he tries to have only one 15-pitch inning. That is why Swindell has pitched complete games of just 2 hours and 3 minutes and 2 hours and 9 minutes.

So far, Swindell has survived three modern developments that pose a danger for pitchers. One is the practice of hurrying young pitchers to the major leagues too fast. "They're not serving their apprenticeship," says Don Drysdale. "Years ago, 25 was a good age to come to the major leagues. Now the pitchers are younger." Another development is the designated hitter. The result of these two developments is that young pitchers whose arms are still maturing find themselves pitching into the eighth and ninth innings more often than is healthy. The third modern development that causes problems for pitchers and skews the development of strong arms is the increased importance of college baseball in the development of players. The most important, and for pitchers the most problematic, aspect of college baseball is the aluminum bat.

Every manager has the sad story of The Bird in the back of his mind. The Tigers' Mark "The Bird" Fidrych pitched 24 complete games in his 28 decisions (19–9) in 1976. That was his first season. It was his last good season. He won only 10 more games over his next, and final, four seasons. "If I were pitching today," says manager Tom Trebelhorn of the Brewers, "I would most assuredly want to pitch in the National League. In the American League I throw extra pitches, extra innings, and I face nine bona fide outs. In the National League, if I am Orel Hershiser pitching at the top of my game, and I face 32 batters in a given game, I don't even face 32 batters. I face the pitcher—if he pitches a good game—maybe three times. Then I face the eighth-place hitter who, some of those times, isn't approaching me as an offensive player. He's approaching me as a defensive hitter trying to work me for a walk or do something else just to get the pitcher up so he will not lead off the next inning. I've had a pretty good night. On another night, when I've not pitched too well, I've given up four runs in four innings, in the American League I might finish that game and get beaten 4–2. In the National

League, if you're down 4–1 and you're not pitching too well, see you later. You don't have those tough innings piled on those tough starts."

If the DH makes the American League permanently prone to overworking pitchers, then Swindell's career has involved double jeopardy. He came to the American League from big-time college baseball. Swindell won 18 in 1988 with his second-best pitch, his slider, severely rationed. It was rationed because of the injury that prevented 1987 from being his first full season. A ligament separated from a bone in his left elbow and he did not pitch after June 30. That injury intensified the suspicions and fueled the prejudices that some baseball people "of the old school" have concerning college baseball programs for pitchers. The complaint concerns two things, the increased pressure to win and the use of metal bats.

Even the most high-powered college baseball programs are nowhere near as big time as many college football programs, and sensible people hope they never will be. But in some conferences, such as the Southwest, where Texas plays, baseball is a serious business, and now that ESPN is bringing college baseball by cable to a national audience, college baseball is going to be modestly big business. It will never be as lucrative as football, but it will bring in some revenue for university athletic departments, and prestige. Therefore winning is taken seriously. A manager with an overpowering pitcher will be tempted to use him a lot, perhaps more than is in the player's long-term interest. Swindell pitched 440 innings in three college seasons. And he was pitching to people swinging metal bats.

Did Swindell pitch too much too soon? He certainly pitched a lot while young. Swindell has been a pitcher since he was old enough to know better (if age seven really is, as the Jesuits say, the age of reason). He was a pitcher in Little League, in junior and senior high school, and for three years at the University of Texas, the mother of power pitchers. As a high school junior Swindell was 14–0 and pitched Sharpstown to the Texas state championship. The next season he lost only one game, and the score of that game was 1–0. However, he was not picked by any major league team in the amateur draft, for two reasons. Major league scouts had doubts about his physique and his velocity. His high school coach, who probably is a better coach than diplomat, remembers Swindell as "plump" and "short and squatty, a Porky Pig type." When he first came to Cleveland sportswriters referred to his "butterball physique." His teammates hung on him a nickname he hated—"Flounder," the name of the fat pledge in the movie *Animal House.*

As a Texas freshman, Swindell asked for and was given uniform number 21, which had belonged to a pitcher who had just left Texas, Roger Clemens. And Swindell became a pupil of a proven teacher, Coach Cliff Gustafson. The 1989 season was Gustafson's thirty-sixth as a college coach and his twenty-third at Texas. He has a mesquite-seasoned voice and an accent as Texas as can be. Good college baseball is, he says, equivalent to "good Single-A ball." Only the best players can step from their junior year in college into the Double-A level.

Gustafson believes that by age 19 a pitcher will be within two or three miles per hour of the best velocity he is ever going to achieve. Swindell was an exception to this rule. Gustafson did not at first regard Swindell as a professional prospect, partly because Swindell was, in Gustafson's words, "kind of pudgy" and partly because Swindell's fastball was not very fast. It was "80, 81 tops." But Gustafson was impressed that Swindell had "excellent control for a left-hander." Gustafson is one of those baseball people who hold to the unshakeable (and unsupported) belief that "most young left-handers have trouble throwing strikes." Why is this? Gustafson is an empiricist, not a theorist: "That's an oddity of baseball. You have a lot of wild left-handers." Or as Ring Lardner wrote, "Shut up, he explained."

Swindell's first outing in his freshman year was against Texas Lutheran College. That team was not a powerhouse, but it was powerful enough. It knocked Swindell around, and out of the game. He pitched next against a genuine powerhouse, Arizona State University, which had two future major leaguers, Barry Bonds and Oddibe McDowell. Texas was down by two runs when Gustafson put Swindell in "for a little more baptism." Suddenly Swindell made what Gustafson laconically calls "quite an adjustment." His fastball zoomed into the high 80s.

Adrenaline can work wonders. But the more of it you have, the more you need prudence. Undergraduates are not long on that. Most undergraduates think they are immortal. Most undergraduate pitchers think their arms are indestructible. "When I got to college I almost never had time to ice it because I was always pitching. There are a lot of big rivals in college. I remember one time when we were playing Houston in Houston. College fans can get real rowdy and I just didn't want to hear them. I wanted them to shut up, so I went down and started warming up on my own. Coach Gus looked down there and I said I was ready and he sent me in." At Texas he occasionally pitched in relief the day after pitching a complete game. Once he pitched a complete game on Friday and the next day relieved in both ends of a doubleheader.

And he was pitching to aluminum bats, which do not break. That fact is even more important than the fact that they put a few extra feet on fly balls and a few more miles per hour on line drives. Because aluminum bats do not break, pitching inside becomes problematic, even futile. Jam a batter on his fists with a pitch that would shatter a wooden bat and he still may be able to put it in play or even over the infield for a hit. That is why college baseball games last so long and why college batting averages are so high—and why professional scouts have such a hard time judging college talent. Because of aluminum bats, college pitchers throw fewer fastballs than they otherwise would. They throw curves, sliders, split-fingers and other breaking balls, and they throw them away from the hitters. This has three pernicious consequences: They do not develop the arm strength that comes from throwing fastballs; they jeopardize their arms with all the torque involved in throwing breaking balls; they do not learn to pitch inside.

Gustafson says he is not sacrificing Texas wins when he encourages his pitchers to put the ball where they will need to put it in professional baseball—inside. Far from costing Texas games, he says, pitching inside makes his pitchers more effective. This is because so few other college pitchers are doing it and so many hitters are, therefore, leaning out over the plate. They find Texas's pitching unsettling. Almost all the players Gustafson recruits "have a burning ambition to be professional players." So "we teach how to pitch in professional baseball," which means "throwing fastballs inside." College pitchers, he acknowledges, "don't like to do it, but they've got to learn."

Swindell learned. He was an all-American selection all three years at Texas, with a 43–8 record and a 1.92 ERA. In 1985, his sophomore year, he won 18 in a row while going 19–1. He is third on the NCAA career strikeout list (behind two pitchers who played four seasons). As the amateur draft approached in June, 1986, Swindell found out which teams had the first three picks. They were Pittsburgh, Cleveland and San Francisco. Then he looked to see which of them could give him number 21. Pittsburgh could not because that number was retired in honor of the late Roberto Clemente. A San Francisco player was using 21. So Swindell hoped to be chosen second. He was.

On the night of August 20, 1986, Swindell was in a Waterbury, Connecticut, hotel sleeping the deep sleep of someone strong, happy and unaware of how fast things can happen in life. Things had happened fast enough already, and would accelerate on the morrow. Less than three months earlier he had been pitching to college boys for the Texas Longhorns. Drafted by the Indians, by August 20 he had pitched the grand total of 18 innings of professional baseball, all of them in Single-A ball, at Waterloo, Iowa. On August 20 he was in Waterbury because he was scheduled to make his Double-A debut the next day. Instead, a telephone call summoned him to make his major league debut—on two hours sleep—in Boston.

His baptism of fire was full of fire, from the Red Sox side. "It was like Vietnam out there," he says. "I'm glad I got out alive." He got out in the fourth inning with the Indians on their way to a 24–5 shellacking. But there was a bright spot. In the second inning he picked Bill Buckner off first. Buckner was then in his eighteenth season in the major leagues. In the midst of a disaster, Swindell had shown some poise and finesse. There was an especially interested onlooker in the Red Sox dugout: Roger Clemens.

Clemens and Swindell, two large, strong Texans, are about as strong as pitchers are these days. But these days are different. What has happened since August 7, 1908, when Walter Johnson shut out the Yankees for the third time in four days? For that matter, what has happened since that day in 1963 when 25-year-old Juan Marichal of the Giants and 42-year-old Warren Spahn of the Braves hooked up in the sort of game that had not been seen for many years and almost certainly will never be seen again. The Giants won, 1–0, on a Willie Mays home run in the bottom of the sixteenth inning. Marichal pitched all the way, throwing 227 pitches. Spahn had thrown 200 pitches when the Giants came to bat in the bottom of the sixteenth.

Twenty-five years later baseball looks a lot different. Roger Clemens stands 6 feet 4, weighs 215 pounds and trains like a demon. He is one of the strongest and most competitive pitchers of this or any other day. In two consecutive starts in July, 1988, he threw 161 and 149 pitches. In his next five starts he lasted just 27 innings. He was 0–5 and 7.33 in those starts. He then went 0-for-August. And by the

All-Star break in 1989 (which he spent at home, not with the All-Star team) he was struggling.

The Tigers' Jack Morris, the winningest pitcher of the 1980s, is one of baseball's workhorses, but the most pitches he remembers throwing in a game are 140. Morris is a fierce competitor who feels that when a relief pitcher comes in for him, he has failed to do his job properly. Tony La Russa calls that attitude "beautiful." He also calls it a mistake. La Russa says he wants all his pitchers to go to the mound thinking they are going to pitch a complete game, but he says he never thinks that way. La Russa's rule is that anytime a pitcher has thrown 120 pitches, he's vulnerable. La Russa remembers a game in which Mark Langston, then with the Mariners, struck out 16 Athletics, but threw 153 pitches doing so. It was a good performance but also a good way to get hurt. "If you have a pitcher who is going to make 30-plus starts for you in a season," La Russa says, "if he is going to be effective for the year and for several seasons, there are going to be a bunch of games in which you can save him 10, 15, 20, 25 pitches, games in which it is not necessary for him to throw those pitches." It is possible to save a pitcher 300 pitches, or the equivalent of three extra starts in which he goes seven or eight innings.

"Back in my day," says Edwards, "everyone told a kid to throw fastballs and change-ups, building his arm strength throwing fastballs. Nowadays you hear somebody say, 'Wow! Johnny is 12–1 in high school' and you go out to see Johnny throw and he throws 100 pitches and 70 of them are curveballs, and the 30 fastballs are about 75 miles per hour. Of course I came from an era when 200 innings was the fifth man on the staff." The fifth man, that is, on a staff built around a four-man rotation.

When Roger Clemens first came up, Gene Mauch told Roger Angell that 25 years earlier every team had three pitchers who could throw as hard as Clemens. Doc Edwards recalls that after the 1964 season the Indians traded Tommy John to the White Sox because he threw only 88 miles per hour. The Indians at the time had Sonny Siebert, Luis Tiant, Steve Hargan, Sam McDowell and Gary Bell, all of whom, Edwards insists, threw in the 90s, as did eight to ten pitchers in the Indians' farm system. Of course John went on to pitch for a quarter of a century more and in most of those seasons he rarely approached even 88 miles per hour.

Leave aside fast pitches and long games. What about long careers?

There are a few records that we can confidently say will never be broken. One is Cy Young's 511 victories. Bert Blyleven had 271 victories by the end of the 1989 season, when he was 38. If he wins 300, he may be the last 300-game winner for a long time—at least until Dwight Gooden grows old. Mickey Welch, a Hall of Famer who was the third pitcher to win 300 games, *completed* his first 105 major league starts. Christy Mathewson had 561 decisions (373 wins, 188 losses) and 435 complete games. Over a 14-year span he *averaged* 26 wins a year. Twenty-one times in this century pitchers have won 30 or more games in a season. But that has been done only three times since 1920: 1931 (Lefty Grove, 31–4); 1934 (Dizzy Dean, 30–7); and in the famous, or infamous, year of the pitcher, 1968 (Denny McLain, 31–6). Johnny Sain was a good pitcher and a great pitching coach. (And he is the answer to a magnificent trivia question: He threw the last pitch to Babe Ruth and the first pitch to Jackie Robinson. Okay, it is a trick question. Sain pitched to Ruth in an exhibition game in May, 1943. Ruth walked.) In 1948, the year the Braves won the pennant on a pitching refrain of "Spahn and Sain and pray for rain," he started 9 games in 29 days. He won 7 of them and lost 2—by scores of 2–1 and 1–0. Since Steve Carlton pitched 304 innings in 1980 no one has pitched 300 innings in a season. It was considered at least mildly marvelous when Roger Clemens put together three consecutive seasons with more than 250 innings pitched and an ERA under 3.00. But Christy Mathewson had 13 consecutive seasons like that and Walter Johnson had 12.

Now, to be fair to today's pitchers, it should be noted that some of these statistics that seem to establish the superior durability of earlier generations of pitchers must be partially discounted, for reasons given by Craig R. Wright. Wright, a statistician and co-author (with Tom House, the Rangers' pitching coach) of *The Diamond Appraised,* notes that in the dead-ball era, before the home-run threat became pervasive, pitchers faced fewer crucial situations, so there was less nibbling at the strike zone and more coasting by pitchers. Wright recalls reading something written by an old-time pitcher— Christy Mathewson, he thinks—arguing that stamina is important because a pitcher must be able to throw as many as 100 pitches in a game. Today more pitches are thrown per batter and 130 to 140 per game is normal. Also, more home runs mean more careful pitching, more deep counts, more walks. More base runners mean more pitching from the stretch, which increases the burden on the arm by decreasing the involvement of the rest of the body. And more base runners also mean more throws from the mound to first.

Big Ed Walsh pitched 464 innings while winning 40 games in 1908. But using an estimate of 2.8 pitches per batter then, and a conservative estimate of 3.5 pitches per batter in 1971 when Detroit's Mickey Lolich pitched 376 innings, Lolich threw about 500 more pitches than Walsh did. Grover Cleveland Alexander's total of 38 complete games in 1916 is impressive, but less so than it would be if we did not know that he threw about 40 fewer pitches per game than are thrown in a normal complete game today. And many of the pitches he threw were fat and slow, allowing weak hitters to dribble the dead (and gray and battered) ball at fielders.

Nevertheless, there is a broad consensus in baseball that there are not as many strong arms as there used to be. That, says Ray Miller, is not a hypothesis, it is a fact, and he thinks he knows why: America is going to hell in a handcart.

Ray Miller, a.k.a. The Rabbit, will be 44 on Opening Day, 1990. He has been the Pirates' pitching coach since October, 1986. Before that he was the Twins' manager for parts of two years and before that he was the Orioles' pitching coach. In Baltimore he coached two Cy Young Award winners (Mike Flanagan and Steve Stone) and five 20-game winners (Flanagan, Stone, Jim Palmer, Scott McGregor and Mike Boddicker). During his tenure the Orioles went to two World Series, 1979 and 1983. Before that Miller was a good Triple-A pitcher who never made it to the major leagues even for, as they say, a cup of coffee. He is a man of many convictions, all of them firm and some of them odd. For example: "There isn't a left-hander in the world that can run a straight line. It's the gravitational pull on the axis of the earth that gets 'em." And he believes in the unity of theory and practice. Tom Boswell reports that when Miller was a roving pitching coach for the Orioles' minor league clubs he had an odd way of organizing wind sprints. He would line up left-handers all on the right side, or on a hill, to balance their gravitational field. "If you don't," Miller patiently explains, "they'll whip out your whole line." Miller believes that left-handers, a persecuted minority, acquire, as a stigma of their servitude, a slight "body lean," the indelible mark of growing up groaning beneath the burdens of life in a right-handed world. (Miller is right-handed.) Miller's physics and sociology may be hard to follow but his thoughts about pitching are as straightforward as a fastball.

The reasons young men do not have arms as strong as young men used to have, according to Miller's doleful analysis, is that there is too damned much going on. The winningest pitcher ever, Cy Young, was also something of an aphorist: "Pitchers, like poets, are born, not made." Actually, pitchers are made from a youth of throwing baseballs. Young people who are headed for professional baseball are not spending the time earlier generations of young people did playing baseball—or even playing catch with their fathers, for that matter. They are playing soccer or competing on swimming teams, or sitting in front of a television set or . . . at any rate, they are not throwing, not developing strong arms. Miller says that back in the better days, when men were men and the world was rational, the biggest kid was made into a pitcher and baseball was the center of his life. Today that kid is apt to be a four-sport athlete. Many baseball people think there are also fewer strong arms than there used to be among outfielders. That, too, indicates that other sports, particularly football and basketball, are taking more of the strongest athletes than they used to. Certainly other sports, including soccer, swimming and tennis are taking the time of even very young children. In eras when childhood was less organized, such children might have been throwing baseballs out in the pasture, when pastures were just a step from many American back stoops. Or the city children would be throwing in vacant lots, when there were more vacant lots.

Jack McKeon, the crusty manager of the Padres, believes that the scarcity of outfielders with strong arms is a result of coaching that is too good, or at least too sophisticated. Coaches, he says, are teaching young outfielders to hit cutoff men too well, so they are not developing the strength for long throws. Ray Miller, education theorist, says that the recent decline of major league pitching is partially a result of "overcoaching" at the Little League level. He says boys are being taught to throw curveballs, knuckleballs, split-fingers. The emphasis, he says, should be on throwing hard and throwing often. And Miller, like most baseball people over 40, tends to see national decline in the rise of the breaking pitch and the fall of the fastball among the nation's young. "It's a statement on society. Everybody is looking for the easy way out. You can't find a big, strong kid who wants to throw year-round, who will stand out in the yard and throw rocks and knock cans down, just making himself bigger and stronger, and throw better."

The first year Miller coached in Baltimore the Orioles' pitchers had 65 complete games. Miller, the sociologist, blames the decline in the number of complete games at least in part on "affluence and the medical profession." He means that there is so much money invested in each player that the teams have doctors—*doctors,* for Pete's sake—in the clubhouses monitoring aches and pains. Talk about Babylonian decadence.

———◆———

Ray Miller, wearing blue jeans and a day's growth of beard, delivered these remarks in a really stupid setting, which is not his fault. He is a baseball person's baseball person and not responsible for the fact that the Pittsburgh Pirates play in a stadium that contains a restaurant that is about as big—bigger, maybe—than the park they used to play in. (What would Honus say?)

Through the restaurant's huge windows people eating lunch can look down to the bottom of the great concrete saucer, down at the artificial turf that is so green in the 1:00 P.M. sunlight it bites your eyes. It is symmetrical and immaculate—the turf, the concrete, the restaurant. It makes you want to mess it up a bit. Fortunately, an unruly force will be here soon. In a few hours a large man of the sort Miller thinks America needs more of will be out there. By about 5:00 P.M. he will be running the stadium steps, Walkman headphones clamped onto his large head, Van Halen hard rock pounding in his ears. Jim Gott, relief pitcher, will be getting himself worked up, getting ready to go to work.

As Earl Weaver says about baseball, "You can't sit on a lead and run a few plays into the line and just kill the clock. You've got to throw the ball over the goddamn plate and give the other man a chance." Baseball has roots far back in this young nation's antiquity. The absence of a clock in baseball is a product of the preindustrial sensibility. Before time was chopped up into units (as production was chopped into units, each timed for industrial efficiency), life was governed by just two things, daylight and its absence. And that (I am needlessly complicating and also recklessly simplifying) is why there are relief pitchers, and especially those large, powerful specimens called "closers." The closer is crucial because of one of the fundamental facts of baseball life: There being no clock, someone has to get the last outs. And they are the hardest to get.

One of baseball's impenetrable mysteries is the origin of the term "bull pen." Some historians believe it comes from the fact that around the turn of the century relief pitchers (to the extent that there were any) often warmed up in front of Bull Durham tobacco signs that were painted on many outfield fences. But as early as 1877 the *Cincinnati Enquirer* used the term "bull pen" to denote a roped-in area in foul territory where late-arriving fans were herded like bulls. Bill James says he has solved another mystery. He knows who invented relief pitching:

> Napoleon. No joke. Napoleon believed that every battle tended, for reasons of its own, to resolve itself into immobile, equal positions; he believed, in essence, in the law of Competitive Balance as applied to a battle. So on the day of a battle he would take two or three regiments of crack troops, and sequester them a distance from the shooting, eating and sleeping and trying to stay comfortable. Over the course of a day or several days, the troops in the field would take positions and lose them and retake and relose them, growing ever more and more weary, their provisions in shorter and shorter supply, and their positions ever more and more inflexible. Finally, at a key moment in the battle, with everyone else in the field barely able to stand, he would release into the fray a few hundred fresh and alert troops, riding fresh horses and with every piece of their equipment in good repair, attacking the enemy at his most vulnerable spot. He did this many times and with devastating effect—and if that's not relief pitching, I don't know what is.

Right. And Wellington won at Waterloo because he had what every team needs, a closer. His closer was Blucher's Prussians.

The relief pitcher originally was a rarity. He was called the "change" because before 1891 substitutions from the bench were permitted only in cases of injuries. When a new pitcher was needed, he came to the mound (actually, the "pitcher's box" as it then was) from another position, and the tuckered-out pitcher went somewhere else on the field. In 1904 the Red Sox played 154 games and Red Sox pitchers had 148 complete games. The bull pen had a six-game season, which means there really was no bull pen. In 1905 the Chicago Cubs' pitchers had 133 complete games. However, early in the century other clubs began to follow John McGraw's example by pressing starting pitchers into service as relievers. The Cubs, whose complete games plunged from 133 in 1905 to 99 in 1910, used Hall of Famer Mordecai "Three Finger" Brown in relief

44 times between 1908 and 1910, years in which he was averaging 32 starts.

The practice of using starters, including stars, as relievers was common for many decades. In 1930 and 1931 Lefty Grove relieved in 29 games. While Dizzy Dean won 30 games in 1934 he also relieved in 17. On the last day of the 1949 season George Kell of the Tigers edged out Ted Williams for the batting title, finishing at .342911 to Williams's .342756. Kell had to get his last two hits off a Cleveland pitcher working in relief: Bob Feller. In fact, 86 of Feller's 570 career appearances were in relief. Early Wynn relieved 79 times, Whitey Ford relieved 60 times.

The first real reliever, meaning the first man who came to the park expecting to make his living by entering late into many games, was the euphoniously named Firpo Marberry of the Senators. As Walter Johnson's career came to a close, Marberry came in to close many of the great man's games. In 1926 Marberry became the first pitcher to get 20 saves. (In 1965 the Cubs' Ted Abernathy became the first reliever to record 30 or more saves in a season. Three pitchers did that in the 1960s. In the 1970s there were fifteen 30-save seasons; in the 1980s, fifty-four.) But Marberry was a starter as well as a reliever. In 1924 he started 15 games but relieved in 35 as the Senators won their first pennant. In 1925, when they won again, he appeared in 55 games. In 1926 he appeared in 64. However, his career was a false dawn for relief pitching as a career. Relievers had to wait more than two decades for the flowering of the craft.

The first modern "closer" was Joe Page of the Yankees, who appeared in 278 games for the Yankees from 1944 through 1950. In 1950 Jim Konstanty appeared in 74 games for the pennant-winning "Whiz Kids" Phillies. In the 1950s, with Elroy Face, Lindy McDaniel and Hoyt Wilhelm, relief pitching became a recognized vocation. Relief pitchers have only recently begun receiving proper recognition. When Whitey Ford rose at the New York Baseball Writers banquet to receive the Cy Young Award for the 1961 season, he said he had a nine-minute speech but would deliver only seven minutes of it. He would let Luis Arroyo, who had saved so many of Ford's wins, do the final two minutes. Through 1989 seven relief pitchers had won Cy Young awards: Willie (now Guillermo) Hernandez, Sparky Lyle and Rollie Fingers in the American League; and Mike Marshall, Bruce Sutter, Steve Bedrosian and Mark Davis in the National League. All these awards were won since 1974. Fingers and

Hernandez also were MVPs. So was Jim Konstanty in 1950. Hoyt Wilhelm is the only relief pitcher in the Hall of Fame. He set a major league record by appearing in 1,070 games for 8 teams in 21 seasons from 1952 through 1972. (Kent Tekulve, who retired during the 1989 season, appeared in 1,050 games in 16 seasons.)

Whitey Herzog, the Missouri Valley epigrammatist, says, "A manager is as smart as his bull pen." Expanding that thought, he says, "When I managed Kansas City I wasn't too smart because I didn't have a closer. I got smarter in St. Louis because I've had Bruce Sutter, Todd Worrell and Ken Dayley. Today managers start with their bull pens and work forward." La Russa says that if he were putting together a pitching staff from scratch, his first priority would be a hard-throwing closer. It is, he says, easier to get to the fifth inning in good shape than it is to get the last six outs of a game. In 1988 La Russa's Athletics set a major league record with 64 saves. In 1989 Oakland's bull pen made a 19-game winner out of Storm Davis, who usually is out of gas, and the game, around the sixth inning. He won 19 games while pitching just 169⅓ innings, probably the fewest ever by a pitcher who won so many. The star of the Athletics' late-inning show has been Dennis Eckersley, the only pitcher to have both a 20-win season and a 45-save season. His 1988 numbers, though overshadowed by Hershiser's, were almost as remarkable. In the 45 games in which he earned saves his ERA was 0.17, one earned run in 53.1 innings. (Baseball's rule makers have tinkered with the definition of a "save" almost as much as the Supreme Court has tinkered with the meaning of "equal protection" of the laws. What should constitute a save is an inherently subjective judgment. For now the rule is this: To get credit for a save a relief pitcher must finish a game and satisfy one of the following three criteria. He must enter the game with the potential tieing run on base, or at bat, or on deck; or he must pitch one inning with a lead of not more than three runs; or he must pitch effectively, in the judgment of the official scorer, for at least three innings.)

When Sparky Anderson managed the Reds in the 1970s he became known as Captain Hook because of his frequent recourse to four relief pitchers to supplement his shaky starters. "What we were doing," he remembers, "was reducing each game to six or seven innings. If I have the bull pen and you don't, you have six or seven innings to beat me." In 1977 the Padres set a major league record with 382 appearances by relievers. In 1987 two teams broke that record (Reds, 392; Phillies, 389). In 1981 some careless person said the Yankees had an "incredible" record of 51–3 in games in which they led going into the eighth inning. But Bill James found that the average record for American League teams leading after seven innings was 49–5. The Cleveland Indians, part of baseball's Third World, were 42–3. And James found that the Yankees' record was 0–41 when they were behind after seven. Again, most teams win about 90 percent of the games in which they are ahead going into the eighth inning. Teams with good bull pens win 95 percent.

Batters are given to complaining that no one ever had it so hard. Actually, today's batters do not have some of the problems earlier batters had. For example, before there were lights for night baseball, back in the days when games took less time than they do now, many games started at 3:00 P.M. In the slanting light and shadows of the late innings, Lefty Grove's fastball probably did indeed look, as one batter said, "like a flash of white sewing thread coming up at you." However, the coming of the division of labor to the pitcher's mound has made hitting harder. Speaking about the role of hard-throwing relief pitchers, Pete Rose, who can not stop picking on Ty Cobb, says, "If Ty Cobb had to hit off those guys, he might have batted .315." Pete has a point. Consider 1930, which was 1968 turned inside out. In 1930 baseball finally did it. It went too far in favor of offense, even for the tastes of the most vulgar offense fanatics. In 1930 the National League—that is right, the *league*—hit .303 and 43 National League players hit .300 or better. Thirty-two American Leaguers and three American League teams hit .300 or better. Was the ball juiced? Probably. And yet there were 1,099 complete games pitched during all that year of cannonading. Both leagues probably hit something like .340 in the fourth and fifth at bats against shell-shocked starters. Today most starters have their pitching arms in ice when relief pitchers put the game on ice.

Since it was first done in 1973, 33 relief pitchers have earned credits (wins or saves) in 50 percent or more of their teams' wins. Peter Gammons notes that, leaving aside the strike-shortened 1981 season, only one team reached the World Series in the 1980s without having a reliever with at least 19 saves. That one team was the 1986 Red Sox, who lost games six and seven of the Series largely because of their bull pen. In 1986 the Twins lost 91 games and finished sixth in baseball's weakest division. They hit .261 with 196 home runs. In 1987 they again hit .261, again with 196 home runs. Were they in a rut? No, in 1987 they were in the World Series, which they won. And some baseball people were prepared to say that the most important difference between the 1986 and 1987 Twins was the addition of one relief pitcher, Jeff Reardon, who came to the Twins in a trade and had 31 saves.

In 1901, 87.3 percent of all games were completed by the starting pitcher. In 1988 only 14.8 were. In 1989 only 11.4 percent were. In the four seasons 1985–88, the Dodgers led the National League in complete games with 133. But by the time you got down the list to the fifth-highest total you were down to the Phillies' 75. The top five National League teams had a four-year total of 478 complete games, an average of just under 24 a season. The difference the DH makes is apparent in the total for the top five American League teams: 643. In the decade from 1978 through 1987 the number of complete games declined 46 percent. In 1978 there were 22 pitchers who worked 250 or more innings. By 1987 the number was 13. In 1988 it was 11. In 1989 it was 7. The major league leader was Bret Saberhagen (262⅓).

The primary reason for this decline is the rise of relief pitching as a respected role in the day-by-day running of a team. And one reason for that rise is the memorable example of the 1980 Athletics. Manager Billy Martin took a talented staff of starters and ruined it with too much work. They had 94 complete games that year, almost twice the number of any other team in the league. By 1983 four of the five starters had sore arms and were out of the rotation.

However, by now there is something of a tradition of wearing out relievers instead of starters. Through 1988 only three relief pitchers had recorded at least 30 saves in four consecutive seasons. (Lee Smith, with the Cubs, 1984–87; Dan Quisenberry with the Royals, 1982–85; Jeff Reardon with the Expos and Twins, 1985–88. In 1989 Reardon became the first to save 30 or more five seasons in a row.) There are several reasons why it is not uncommon for a relief pitcher to go from hotshot to has-been, from (as one player put it) "Cy Young to *sayonara.*" One reason is the mental strain of relief pitching, most of which is done in high-pressure situations with the game on the line. Another reason is the physical wear and tear. The better a relief pitcher is, the more often a manager, living for the moment, is apt to use, and eventually abuse, him. Third, a relief pitcher, more than a starter, can get by relying on a particular pitch, such as Bruce Sutter's fork ball, or even a quirky delivery, such as

themselves in 1989, although each took a while in baseball to get there. Both Miller and Gott are no-frills people. They subscribe to the straight-ahead approach to their business. Like the Pirates, they are hard-core baseball.

The Pirates originally were called the Alleghenys. Imagine, a team named after some mountains that are, as mountains go, not much. (Could have been worse. The Brooklyn Dodgers once were the Bridegrooms.) Some franchises are strongly associated with particular parts of the game. When you think of the Dodgers you think of a tradition of pitching, particularly Koufax and Drysdale. When you think of the Pirates you think of hitting, from Willie Stargell and Roberto Clemente back through Ralph Kiner and the Waner brothers (Paul and Lloyd, Big Poison and Little Poison), Pie Traynor and Arky Vaughan and, most of all, the man Branch Rickey and some others say was the best player ever, Honus Wagner.

Pittsburgh's hard-core baseball tradition is best seen far from Pittsburgh, in the Florida town where the Pirates train. A sign on the left-field fence says Bradenton is "the friendly city" and, for good measure, "a little bit of paradise." Perhaps. But the best part of Spring Training in Bradenton is that it still has some of the scruffiness associated with life in what used to be baseball's slow lane. More and more communities have cottoned on to the fact that Spring Training can be big business and have lured teams with posh training "complexes." Crowds are so big in some places that there are ticket scalpers. Oh, well. All this is probably progress, but Bradenton's McKechnie Field, located in the midst of the hum of ordinary commerce and living, should be preserved for the flavor of Spring Training before it became upscale.

Alas, Pittsburgh, like so many other cities, suffered terribly at the hands of baseball vandals in the late 1960s and 1970s. Not since Cromwell's troops, their puritan sensibilities offended by beauty, went around smashing decorative art in churches has there been an act of folly comparable to the abandonment and destruction of Forbes Field, the Pirates' home for generations. The outrage was made worse by the replacement of Forbes Field by Three Rivers Stadium. Forgive my intensity, but a fan remembers with special fondness the ballpark where he saw his first major league game. My first was in Forbes Field in 1950. The loudspeakers were pouring forth the pop song of the moment ("Good Night, Irene") as the 9-year-old from central Illinois entered. He left after the Pirates rang up a thumping victory over the Cardinals, one of only 57 Pirate wins that year. Forbes Field was one of those old parks that combined a sense of spaciousness with a feeling of intimacy.

Three Rivers Stadium was opened in 1970, which means it was dreamed up in the 1960s, which is no excuse but explains a lot. Almost everything about the 1960s, from politics to popular music to neckties, was marked by wretched excess. It was, of course, a decade in love with professional football. It is to baseball's credit that when the times were out of joint, baseball was out of step. As Bill Veeck said, "The Sixties was a time for grunts and screams. . . . The sports that fitted the time were football, hockey and mugging." Three Rivers Stadium was built to accommodate both football and baseball. Big mistake. And speaking of mistakes (there are so many to speak of), there were those Pirates uniforms. From 1977 through 1979 the Pirates pioneered new forms of gaucherie in their three uniforms (one yellow, one black, one white with pinstripes) and two styles of hats. Could there be a more complete contrast with the sedate, unchanging vestments of the Dodgers? In many ways Gott offers a complete contrast with Hershiser. Hershiser is intergalactically famous. Gott is not. No Bob Hope specials for him. Hershiser works in one of the nation's two biggest media markets. Gott worked in one of the smallest of the 26 major league markets. Los Angeles is synonymous with glitter. It should not be. It is as much the home of gang war as of Hollywood. (Gott, by the way, was born in Hollywood.) Pittsburgh is synonymous with sweat and soot. It should not be. The image of Pittsburgh as the Steel City is more than a generation out of date. No steel is made within the city limits. There is only one producing steel mill in the metropolitan area. The city's largest employer is the University of Pittsburgh. But the biggest contrast between Hershiser and Gott is in what they do. Hershiser has a star's job: starting pitcher. Gott's job is to prevent disasters and sometimes tidy up messes that other pitchers have made. Hershiser has the glamour of a surgeon. Gott is one of those harried doctors you see—and are mighty glad to see—coping with crises in busy emergency rooms. When major league managers reach for the dugout phone to call the bull pen they should dial 911. The Book of Job—the relief pitcher's handbook—got it right: Man is born unto trouble as the sparks fly upward.

You do not have to be a bit touched in the head to want to earn a living as a reliever, but many relievers seem to be. There is a tendency for relief pitchers to seem a bit mad—mad meaning angry (Goose Gossage), mad meaning crazed (Sparky Lyle), or both angry and crazed (Al Hrabosky). Moe Drabowsky collected the phone numbers of bull pens all over the major leagues and enjoyed lightening the burden of boredom by calling bull pens in other cities. Imitating the voices of various coaches, he would order relievers hundreds of miles away to start warming up.

Gott, too, tends toward the manic, another complete contrast with cool-hand Hershiser. "My father was a very hard worker, came from nothing and made a lot of money. You don't listen to parents when you are growing up, so my dad found other people for us to listen to." Gott's brother went to golf camps and twice won the California state high school golf championship. Gott went to baseball camps. As a junior in high school he went out for football for the first time. He did it on a dare. Someone challenged him to prove that he was tough enough to play. He could play. As a senior he was all-conference. UCLA recruited him as a defensive end and middle linebacker. But his father had been a baseball prospect who injured his arm just at the time he was about to make the transition from amateur to professional ball and he wanted one of his children to be a ball player. "My brother," says Gott, "is an introvert and went into golf." Gott is not an introvert. For a while during his, shall we say, vigorously lived youth, which extended well into his twenties, Gott was, he admits, "the classic million-dollar arm with the ten-cent brain." He will be 30 on Opening Day, 1990, and he is still not your typical sight when he arrives at the mound.

It is one of the oldest sayings in baseball. It is what innumerable coaches and managers have said (or are said to have said) to innumerable pitchers having problems: "Babe Ruth is dead—throw strikes." It is said that Art Fowler, Billy Martin's Sancho Panza and pitching coach at various stops in Martin's career, was once approached before a game by a young pitcher who said: "In the late innings I seem to lose my control. I'm doing something wrong—opening my shoulder or otherwise developing a flaw in my mechanics. Watch me closely tonight and see if you can spot the problem." Around the seventh inning the young pitcher did indeed lose his control and walked three people. Fowler came to the mound and the young pitcher asked anxiously, "What am I doing wrong?" Fowler, drawing upon years of experience, said, "You're walking people and Billy's pissed."

Fans are forever wondering what gets said to a relief pitcher when he comes to the mound in a difficult situation. With Gott, says LaValliere, "I just try to stop him from snorting. He comes in like a horse, running in from the bull pen. He's huffing and puffing, so the first thing I want to do before I go back to warm him up is let him catch his breath a little bit." Doesn't that surge of adrenaline make it hard for him to keep his mechanics stable? "That is one reason why he has to throw from a stretch even when he is starting an inning. He gets so excited he really couldn't keep all the body parts going in the same direction enough to throw strikes." Steve Carlton used to go into a semi-trance of concentration before a game. But Carlton was a silent, solitary, withdrawn man most of the time. Gott is the soul of sociability, up to a point. "You can talk to him in the bull pen until up around the seventh inning," says LaValliere. "Then he goes into a kind of trance. When he finally gets the phone call, he works himself up. He has to be in fourth gear when he comes in." Gott says, "We're little kids playing a little kid's game. Why shouldn't we show emotion?"

There is an answer to that question. Showing emotion is just *not done* because baseball is such a humbling game. The exultation of success is going to be followed in short order by the cold slap of failure. Any team's success. Anyone's success. So why get high when a low is just around the corner? Baseball is a life best lived in an emotionally temperate zone. Still, relief pitchers and especially closers can be forgiven for being different. Gott sure is. The highlight of his 1989 season may have been painting the horse's testicles silver. And even that, although worth doing, did not go right. Wrong color. No one got gold paint.

When visiting teams leave their hotel in downtown Chicago, heading for Wrigley Field, their bus takes Lake Shore Drive, getting off at the Belmont exit, where there is a statue of General Philip Sheridan on a horse—an anatomically correct horse. A few years ago a tradition got started involving the horse. It was said that things would go better for a team that season, and that the team's rookies would have long careers, if during the team's first visit of the season to Chicago, the rookies painted the horse's testicles the team colors. The rookies would go out to perform this rite, the veterans would alert the police, the rookies would get hauled into the station house where they would sign the baseball celebrity prisoner book, and that would be that. A good time was had by all. In 1989 Gott, who is not a rookie, went along with a rookie to do the job. But the visiting clubhouse man got silver paint. The Pirates' colors are black and gold.

Gott had flown back from Pittsburgh to Chicago to do the daring deed. He had originally left the team in Chicago and flown to Pittsburgh to see a doctor, who promptly put Gott on the 15-day disabled list. He had tenderness in his elbow and the doctor hoped that all it would require would be a short rest. But Gott flew on from Chicago to Los Angeles to see a specialist in pitchers' problems. The specialist saw the need for a simple, 45-minute operation. However, when the specialist got into the elbow he saw a lot of debris (bone chips) and loose ends and frayed things. The operation took four hours and Gott went home with his arm in a cast, his season a shambles and his career on hold.

Gott is a grown-up. He knows the risks of what he does. Pitchers get hurt. They break. They wear out. A 30-year-old pitcher probably has an arm a great deal older than that.

Ron Fairly, a broadcaster of Giants games, once said, "Bruce Sutter has been around a while and he's pretty old. He's 35 years old. That will give you an idea of how old he is." Even with modern conditioning techniques and nutrition plans, even with the care players take to prolong today's lucrative careers, 35 is the sear, the yellow leaf. This is especially true for a pitcher, who lives by abusing his throwing arm. "Your arm is your best friend," says Tom Seaver, "but in the end you've got to treat it as if it was your worst enemy." That is, taking up pitching as a career is deciding to injure yourself every four or five days. Throwing a baseball is a highly unnatural act. As the arm accelerates past the ear, it gains terrific speed and then changes direction, turning down and decelerating sharply. Muscles stretch and tear and bleed. And that is when everything is going well. Lots of blood and other stuff must then be given time to go away—time, and encouragement. Ice and heat and exercise and massage and sound waves and other things are used to help the healing process.

Roger Angell reports that when, during the 1978 season, the Yankee team physician put Catfish Hunter under anesthesia to manipulate his damaged pitching arm, the physician was so startled by the popping noise when he broke the old adhesions in Hunter's shoulder that he thought he had broken one of Hunter's bones. And muscles are not the only things that suffer wear and tear. Sandy Koufax retired at age 30 at the end of a season when he won the pitcher's triple crown. Never mind the numbers, he knew his arm was worn out. By October, 1966, his left elbow had suffered so much traumatic arthritis that his arm had begun to turn inward and he had to shorten the left sleeves of his coats. There was nothing Koufax could do about his elbow except take too many cortisone shots, which could have crippled him. He refused to run that risk.

Nowadays much more is known about the mechanics of pitching, how to minimize physical stresses and how to recover from their ravages. "Back in the old days," Roger Craig remembers, "the pitching coaches didn't really care about your delivery or your stretch position. They would just run you to keep you in shape. They didn't worry about mechanics." Another change in pitching concerns medicine. Roger Craig pitched for 12 years with six National League teams. He pitched and lost the last game the Brooklyn Dodgers played in Philadelphia. "About the third or fourth inning," he recalls, "I snapped something in my shoulder that I now know was a rotator cuff. In those days you never heard of that. If that had happened now they would have gone in and 'scoped' [arthroscopic surgery] it. I pitched the last seven, eight years I was in the major leagues with a sore arm."

It is remarkable how recently ice and weights became part of pitchers' regimens. Until recently baseball has been backward about exercises. Unlike in football, where exercise programs have been devised to enhance performance, baseball has regarded exercise as primarily corrective, something you do when something has gone wrong. After a game, Hershiser, like most pitchers, ices his shoulder with a huge pack taped to his upper torso and he ices his elbow in a tub on a table. This cuts down the swelling and begins the healing, a practice begun on the Dodgers remarkably recently, in the 1960s, by Don Drysdale and Sandy Koufax. The day after pitching is the off-day on which Hershiser works hardest: He has the most time to recuperate before his next start. He no longer is sore the day after a game, which he attributes to the work he has done with free weights and Nautilus equipment. The work develops strength and flexibility and long, lean muscles. Before he began weight training he was so stiff on mornings after games he could barely get out of bed. He does a free-weight program for his shoulder and rotator cuff, another for the elbow and ulnar nerve. For pitchers, that cuff and that nerve are the parts that are most apt to suffer incapacitating or even career-ending injuries. For cardiovascular conditioning Hershiser uses a Versiclimber, a sort of treadmill in the form of a ladder. He calls it "a way of climbing a mountain without going anywhere." He also uses a stationary bicycle.

Gott also does all that stuff, and more. In the spring he thought a cortisone shot would put the pain away and let him pitch as though everything inside his arm was all right. He prepared for an appearance against the Texas Rangers by wearing, strapped to his forearm, a gadget that sent healing sound waves into his arm. At the Rangers' posh Spring Training complex at Port Charlotte, Florida, Gott came in for an inning of work in the eighth with the Rangers leading, 6–4. He got two quick outs, then surrendered a solid single, balked the runner to second, gave up a run-scoring single, then a run-scoring double. Two runs on three hits. After the game in the clubhouse Ray Miller said, "I'm not worried about Jimmy. What he needs is 50,000 in there." Miller means that Gott needs the presence of a crowd—the more the merrier; 50,000 if possible—to get himself pumped up. But Miller should have been worried.

After Gott went on the disabled list, Jim Leyland said he was not surprised: "I was suspicious because of his control. You don't have to be a rocket scientist to figure out that when a guy starts his motion and then pulls his arm in because it hurts him to leave it out, or he leaves his arm extended because he doesn't want to pull through, something hurts and it makes him wild. Being wild is very uncharacteristic of Jim Gott. If there is one thing he can do it is throw strikes." Gott will be back, running the Dodger Stadium steps with Van Halen reverberating in his head, and throwing strikes, abusing his arm for a living, and loving it.

———◆———

The way to minimize arm abuse is to pay attention to the way the arm bone is connected to the shoulder bone, and the way all the bones go together, right down to the leg bones. As Shea Stadium's loudspeakers blare Jan and Dean's "Surf City" into the fetid air of Flushing—the surf city by Flushing Bay—Hershiser raises his voice to make himself heard, explaining pitching mechanics with reference to "the law of the flail." A pitcher's body works, he says, like a catapult or whip. The reason a whip snaps is that the tip of the whip accelerates when the handle stops. A pitcher's planted front leg is the handle; the arm is the end of the whip. "That's why they say a pitcher is only as good as his legs."

Be that as it may, Ray Miller believes that the key to velocity is arm speed. "Willie Mays used a 32-ounce bat. Mickey Mantle used a 34- or 32-ounce bat and hit the ball as far as anyone who ever lived. So what's the size of the bat got to do with it? It's the speed of the bat at contact. And it's the speed of the arm as the ball leaves your hand." Miller is a man worth listening to. He says a pitching coach contributes to a 20-win season this way. Assume 35 starts a year for a strong pitcher. If he is lucky he will have his best stuff perhaps 15 times. If the pitcher is working for a good team, he may win 10 of those. On the other 5, says Miller, you may pitch reasonably well but may pitch against Hershiser and lose. On the other 20 starts, that's where the pitching coach comes in.

Miller comes into any relationship with a pitching pupil with a simple credo: "Throw strikes, change speeds, work fast." That's it. End of science. No philosophy.

Throw strikes, starting with the first pitch. In 1988, 43 percent of all first pitches were balls. But 25 percent were called strikes, 6 percent were swinging strikes and 12 percent were fouled. So 43 percent of first pitches resulted in 0–1 counts. The other 14 percent of first pitches were put in play. In the fifth game of the World Series, Hershiser worked on short rest, after an exhausting September and the draining seven-game League Championship Series. The Athletics came out trying to "run the count," to take a lot of pitches and make him work. But that strategy would work only if Hershiser could not get the first pitch in. He got it in.

In a nine-inning game, Hershiser usually throws 110 to 115 pitches. That is on the low side for complete games by major league pitchers. It is low because, although he consistently ranks among the league leaders in strikeouts, he does not consider himself a strikeout pitcher. "Batters know I come after them with first pitches so they are swinging and I get a lot of first-pitch outs." If a pitcher gets the first strike on a batter, he can miss with the next three before he is in dire straits. If he gets one more strike the batter is in dire straits. A pitcher ahead 0–2 should rarely fail to retire the batter. Probably the stiffest fine in the history of baseball was levied by Giants manager Mel Ott on pitcher Bill Voiselle, who gave up a home run to a Cardinals batter on an 0–2 pitch. The fine was only $500 but it concentrated Voiselle's mind wonderfully. He was making $3,500 that season. Ray Miller probably approves of Ott's criminal-justice system. Miller is a first-pitch fanatic. "It's 90 percent of the game— strike one. If you throw strike one you've got five possible pitches left to throw for two strikes." And "there are always about 12 million guys in baseball who are first-pitch fastball hitters. If you don't throw them a fastball on the first pitch you eliminate about 75 percent of their game plan."

But what if personal experience, or information from the advance scout, indicates that a particular batter is jumping on first pitches? "There are two theories of pitching," Hershiser says. "One is that you try to convince the batter that a particular pitch is coming and you throw something different. The other theory, that you don't hear as much but that I use, is that if the batter expects a particular pitch, you throw it, but you throw it in a place where he can't hit it." That is: Know what a batter wants or expects and throw the ball *almost* there. If he is a high-ball hitter, throw it a bit too high. His eagerness will prevent him from laying off it, but it will be hard to hit well. Davey Johnson, the Mets' manager, says the same thing in baseballspeak: "If a guy is a first-ball, fastball, high-ball hitter, and you are a fastball pitcher, give him a first-ball fastball a little higher than he likes it and see if he'll bite on it rather than hook [curve] him and miss, hook him and miss, and then give a cherry [unconvincing] fastball."

Hershiser wants to learn what a batter is thinking during *this at bat*. "If a guy is a good first-pitch fastball hitter, I know it and he knows it, and I throw a fastball right down the middle and he takes it, that tells me his thinking is different this at bat. He thought I was going to throw him a curve because he knows that I know he's a first-pitch fastball hitter and he was sitting on a curve—he took a pitch he normally swings at. He's looking for something else and that gives you a clue to his thinking." Unlike a lot of pitchers—and batters—Hershiser can not call up from memory at any time a sequence of pitches, or remember the nature of a particular pitch that got an out, or got hammered. But he can do that when he is on the mound. "It just comes to me. The situation has been re-created and it just all clicks in." Any pitcher must draw upon memory, he says, and continues, "In the big leagues, no one has enough talent to overcome slumps just by kicking it in and overpowering people."

There are various ways of learning what a hitter is looking for. Jim Lefebvre says that a really observant pitcher can tell by the way a hitter takes a pitch what the hitter is looking for that day. Hershiser has talked to hitting coaches to learn about pitching and has learned to watch a batter's check swing. The batter has been fooled; he did not understand where the ball was going. But where his bat was going tells you where he wanted the ball to be. It tells you if he is looking for a high or low pitch. When a left-handed hitter lines a fastball foul into the stands on the third-base side, either he did not get his bat up to the speed required for the fastball or he was looking for an off-speed pitch. It does not matter which is the explanation. The lesson is: more fastballs, and keep them outside, where a slow bat will never catch up with them.

"I lockered next to Sal Maglie in Brooklyn," Don Drysdale remembers, "and he had a theory that stuck in my mind. He said that if you're ever in doubt about what the hitter is looking for, always watch his feet. Take your first pitch and go low and away for a ball and watch the hitter's feet. If he's moving into the pitch so he can cover the outside corner, he's told you that he's looking for a pitch that is going to be out over the plate or down and away. He's going out to cover that zone. If he's coming straight at you, you learn nothing. If he's pulling out [a right-hander striding slightly toward third; if a left-hander, toward first], he's looking for you to crowd him."

A first-pitch strike to the leadoff batter in an inning is a big first step toward the out that makes life a lot easier. Hershiser says that one of the keys to pitching is to get the first batter in each inning out. "Never walk a leadoff batter because he scores about 80 percent of the time. Even a good pitcher gives up an average of about a hit an inning. You give a guy a free pass and they advance him one base with an out, now where is your hit-an-inning going to come? It's going to come and you're going to give up a run."

As the strike zone has become smaller and hitters have become stronger, and less fearful at the plate, pitchers have had to pitch more carefully, nibbling at the strike zone (what is left of it). So they have more frequently fallen behind in the count to more confident hitters. However, a pitcher with good control can often influence the size of the strike zone, at least for part of a game. Once a pitcher has shown a batter and the plate umpire that he wants to get the first strike in, and that he will continue to throw strikes, he is apt to influence their decisions about pitches at the edges of the strike zone. He can, in effect, enlarge the strike zone. "If you're consistent in an area," says Hershiser, "that part of the strike zone will become bigger because you have proven that you can hit that area, so the umpire gives you the benefit of the doubt. When you are all over the place, you're less apt to get strikes called on close pitches. You get more close pitches called strikes the more consistent you are in hitting the glove."

There may be nothing a pitcher can do to make some umpires expand the strike zone. However, when the pitcher gets ahead of the batter in the count, the batter will expand the strike zone on his own—he will swing at borderline pitches that are too close to risk taking. Every hitter goes to the plate determined to do what dozens of coaches, from Little League to the big leagues, have urged: "Be selective." But that is devilishly hard to do with two strikes on you. Mike Scott recalls one umpire, the late Lee Weyer, who had an enormous strike zone. The pitchers knew it, the hitters knew it, and the games went fast because anything around the plate was a strike, so the hitters were always swinging.

Throw strikes? Piece of cake, said Satchel Paige, because "home plate don't move." In a reasonably good game, Hershiser will face 35 batters and will be ahead in the count to at least 25 of them. Paige probably did even better. He would warm up by pitching over a matchbook. Whitey Herzog tells the following story about something Paige did when he, Herzog, was playing for the Miami Marlins:

> The Marlins once had a distance-throwing contest before a night game. [Don] Landrum and I had the best arms of any of the outfielders. We were out by the center-field fence, throwing two-hoppers to the plate. Ol' Satch came out, didn't even warm up, and kind of flipped the ball sidearm. It went 400 feet on a dead line and hit the plate. I wouldn't believe it if I hadn't seen it.
>
> We were on the road in Rochester one night, screwing around in the outfield. They had a hole in the outfield fence just barely big enough for a baseball to go through, and the deal was that any player who hit a ball through there on the fly would win $10,000. I started trying to throw the ball through the hole, just to see if I could. I bet I tried 150 or 200 times, but I couldn't do it, so I went back to the dugout.
>
> When Satch got to the park, I said, "Satch, I bet you can't throw the ball through that hole out there."
>
> He looked out at it and said, "Wild Child, do the ball fit in the hole?"
>
> "Yeah, Satch," I said. "But not by much. I'll bet you a fifth of Old Forester that you can't throw it through there."

"Wild Child," he said. "I'll see you tomorrow night."

So the next night Satch showed up for batting practice—first time in his life he'd ever been that early. I took a few baseballs, went out to the outfield, and stepped off about 60 feet 6 inches, the distance from the mound to home. Satch ambled out, took the ball, brought it up to his eye like he was aiming it, and let fire.

I couldn't believe it. The ball hit the hole, rattled around, and dropped back out. He'd come that close, but I figured it was his best shot.

Satch took another ball and drilled the hole dead center. The ball went right through, and I haven't seen it since.

"Thank you, Wild Child," Satch said, and then went back into the clubhouse.

Control isn't what it used to be. But to repeat, the strike zone (smaller) and the batters (larger, less fearful) aren't what they used to be either. So there are more walks. But come to think of it, that may not mean worse control. It may mean more nibbling—more well-controlled pitches near but not too near the corners. In any case, some of the records of the past masters of control are amazing.

In two seasons, 1913 and 1914, when his records were 25–11 and 24–13, Christy Mathewson walked fewer men than he had victories (21 in 1913 and 23 in 1914). In 1913 Mathewson allowed just 0.62 walks per 9 innings pitched, a single-season record. Only 22 pitchers in this century have allowed less than 1 walk per 9 innings over a season. Only 3 of those 22 have done it since 1920, the dawn of the age of offense. The great achievements of control include the 7 innings Stan Coveleski pitched without a single pitch called a ball. Babe Adams in 1920 and Cy Young in 1905 pitched 21 and 20 innings, respectively, without a walk. And in 1933 Carl Hubbell pitched an 18-inning shutout without a walk. The modern era does have one hero of control: Ferguson Jenkins is the only pitcher in history to have more than 3,000 strikeouts and fewer (just three fewer) than 1,000 walks.

For most mortals, control is a sometime thing. It comes and goes. Tom Seaver said that when he had his best control, he could pitch within a quarter of an inch of a spot nine times out of ten. Hershiser illustrates his best control by holding his palm forward, as a catcher holds a mitt, and rotating his wrist without moving his forearm. He says that when his catcher has given him a target with the mitt, the catcher should be able to receive eight out of ten pitches with no more movement than twisting the wrist, leaving his forearm immobile and moving the mitt about an inch.

When a pitcher does not have good control—when home plate seems to be moving—it may or may not be nice to have an infielder like Davey Johnson. Johnson was second baseman for the Orioles in some of their salad seasons (1965–72). He also was a math major at Texas A&M. Imagine the puzzlement of Dave McNally, an Orioles pitcher, the day he was having control trouble and Johnson trotted in to the mound to suggest that McNally give a thought to the theory of "unfavorable chance deviation." No jury would have convicted McNally, who had other things on his mind, if he had murdered Johnson right there on the mound. But Johnson had a point. "A pitcher," says Johnson, "is in an 'unfavorable chance deviation' if he's aiming at a particular area and he's missing by X on each side. If he's trying to go on the inside corner, he either is missing six to eight inches inside or right over the heart of the plate. So if he aims over the heart of the plate, he'll hit the corners. So I told McNally he was in an 'unfavorable chance deviation,' to just throw it down the middle. He said, 'Get back to second base.'"

Control does not mean always throwing strikes. Rather, it means throwing enough strikes to get hitters to swing at balls. To do that, change speeds.

Warren Spahn pitched for 21 seasons and won 363 games. If he had not missed three seasons because of military service during World War II, he would have far surpassed Christy Mathewson and Grover Cleveland Alexander's 373 wins as the National League's winningest pitchers. Spahn's craft was subtle. His explanation of it is concise: "Hitting is timing. Pitching is upsetting timing." Sandy Koufax says, "Every pitcher's best pitch is his fastball. It's the fastball that makes the other pitches effective. Hitters must look for it and try to adjust for a breaking pitch. While they are looking for the breaking pitch, the fastball is by them before they can adjust." Ray Miller produced a compilation of every pitch thrown by all the Orioles' 20-game winners. He learned, with the delight that any theorist feels when facts confirm his beliefs, that all of them threw at least 60 percent fastballs in those seasons of maximum success. Changing speeds can mean mixing up the kinds of pitches you throw, or changing the speed at which you throw one kind of pitch.

Miller believes that "offensive" pitching is not coming at the batter with hard stuff. Rather, it is coming at the batter with all sorts of stuff. And "defensive" hitting is not a batter biding his time waiting for the pitch he wants. Rather, defensive hitting is nervous, uncertain swinging at pitches anywhere near what the batter prefers. Jim Palmer estimates that half of all swinging third strikes are defensive swings at pitches outside the strike zone. "When pitchers are offensive," says Miller, "the batters become defensive. When you change speeds, batters swing more."

Most baseball people say a good starting pitcher needs only three pitches. Hershiser has four: the two fastballs (the hard one that sinks and the "cutter" that sort of slides), the curve and the change-up. However, his curve is really several pitches because he can "tighten" the break. "If the hitter is the kind who reacts early to the ball when it leaves your hand, I'll throw more of a sweeping large curveball. If it's a good disciplined hitter who reads that pitch very well, like a [Keith] Hernandez or [Kevin] McReynolds, or a Punch-and-Judy–type hitter who really stays in there and fights you off, I shorten the break to get the ball to look like it's really going to be a strike the whole way and then quickly break at the end." Because Hershiser changes the trajectory and velocity, "there might be ten different curveballs in my arm."

Hershiser, says Drysdale, is in "the low end of the power-pitcher category," but batters know that what they face when they face him is "not a comfortable 0-for-4 but a bastard 0-for-4." That is, they are going to be jammed, struck out, they will swing at curveballs in the dirt, they will break their bats, they will be made to look foolish.

Fiddling around with a radar gun one day, Hershiser concluded that a ball must be thrown 40 miles per hour to get from the mound to the plate in the air. He says that there is about a 10-mile-per-hour difference between his fastball and his curve. There are always some pitchers of whom it is said: If you are going to get them you have to get them early in the game. Often these are pitchers who throw too hard when they come in from their pregame pitching in the bull pen, pumped up and rarin' to go. They may throw their curves so hard that those pitches straighten out, or their sinker so hard it doesn't sink. The serious use of the radar gun is less to measure the velocity of a pitcher's fastest pitch than it is to measure the difference between a pitcher's fastball and his change-up, or between his fastball and his curve. Some differences are too small and others are too large to be of maximum effectiveness in upsetting a hitter's timing. A radar gun can pick up the fact that a pumped-up pitcher is throwing too hard.

The new high-tech aspect of baseball is, in Tony La Russa's view, just "backing up observation with numbers." Many experienced baseball people can watch a pitcher for a few minutes and estimate his velocity within one or two miles per hour. They can watch a pitcher's release and tell if he is quick or slow, if he can be run on or not. The backup by technology becomes most effective when, during a game, the manager, with much on his mind, can be told that between the seventh and eighth innings his tiring starter lost three miles per hour off his fastball, or that the opposing pitcher did. Clever pitchers, especially now that pitchers work constantly with radar guns pointed at them, complicate things by masking fatigue. Tom Seaver, generally regarded as the most thoughtful pitcher of the modern era, would save in his arm a few full-power pitches for late in the game, when batters were adjusting to any loss of velocity that the radar gun had recorded. Hershiser throws his fastball at maximum velocity (around 94 miles per hour) only about five times a game. Usually he throws it at 85 percent of maximum velocity because he wants the option of going up in speed late in the game, when it will be, in effect, a new pitch. Jim Palmer would do something like that during an entire game. On days when he did not have a good fastball he would slow his other pitches down proportionately and still pitch effectively.

Hershiser thinks of a game as a tennis match, with three "sets," each consisting of three innings. He tries to save one pitch to introduce into the second "set" and another to introduce into the third. By varying his repertoire within a game, he makes himself his own relief pitcher in the sense that the second, third and fourth times through the lineup the opposing hitters still do not quite have the advantage of a second, third and fourth look at his complete repertoire.

The pitcher's most formidable new weapon in the postwar era has been the slider, a fastball with a tight spin that can break six inches horizontally and vertically. Hershiser does not throw it. The second most important new pitch has been the split-finger fastball. Hershiser does not throw it either. Why this unilateral non-armament? The answer is: Why take risks when there is no need—not yet, at least. The risk Hershiser sees with a slider is the need to alter his mechanics, and the additional strain put on the arm and elbow by the act of imparting spin to the ball. The split-finger, Hershiser says, dangerously tightens the arm from wrist to elbow when the ball is wedged between the index and middle fingers. (Try it; it does.) When will he throw one or the other or both of those pitches? "When I start getting hit around. You know what I said about having a repertoire within a game, and when to show it? You should have a repertoire within a career. All the guys who pitch 15, 20 years make adjustments on a 3-to-5-year basis. They come up with a new pitch, new angle, new style. There's no way I can get [Keith] Hernandez out for 10 years pitching the same way. There's no way we can play in the same league because all the information is not coming to my favor. It's coming to his favor. So I've got to create some new information. He's the one learning. I'm not learning. Batters don't change. That's why knuckleball pitchers, screwball pitchers and speciality-pitch pitchers do so well. Because batters won't change that one day and risk ruining the other four. Charlie Hough goes out and throws that floater and everybody says to himself, 'Come on, just stay back, maybe change your swing, maybe crouch a little, move up on the plate.' But the batter gets up and thinks, 'I've never been in this part of the batter's box before!' "

Work fast.

Work fast for many reasons, not the least of which is that a pitcher is only as good as his defense. Good defense is a matter of concentration and anticipation. A pitcher who dawdles puts his defense to sleep. A pitcher working fast sets a tempo that keeps people on their toes. Miller says an average major league game has 13½ pitches per half inning, or around 120 in nine innings. So 120 times the seven players behind the pitcher "set up" on the balls of their feet. Working fast also helps a pitcher maintain his mechanics once they are in tune. Hershiser says he is "mechanically conscious" when on the mound. He puts on his computer disks his postgame recollections of successful adjustments he has made in his delivery during games. "When I'm not in a groove I make adjustments on every pitch. 'You didn't stay on top of that pitch, so the next time you throw a curveball make sure you get your arm up. And the way you get your arm up is not by just thinking it. This is what you need to do: Stay back, allow your hip to move out first, don't put your shoulder in front of your hip. You have to feel the weight on the inside part of your foot. That allows your hip to slide out.' There are different keys I have learned that will bring me back in sync on a certain pitch. If my sinker is just going sideways instead of down, I know I need to get more on top of the ball, not with arm angle but with hand discipline."

There are people who believe that the plodding pace of games set by White Sox catcher Carlton Fisk works, like a basketball coach calling time out when the other team is on a roll, to make it difficult for opponents to generate momentum for a big inning. But Hershiser is a man after Ray Miller's heart. According to Dempsey (who was the catcher in Baltimore when Miller was coaching there), Hershiser "wants the ball and to get right back up on the mound."

◆

On the mound Hershiser seems to be all business. Seems to be. Actually, he has fun there. Often when he steps on the rubber, he drops his head, which suggests solemnity. Actually, he is avoiding the distraction in front of him—the umpire standing up, the catcher getting set, the batter digging in and the television and other cameras and radar guns and equipment and activity that are often behind the screen directly behind home plate. "When I lift my head, they are waiting for me." Off the field, Hershiser is a formidable businessman. And because of his religiosity, an aroma of incense and an aura of sanctity cloak his public persona. This is unfortunate. He has a dry wit that surfaces constantly in conversations. Once on a team flight, when some of the players were flirting with the flight attendants (or perhaps it was the other way around in the friendly skies that day), Hershiser said, "You're writing about men at work? How about men at play?" Hershiser's wife, Jamie, comes from Mattoon, Illinois. A sign on the interstate highway that passes near Mattoon notifies drivers that the town has "Food, Gas, Lodging." "All three," says Hershiser with a tone of mock wonderment.

On Friday morning, July 21, 1989, the Dodgers awake in the Gateway Hilton, just a ten-minute walk across a bridge from Pittsburgh's Three Rivers Stadium. They are to play a doubleheader that night and another on Sunday as part of an unusual six-game series, the result of rainouts. The Dodgers' pitching staff is toiling with little support from Dodgers hitters, which is why the Dodgers are in fifth place, 13½ games behind the division-leading Giants and only 3½ games ahead of the last-place Braves.

However, this morning Hershiser is going to have fun. He is going to watch a tape he has not watched before, a tape of the seventh game of the 1988 Dodgers-Mets League Championship Series. He pitched that game. On the screen the tape shows Tommy Lasorda pacing and fidgeting nervously before the first pitch. Hershiser, watching with quickly mounting interest the events of nine months ago, says to the Lasorda on the television screen, "Don't worry. We win, 6–0."

"Before the game they [the Mets] came out with quotes that 'we're not worried because we've got Hershiser figured out.' I took it to mean that they were going to try to take my sinker away from me by the left-handers crowding the plate—Strawberry and Backman and Dykstra and Hernandez and Jefferies and Mookie Wilson." Also, Mets manager Davey Johnson had said that Hershiser must be tired. That, Hershiser thought, meant that the Mets would assume that he would rely entirely on his sinker away. So he decided to disabuse them of this idea by pitching inside more than he normally would early in the game.

"I wasn't tired," he says. "I was going on adrenaline. In fact, early in the game I wasn't throwing the ball really well because my adrenaline was so high. My ball wasn't sinking, it was going sideways. I was throwing too hard, and when I throw too hard my mechanics can move sideways, so the ball goes more sideways." His shoulders were tilting down toward first base instead of staying close to parallel with the ground. "When your mechanics are slowed down and you stay within yourself"—the phrase "stay within yourself" recurs constantly in players' talk, as we shall see with Tony Gwynn—"you can create the proper angle. But if I start to rush and overthrow, most of my motion becomes lateral. Just as my arm is starting to come forward, my left shoulder is already flying open [turning to Hershiser's left]. I am firing too early and killing my whole left side. I'm not going to have any left side to throw against." That is, because his left shoulder has turned too far too soon, his torso is out in front of his arm, leaving the arm to do too much of the work, unassisted by the position of his frame. When that happens, everything he throws—the curve, the sinking fastball—is harder and, for that reason, flatter than it should be. Against the Mets his curveball was rolling out of his hand and drifting high and inside to right-handed hitters. He can not quite remember but he thinks he went into the Dodger Stadium tape room between innings early in the game to watch what he was doing wrong. However, he says, there are limits to what you can do to iron out imperfections. "Sometimes you're human and just don't do it. No matter how much thinking and practicing you do, no matter how ready you are, you just don't do it."

Hershiser was not the only player who was feeling the heat of that winner-take-all seventh game. "See, that's uncharacteristic for Keith [Hernandez]. You can tell it's the adrenaline of a big situation. I've thrown three pitches at a 3-and-2 count and he swung at [and fouled off] all of them, and two of three or maybe three of three have been balls. In the regular season he'd just be flipping his bat and taking his walk—he's got a great eye. He's swinging before he's decided it's a strike. He's just pumped up—game seven."

The Mets did not score in the top of the first. The Dodgers scored one run in the bottom of the first. The Mets did not score in the top of the second. In the bottom of the inning the wheels came off the Mets. There was an error, a defensive mix-up that turned a sacrifice bunt into a hit, and the Dodgers scored five runs. On the bunt the batter, Alfredo Griffin, should have been called out without the Mets doing anything right. Griffin did something very wrong. When he squared around to bunt his left foot was a foot out of the batter's box, directly in front of the catcher. If the umpire had noticed, Griffin would have been called out. But when you are hot you are lucky and the Dodgers (remember, there will be those 11 hits in 15 hit-and-run attempts in the World Series) are very lucky-hot.

When the second inning ends the score is 6–0, as it will be at the end of the game. But pitching with a five-run lead is, says Hershiser, its own kind of burden. The pitcher's basic job is to keep the game close, keeping his team in the game until its batters produce some runs. In the 169th game of the Dodgers' season, it was no longer up to the hitters to win the game, it was up to him not to lose it. "A lot of pitchers," says Hershiser, "when they get a big lead, they say, 'Let's just go with the odds of baseball. Throw the ball hard down the middle and let them hit it. Let them swing the bats and make outs. If they don't make outs, we'll go back to pitching.' A lot of times they go directly to their fastballs and throw a lot of strikes right over the plate, and then, later, when they get into a jam, they don't have their other pitches with them anymore and the other team gets a chance to catch up. So when we get ahead I do the opposite. I go to every pitch possible. I go to my fourth- and fifth-best pitches, just to keep the repertoire ready. They are pitches I normally don't use in key situations, but the lead has given me a chance to not worry about getting beat on my fourth or fifth pitch, or about giving up a one-run home run on my slowest of slow curveballs. Then I'm prepared for the jam, and the batters have seen a lot of different pitches in at bats before the jam and they have doubts in their minds. 'Boy, he has never thrown me that before.' 'I've never seen him throw a curveball that slow.' 'He's never thrown me back-to-back change-ups.' "

On this morning in Pittsburgh Hershiser watches the videotape as the Mets' Gregg Jefferies hits a long fly to right field off a change-up. Jefferies was out in front of the pitch. It was the second consecutive change-up Hershiser had thrown to him. Jefferies was not expecting two off-speed pitches in a row. Expecting something faster, he had the head of his bat about four inches too far out over the plate. It was in the hitting zone before the ball was. Hitting is timing. Hershiser upset Jefferies's timing.

On a 3–2 pitch with two outs, Kevin Elster got a single off a fastball right down the middle. "Three-and-2, two out, nobody on, I'm not going to show him a pitch I might need to get him out in a jam. If it's runners on second and third and two out and I need to get him out, he'll get a breaking ball or a real my-pitch sinker low and away." Husbanding his better pitches, anticipating the possibility of trouble later, was pure Hershiser.

Later in the game, with Darryl Strawberry up with a 3–1 count, catcher Mike Scioscia called for a sinker away. Hershiser preferred to throw a change-up, and did, without telling Scioscia. Scioscia, annoyed, stepped out in front of the plate and fired the ball back at Hershiser faster than Hershiser had thrown the change-up. Watching this scene on tape, Hershiser laughs merrily: "Wham! He airs it back at me as if to say, 'What are you doing out there?' With men on base it [throwing a pitch Scioscia had not called for] doesn't matter because I'm not screwing him up as far as his rhythm to throw someone out. I'm screwing up the infielders a little bit because they might be shading the opposite way instead of to pull with the change-up. But I do it because when I get a rhythm I don't want to stand there and shake my head because I might lose that feeling—the flow." The change-up that he threw was a strike. The next pitch was a curveball for a called third strike, the pitch of a pitcher at the peak of his performance. "A 3–2 curveball with a 6–0 lead!" He laughs delightedly, as though seeing all this for the first time.

With two outs and one on in the top of the ninth, with the Mets' Lee Mazzilli up with an 0–2 count, with the crowd on its feet and the Mets one strike away from winter, Hershiser hits Mazzilli. That happened because before the pitch "I decide I'll let my game face off and I walk around the mound and take in the whole situation, the standing ovation, with our team going nuts and their team all depressed. I almost started to cry, and that's when I stopped it and put my game face back on. And then I get back on the mound and throw the pitch. It's a fastball inside. Scioc [Scioscia's nickname; pronounced Sosh, rhymes with gauche] calls the sinker inside but I threw the cutter [cut fastball]. Scioc comes halfway to the mound and I walk out to meet him. He says, 'I wanted the sinker inside!' I say, 'Well, I threw the cutter—I wanted to make sure I got it in.' He says, 'But you might hit him if you do that.' I say, 'I *did* hit him.' It was hilarious." In Spring Training Hershiser told Mazzilli what happened and apologized. Mazzilli thanked Hershiser for sparing him the indignity of being the last out of the Mets' season.

It was a movie with a happy ending, in the Hollywood tradition. But now, back in real time, it is time to get his contact lenses, put his wire-rim glasses aside and go across the river to Three Rivers Stadium, to work.

———◆———

Looking out across the Three Rivers diamond, Ray Miller says, a trifle wistfully, "I've got this little spiel when a guy comes up from the minors. When I'm walking him in from the bull pen, right before the game starts, I say, 'You know, I never got to do this, what you're doing today. But don't be nervous. You're working on a perfect mound. You have the best defense you've ever had behind you.' Then I go to the dugout and smoke fourteen cigarettes." Don't be nervous? Hard not to be. The pitcher's mound is where the pressure is constant.

The pressure of the 1988 season produced sufficient heat to temper the steel in Hershiser. "I know about myself that I can perform under any pressure. I found out I loved it. And the thing about the game I love even more is competition. I want to be in there. In the eighth inning in game five [the final game of the Series] when Canseco and Parker were coming up, runners on first and second, in a hole I'd put myself in, I wanted to be out there. I wasn't looking to Tommy and saying, 'This is scary, I don't want to be out here.' " A year ago, would he have looked and said that? He pauses to consider, then says softly, "I wouldn't have complained about losing the ball." He adds, "I am at the point in my career now that I will complain when they take me out. They come out to the mound and I make sure they see in my face and in my actions that I want to stay there, no matter how I feel. I have no fear of failure now. You get to a point in your career when you know you are going to be a big leaguer, you know you are going to have a job. So where is the fear of failure? The fun is competing, so why get out?"

The 1989 season was bound to be a special kind of challenge, the challenge of pursuing excellence while knowing that he had hit a peak he would not reach again. "I got all that after 1985 when I was 19–3, 2.03. People came to me and said, 'What is it like to have the best year of your career in your second year? It's all downhill from here.' And I said, well, you never know." Indeed, no one in 1985 could have imagined what was coming in 1988. In December, 1988, Hershiser was in Washington, D.C., to attend Ronald Reagan's last State Dinner, which was for Margaret Thatcher. He said, "Someone asked me at a speaking engagement two nights ago what are my goals now after accomplishing so much. I said I want to be the best Orel Hershiser I can be."

There is a Jewish parable about Moshe, a humble shoemaker who, after dying, finds himself about to meet his Maker. He begins to utter self-deprecating laments and excuses for his failure to have made more of himself in life. Whereupon he is warned: "When you are in His presence He will not ask you why you were not Moses or King David or one of the Prophets. He will ask you why you were not Moshe the shoemaker." The point is that the point of life is not to be great but to be all that you can be. That is hard work. And as is well known, the harder one works, the luckier one becomes. "Whatever you do, do it well. Everyone says, 'This is a big game' or 'This is not a big game.' I say to myself, 'It's a big game because it's the only game—it's the only game we can win today.' "

Pitching, like politics and marriage and other difficult undertakings, illustrates the axiom that "the perfect is the enemy of the good." Which means: In the real world, be ready to settle for something short of everything. "There are pitchers," Rick Dempsey says, "who, when you score a run off them, you can see you've ruined their perfect day and they lose their competitive edge. Then the dam breaks and they give up six, seven runs." Does Hershiser go to the mound in the first inning planning to pitch a complete game? "A perfect game," Hershiser replies. "If they get a hit, then I am throwing a one-hitter. If they get a walk, it's my last walk. I deal with perfection to the point that it is logical to conceive it. History is history, the future is perfect."

3

THE BATTER

◆

Tony Gwynn's Muscle Memory

Early in the 1989 season Tony Gwynn hit home runs in consecutive games and was even more displeased with his hitting than he generally is. The second home run came after an afternoon spent toiling to remove the flaws in the way he had swung the bat in the game in which he hit the first one. He knew the flaws were there. In fact, the home run was evidence that he was not hitting the pitches he wanted to hit in the way he wanted to hit them. So the afternoon before the night when he hit the second home run, he went to work early, several hours before game time.

The previous night he had hit two balls hard. One pleased him, the other distressed him. The pleasing one was an out, the distressing one was a home run. When he hit the ball hard for an out, as he started his stride forward his hands moved in the opposite direction. They came back so he could keep the bat back long enough to "inside out" the ball to left field, lashing a line drive that was caught by the left fielder. To "inside out" is to sweep the bat through the strike zone at a slight angle, from the back inside portion of the plate toward the outside front portion. When a left-handed hitter does that, he has power to the left side of the diamond.

On the home-run swing his hands came forward too soon. That is what he means by being "out in front." He drove the ball to right field. Sure, it went over the fence, but he knows that over the course of the long season, hitting the ball that way is a recipe for the sort of frustration he experienced in 1988. "When my hands don't go back I have this kind of loop in my swing." Call it a flawed 1980s swing or a satisfactory 1950s swing. In the 1950s, when parks were smaller and home runs were emphasized, uppercutting the ball was not considered such a vice. Be that as it may, Gwynn will not stand for it. Besides, he is mired in a .360 slump. (Ball players are never just in slumps; they are always "mired" in them.) So he came to the stadium this day shortly after noon. There was work to do before the playing began.

"Hitting," says Jim Lefebvre, "is a summation of internal forces. It's everything. It's not just hands or wrists. You have to get the whole body into it." Lefebvre says hitting is the most overcoached and undertrained facet of baseball. He means there is too much theory and too little hard, humdrum repetition, the blister-causing tedium that builds up muscle memory. He may be right, but not about Gwynn, who is baseball's Mr. Humdrum. Gwynn's repertoire of repetition begins beneath the stands at San Diego's Jack Murphy Stadium.

A modern major league stadium, such as Jack Murphy, is a complex edifice containing many surprises in its nooks and crannies. On Opening Day, 1989, 19 skunks were evicted from it. It is a very Nineties place. Sushi is served at one of the food stands and there are diapering tables in the men's as well as women's rest rooms. Deep beneath the stands there is a clean, well-lit room that was prepared by the Padres to satisfy Gwynn, who asked for it for several seasons. It is a long, narrow batting room, big enough for a pitcher's mound at regulation distance from a plate, and an "Iron Mike" pitching machine with a capacity for about 250 baseballs. The room is lit at 300 candle feet, exactly as the Jack Murphy field is lit, so a player expecting to pinch-hit can come to the room during a game to take practice swings. This afternoon Gwynn is trying to wear it out—the machine and the netting that captures the batted balls. He also is wearing out several Padres relief pitchers who have not been used much in recent games and do not mind satisfying—well, trying to satisfy—Gwynn's voracious appetite for pitches to hit.

The Padres did Gwynn's family a favor by building the batting cage. Gwynn has been known to show up at a social event with a batting glove hanging out of his hip pocket, having stopped somewhere on the way for some swings. Around midnight after a San Diego game a few years ago, one of Gwynn's associates at the San Diego School of Baseball was driving by the building where the school's pitching machines are and was annoyed to see the lights on.

Assuming that some kids had neglected to turn them off, he stopped to do so. Inside he found Gwynn standing in his street clothes, with a paper cup between his feet so he could swing and spit at the same time without making tobacco stains on the floor, taking some swings before heading home. With the new batting room at the Stadium, the Padres and Mrs. Gwynn and his son and daughter at least know where he is when he is not at home.

During the first days of the 1989 season, Gwynn spent so much time using the new batting room (he went there for extra hitting after the opening night game) that a teammate said, "He wants the hits to land and spin a certain way." The room is not a restful place to be. The pitching machine, with its cranking, clanking arm, is noisy. The crack of the bat on the ball, so pleasant in the open air, is a jarring concussion in the concrete enclosure. Baseball's violence—the slash of the ball on a tight arc toward the plate, the ricochet of the ball off the bat—is intensified in the glare and confinement of the room. But a teammate who is waiting to hit provides a softening musical background.

John Kruk is, like Gwynn, compact, only more so. He is 5 feet 10 and about 200 pounds. In the clubhouse, where politeness is not mandatory, it is said that he not only has his number but also his picture on the back of his uniform. His number is 8. In a few weeks there will be a new name on the front of his uniform—Phillies—but this day, with no trade or much of anything else on his mind, Kruky, as his teammates call him when not calling him Snack Bar, is waiting his turn with the machine and passing the time singing country music in a soft falsetto: "She looks great in her tight jeans. . . . Everything I buy has a foreign name."

Gwynn hits off the machine until a relief pitcher, Mark Grant, arrives to throw to him. Grant is a large, amiable young man with the kind of flat-top haircut that was fashionable in his hometown of Joliet, Illinois, before he was born. In his locker he displays prominently his favorite book, Dr. Seuss's *Green Eggs and Ham.* As he pitches, Gwynn reads Grant's pitching motion. Gwynn identifies and calls out, in the middle of Grant's deliveries, the kinds of pitches Grant is in the process of throwing. Grant is distressed (well, as distressed as a Dr. Seuss fan can be, which is not very) by this evidence that he is tipping off his pitches, but he is pleased to receive a clinic from Gwynn. While Grant pitches, Gwynn explains what he is seeing: Grant's arm is less extended than usual when throwing one kind of pitch, his grip on the ball is too visible on another.

Gwynn also enlivens the batting session, with the machine and with Grant, by calling out different game situations as the balls come flying at him. "Man on second, no one out . . . man on third, one out . . . infield in, man on first, nobody out . . . man on third, two outs . . . first and third, one out . . . man on first, two outs . . ." He can tailor his swing to the situation.

A matter of minutes after he began in the batting room he was drenched with sweat. By the time he left the room he had taken more than 200 swings, for the fifth time in as many days. Those 1,000 swings were taken before and after full workdays. When he left the room it was 2:45 P.M., 4 hours and 15 minutes before game time. Still ahead was outfield practice. Oh, yes, and batting practice.

"I remember," says Gwynn, "when they asked Pete Rose what do you think about Gwynn taking batting practice every day. He said, 'He'll learn, the more he plays the more he'll realize he doesn't need batting practice every day.' Pete's got more hits than anybody but I just don't feel I'm prepared unless I'm doing what I can to be a little bit smarter, a little bit better, a little bit more prepared. I have been brought up in the game to do every little extra thing, get every bit of extra knowledge that can help you get a base hit in a key situation." As the twig is bent. He was brought up at home like that. "I think my parents gave it to me. I remember when my mom started to work. She used to be at home, then she got a job in the post office. When she went to the post office she wanted to be *prepared.* She'd give me the test she had to take and I'd read off the streets and she'd tell me where they connect or whatever. I think it rubbed off."

According to Professor Carl Ojala of Eastern Michigan University, in the 1950s California replaced Pennsylvania as the richest source of players. Since 1876 the top 10 states are: California, Pennsylvania, New York, Illinois, Ohio, Massachusetts, Texas, Missouri, Michigan, New Jersey. Today California, with 12 percent of the nation's population, produces more than 20 percent of the major league players and Southern California produces most of those. Two are from the same home in Long Beach. Because Tony Gwynn's father was away from the house from 7:30 A.M. until 5:00 P.M., and his mother worked from 5:30 P.M. until 3:00 A.M., he and his brother Chris, now with the Dodgers, had a lot of time to fill playing. What Tony played most was basketball, which turned out to be a good apprenticeship for baseball. As a point guard in basketball he developed strong wrists from a lot of dribbling. Because of his wrists he has never suffered from what he calls "slow bat syndrome." And the quickness required of a point guard became the basis of Gwynn's baserunning skills. He was a good enough basketball player to be drafted by both the Padres and the San Diego (as they then were) Clippers.

You would not know by looking at him that he is such a superb all-around athlete. It is a bit much to say, as has been said, that his is "a body by Betty Crocker." His 200 pounds are packed on a 5-foot-11 frame. He is thick around the middle and in the thighs—not Kirby Puckett thick, but thick nonetheless. However, a batter hits with his whole body, with hips and legs as well as wrists and arms and shoulders, so no one in San Diego has any reason to complain about how Gwynn is put together.

Emotionally, he is perfect. Gwynn is an almost unfailingly cheerful man who is almost always trying to be morose. Trying but failing. He may be the most liked player in baseball. That is because of the radical difference between his amiableness toward others and his severity toward himself. His ability to combine intense competitiveness and agreeableness makes him the antithesis of the best player in history to combine, as Gwynn does, a high batting average and a lot of stolen bases. Ty Cobb was so detested that in 1910, when Napoleon Lajoie was in a close race with Cobb for the batting title, the St. Louis Browns' third baseman played extraordinarily deep on the last day of the season so Lajoie could drop seven consecutive bunt singles. They were not quite enough. Lajoie finished at .384, Cobb at .385, but only because the president of the American League, Ban Johnson, was bothered by what the Browns had done. Johnson credited Cobb with a couple of extra hits, enough to put him a point ahead. But before Johnson did that, when it looked as if Lajoie had won, Lajoie received a congratulatory telegram signed by eight of Cobb's Tiger teammates. They were not amused by Cobb's habit—so they said—of not swinging on hit-and-run plays when the pitch was not to his liking, and they resented his decision to sit out the last two games of the season in an attempt to protect his batting lead.

It is inconceivable that Gwynn would ever do either of those things. In September, 1989, at a point when Gwynn was in a nip-and-tuck race for the batting title, he was hurting. His right leg was sore from two foul balls, one off his ankle bone, the other off his toe. The one off his toe made it hard for him to get his shoe on. An even more serious problem was that his left Achilles tendon was so sore he could not push off properly when swinging. This injury was driving down his batting average but he refused to miss a game until his manager insisted. Then he sat out only two games before limping back into the lineup. He won the batting title anyway, catching and passing Will Clark with two 3-for-4 games on the last weekend of the season. Clark said, "I lost to the best."

———◆———

There are some wonderful high-average hitters today. Through 1989 Wade Boggs had the fourth-highest career average (.352) in baseball history. In 1989 he became the first player in the modern era (since 1900) to get 200 or more hits in seven straight seasons. Kirby Puckett's .356 average, in 1988, was the highest for a right-handed batter since DiMaggio's .357 in 1941 (when he lost the batting title to a left-hander, Ted Williams, by 49 points). By May 7, 1989, Puckett had played in five full major league seasons. By then he had 1,062 hits. Only one player, Joe Medwick, ever got more hits (two more) in his first five years.

According to Roger Craig, Tony Gwynn is "the best pure hitter in this league." Actually, Gwynn may be the best pure hitter in baseball today, and with his baserunning, he may be the best offensive player. Consider his luminous 1987 season, when he became the first National League player ever to hit as high as .370 while stealing 50 bases (56, actually). Gwynn's .370 in 1987 was the highest National League average since Stan Musial's .376 in 1948. Gwynn's .370 was the second-highest single-season average in the decade, second to George Brett's .390 in 1980. Gwynn became only the seventh player in history to win two batting titles by 30 or more points. In 1987 it was not until the third week of July that the Padres had a team winning percentage higher than Gwynn's batting average, .366 to .362. Characteristically, Gwynn used the Padres' bad record as a way to make light of his achievement. "I think it's easier to concentrate when you're getting smoked every night than it is when you're right in the heat of a pennant race. You can just be relaxed and swing the bat. When I hit .370 it was easy to relax and play the game and have fun."

It is sometimes said that a batter can expect to have three slumps a season. In 1987 Gwynn did not have any, unless going 0-for-8 counts as a slump. He hit safely in 82 percent of the 155 games he batted in. He never went more than 8 at bats without a hit. He ranked second in the league in stolen bases (56), triples (13) and on-base percentage (.447); he ranked fourth in runs scored (119), tied for eighth in doubles (36) and tenth in walks (82). He struck out only 35 times in 589 at bats, once every 17 times up. Those last two numbers—the large number of walks and small number of strike-outs—go a long way toward explaining all the preceding numbers.

Walking is part of a batter's duty. Steve Garvey, who was Gwynn's teammate for five years, collected 2,599 hits and had six 200-hit seasons, but he would have been a more valuable asset to his team if he had walked more. He walked only once per 18.44 at bats. Ted Williams's average was once per 3.82. "[Stan] Musial," says Earl Weaver, "was the best at adjusting once the ball left the pitcher's hand. He'd hit the pitcher's pitch. Williams was the best at making them throw his pitch. He didn't believe in adjusting. If it wasn't the pitch he wanted, he knew enough to walk to first base. That's why he hit .406."

Baseball needs more walks and fewer strikeouts. Forty-four times hitters have slugged 20 or more home runs in a season while having fewer strikeouts than home runs. But aside from the Royals' George Brett in his sensational 1980 season (.390, 24 home runs, 22 strike-outs), no one had done it since 1956, when both Yogi Berra and Ted Kluszewski did it. Clearly many of today's home-run hitters are conceding less with two strikes on them; they are more determined to hit home runs, regardless of the cost, than sluggers used to be. Only five players—DiMaggio, Gehrig, Kluszewski, Johnny Mize, Mel Ott—have hit 40 or more home runs while striking out 40 or fewer times. Kluszewski did it three times. The last time he did it was in President Eisenhower's first term—1955. The trend is against that kind of 40-40 season. In 1987 Andre Dawson with 49 home runs and George Bell with 47 became the fifth and sixth players in major league history to have more home runs than walks. That is a sign of indiscipline, but they were rewarded with MVP awards.

Baseball needs subtle standards by which to judge players' seasons and Tom Boswell has provided one. He has devised the statistic "total average" (TA). Boswell reasons that baseball's two basic units of measurement are the base achieved and the out made. Each base is a step closer to a run scored, each out is a step closer to an inning ended. Total average is simply the individual's ratio of bases accumulated for his team to the outs he costs his team. Walks, stolen bases, even being hit by pitches increases your base total average, as Boswell calculates it; but being caught stealing adds an out and grounding into a double play adds two outs. Total average is well suited to the era of artificial turf because it gives special weight to speed, both in terms of bases stolen and double plays avoided. (Being caught stealing not only creates a total average out, it erases a base runner, so getting caught hurts total average by simultaneously adding an out and subtracting a base.) Boswell believes that any player with a TA over .900 is producing at a Hall of Fame level. An .800 TA is All-Star level. Year in and year out the major league average is about .666. Only 17 players in history have compiled career TAs over 1.000. In 1987 Gwynn's TA was 1.086.

In his career through 1989, Gwynn had a better than .300 average against every National League team. By winning the 1989 batting title he became the first National League player since Musial in 1950–52 to win three consecutive titles. (That is good company. Carl Erskine, the Dodgers' pitcher, said, "I've had pretty good success with Stan—by throwing him my best pitch and backing up third.") And what has all this earned Gwynn? He is called "the West Coast Wade Boggs." That is because Gwynn practices his craft at the wrong edge of the continent.

In America news still travels east to west. It is hard for Gwynn to get proper attention for his craftsmanship when he plays in a city with a desert to the east, Japan to the west, Mexico to the south and two other major league teams in the urban sprawl to the north.

———◆———

After Lee Smith, the big relief pitcher who had many successful seasons with the Cubs, won his first game for the Red Sox, he gave credit to a little boy in the bleachers. Smith said that as he was leaving the bull pen a boy about seven years old leaned over the rail and shouted, "Lee, stay within yourself." Smith said that was the secret of his success that day. Does that seem implausible? Not to me it doesn't. Any properly raised American child would have said the same thing. "Stay within yourself" is baseball's first commandment. It means: Do not try to do things that strain your capacities and distort the smooth working of your parts—what players call "mechanics." Polonius could have been a baseball coach. Of all his bromides, "To thine own self be true" is the most memorable. It means what baseball players mean when they mutter to themselves "stay within yourself." Players, at least at the major league level, are severe realists about themselves. They have been playing this difficult game for so long—even the 22-year-olds have—that they know there are players better than they are. Or, to be precise, they know there are many players who can do many things better than they can. Baseball has many roles, plays, skills and situations. Major league players know that they have mastered enough of them, often barely enough of them, to be in the major leagues for a while. They know what they can do and what they can not. To "stay within yourself" is to keep your balance. A player's reach should not exceed his grasp.

But at one point in his career Gwynn was tempted to overreach. When after his sensational 1987 season he finished only eighth in the National League MVP voting, he succumbed, if only briefly, to bitter thoughts. He began to think that in order to get the respect that any artist worth his salt craves, he would have to truckle to contemporary prejudices and vulgar tastes—he would have to start hitting home runs. (It was either that or tow San Diego around the Cape of Good Hope and tether it to Manhattan, where the media might notice him.) In fact, he could become much more of a power hitter by changing his stroke. He has the strength to hit for distance, and other players have made mid-career changes in the way they swing.

When Kirk Gibson went from the Tigers to the Dodgers in 1988, he shortened his swing slightly, making it more compact and quicker. He knew he was going to see more fastballs in his new league. This is in part because it is a league with parks that reward a running game, and the quicker the pitcher gets the ball to the catcher, the quicker the catcher can get it on its way to second base. But the large number of fastballs in the National League also has something to do with the fact that by 1988 that league's umpires had produced a strike zone even smaller than the one in the American League. Pitchers presented with this shrunken target were increasingly reluctant to try to throw curveballs into it.

Carlton Fisk was the Red Sox catcher for nine seasons. He had a compact, chopping swing perfect for Fenway Park, perfect for chipping fly balls off or over The Wall. Then in 1981 he went to the White Sox, to a spacious park. (The Sox career records for home runs was Harold Baines' 186 until Fisk broke it in 1990.) After a few games at Comiskey Park Fisk saw that his stroke was a harmless fly ball stroke in his new home. He soon put himself in the hands of Charlie Lau, the White Sox batting coach. Lau's fame rested primarily on his ability to coach players who are willing to sacrifice some power for higher batting averages, but in this case Lau's aim was to help Fisk power the ball out of his new park. Together they reconstructed his swing. Tony La Russa, then manager of the White Sox, remembers returning to the Sox Spring Training camp at Sarasota from a game in Fort Myers when Lau and Fisk had stayed in Sarasota. The Sox bus pulled in at about 6:30 P.M. and, recalls La Russa, "that day it was almost Eliza Doolittle. It worked. That was it." Fisk would become a slugger and would go on to break the career record for home runs by a catcher.

During the winter of 1987–88 Gwynn decided to leave superb alone. He would settle for being the best Tony Gwynn in baseball. He knew that hitting home runs was not his natural bent. In 1984 only 36 of his 213 hits were for extra bases. (Only 11 players in history have had 36 or fewer extra-base hits in a 200-hit season.) And he knew that hitting a dozen, maybe even two dozen more home runs might not help him much in his quest for recognition. In 1987 Wade Boggs won his fourth batting title in five years, batted .363 with 24 home runs, and he finished ninth in the MVP voting. Gwynn also knew that home runs in quantity are not necessary for his team to do what he hungers to do—win. When the Padres won their only pennant, in 1984, they had fewer home runs than the last-place Giants. And in 1987 all of baseball had seen how far a team could go powered by players who were not power hitters. The 1987 Cardinals came within one game (game seven of the World Series) of proving themselves to be baseball's best team. Yet they were last— yes, twenty-sixth—in home runs. They hit only 94, and one man— Jack Clark—hit 35 of them.

A hitter's job is to contribute to run creation. Hitting safely does that, so batting average is a good measurement of a hitter's value. It is a good measurement but it is insufficient, for two reasons. First, not all hits are equal. Second, not all failures to hit are equal. Not all hits are equal, for two reasons. Some hits carry the hitter to more bases, closer to a run. And not all hits occur when they would be most productive—particularly, when runners are in scoring position. Baltimore's Jim Gentile was hardly a household word in his day and today his name certainly does not spring to mind when thoughts turn to remarkable hitting records. But in 1961, when better hitters were making bigger headlines, Gentile set an interesting record— the best ratio of RBIs to hits, an astonishing .959. He drove in 141 runs while getting just 147 hits.

Not all "failures" are really failures. Some of them contribute to run creation. Official scoring reflects this by not charging an at bat when the hitter delivers a sacrifice or sacrifice fly. But a hitter who, with no outs and a runner on second, gives himself up by grounding to the right side of the infield, thereby enabling the runner to advance to third, has "failed" to get a hit but has succeeded at the team project of advancing the process of run creation. One night in 1989 in a 5–1 Padres win over the Reds Gwynn had this batting line: 4 at bats, 0 hits, 0 runs, 3 RBIs. He drove in runs with two infield groundouts and a sacrifice fly. That batting line shows why the only certain failure for a batter is the failure to put the ball in play. By the way, the night before Gwynn's 4-0-0-3 night, Darren Daulton of the Phillies went 5-for-5 but neither drove in nor scored a run.

Gwynn became one of the National League's premier players in 1984 at age 24. In the six seasons 1984–89 he hit just 43 home runs, 7 per season. He had 362 RBIs, an average of about 60 a season, a respectable total. He scored 550 runs, or 91 per season, an excellent total.

Batters who, like Gwynn, bat near the top of the order, want to combine power and speed and a discriminating eye that enables them to receive a lot of walks, thereby further fattening their on-base percentage. Davey Johnson remembers playing in Atlanta with Ralph Garr, a leadoff hitter, who in 1974 hit .353. But Garr was not as good a leadoff man as he should have been that year because he walked only 28 times and he struck out 52 times. He should have been batting lower in the order, a better place for someone who can not resist hacking at anything thrown near him. The best leadoff man Johnson ever saw was the Giants' Bobby Bonds in 1973, the season Bonds almost became what Canseco became 15 years later, baseball's first 40-40 (home runs and stolen bases) man. Bonds hit .283 but that is only part of the story. Pitchers did not want to pitch to him because he had enough power to hit 39 home runs that year. So they walked him 87 times. But they hated doing that because he had enough speed to steal 43 bases that year.

Any batter would like to make pitchers as anxious as power hitters do. Hear Hershiser on that subject: "Power hitters, in general, if you make your pitch, you get them out. If you make a mistake it will hurt you bad. When I make a mistake to a singles hitter, he hits it for a single. When I make a good pitch to the next singles hitter, he hits it on the ground and I get a double play and it erases the hit. I make a mistake to a power hitter, he hits it out of the park or for a double and I have no way of getting a double play to erase the hit. With singles hitters the odds are in my favor. If they keep hitting the ball on the ground, sooner or later they are going to hit one at somebody for a double play. Or I'll get the lead runner. But as soon as power hitters hit the ball in the air and they get a double or triple, there is no force play anymore, they can advance with an out and score a run." Ah, but what if that singles hitter steals second, turning that single into a two-stage, delayed-action double? Then there goes the force play, there goes the double play.

Gwynn has what is called "gap power," the power to drive hits between outfielders. It is often less spectacular but is almost always more productive than mere "warning-track power," the power to make noisy outs. Through 1989 Gwynn had 192 doubles and 51 triples. Harmon Killebrew, who hit more home runs than anyone else in the 1960s, is a suitable symbol of big bang baseball: 8,147 at bats, zero sacrifices. Gwynn, with his high average and large number of stolen bases, is a suitable symbol of the direction in which baseball has moved.

———◆———

Eight decades ago (or so the story is) an extremely fat baseball fan, finding his seat at the park confining, heaved himself to his feet to stretch. It was the seventh inning. Because the 300-pound fellow was the President of the United States, everyone around him stood up respectfully. William Howard Taft thereby started a useful tradition, which is more than can be said for many presidents.

One should not tamper with traditions, but it has been suggested that the seventh-inning stretch should be moved to the fifth inning because games today are, on average, about 45 minutes longer than they were in Taft's time. Games have been becoming longer partly because fewer hitters are swinging at first and second pitches. Information is one reason more batters are waiting longer before they start swinging. They know, or think they know, pitchers' patterns, so they sometimes think they gain an advantage on the pitcher by going deeper into the count. Because batters are going deeper into the count, there are more walks and strikeouts, both of which take time. And the increased emphasis on base stealing has pitchers throwing over to first more frequently to hold runners on. Furthermore, Keith Hernandez says that because of advance scouts "the first game of a series becomes a feeling-out process. You might take more pitches to see what they're thinking."

The man standing behind the batter and facing the pitcher—the umpire—may be thinking, or at least acting, in a way that both the batter and the pitcher need to be aware of.

"Baseball," said Bill Veeck, team owner (Indians, Browns, White Sox) and innovator, "is almost the only orderly thing in a very unorderly world. If you get three strikes, even the best lawyer in the world can't get you off." Yes, but like the law, the rules of baseball are not as neat in practice as they are on paper. And the rules, like the law, are not, alas, the same for all people. The mighty have things better. As we have seen already, the history of the strike zone is another episode in the struggle to use written law to define and confine elusive reality. But law can be shaped by the discretion of judges (umpires, in this case). The formal definition of the strike zone has not meant much. When the *de jure* zone extended from the top of the batter's shoulders to the bottom of his knees it was nearly twice the size of today's *de facto* strike zone. One way umpires have contracted the zone is by using the elasticity inherent in the need to define where the shoulders are relative to the knees when the batter is in his natural stance, or the stance as it is when the batter is in the act of swinging.

Culture follows the law and so today most pitchers are low-ball pitchers. The great pitch of the 1980s was the split-finger fastball, which sinks. Most hitters are low-ball hitters. Otherwise they would not be in the major leagues. To see how much has changed in a short time, look at Ted Williams's book *The Science of Hitting,* published in 1970. In it Williams produced a famous picture of the strike zone filled with baseballs. The zone was divided into different colored sections to show the various percentages he would hit if he swung at pitches delivered there. His strike zone is 11 rows high. The top four rows, filled with balls marked with averages from .300 to .400, are out of the strike zone as umpires call it today, just two decades after Williams wrote that book. Williams had to cope with a larger strike zone than exists today but that was not a handicap because he liked to hit high pitches. The strike zone, he wrote, "is approximately the width of seven baseballs, allowing for pitches on 'the black' being called strikes. When a batter starts swinging at pitches just two inches out of that zone, he has increased the pitcher's target from approximately 4.2 square feet to about 5.8 square feet—an increase of 38 percent. Allow a pitcher that much of an advantage and you will be a .250 hitter."

There is evidence that umpires give the best batters a smaller strike zone than other batters must cope with, and give the best pitchers bigger strike zones to throw to. Once a flustered rookie pitcher was facing Rogers Hornsby and threw three consecutive pitches that were close to the plate but were called balls. The rookie complained and the umpire responded, "Young man, when you pitch a strike, Mr. Hornsby will let you know." Fine pitchers, too, get some deference from umpires. The Tigers' Jack Morris says he gets, in general, a bigger strike zone as an established veteran than he had as a rookie "and it should be that way." He says, "Early in the game you establish yourself. I'll throw two balls right on the corner. They might be balls. But I throw a third one there, it might become a strike because I have shown the umpire that I can put the same pitch in the same location three times." Morris, therefore, does not complain when the practice of umpires deferring to established stars works to the advantage of some hitters. "My first two years," Morris remembers, "when Carl Yastrzemski was up, if Carl didn't swing, it was not a strike. And I mean to tell you I threw balls right down the middle of the plate, belt-high, and you could not doubt it, but if Carl didn't swing, it was not a strike."

There once was a judge who liked to say, "In my youth, when matched against a more experienced attorney, I lost many cases I should have won. But later, when I became an experienced attorney and was matched against attorneys fresh from law school, I won many cases I should have lost. Thus justice was served." Over a long career, things even out.

Strike zones vary, over time and with different umpires. Batting conditions vary in other ways, too. Referring to differences between batting conditions in ballparks, Bill James says what Ping Bodie said when Walter Johnson struck him out: "You can't hit what you can't see." Visibility varies significantly from the best parks (Royals Stadium) to the worst (Shea Stadium). The huge foul territory in Oakland's Coliseum probably knocks 5 to 7 points off batting averages because of pop fouls that would land in the seats in many other parks. The narrow foul territory in Fenway Park probably adds as much. Since World War II the Red Sox have had 18 batting champions (through 1989), although Ted Williams and Wade Boggs would have prospered anywhere. Five to 7 points are a lot, given that there may be only a 15- or 20-point spread between a good hitting team and a poor hitting team.

The ball carries better at higher altitudes (Atlanta–Fulton County Stadium is baseball's highest, 1,000 feet above sea level). Yankee Stadium's deep power alleys clearly hurt Joe DiMaggio, who hit 213 home runs on the road and only 148 at home. Bill James notes that when Joe DiMaggio and Ted Williams played in neutral parks (that is, excluding Fenway Park and Yankee Stadium), DiMaggio outhit Williams .333 to .328. With Fenway as his home park, DiMaggio might have hit more than 600 home runs. A tragic automobile accident may have prevented the most freakish playing field of modern times from making a mockery of one of baseball's most revered records, the record for most home runs in a season. The year the Dodgers moved from Ebbets Field to the Los Angeles Coliseum, with its ludicrous 250-foot left-field line, Don Drysdale's ERA soared to 4.17 from 2.69 the previous year. If Roy Campanella, master of high-arc home runs, had not been paralyzed in an automobile accident the winter before that first Coliseum season, he might well have beaten Roger Maris in the race to break Babe Ruth's single-season home-run record.

The era of exotic park effects is over. Fenway is the last park with a dominating peculiarity—The Wall, 315 feet down the left-field line—that influences batters and pitchers and managers in many ways. All parks built after 1958 have been required to have foul lines at least 325 feet long and a center-field fence at least 400 feet from home plate. Today the most important variable is the playing surface: grass or plastic. In the National League the player who hits the most doubles is almost always someone who plays his home games on artificial turf. In fact, since 1970 only Bill Buckner with the 1981 and 1983 Cubs has been an exception to that rule. The parks with artificial turf are generally more spacious than those with grass, so the running game is apt to be emphasized on offense. And turf teams need speed to cover the large outfields. Thus turf teams are generally quicker, so their hitters get from home to second quickly while batted balls are rattling around on the large carpeted outfields.

Such parks may offend purists, but they may also be conducive to virtue. Bill James, who is a ballpark determinist, believes that parks can even shape the souls of players, and hence the morales of teams:

> I have speculated before that the historical tendency of the Boston Red Sox to split into civil camps of stars and scrubs might be related to the park in which they play. Whereas the Houston Astros play in a park in which an offense consists by necessity of one man who gets on base, one who moves him along, and one who brings him around, Fenway Park rewards and thus encourages players who act as individuals, since they can create runs by their individual acts.

That may be, but Gwynn's preference for particular parks is less esoteric. His favorite parks away from home are Atlanta and Cincinnati. "They have big gaps and I'm a gap hitter. Any park that has a 385-foot alley, you've got to love." The crucial variable is not the playing surface—Atlanta is grass, Cincinnati is plastic—but the configuration of the park. That matters most in turning singles into doubles and doubles into triples. Regarding Gwynn's bread and butter, the humble but useful single, he is one of those batters who is amazingly indifferent to the differences between batting conditions in his home park and all the rest. Stan Musial may have been baseball's most consistent hitter, at least as measured by this stunning statistic: He had 3,630 hits, 1,815 at home and 1,815 on the road. Pete Rose's 4,256 hits were divided between 2,123 at home and 2,133 on the road. Al Kaline's 3,007 included 1,508 at home, 1,499 away. Through 1989 Gwynn's hits were distributed 674 at home and 680 away.

◆

A batter's experience at the plate can be unpleasant. The first chapter of Leonard Koppett's *A Thinking Man's Guide to Baseball,* published in 1967, opens with a one-word paragraph: "Fear." Koppett continues, "Fear is the fundamental factor in hitting." The fear is instinctive and reasonable. A baseball is hard and is thrown hard. If it hits you it always hurts, it sometimes injures and it can kill. Tony Kubek says that although almost all players deny it, the "fear factor" is large in baseball. It is more important in baseball than in any other sport. Kubek says, "I remember, years and years ago, when I was first breaking in, Mantle telling me that at least once a year and maybe more 'I wake up screaming in the middle of the night, sweating a cold sweat, with the ball coming right at my head.' "

Even the most gentlemanly pitchers can be provoked to use fear. Kubek says that Sandy Koufax, "who could throw a baseball maybe better than anybody in history," once threatened Lou Brock just because Brock stole a base in a crucial situation. As Brock was dusting himself off at second, Koufax turned to him and, according to Kubek, said, "Next time you do that I'm going to hit you right in the head." Brock stole another base against Koufax. He then became the only man Koufax ever hit in the head. Brock stole no more bases off Koufax.

Of course it is batting, not baserunning, that usually brings what used to be called "bean balls" and now is referred to as "chin music." As was mentioned earlier, there is a particular style of batting that pitchers find especially problematic, and provoking. It is that Charlie Lau style, in which batters dive in over the plate to enhance bat coverage of the outside corner. A batter diving in causes a pitcher to come inside to drive the batter back. Close observers of the game detected a pattern: Teams coached by Lau had an unusual number of hit batters and bench-clearing dust-ups. Andre Dawson of the Cubs is a "diving" batter. It was in a game against the Padres at Wrigley Field that Dawson, diving in against the pitches of Eric Show, was hit in the face by a slider. Gwynn remembers that day clearly because the Cubs' pitcher, Scott Sanderson, tried to retaliate. Sanderson's principle of proportionality identified Gwynn as the Padre of Dawson's stature. "Sanderson was taking potshots at me the day Dawson got hit. He was buzzing me. I got in my same stance. I was still diving over the plate. I took a couple of fastballs running in right at my chin. I got out of the way. If I get hit, I'm not going to get it in the head."

Is there ever a trace of fear in Gwynn when he goes to bat? "Not at all," he says with a firmness convincingly free of bravado. "I just feel I'm quick enough to get out of the way." The most he will concede is this small caveat: There is a certain, well, not fear but perhaps anxiety "when you go up to the plate against a left-hander you've never seen before and he's got a funky delivery and you see a curveball coming right at you and you flinch and it comes over for a strike." But flinching is not fear.

A batter's experience at the plate can be considerably influenced by who bats before him and who bats immediately after him. As Tony La Russa says, the ideal place to hit is behind Rickey Henderson and in front of Don Mattingly: Henderson gets on base and bothers the pitchers, who have trouble concentrating on the hitter and are reluctant to throw breaking balls lest Henderson steal second standing up. So they are going to throw the next batter a lot of fastballs and will throw them in the strike zone lest they walk the batter and bring up Mattingly with two runners on. In the second half of the 1989 season, after Henderson was traded from the Yankees to the Athletics and after the injured Canseco returned to the lineup, the happiest man in America was Carney Lansford, who found himself batting just behind Henderson and just in front of Canseco. Lansford finished three points behind Puckett in the batting race; just two more hits in the same number of at bats and he would have won.

Baseball often is subject to a domino effect, for better or for worse. This was demonstrated, at the Cardinals' expense, in the 1985 World Series. During the League Championship Series Vince Coleman collided with a tarpaulin (or it with him) and he was injured. When the tarpaulin ate Coleman, it also ate Willie McGee. Batting without Coleman on base, McGee saw fewer of the fastballs he had devoured during that MVP season. And because Coleman was not on first with a first baseman holding him, McGee did not have a hole to hit through on the right side. And the pitcher was not a nervous wreck. The "tarpaulin effect" trickled down to the third (Tommy Herr) and fourth (Jack Clark) hitters. The Royals should have voted the tarpaulin a share of the Series take.

For Gwynn the ideal situation is to bat right after someone who has a high on-base percentage and is a base-stealing threat—someone like Alan Wiggins in 1984. In that pennant-winning season Wiggins stole 70 bases and scored 106 runs. The effect of someone like Wiggins batting in front of Gwynn is reinforced by having a power hitter batting behind him, someone like Jack Clark, if Clark is having a good year. (Whether Clark has a good year depends in part on whether the man batting behind him is enough of a threat to cause pitchers to throw strikes to Clark rather than walk him.) Having a power hitter behind Gwynn would make pitchers more wary of walking Gwynn, even if Wiggins, by stealing second, had opened up first base. (In 1961 Roger Maris hit 61 home runs but never received an intentional walk. That is one advantage of batting with Mickey Mantle leaning on one knee in the on-deck circle.)

If there is a runner on first when Gwynn comes to the plate, the pitcher has a problem. "Usually with a runner on first and no outs, or one out, they're going to pitch to a left-hander away," Gwynn says. "They want him to hit the other way." Away, that is, from the hole created by the first baseman holding the runner on first. But that puts the pitcher in the position of serving up Gwynn's preference—the outside pitch he can drive to left with his inside-out swing. The pitcher's position is made worse if the runner on base is a base-stealing threat of the sort Alan Wiggins was in 1984. "We haven't had a guy like Wiggy since he left. Having a guy like that in front of you can open up some things for a hitter." That is putting it mildly. If the runner on first is as fast as Wiggins was, the pitcher's problem is compounded because Gwynn can guess—actually, he is not guessing, he knows—what array of pitches will be coming his way. He is going to see a high ratio of fastballs to breaking balls. (Unless, of course, the pitcher has an exceptionally quick release time to the plate and can stay with breaking pitches.)

Having Wiggins on base was, on balance, very good for Gwynn, but it was not an unmixed blessing. Gwynn's first thought when he came to the plate with Wiggins on base was to take at least one pitch so Wiggins could have a chance to steal. Pitchers—they are not dummies—knew this. They would put the first pitch over the plate so he often found himself batting behind in the count before he buckled down to the main business of putting the ball in play. "At times in 1984 I'd see out of the corner of my eye that Wiggins had got a great jump, so I'd take the pitch even if I already had a strike on me." Then, with the runner on second and no one out, Gwynn's job was to get the runner over to third. Gwynn would have two strikes on him, but felt that in such a situation hitting with two strikes was not much different than hitting with no strikes because "all you had to do was put your bat on the ball. Wiggins was so fast, no one was going to throw him out at third."

When Wiggins went from the Padres to the Orioles in the middle of the 1985 season, Gwynn had to become a better hitter. Suddenly, hitting was a more complicated business because he no longer got the steady diet of fastballs that pitchers threw to him when Wiggins was on base. How soon did he notice the difference that Wiggins's departure was going to make? Gwynn snaps his fingers by way of saying: instantly. "As soon as he was gone, the fastballs ceased coming. When he was here I knew I could go up there with him on base, take a fastball, take another fastball, 2-and-0, take another one, 2-and-1, and know I was still going to get another fastball. Knowing that I'd get all fastballs outweighed the disadvantage of not being able to swing early in the count. I'd take until I had a strike on me. If I never got a strike, I'd walk on four pitches because I wasn't going to hack until I gave him a chance to steal or I had got a strike. If Wiggins stole second and I didn't have a strike on me, I'd take another pitch so he could steal third."

Gwynn's control of the bat makes him a good hit-and-run player. The most important thing in a hit-and-run situation is not what you do but what you avoid doing. You avoid swinging and missing and you avoid hitting the ball hard in the air to the infield. A swing and a miss or a line drive to the infield is trouble for a runner in motion. The Padres experimented briefly with having Gwynn give his own hit-and-run sign to a runner on first. But the first time he tried it, the runner missed the sign—fortunately, as it turned out. Gwynn hit a ball through the middle. If the runner had got the sign and started for second with the pitch, the second baseman would have been moving toward the middle to cover second base and would have fielded Gwynn's ground ball, perhaps for a double play. But the runner was not moving, so neither was the second baseman, and the ball went through for a hit.

Gwynn reads the other team's pitching intentions toward him by watching the middle infielders. "If they play me up the middle they are planning to start me inside and get me out away. If they are playing me in the holes they will pitch me inside, thinking that if I pull it, it will go into the hole on the right side, and if I go inside-out I'll hit it in the hole on the other side." When Gwynn comes up with a man on first in a running situation, the other team's shortstop usually doesn't plan to cover second. "Usually they're going to pitch me away and have the second baseman cover." Often Gwynn will try to go to right field, through the hole created by the first baseman holding the runner on first and the second baseman breaking over to cover second. Often Gwynn will take a few pitches to give the runner a chance to steal. "But once I get a strike on me I can't do that anymore"—at least, not with Alan Wiggins gone. Then he has to see several things, almost simultaneously, that are not in a single field of vision. "Out of the corner of my eye I can see the runner going and I can shift my vision quickly to the pitcher again, and try to see who is moving, who is covering [second]. Sometimes, like in 1984, I guessed right and hit to the hole. But since Wiggy has been gone, I haven't done that too much."

La Russa in the dugout: A modern manager's paperwork is never done.
(Michael Zagaris)

Above: The man and the man-child: La Russa talks, Jose Canseco listens. (V. J. Lovero/*Sports Illustrated*)

Right: La Russa: With his ample dark hair and thick eyebrows, and the bill of his cap pulled low, keeping his eyes in perpetual shadow, his watchfulness has an aspect of brooding. (Courtesy of the Oakland Athletics)

Top: Rene Lachemann, coach, and Terry Steinbach, catcher, prepare for a game. (Michael Zagaris)

Right: "You know how you pitch Mike Schmidt?" asks Jim Lefebvre rhetorically. "Hard fastballs inside, sliders down and away. You know how you pitch Henry Aaron? Willie Mays? Hard stuff inside, soft away. You know how you pitch Willie Stargell? Hard stuff inside, soft away. You know how you pitch God? Hard stuff inside, then down and away, and if you get it there you'll get Him out. Even though He'll know it's coming. Or at least they say He knows." (Courtesy of the Oakland Athletics)

Bottom: Dave Duncan, the Athletics' pitching coach, with his best pupil, Dave Stewart, the 1989 World Series MVP. (John McDonough/*Sports Illustrated*)

Above: Coach, catcher and pupil: Ron Perranoski and Rick Dempsey
with pitcher William Brennan. "You've got to concentrate on each
play, each hitter, each pitch," says Dempsey. "All this makes the game
much slower and much clearer. It breaks it down to its smallest part.
If you take the game like that—one pitch, one hitter, one inning at a
time, and then one *game* at a time—the next thing you know, you look
up and you've won." (Tom DiPace)

Right: Hershiser pitching: Pitching, like politics and marriage and other
difficult undertakings, illustrates the axiom that "the perfect is the enemy of
the good." Which means: In the real world, be ready to settle for something
short of everything. But Hershiser is reluctant to settle. Does he go to the
mound in the first inning planning to pitch a complete game? "A perfect
game," Hershiser replies. "If they get a hit, then I am throwing a one-hitter.
If they get a walk, it's my last walk. I deal with perfection to the point that
it's logical to conceive it. History is history, the future is perfect."
(Paul Richards/UPI/Bettmann Newsphotos)

Top: Davey Johnson, the Mets' manager, and Dwight Gooden, a pitcher to whom Johnson does not need to recommend the theory of unfavorable chance deviation. (Adam J. Stoltman/Duomo)

Bottom: Roger Craig is manager of the Giants and Edison of the pitchers' guild. He was pioneer and proselyte of the split-finger fastball. (Robert Beck/Allsport USA)

Top: Swindell knows that high velocity is nice but it is no substitute for *pitching*. (Charles Bernhardt/Allsport USA)

Bottom: "We're little kids playing a little kid's game," says Jim Gott, relief pitcher. "Why shouldn't we show emotion?" There is an answer to that question. Showing emotion is just *not done* because baseball is such a humbling game. Gott earned 34 saves in 1988. In 1989 he pitched two-thirds of an inning. After the 1989 season he became a Dodger. (Peter Diana)

Top: Tony Gwynn is congratulated by Will Clark after beating Clark for the 1989 National League batting title in his last at bat of the season. The first-base coach is Greg Riddoch. An opposing catcher says of Tony Gwynn: "Out of 650 at bats in a season you will fool him maybe ten times." Ten times is less than twice a month. (Kirk Schlea/Allsport USA)

Bottom: Tony Gwynn at work on the base paths. Baseball connoisseurs consider baserunning the purest baseball achievement because it is the facet of the game in which luck matters least. (Walt Frerck/UPI/Bettmann Newsphotos)

Tony Gwynn awaiting his two-tenths of a second: A 90-mile-per-hour fastball that leaves a pitcher's hand 55 feet from the plate is traveling 132 feet per second and will reach the plate in .4167 second. A change-up or slow breaking ball loitering along at 80 miles per hour travels 117.3 feet per second and will arrive in .4688 second. The difference is .052 of a second and is crucial. Having decided to hit the pitch, the batter has about two-tenths of a second to make his body do it. The ball can be touched by the bat in about 2 feet of the pitch's path, or for about fifteen-thousandths of a second. (Robert Beck/Allsport USA)

Top: Cal lunges to his right: His is a deceptively bland countenance. The blandness is actually a quiet force, a kind of confidence that comes only to athletes and other performers, and only to a few of them. It is confidence in *being able to do it.* (Jerry Wachter/Baltimore Orioles)

Bottom: Two Ripkens (Bill left, Cal right), two outs. (Jerry Wachter/Baltimore Orioles)

Assuming an average of 130 pitches per game over a 162-game season, Ripken tenses, rocks forward on the balls of his feet and begins to lean or move in toward the infield grass, or to one side or the other, 21,000 times each season. Ripken has rocked forward on the balls of his feet more often than any other player since May 30, 1982—the day his consecutive-game streak began. (Tom DiPace)

Top: Ray Miller, a.k.a. The Rabbit, is a philosopher, scientist, social scientist, education theorist and pitching coach. "I don't understand how anyone hits a baseball," says Miller. "You play golf and the damn thing is sitting there and all you've got to do is hit it and that's hard enough." (Peter Diana)

Right: Milwaukee's manager Tom Trebelhorn. Before the Brewers there was Boise, and teaching Rickey Henderson the takeoff sign. "Baseball has got to be fun, because if it is not fun, it's a long time to be in agony." (Tom DiPace)

Bottom: Cal Ripken, Sr., is a former minor league catcher who looks like something whittled from an old fungo bat. When tanned, his skin is the color of a new baseball glove, but it has the wrinkles and creases of one that's seen a lot of hard use. Any reader of John Tunis's boys' books knows that a short, scrappy former catcher should be "bandy-legged." Cal, Sr., is. (Jerry Wachter/*Sports Illustrated*)

Tony Kubek: "The game lends itself to sitting around." (Courtesy of NBC Sports)

Is there much guessing? Doesn't the second baseman generally cover, because of Gwynn's preference for going to left? "Usually—unless they're going to throw me a breaking ball, especially one inside. Then the shortstop is going to cover." Gwynn has time to change his plan because his plan includes anticipating the need to adjust. "I'm going to go up there and look for a fastball and adjust on anything else. If I can pick it up early enough, then I can adjust and try to hit the hole of whoever is covering." But usually he does not recognize the rotation of the ball. And he insists that the pitcher's arm speed is not the clue. What tells him? "The ball. Not his arm, not his motion, just the ball. You see it out there when he lets it go. You see something that tips you off." He can not say what it is or what he then does. "I see it and I react. You recognize what it is and your hands and body take over." He has then entered the realm of muscle memory. "I'm going to take my stride and my hands are going to go up, and then I recognize the pitch, then I'm just going to stay there until it's time to swing the bat." He is talking about staying there poised to swing, letting time pass, for a fraction of a tenth of a second.

Suppose Gwynn is on first and a left-hander is pitching to a fastball hitter with power, and the count is 0–2. The chances are the pitcher will not throw a fastball. He might go to a breaking ball, changing his release time from 1.3 to 1.32 seconds. Even that minute difference makes that a better pitch to run on. Except—there is always a complication—the situation as described is a good one for the other team to pitch out because the pitcher, being ahead in the count, can afford to waste a pitch.

———◆———

In the *Official Baseball Rules,* section 2.00 deals with definitions of terms, including these two:

A BATTER is an offensive player who takes his position in the batter's box.

BATTER-RUNNER is a term that identifies the offensive player who has just finished his time at bat until he is put out or until the play on which he became a runner ends.

A good batter spends a good deal of time as a batter-runner. Baserunning is as much a Gwynn speciality as getting on base. It has been said that baseball connoisseurs consider baserunning the purest baseball achievement because it is the facet of the game in which luck matters least. Leonard Koppett is correct: Maury Wills breaking Ty Cobb's record by stealing 104 bases in 1962 was a more spectacular achievement than Maris breaking Ruth's record the year before. Today baserunning, and especially base stealing, is a more important part of baseball than ever. This is so for several reasons, the first of which is the increased emphasis on speed generally.

Two tennis terms can usefully be applied to baseball—"forced errors" and "unforced errors." Speed on offense, at bat and on the bases, can force errors on the defense by spreading general anxiety and forcing defenders to make perfect executions in particular cases. Reggie Jackson, who can not be accused of underemphasizing the importance of power, is mightily impressed by the sort of speed possessed by Vince Coleman. Jackson notes that in 1988, 34 of Coleman's 160 hits never left the infield—they were infield hits and hits on bunts. Take those away and Coleman would have hit .205 instead of .260. "So he ran .55 points. He's got to hit .200 and run .100 to bat .300."

Houston's Mike Scott says, "Coleman can outrun the ball." In 1987 Coleman stole successfully 19 consecutive times *on pitchouts*. Coleman has led the league in stolen bases every year he has been in the league. He reached 400 stolen bases (407, actually) in four seasons. In 1988 he would have been the leading base stealer on two major league teams just with his 24 steals of third. And he wasted no time in April, 1989, picking up where he had left off six months earlier. In the first inning of the first game of the 1989 season he stole second and third. It was the fiftieth time in his short career (he was just beginning his fifth season) he had done that. As he dusted himself off at third his career record against the Mets was 40 steals in 41 attempts. By midway in the 1989 season he was breaking a record— his own record—every time he stole a base. It was the record for consecutive successful steals. On July 28 the streak ended at 50. A player like Coleman (Rickey Henderson of the Athletics is another, Tim Raines of the Expos is a third, Gerald Young of the Astros is a fourth, and there are others) is a physical phenomenon new to baseball. He is a player so fast, and so technically accomplished at getting a jump, that he changes—shatters, almost—the magical balance struck by Alexander Cartwright when he put the bases 90 feet apart.

Tom Boswell believes that this has gone too far. He proposes eliminating the balk rule. That would, he believes, put mediocre base stealers out of business and restore the equilibrium of 90 feet. However, there are less drastic measures that can, and have in the past, been taken. The balk rule is as elastic as umpires want it to be. The National League, in effect, recently altered the rule by different enforcement. The league began enforcing tougher balk rules to give base runners more of a break. They were trying to reacquire the reputation they got from the legs of Jackie Robinson, Lou Brock and Maury Wills—the reputation as a league of dash and daring-do. Kubek also believes (perhaps this is an old American Leaguer's bias) that the National League panicked when Rickey Henderson burst on the scene as a base stealer. National Leaguers thought: Good grief! The American League, with its smaller parks, is the home-run league and now it is stealing our glory by stealing bases.

Catchers probably would, to a man, rally to Boswell's proposal for eliminating the balk rule. Not long ago a competent catcher was expected to throw out 50 percent of runners attempting to steal. In 1989 the major league's best was the Royals' Bob Boone at 42.3 percent. American League catchers averaged 29.2 percent, National League catchers 31.9 percent. Those numbers are produced in part by the decline in the quality of catching, as will be noted in the next chapter. But the numbers also reflect the fact that runners are faster and, more important, that they have more information. For both reasons, expectations and standards have changed.

When Jose Canseco, the model of the modern sprinter-slugger, had his 40-40 season, Mickey Mantle mused—he was serious—that if he had known folks would make such a fuss about that achievement, he would have done it a few times. He certainly could have. The fact that Mickey Mantle, one of the finest players ever and certainly the swiftest slugger, stole only 153 bases in 18 seasons is partly explained by the fact that he had bad legs. A bone disease made every step painful and his managers wanted to avoid injuries that would make matters worse. But more than mere fear of injury (although that played a part) explains the fact that Joe DiMaggio, universally regarded as a brilliant base runner, stole a total of just 30 bases in his 13 seasons. In three seasons he stole none. In three others he stole only one. Ralph Kiner is second only to Babe Ruth on his ratio of home runs to at bats. Five times he hit 40 or more in a season, including 51 in 1947 and 54 in 1949. His career high in stolen bases also came in 1949. It was just 6. Not even accomplished base stealers stole many by today's standards. Jackie Robinson's best season total was 37. Willie Mays led the league four times with 40, 38, 31 and 27—a total of 136 bases, just six more than Rickey Henderson stole in 1982.

One reason expectations have changed is that the talent pool has changed. In 1947 Jackie Robinson broke baseball's color barrier and was the National League's stolen base leader. In the next 42 seasons, through 1988, the two leagues awarded 84 stolen base titles. Seventy-seven of them went to black or Latin players. No one knows why, for example, blacks are America's best sprinters, but no one doubts that they are.

Another reason why more is now expected in the way of stolen bases is that we now know that more is possible. And more is possible because more is known. There is more information about what particular pitchers and catchers can and can not do.

Information is one reason why, after the 1989 season, Gwynn was the second player in half a century (Rod Carew was the other, though he finished his career at "only" .328) to have a career average of .330 and 200 stolen bases. Gwynn, says McKeon, "is on his own. He can go anytime." His decision to go depends, in part, on the game situation. However, if Gwynn is a runner on first base and there is no one on second, he will be somewhat inhibited about stealing if there is a power hitter coming up next. He does not want to get caught stealing when the batter is someone who can drive him in from first base. And he certainly does not want to get caught stealing with two outs. So having Clark come to the plate right after him does inhibit Gwynn's baserunning a bit. "I don't want to take the bat out of his hands." But he is not very inhibited. He is now so confident of his ability to read pitchers' movements on the mound that he is not going to get thrown out often. "In a first-and-third situation, if I'm on first, if I steal early in the count, and they're behind in the count, they're just going to walk Clark. So I wait until it gets to be two strikes. If they're ahead 0–2 and I take off and the pitch is a ball, I don't think they'll walk him 1–2."

Gwynn continues: "I usually don't like running on a 1-and-0 count. The pitcher might throw the batter a good pitch to hit and the fact of me going might take the hitter's concentration off hitting that pitch. One-and-1 is a good pitch to go on. They might pitch out, sure. But with a guy like Kruky [John Kruk] hitting they're not going to come right down Broadway with it. They're going to try to throw a breaking ball."

Gwynn's decision to try to steal also depends on what he knows about the pitcher's and catcher's "release times." That means it depends on what he and Greg Riddoch, first-base coach and then manager, have seen on the field and on tape.

Let us here deal with the basic data. While the runner on first who is thinking about stealing is thinking about 90 feet, the catcher is thinking about 127 feet 3⅜ inches—the distance from home plate to second base. And the catcher is hoping that his pitcher will *hurry up*. Hurry, that is, in getting the ball to the plate. That does not mean abandoning breaking balls and just throwing fastballs with a runner on first. Rather, what is meant by "quickness to the plate" is a good "release time," the time that elapses from the instant the pitcher, in the stretch position, begins his move to the plate—the instant the "discernible stop" at the belt ends—to the moment the ball hits the catcher's mitt. The runner on first wants to know that time. A time of 1.2 seconds is good, 1.3 is average and anything higher is an invitation to run. The runner also wants to know the catcher's release time, "pop to pop"—that is, from the time the ball hits the catcher's mitt to the instant his throw pops into the glove of the shortstop or second baseman covering second. That should be two seconds flat, or less. For this reason you may see a coach standing on the mound at Spring Training with a basketful of baseballs, pitching to a catcher. There is no batter; another coach stands next to the catcher, a stopwatch in hand; and an infielder stands at second base. The coach with the watch is measuring the "pop-to-pop" time. It is a measurement not only of the power of the catcher's arm, but also, and at least as important, of the quickness of his "release." What goes into a "release" includes three things.

First, how quickly he grabs the ball from his glove. This is especially important in the second decade P.B.—Post Bench. Johnny Bench, probably the greatest catcher ever and certainly the best of the postwar era, popularized the practice of catching the ball one-handed, with the "meat hand" (that phrase is not one of baseball's lovelier locutions) held back at the catcher's side, out of harm's way. Now, catching is for those who, like John Paul Jones, want to make a vocation of going in harm's way. The commonest harm to catchers comes from foul tips. They can break fingers, tear fingernails and do lots of other damage to the unprotected hand. That happens less now, thanks to Bench. But his style of catching requires special speed in plucking the ball from the pocket of the mitt. The second factor determining a catcher's "release time" is how fast he rises and turns as much as he needs to before throwing. The third factor is the swiftness and compactness of his arm motion in sending the ball on its way. So the coach with the stopwatch will tell the catcher, "1.94, not bad . . . 2.12, you'll not nail many people with that . . . 2.04, not good enough . . . good: 1.85 . . ." The difference between "not bad" (1.94) and good is nine one-hundredths of a second.

Pitchers' and catchers' release times are relatively new considerations in baseball. When Roger Craig was pitching in the 1950s, did anyone ever tell him his release time? "No, they didn't know what that was." One of the first people to time pitchers' moves to the plate was Lou Brock, who would do it while in the dugout during the years when he was setting stolen base records. Roger Craig, a former pitcher, and a censorious one at that, says you too often see the following sequence of events: The pitcher is slow to the plate, the catcher has to hurry his throw, the ball sails or skips into center field, the runner goes to third and scores on a sacrifice fly. "People then say the catcher lost the game. Actually, the pitcher did." A catcher with a lightning release time and a cannon arm can at least partially make up for a pitcher's deficiencies. By mid-August, 1988, Benito Santiago, the Padres' catcher, had picked off eight runners—five of them at second. The eighth was the Mets' Wally Backman, nailed by a throw Santiago had gunned to second from his knees. In the same game Santiago threw out Howard Johnson trying to steal. Later in the game Johnson said to Santiago, "I'm never running on you again." And Backman said, "I had a stopwatch on [Padres pitcher] Andy Hawkins. It was taking him 1.5 seconds to come to the plate. Now, 1.3 is borderline and 1.5 you should steal standing up. Santiago throws out HoJo [Howard Johnson] easily. The guy is unbelievable." The guy's pop-to-pop time compensated for Hawkins's sluggish move to the plate.

According to Craig, "The average pitcher's release time today is 1.35 seconds. Rick Reuschel's is the greatest. He gets rid of the ball quicker than any pitcher I've ever seen, around 1.1 to 1.2. The average is 1.35 to 1.4. We find a guy in the 1.5s and we're going to run on him." Some pitchers have two release times, say, 1.3 if they think the runner is a threat to steal, 1.5 if not. Others are 1.3 with a runner on first but are a more relaxed 1.5 with a runner on second. An observant advance scout can tell his manager that although particular players probably can not steal second off a particular pitcher, they probably can steal third.

"Let's take Coleman," says Greg Riddoch, referring to Vince Coleman, lead sprinter on the Cardinals' track team. "From his stealing lead he is 2.9 seconds to second base. Tim Raines [of the Expos, the last man to lead the National League in stolen bases in the era B.C.—Before Coleman] is 3-flat to 3.2. Knowing those facts, I can predict, with the pitcher's and catcher's release times, whether we have a chance to get him. So now let's say our pitcher is 1.2 to the plate and our catcher is 2-flat. Cumulatively that's 3.2 seconds. Now, you take Tim Raines, who's 3.2 to second at his slowest. You have to be perfect to get him. That tells me what I have to do to try to hold Raines on first. I don't want to show him the same move twice in a row. Most base runners, give them the same move twice in a row, they're gone. So before the first pitch I just hold the ball. The second pitch I throw over to first base. The third pitch maybe I throw to first again. The fourth pitch maybe I quick-pitch to the plate. By mixing his moves the pitcher makes it difficult for the runner to narrow the calculation of when to go." And it tells the pitcher's manager when it might be best to call a pitchout.

Riddoch is an example of those baseball people who matter at the margins of a sport where marginal differences matter a lot. He was born and still lives in Greeley, Colorado. After graduating from the University of Northern Colorado he signed with the Cincinnati Reds organization. He never made it to, or even close to, the major leagues. However, in baseball there is no sting to the adage that "those who can, do; those who can't, teach." In baseball, those who never could do it with major league proficiency, no matter how hard they tried, often are the ones who can teach it well. They can because for them striving was largely a matter of the mind.

It is a small, cozy world, this community of baseball. Riddoch, who worked for the Reds for 18 years, managed in their minor league system for 9 years, with stops in Seattle, Washington, and Billings, Montana, and Eugene, Oregon. In Eugene he managed against Walla Walla when Gwynn was in his rookie year in professional baseball. Riddoch talks in the quiet, flat tone of someone trained to be orderly, which he has been. He has a B.A. degree in business administration and a master's degree from Colorado State in education administration. He taught psychology and coached for 13 years at the high school level. "I'm a detail person," he says. Gwynn says Riddoch's eye for details helped him steal 56 bases in 1987, Riddoch's first season as a Padres coach.

On a warm May morning in the visiting team's locker room at Wrigley Field, Riddoch was an island of soft-spoken calm as the younger men arrived to dress for the day game. Some of the early arrivals played cards and others played fast-and-loose with the rules of nutrition, washing down jelly donuts with sodas. Looking around him, Riddoch said that people in every industry, every business are looking around at one another and wondering why some are successful and others are not. The answer, he said, is that we are all creatures of habit, but successful people make a habit of attention to detail. "In our industry, when a pitcher is going to try to pick a runner off first base, he's going to try to set up that runner with something so that he can make his best move at the right time." So Riddoch videotapes all opposing pitchers' moves to the plate and to first base. There is always a tiny telltale tip-off. "We communicate 90 percent of what we do nonverbally. We communicate with body language or voice language—tone of voice." Pitchers communicate more than they want to. A right-handed pitcher, with his back to the runner on first base, may betray his intentions because today's uniforms are so much tighter than the old-fashioned flannels. Yogi Berra says, "If a pitcher's uniform fits too good, the base runner can see his buttocks tighten up just before a pickoff attempt." A pitcher's smallest mannerisms can reveal various intentions. Enough becomes predictable to narrow the odds against—in baseball the odds are almost always against—success. If Riddoch slows down the tape of a pitcher's motion he is always going to find a fingerprint of intention.

In 1987 and 1988, his first years of on-field duties with the Padres, Riddoch often spent several hours a day studying videotapes in slow motion. Pat Dobson, a former pitcher who is now the Padres' pitching coach, sometimes watched with him. Riddoch was content to pick up one clue in four hours. One pitcher might bring his hands to a slightly different stop position—slightly higher or lower—when he is going to throw to first rather than to the plate. Or the clue might be a slight tilt to the pitcher's shoulders, or where he puts his foot on the rubber, or even how his toe is pointing when he lifts his front leg. (That last is, he says, a dead giveaway for one particular "left-hander who is extraordinarily successful in this league." He will not say who it is. Loose lips sink ships.) "There are always some players," Riddoch acknowledges, "who think this is 'Joe college' stuff." But more and more players have, like Gwynn, gone to college. Since 1973 a majority of the players signed from the amateur draft have had some college experience. In the 1980s the average has been around 80 percent.

A lot of people in baseball know many of the things that can be learned from what Riddoch does with the videotape but, he says, they fail at the discipline of "staying on task." They do not do the detail work day in and day out, every inning. That is a habit he developed by being, as he puts it, "a limited-tool player. In order for me to compete, I had to have an edge. I wasn't fast but I could steal 15, 20 bases just knowing pitchers' moves." Riddoch coaches first base, so he is in a position to shout what he sees to his runners. "Some pitchers do a jump, a spin move to first. In order to do that, the back heel has to raise to step off the rubber." The raising of a heel brings a shout from Riddoch, calling the runner back to first.

When Gwynn gets to first, Riddoch may say, "Watch the back heel." If, when watching the heel, Gwynn sees any motion other than the significant lift of the heel, he knows that the ball is not coming to first, so he can lean toward, or go toward, second. There are more clues to pick up from right-handed pitchers because they have a more complicated task in throwing to first. They begin with their backs toward first. Riddoch says the left-hander's move is more troublesome because a left-hander is facing the runner and (here you hear the aggrieved voice of the First Base Coaches' Guild) umpires rarely call balks on left-handers.

Two months after I talked with Riddoch in Chicago, Gwynn talked to him in San Diego, on the diamond, in a game. Gwynn was on base; Nolan Ryan was pitching for the Astros. Riddoch, said Gwynn, sometimes takes a stopwatch out to the first-base coaching box to measure release times. "I'll bounce back to the bag and he'll go"—here Gwynn simulated silently mouthing the words "one-five-four"—"so I know that if I can get to second in three-flat, I can beat it." In fact, Riddoch had timed Ryan at 1.54 and Gwynn stole second. Pitching is a matter of rhythm and if a pitcher is intending to break his rhythm and throw to first, he will reveal his intentions with some small detail. Always? "Always," says Gwynn, with serene, smiling finality. "A lot of people can't believe that, but if you look at the tape, every time there is something he does to tip it off. There's guys like, well, a pitcher for Houston, who when he comes to first his toes point in a particular way—down. When he goes to home you see the bottom of his shoe." Who is this fellow? Another Gwynn laugh. "I can't say because he might read this."

———◆———

Pitchers complain, with reason, that the world is plotting against them. (Remember: Paranoiacs can have real enemies.) But batters, too, have had some setbacks. If hitters repine for what really was their golden age, they repine for the years between 1870 and 1887, that paradisiacal era when the batter was entitled to tell the pitcher where in the strike zone—high or low—he wanted the ball thrown. And even until 1901 batters had better conditions than today. Not until 1901 (in the National League; 1903 in the American League) were the first two foul balls counted as strikes. This rule change was made in response to the perverse genius of a few players such as Roy Thomas, a Phillies outfielder who once fouled off 22 pitches before walking.

Furthermore (since we are giving batters their turn at baseball's wailing wall), batters are always on the defensive. Baseball's fundamental act of offense—swinging at a thrown ball—is essentially reactive. Lou Brock said that there are only three things involved in hitting—the pitcher, the ball and the batter—and once the ball is released from the pitcher's hand there are only two, and the question becomes who is better, you or the ball. Usually, the ball is. The major league average for batting failure is about 74 out of 100 times. About 7,000 men have come to bat in the major leagues. Eight of them managed to bat .400 over a full season. As Reggie Jackson says, if you play for 10 years and have 7,000 at bats and 2,000 hits you have had a pretty fair career but "you've gone 0-for-5,000." Never mind getting hits. How about putting the ball in play? Mickey Mantle once said, "During my 18 years I came to bat almost 10,000 times. I struck out about 1,700 times and walked maybe 1,800 times. You figure a ball player will average about 500 at bats a year. That means I played seven years in the major leagues without even hitting the ball." Once, after striking out swinging at three bad pitches, Yogi Berra had the brass to ask indignantly, "How can a pitcher that wild stay in the league?" Berra was so gifted at hitting pitches that were out of the strike zone that Mel Ott swore Berra got hits on pitches that, if they had not collided with his bat, would have been wild pitches, colliding with the backstop. But the answer to Berra's question is: Such pitchers stay in the major leagues because there are a lot of hitters who, like Berra, do not discipline themselves to swing only at what is in or near the strike zone and who, unlike Berra, do not have the talent to compensate for their indiscipline. Catcher Terry Kennedy, who was Gwynn's teammate before moving to Baltimore and then San Francisco, has now seen Wade Boggs up close and offers this comparison: "Gwynn is so aggressive, sometimes you can get him to swing at a bad pitch. Wade Boggs *never* swings at a bad pitch." Boggs's discipline is apparent in the way he "works the count." This, like almost everything else about Boggs, has been noted by Chuck Waseleski, known to readers of the *Boston Globe*'s sports pages as "the maniacal one." He lives in Millers Falls, Massachusetts, and is the business manager of an engineering firm. In his spare time, which he seems to have a lot of, he crunches numbers in ways they have rarely been crunched before. For example: In 1989, in 742 plate appearances, Boggs swung at the first pitch just 50 times. He put the first pitch in play just 29 times. Kirby Puckett put the first pitch in play 176 times. Puckett's impatience, if that is what it was, did not prevent him from batting .339 and becoming the first right-hander to win the American League batting title since Carney Lansford in the strike-shortened 1981 season, and the first in a full season since Alex Johnson in 1970. It makes you wonder how high his average might have soared if he had been more patient. Patience is an important part of Boggs's style. In 1989 Boggs demonstrated the importance, at least to him, of being ahead in the count. Here, compiled by Waseleski, is Boggs's batting average by count:

0–0	.321	1–0	.354	2–0	.219	3–0	.000
0–1	.281	1–1	.347	2–1	.453	3–1	.419
0–2	.219	1–2	.181	2–2	.388	3–2	.356

Note the difference between the counts 1–2 and 2–1. Boggs can be patient at the plate because he is a fine contact hitter. In 1989 he swung and missed just 58 times in 1,191 swings. And yet he failed to get hits 67 percent of the time. Why? Because hitting is hard.

In the section of the rule book devoted to instructions for umpires there is this unequivocal and unexceptionable advice: "Keep your eye everlastingly on the ball." Easier said than done. Easier for umpires, who are looking directly at the pitcher, than for batters.

Following the flight of the ball is much more difficult for a batter. He is standing sideways, looking to his left or right, and, when swinging, trying to make an educated guess, and read the pitcher's motion and release point, and then the rotation of the ball (for example, the small red dot made by the seams on the tight rotation of a well-thrown slider), and then striding and holding his hands just right just long enough and turning his hips and then his upper body in the precise flow of energy while keeping his head down and keeping his eyes everlastingly on the ball. All the batter usually knows for sure is that the pitcher is trying to trick him, and occasionally to frighten him, and every once in a while to hit him with a hard, swiftly moving object.

The distance from the front edge of the slab of rubber on the pitcher's mound to the back of home plate is 60 feet 6 inches. Suppose a pitcher throws directly over the top, fully overhand, and releases the ball at least 7 feet above the level of the plate (counting the 10-inch height of the mound) and about 55 feet from the plate. The belt-level top of today's strike zone is about 3½ feet above the plate. That means the ball moves 3½ feet vertically while traveling 55 feet horizontally. And that does not include the irregular motion imparted to a slider, a curve, a split-finger or even a plain fastball by its velocity.

In the major leagues, what makes all the difference is the movement the ball makes—or fails to make—as it passes over the plate. In 1951 Warren Spahn was pitching for the Boston Braves at the Polo Grounds when the Giants sent to the plate a rookie who was 0-for-12. Spahn threw the ball and the rookie crushed it. Willie Mays's first hit was a home run off a Hall of Famer. Spahn later said, "For the first 60 feet it was a hell of a pitch." (Later, remembering that Mays was hitless in his young career when he came to the plate, Spahn said, "I'll never forgive myself. We might have gotten rid of Willie forever if I'd only struck him out.") A 90-mile-per-hour fastball that leaves a pitcher's hand 55 feet from the plate is traveling 132 feet per second and will reach the plate in .4167 second. A change-up or slow breaking ball loitering along at just 80 miles per hour travels 117.3 feet per second and will arrive in .4688 second. The difference is .052 of a second and is crucial. Having decided to try to hit the pitch, the batter has about two-tenths of a second to make his body do it. The ball can be touched by the bat in about 2 feet of the pitch's path, or for about fifteen-thousandths of a second.

So anyone who hits a ball thrown by a major league pitcher—who even just puts the ball in play—is doing something remarkable. The consistently good hitters are astonishing.

Musial once told a rookie, "If I want to hit a grounder, I hit the top third of the ball. If I want to hit a line drive, I hit the middle third. If I want to hit a fly ball, I hit the bottom third." You can imagine how helpful Musial's advice was to a mere mortal. Gwynn picks up the rotation of the pitch only about 20 percent of the time. Usually he just tries to follow the flight of the ball. "If Gooden's curveball starts out pretty high, chances are it's going to finish down somewhere. So it's either a big mistake or a good curveball." What Gwynn's opponents respect most about him is how rarely he is fooled by such a pitch, or any pitch.

Jim Lefebvre recalls what he calls the expression of "ultimate respect" in a team meeting. In 1965, his rookie year with the Dodgers, the team would discuss how to pitch and defense each team the first time the Dodgers met them. "So we are going through the league. 'Willie Mays. Hard stuff way inside. If you miss you'd better miss in, so he can't get his arms out. You get the ball out over the plate, it will take you a five-dollar cab ride to find it.' And I'm thinking, 'Wow! Willie Mays.' And we go through the other guys— McCovey, Banks—as the other teams come through. The last team to come through is the Braves. 'Eddie Mathews. Great high fastball hitter, you gotta do this and this and this.' So all of a sudden Henry Aaron's name comes up. Bad Henry. Here we are with all those great pitchers—Koufax, Drysdale, others—and the room went dead silent. Nobody said a word. Then someone said, 'When he hits one, make sure nobody's on. Next.' "

When asked how he pitched to Mickey Mantle, Frank Sullivan of the Red Sox said, "With tears in my eyes." When Davey Johnson, the Mets' manager, was asked how to pitch to Gwynn, he laughed and said, "Throw it down the middle and hope it confuses him." Johnson says he has seen the likes of Gwynn before, in Tony Oliva of the Twins and Rod Carew of the Twins and Angels. He recalls that in pitching against them the sensible theory was: "Let's not get cute. Throw it right down the middle because that will confuse them. They're not going to know what field to hit it to. If you threw Oliva the up-and-in pitch, he'd hit it to left field, like Gwynn does. Oliva used to pull low-and-away breaking balls. There was no way to defense them. They had great hand-eye coordination and what I call 'barrel control,' putting the barrel of the bat right on the ball. That's why I say with guys like Gwynn, throw it down the middle and hope they hit it at someone."

Mike LaValliere, the Pirates' catcher, says of Gwynn, "He's one of the few guys in the league there is no 'book' on. He's like Keith Hernandez. He's going to get his hits and you just hope no one's on base. He has such a short, compact swing and such a good idea of the strike zone that you are not going to fool him often. Out of 650 at bats in a season you will fool him maybe ten times." Ten times is less than twice a month.

There are similarities between Gwynn and George Brett. Brett was the last man to flirt with a .400 season by being over .400 at one point in September. A pitcher once said of Brett, "The only way to pitch him is inside, so you force him to pull the ball. That way the line drives won't hit you." Jim Frey, who managed Brett for a while with the Royals, was asked what advice he gave Brett about hitting. Frey said, "I tell him, 'Attaway to hit, George.'" He has more power than Gwynn but they are similar in keeping their hands back, even when fooled by a pitch. Even if, when they are fooled, they are far out in front, with their weight shifting toward their front foot, their hands are still back. Thus they still have a chance to compensate and slap the ball by snapping their wrists. Batters who bring their hands forward too fast are finished with a pitch when they are fooled by it.

Gwynn, like Brett and Boggs, has one important natural advantage. He is left-handed. That is not always an advantage in baseball. Indeed, it can be argued that baseball has a built-in bias against left-handers. This bias is glaring, for example, in the fact that the bases are run counterclockwise. This custom reflects the convenience of right-handers who want to be infielders. Almost all infielders other than first basemen are right-handed because on most plays they can throw to first without turning their bodies as far as left-handers would have to. The consolation, such as it is, for left-handers playing defense is that they are suited to first base because their glove hand is on the side the throws come from, and they can throw more easily than right-handed first basemen could to start the 3-6-3 (or 3-4-3) double play.

However, left-handers get their revenge as batters. At the plate they stand a step closer to first and the momentum of their swing causes them to uncoil moving toward first. As a result, the average left-hander among today's major leaguers gets there a full tenth of a second faster than the average right-hander (4.05 versus 4.15). Until 1870 the left-handers' advantage in the sprint to first did not matter so much because running to first was not the headlong dash it now is. Until 1870 a batter could not overrun first base without being tagged out.

Another advantage for today's left-handed hitter is that he faces right-handed pitching about two-thirds of the time, so most of the breaking pitches he sees are moving in toward his power. These facts help explain why in the postwar (1946–89) era 55 of the 88 league batting championships have been won by left-handers. Kevin Kerrane, professor of English at the University of Delaware and baseball scholar, notes that 34 of the 55 were won by long-range strategic thinkers like Ted Williams, George Brett and Wade Boggs, who, although they throw right-handed, had the wisdom as children to become left-handed hitters. (There have been few "reverse crossovers," players perverse enough to throw left but insist on batting right. Rickey Henderson is one. Another was a thin fellow who played first base for Yale, George Bush.)

◆

About one thing Karl Marx, a lefty, was right. Change the modes of production and you will change the nature of work, and consciousness. Baseball's two fundamental tools are the ball and the bat. Neither is what it used to be. Although baseball adopted a cork-centered ball in 1910, aggregate major league averages did not jump until 1919. Remember, we have agreed to credit (or blame) Australian yarn. In any case, the advent of the lively ball changed almost everything in the game. Bats, too, have changed, but not, as the ball did, suddenly. So it is difficult to determine exactly when and how the changes began making differences.

Let us begin at the beginning, and I mean the Beginning. The Big Bang got the universe rolling and produced, among the flying debris, the planet Earth. It (and here we may have evidence of a kindly Mind superintending things) is enveloped in a thin membrane of atmosphere. The membrane is not too thick to keep out necessary energy and not too thin to let in lethal rays. And it is just right to cause raindrops to patter on Pennsylvania ridges where ash trees grow. They grow surrounded by other trees that protect the ash from winds that might twist and weaken them. In this protection they grow straight toward the sunlight. The result is wood wonderfully suited to being made into baseball bats. I think that I shall never see a tree as lovely as these things made from them.

The bats in use at any time, unlike the balls, have important differences. This is so because players are keenly interested in, and occasionally neurotic about, these instruments by which they pursue an acceptable rate of failure at the plate. Shoeless Joe Jackson believed that his bats had to winter in South Carolina to stay warm. (Don't snicker unless you, too, have a .356 career average.) Richie Ashburn slept with his bats, but only, he says chastely, on the road. Orlando Cepeda used to discard a bat after getting a hit. His reasoning (in which I find no flaw) was that there are only so many hits in a bat; you can not know how many; so why risk using a bat from which all the hits may have been wrung? Ted Williams is said to have shipped some bats back to Louisville because the lathe operator had made a mistake of five-thousandths of an inch when turning the bat handles.

Gwynn has a more relaxed relationship with his bats. One day at San Diego State, just after basketball season, he wandered into the storeroom looking for a bat and picked up a little aluminum thing with a heavyweight name. The "Tennessee Thumper" weighed 31 ounces and was 32 inches long. Thus began a happy relationship between a young man and a piece of metal. When he became a professional and had to switch to wood he picked a bat of the same length and weight. He still wants his bat light but with a big barrel. So instead of achieving lightness by having the barrels of his bats shaved, as many hitters do, he has them "cupped," with a portion of the end of the barrel hollowed out like the bottom of a wine bottle. The only change he has made he made in 1984, when he decided his bat was "too quick" on his swing. He changed to a bat that, like the old one, weighed 31 ounces but was half an inch longer. It is, by the standards of olden times, a twig. The young Babe Ruth supposedly used a 52-ounce bat. Later he used bats "only" 44 to 48 ounces.

But mighty records can from little bats spring. Wee Willie Keeler used a 30½-inch bat, but he was just 5 feet 4½ and weighed only 140 pounds. And his bat was big enough for eight 200-hit seasons. Joe Morgan, the career home-run leader among second basemen, used an even lighter bat—30 ounces. Ernie Banks's 32-ounce bat propelled 512 home runs. In the 1950s Banks and Henry Aaron exemplified a new kind of power hitter. They used thin-handled bats that they whipped with their quick, strong wrists.

Thin-handled bats break—often. But all bats are breakable. On July 15, 1887, Pete Browning, an outfielder for the Louisville club, broke his bat. A fan who also was a wood-turner made Browning a new one. The fan's name was John Andrew (Bud) Hillerich. Browning went 3-for-3 in his first game with the new bat and he soon became known as "The Louisville Slugger." So did his bat. A company, and one of America's most famous trademarks, was born.

For many years bats did not break nearly as often as they do now. Lefty Gomez, the Hall of Fame wit and pitcher, said he broke only one bat: "I ran over it backing out of the garage." There have been people who, unlike Gomez, were good at bringing their bats into contact with pitched balls and broke remarkably few bats. Bill Terry used only two bats in 1930 while hitting .401 with 254 hits. Ira Berkow, sports columnist for *The New York Times,* reports that Joe Sewell, the last living member of the 1920 Indians' team that beat the Dodgers in a seven-game (5–2) World Series, still has in a glass case at his home in Mobile, Alabama, the one bat he used throughout his 14-year career. It is long (35 inches) and hefty (40 ounces) and must be enjoying retirement because it had a hard working life: Not only did it bang out 2,226 hits but it was constantly making contact. Sewell struck out only 114 times in 7,132 at bats, the fewest strikeouts recorded in any extended career. The fact that Jim Rice several times snapped bats on checked swings may reveal as much about the nature of today's bats as about Rice's wrists, powerful though they undoubtedly are. Bo Jackson is an impressive specimen, but when he breaks bats over his knee, and even over his head (wearing a batting helmet), one does wonder about the wood, or whether today's batters have gone a bit too far in favoring thin handles. Whatever the reason for so many bats breaking (some baseball people say that wood isn't what it used to be), the fact that so many are breaking has an interesting consequence. A college player's baseball education begins when he leaves school—and it begins immediately.

"I learned the day after I was signed, in Walla Walla," Gwynn says. "The first hack I took in batting practice I got jammed, tried to fight it off, shattered my bat, stung my hands. I took that one swing and that was it. You realize you're not going to make a living swinging a bat like that. You've got to get the barrel of the bat on the ball.

In college I hit the ball the other way but didn't get to use the barrel of the bat often. With aluminum you can get jammed and fight it off and still loop one over the third baseman's ear. The pitcher makes a great pitch and you get a hit."

Greg Swindell had the same sort of startling experience, but from the pitcher's point of view, so it was a pleasant surprise. Before he became a professional, Swindell had pitched against wooden bats only in University of Texas alumni games. In his first game at Waterloo, Iowa, he hummed a fastball in on the fist of the first batter he faced as a professional. A fragment of the man's bat flew over Swindell's head. "I got four or five bats that day," he says, savoring the memory. And he is still at it, and still counting. In one 1988 game in Minnesota he counted 12 bats he cracked or shattered. Ben McDonald, the 6-foot-7 pitcher from Louisiana State University, the first pick in the 1989 draft (the Orioles picked him), said he frequently talks with his friend Andy Benes, the first pick in the 1988 draft (the Padres picked him). "When I talk to Andy, that's all he talks about. He says he's breaking four or five bats every time out. I want to throw to some wood, saw some off in somebody's hands."

There are people—let us hope they are not prophets—who say pitchers had better hurry up and have the pleasure while it is here to be had.

In July, 1989, civilization was rocked by Peter Gammons's report in *Sports Illustrated* that aluminum bats are advancing on the gates of professional baseball. Gammons said that some minor leagues are flirting with the idea of abandoning wood bats in favor of aluminum, and that within a generation the major leagues may ring with the ping of metal on horsehide (so to speak: remember balls have been wrapped in cowhide for years). Aluminum bats are used everywhere outside of professional baseball, from Little League through college. Hillerich & Bradsby, makers of the Louisville Sluggers (which, by the way, are no longer made in Louisville but across the Ohio River in Indiana), used to make 7 million wood bats a year. Now it makes 1.5 million, of which 185,000 go to the major leagues. The company makes aluminum bats by the millions but makes them far from the American heartland, in Southern California, land of novelties and regrets. The reason for the popularity of aluminum bats is that they do not break, and so they cut costs. But a switch in professional baseball from wood to aluminum would make a bad and deteriorating situation worse. It would sacrifice much on the altar of parsimony—and at a time when baseball is rolling in money.

Allowing aluminum bats into the major leagues would constitute a serious degradation of the game, and not just for aesthetic reasons. But let us begin with them. Aesthetic reasons are not trivial. Baseball's ambiance is a complex, subtle and fragile creation. Baseball's sounds are important aspects of the game, and no sound is more evocative than that of the thwack of wood on a ball. It is particularly so when it is heard against the background sizzle of crowd noise on a radio broadcast, radio being the basic and arguably the best way to experience baseball if you can not be at the park. To a person of refined sensibilities, aluminum hitting a ball makes a sound as distressing as that of fingernails scraping a blackboard.

The other reasons for resisting any attempt to introduce metallurgy into the major leagues concern the safety of the players and the artistry of the game. An aluminum bat is lighter than a wood bat of the same length by two to four ounces. That makes for greater bat speed, which is the key to power. Also, the "sweet spot"—the impact point for maximum power—is larger on aluminum than on wood bats. You might think that major league batters would welcome the change. But hear them.

Scott Bradley of the Mariners, who played baseball at the University of North Carolina at Chapel Hill, told Gammons, "If you hit a ball right with a wood bat, it'll go about the same distance as a ball hit with aluminum. But with wood you have to hit it right. You have to use your hands to get the bat head out and hit it on the sweet spot. . . . With aluminum, you can make contact almost anywhere on the bat and get the ball through or over the infield. Watch a college game and see how many hitters get jammed and still hit flares into the opposite field." Watch a college game? Better cancel some appointments. College games are, not surprisingly, longer than major league games. However, aluminum bats might speed up the games in one way: There would be fewer walks. Why walk when the metal bat raises the odds that merely making contact will result in a hit?

Bradley is dead right: With a wood bat you have to do things right. Aluminum bats reduce the importance of craftsmanship. Tom Grieve, general manager of the Rangers, told Gammons that an aluminum bat's sweet spot is so big, "with an aluminum bat most kids can take the same swing at every pitch. When they see that they have to hit the ball on a certain spot on a wood bat, they find out they have to swing differently, according to the pitch." The Yankees' Don Mattingly, one of the game's artists, said simply, "It takes all the art out of the game." The difference between hitting with wood and aluminum is comparable to the difference between a real pitcher and a mere thrower. You say Pete Incaviglia breaks nearly 40 dozen bats in a season? That will not break any bank and should not break any hearts. A glance at his strikeout totals shows the way he breaks bats: He is an undisciplined hitter who never properly learned his craft in the minor leagues. He went straight from Oklahoma State University and aluminum bats to the big leagues.

Put aluminum bats in the hands of major league hitters and you may have many tragedies of the sort that felled Herb Score. The pitcher's rubber is still 60 feet 6 inches from home plate, but batters are bigger and stronger than ever. Ken Griffey, Jr., of the Mariners says, "You'd better move the mound back 10 feet. And give everybody life insurance because somebody will get killed." Joe Carter of the Indians, who the week Gammons's article appeared hit 5 home runs in 6 at bats, says, "You'd have a lot of dead pitchers and third basemen. Imagine Bo Jackson with an aluminum bat. You're talking 600-foot home runs." Dave Parker, now with the Milwaukee Brewers, remembers taking batting practice in Pittsburgh with aluminum bats. In 20 swings he hit 13 balls into the seats, 7 of them into the third tier at Three Rivers Stadium. "If they let them in," he says, "I'd have notches in my bat. I'd kill someone." ("But," said Merv Rettenmund, the Athletics' hitting coach, "it's [the victim's] a pitcher. They deserve it.") Tim Flannery, a Padres third baseman who thinks that the hot corner is hot enough, thank you, says, "They better get softer baseballs." Greg Minton, an Angels relief pitcher who thinks he already has enough to repent of, says, "I've already killed enough first and third basemen with hanging sinkers. I don't want to see my infielders playing short left and short right."

We already see what aluminum bats do to pitching. They produce pitchers with inferior fastballs and arms often prematurely worn out from the torque of throwing too many breaking balls. We already know what this, combined with variants of the Charlie Lau style of hitting, produces: batters diving in to hit pitches in the outside part of the strike zone, and diving batters getting hit by inside pitches that are not much out of the strike zone, and brawls and warnings from umpires, and the migration of the strike zone. Mike Boddicker of the Red Sox says the strike zone has moved horizontally as well as vertically. Not only is the top of the zone at the belt, the inside edge of the zone is, for most umpires, at least two inches out over the plate. "A majority of umpires won't call strikes on the inner few inches of the plate." Hershiser's opinion about umpires' practices is more tempered. "My theory on the inside-outside corner is that on the inside part of the plate you need to have the whole ball on the plate. On the outside corner the ball only needs to touch the plate." Still, Hershiser, like Boddicker, believes that even some inside pitches that are strikes are now problematic. One source of this problem, starting a long way below the big leagues, is the aluminum bat, which prevents too many pitchers from learning how to shade the inside slice of the plate. Playing college baseball, Incaviglia remembers fondly, "You never had to worry about getting jammed. You never worried because it never happened." It never happened because of what he held in his hand.

Baseball is like a mobile: Jiggle something here and things move over there. Everything is related to everything else. So, naturally, aluminum bats change fielding as well as batting and pitching. Infielders facing aluminum bats rarely need to charge balls because balls get to them so quickly. Major league infielders on artificial turf already play deeper than on grass. Add aluminum bats and you will, in effect, subtract a couple of infielders and add a couple of outfielders.

Aluminum bats have made it difficult for major league scouts to evaluate high school and college talent. In fact, major league baseball subsidizes the Cape Cod League and seven other leagues where outstanding prospects can play in the summer without losing their college eligibility. Those leagues use wood bats. Now that major league baseball is feeling flush (and if it isn't, it should be) it should work out some way to subsidize a comeback by wood bats. Surely major league baseball could help colleges put the aluminum bats back into the bat racks for good.

Why is anyone even considering the cockamamie idea of aluminum bats in professional baseball, all the way up to the major leagues? The reasons given are remarkably unconvincing.

It is said that the world is running out of suitable wood for bats. But wood is a renewable resource. Need more trees? Plant some, for goodness' sake. If the price is right for a product (we are not talking about platinum, we are talking about wood), people will produce it. Hillerich & Bradsby says it could continue making wood bats for the major leagues if it charged $40 rather than just $16.50. So? Charge it. Millionaire utility infielders playing for franchises that have sextupled in value in one decade can come up with the extra $23.50. A major college baseball program that includes a fall and spring schedule (most colleges do not play in the fall) might go through 50 dozen $14 bats (college bats are cheaper than the ones the major leagues use) for an annual cost of $8,400. But that cost is small beer for a major college athletic department. And what is big-time football for if not to subsidize more civilized sports? *USA Today* reported that the California Angels, for example, expected to use 172 dozen bats during the 1989 season, at a cost of about $35,000, but would need only a few dozen $60 aluminum bats and would save $33,500. Big deal. The sum that would be saved is a lot less than is earned in one season by the hot cinnamon bun concession stand (or the baked potato stand) at Anaheim Stadium. America's real (adjusted for inflation) GNP has doubled in the last 30 years, leisure dollars flowing toward sports have increased even more than that, major league baseball's attendance has increased for four consecutive seasons, revenues from licensing of major league products are soaring, television revenues will double between 1989 and 1990 (we are talking about numbers with three commas—billions) and yet baseball can not afford proper bats? Be serious.

There is a consensus that in the late 1970s aluminum bats were made significantly more lively than they had been. (Can a bat be "juiced"? What is the world coming to when we have to wonder about that?) Manufacturers of aluminum bats, who have an incentive to say soothing things, say they can make bats with a wide variety of characteristics, including those of wooden bats. But would batters in pursuit of their own interests (and offense-crazed owners in pursuit of even higher attendance) want anything less than the maximum potency from bats? Would major league baseball really do with bats what it has done with the ball—write narrow tolerances for what is permissible? And in the unlikely event that major league baseball was inclined to do that, how exactly would it work? Players come in different sizes and strengths and tendencies and inclinations. Therefore, bats must come in a wide variety of lengths and weights and handle widths.

Do we want major league teams that have, as some college teams do these days, *team* batting averages above .340? (In 1979 the Wichita State Shockers had a team average of .384.) Aluminum bats would rewrite the record books and, more important, would make records less interesting because they would be less instructive. Advocates of aluminum bats say that differences in the parks—say, between Fenway and the Astrodome—already make comparisons of records difficult. True, but that has always been so. Mel Ott hit 511 home runs playing half his games in the Polo Grounds with its short foul lines. Across the Harlem River, Joe DiMaggio had hundreds of potential home runs swallowed up as fly outs in the vast power alleys of Yankee Stadium. But at least Ott and DiMaggio used essentially the same equipment. And although parks have changed a lot over the years, they have changed gradually. There was not a stark demarcation between one era of parks and another. Only once since 1900 has there been an abrupt change in conditions, a change that divided all that happened before from all that has happened since: the introduction of the lively ball. So modern baseball has had just two eras. Aluminum bats would be another radical rupture. They would add a third disorienting disjunction to baseball's story. They would dilute baseball's intensely satisfying continuity and thereby would render much less interesting the comparison of players' performances. Those comparisons nourish interest in the game as it passes down from generation to generation and they sustain fans in the fallow months of the off-season.

So where are we headed? To a future of batters diving across the plate toward the outer edge of a moving strike zone, taking long looping swings and spraying hits—ping! ping! ping!—off a series of weak-armed breaking-ball pitchers? Wade Boggs believes that if aluminum bats come to the big leagues "there will be another .400 hitter." Sure, but will anybody really care?

———◆———

What is Gwynn's weakness? He says that through his first five years the hardest pitcher for him to hit—hardest to hit for reasons other than velocity (meaning the hardest for him to hit other than Nolan Ryan)—was John Tudor. Speaking in 1988, Gwynn said: "He's the only pitcher who has a pitch I can not hit. It's his curveball. I have fouled it off but I don't think I have ever put it in play." Fortunately for Gwynn, Tudor does not seem to have taken proper notice. "The last time we faced him in St. Louis [shortly before Tudor was traded to the Dodgers] we had runners on second and third with two outs and he threw me the curveball for a strike, then a fastball that ran in on my hands. I tried unsuccessfully to bunt it and was 0-and-2. So

I was looking breaking ball because I have never hit it. Instead, he threw me a fastball in on my hands, I fought it off, it went in the hole, off Ozzie's [Smith] glove, and we got two runs." Gwynn's complete recall is tinged with disbelief and disapproval of Tudor's failure to remember Gwynn's weakness. "Any pitcher who has pitched that long and been that successful, you would think has got to realize I can't hit that breaking ball."

Is there a Gwynn strength? "Anything hanging," he says laughing. Well, yes, of course: a pitcher's mistake. But what else? He likes fastballs up in the strike zone. "I hit the other way best. It's easy for me to take that fastball that's thigh-high and fight it off and go to left field."

A basic pitching strategy is to use off-speed curveballs and change-ups to get a batter shifted onto his front foot to slow his bat down. The batter wants to stay back as long as possible so his bat will be accelerating on contact. For every good hitter, batting is a matter of patience. It is especially so for Gwynn. Every good hitter must wait as long as possible for his pitch, or for the pitcher to make a mistake. He must wait for particular counts or circumstances that shift, however slightly, the balance of the competition toward the hitter. But Gwynn must be patient in another sense. Even after he has locked his eyes on a pitch that he has decided he wants to hit, he still must wait longer than most batters before swinging. In Ted Williams's four-word formulation, one key to hitting is: hips ahead of hands. But when a left-handed hitter is "going the other way," to left field, he prefers an outside pitch, and Gwynn says, "On an outside pitch you want your hands to lead and the barrel of the bat to trail." The barrel of Gwynn's bat trails his hands by about ten inches. When trying to hit to left, Gwynn is, in effect, pushing back the pitching rubber, perhaps half a foot farther from the plate. He is using his quick bat—those basketball dribbler's wrists again—to allow him to wait on a pitch and hit it when it has passed over most of the plate.

The late Charlie Lau would take a .250 right-handed pull hitter and teach him to hit to right. Lau would tell the right-hander that every time he does that with a runner on first the result will be first-and-third, whereas if he pulled the ball through the infield on the left side, the result would be just first-and-second because of the short throw from left field to third. And in the process of learning to "go the other way" the .250 hitter becomes a .280 hitter. A pitcher who knows he is facing such a hitter will throw him sliders breaking down and in. Perhaps the hitter can "inside-out" a fastball to right, but not a slider that is down and in.

Gwynn says, "I stand in the middle of the batter's box. You see a lot of guys dig that white line out and stand in the back to give them more time. I thought about doing that, but I'm so used to hitting up closer that if I change it's going to throw my timing off. I would have to wait that much longer and as you can see from some of these tapes I have a tough enough time waiting. Also, I've got a little bat, so I've got to be able to cover both sides of the plate." When his swing is mechanically sound, his front leg is stiff, or solid, and he's deriving power from the drive of his back leg. Furthermore, the barrel of the bat is behind his hands. The instinct in hitting is "hurry up because the ball is hurrying." Every fiber of a hitter's being urges him not to hesitate. In this regard Gwynn's batting style is true to Ted Williams's formula: "Wait-wait-wait and then quick-quick-quick." Gwynn will "turn" on a ball inside—that is, he will try to pull it. But he prefers to get his hands out and "go the other way," to left. He has so much power, even going to the opposite field, that opponents play him deep. And most of the hits he gets are line drives, over the infield or through the hole between short and third. So if the other team plays the outfield shallow on him, he can hit over their heads for at least a double. Late in a close game, especially, Gwynn must be played deep. So he has three different tendencies: Pitch him inside and he can pull; down the middle and he can go up the middle; pitch him away and he will go the other way. Three tendencies almost amount to no tendency. So a team can pitch him away and play him away, letting him do what he wants and counting on defensive positioning to contain him.

In theory, everyone can be contained. "You know how you pitch Mike Schmidt?" asks Jim Lefebvre rhetorically. "Hard fastballs inside, sliders down and away. You know how you pitch Henry Aaron? Willie Mays? Hard stuff inside, soft away. You know how you pitch [Willie] Stargell? Hard stuff inside, soft away. You know how you pitch God? Hard stuff inside, then down and away, and if you get it there you'll get Him out. Even though He'll know it's coming. Or at least they say He knows." Lefebvre's point is practical, not theological. It is that hitting is so hard that when a major league pitcher is doing what he wants to do, he is probably going to get you out. So hitting is usually a matter of being prepared to pounce on pitchers' mistakes. "Why worry about that high fastball up and in or that nasty slider low and away? Look for a zone you can handle. Be ready and patient and wait for a better pitch—a mistake. Until there are two strikes. Then it's survival."

Almost every hitter has what baseball people call "a hole in his swing." Often a hitter's strength and his weakness are inches apart. Dr. Robert William Brown, cardiologist (after he was the Yankees' third baseman and before he was president of the American League), once said, "The art of hitting is getting your pitch to hit." Lew Burdette, the Milwaukee Braves' pitcher, said, "I make my living from the hungriness of hitters." He meant that hitters are vulnerable when they will not wait—will not wait for the pitch they can hit.

All pitchers know that most batters look for the fastball and adjust down. Most mortals, that is. Henry Aaron once said, "I never worried about the fastball. They couldn't throw it past me. None of them." That was true, but that was Aaron, he of the phenomenally quick wrists and whippy, thin-handled bat. The strength of those wrists was the serendipitous result of a mistake that could not be repeated with today's coaching of kids from an early age. When Aaron first began playing, and until he signed a professional contract, he did not know how to hold the bat. His mistake was not a matter of mere nuance. *He did not know which hand went above the other.* That is right: He was a right-handed hitter who put his left hand over his right hand on the bat handle. Try it, but try it carefully. You can wrench your wrists swinging that way. You can also develop extra strong wrists by trying to overcome the handicap of swinging that way.

Getting a fastball past Aaron was, as folks said, like sneaking the sun past a rooster. Again, let us be clear about what a fastball is. A 96-mile-per-hour fastball goes from the pitcher to the plate in 0.42 second. The batter has approximately 0.17 second (give or take, say, two one-hundredths of a second) to decide to pull the trigger. Then he has perhaps 0.2 second to bring the bat around. "It's easier to hit a breaking ball than a fastball," says Gwynn with laconic matter-of-factness, "because you get more time to look at it." What exactly is he talking about, "more time"? Even a slow 80-mile-per-hour curveball gets from the pitcher's hand to the plate faster than you can say "curveball." And because hitting is timing and pitching is upsetting timing, a pitcher needs high velocity less than he needs a variety of velocities.

A pitcher with such a variety may be unimpressive—to everyone but batters. Casey Stengel said his slow-throwing Eddie Lopat made it look so easy ("Looks like he's throwing wads of tissue paper") that "every time he wins a game, fans come down out of the stands asking for contracts." However, Lopat was a master at changing speeds and locations. Ray Miller cites Tommy John as an example of what can be done with just two pitches, a little slider and a little sinker, neither of them overpowering. "He'll throw his sinker from 65 miles per hour to 80. One hard, one slow, one in between, so you are saying to yourself, 'Don't get out too soon or your hit is on the ground.' So you stay back and wait and he puts a little bit more on and you wait too long and pop it up." Look, says Lefebvre, drawing his lesson in the dust with a bat handle behind the batting cage one day at the Oakland Coliseum, Tommy John is going to rely on slow sinkers, slow curves and sliders. It would be silly to be looking for fastballs. John wants you to swing at those around the knees, but the ones that start at the knees wind up around the ankles. So look for pitches around the middle of the plate, out and up. But with a Roger Clemens, a power pitcher, look for the middle of the plate, down. If the ball is up, take it.

"The toughest thing to judge," says Miller, "is velocity. Good hitters see the ball right out of your hand. They recognize a breaking ball or fastball immediately." That is why a change-up is effective. As soon as the batter recognizes a fastball he still has a second order of uncertainty: What kind of fastball? What is important in a change-up, says Miller, is "the speed of your arm after the ball leaves your hand. That's what convinces the batter." Before a pitcher gets to the major leagues he tries to throw what the batter is not looking for. Once in the major leagues no pitcher can be said to know his craft unless he knows how to get a hitter in a situation in which the pitcher knows what the hitter is looking for and can give it to him— with something taken off or added. Miller gives the example of using a "BP fastball," meaning a slow, batting practice fastball. You have a two-run lead but there is a runner on second, Canseco is up. A mixture of 90-plus-mile-per-hour fastballs and breaking balls brings the count to 3–1. Canseco knows he's the potential tieing run and that the pitcher does not want to risk walking him with a breaking ball. That would bring up McGwire, who is as menacing as Canseco. "Now, with the same delivery that you've been throwing a 91- or 92-mile-per-hour fastball, you throw an 80-mile-per-hour fastball on the outside part of the plate. The same motion but you just don't 'finish' the pitch, you just kind of kill it. Canseco starts for the hard one, he reaches for it but has to slow down a bit. He hits a fly ball and yells at you, 'Throw the damn ball!' That's what pitching is all about, the deception of speed."

Remember, that is why good hitters like Gwynn are prepared to take a few pitches to gauge velocity, even at the cost of finding themselves behind in the count. They have such confidence in their skills that they think the information they gain more than makes up for their reduced margin of error.

"Early in the game," says Gwynn, "I want to see a few pitches. I want to see what kind of velocity he's got on his curveball. But later in the game I go up hacking." Because deciphering the velocity, and hence the probable movement, of a pitch is so important in batting, it can be extremely useful for a batter to know in advance—before the ball is released—what kind of pitch is coming. Give a Ruth or a Mantle that kind of information and the batter-pitcher confrontation becomes a mismatch. There is a famous story of Babe Ruth noting that a particular pitcher bit his tongue when throwing a curve. Mickey Mantle, who was an extraordinarily acute observer of pitchers' mannerisms, saw that Camilo Pascual had two different mannerisms with his mouth when throwing two different pitches.

Kubek remembers that in 1961 Bob Turley hurt his arm and was going to go home and have surgery, but manager Ralph Houk told him to stay with the team and continue doing what he did so well. Turley was a master at reading the movements of opposing pitchers and calling the pitches that were coming. He called the pitch that Roger Maris hit for his 61st home run. That is, he signaled to Frank Crosetti, the Yankees' third-base coach, who passed a sign to Maris, who, as a left-handed hitter, was facing Crosetti. "Turley said, and I believe him," Kubek recalls, "that he could watch any pitcher in baseball—this was before we used tapes much—and pick up his pitches. He would watch the way the pitcher held the ball in one way and then another, moving from one spot on the rubber to another, the way the catcher moved, always something. Maris didn't like it until Turley proved that he was 99.9 percent accurate. Turley claims he called the pitch on 100 of Mantle's home runs." Turley would whistle when a fastball was coming. Silence meant a breaking ball.

It may seem odd but it is the case that Gwynn does not want the sort of help that Turley provided the Yankee hitters, or that runners on second stealing signs provide to hitters on many teams. Gwynn's explanation for not wanting advance information is not convincing: "You're not going to hit with runners on base all the time. You're going to have to go up there sometimes on your own." True, but one does not normally spurn occasional help merely because one can not have constant help. Some hitters, Gwynn says, watch how a pitcher grips the ball and then watch to see if he moves his hand in a way that indicates he is changing his grip when the ball is hidden in the pocket of his glove. Gwynn pays no attention to that either. The real reason he does not want such information about what is coming at him from the pitcher's hand is that he has an interesting intuition about the delicate mental equipoise that is needed for hitting. He has so much confidence in his muscle memory, he believes that his best chance of hitting the ball is when he sees it leave the pitcher's hand and reacts. His ability to see it depends on work done—with batting machines, with videotape—before he gets to the plate. His reaction depends on his analysis of what this particular pitcher does. That is enough. If he does his work well prior to coming to the plate, he does not need what he can not always rely on—information about the particular pitch that is coming.

"I don't understand how anyone hits a baseball," says Ray Miller. "You play golf and the damn thing is sitting there and all you've got to do is hit it and that's hard enough." It is amazing that batters have as much confidence as they do. Confidence is a sometime thing; it comes and goes. A batter who has it probably has it because, as batters say, he is "seeing the ball well" at the moment. As Red Schoendienst was in July, 1950. The 1950 All-Star Game in Chicago's Comiskey Park was won, 4–3, by the National League when the Cardinals' Schoendienst hit a home run on the first pitch of the fourteenth inning. Late in the game Schoendienst, sitting in the dugout next to Duke Snider, said, "See that guy in the red sweater in the third row of the upper deck in left field? If I have to hit right-handed, that's where I'm going to put it." His home run landed two feet away from the red sweater.

When batters are hot they say they are "in a groove." Again, listen to the common, natural language of a craft. It tells what it feels like on the rare occasions when everything feels right. A groove is something especially smooth, a path that guides movement effortlessly. To be in a groove is to have all one's "mechanics" flowing together. "Mechanics" that flow? No, to be in a groove is not to be mechanical, it is to be animal, with the grace that only something living can have.

Batters become obsessive about good "grooves" once they get into them. In 1961, when Roger Maris was chasing Ruth's record, he batted behind Tony Kubek and generally put his back (left) foot in the same spot in the batter's box that Kubek dug with his foot. If Kubek changed his position even slightly, Maris would come back to the dugout after batting and ask why. It is obvious—the evidence is in the box scores—when a batter is in a groove. Some opponents will try to dislodge him from his groove. "There are," says Cal Ripken, Jr., "a lot of mind games involved in baseball, for example against a batter who is hot. I learned this the hard way. In 1987 I was hot as anything for a while, hitting home runs and with a high average, driving in runs. So in one game in California Ruppert Jones of the Angels hits a double, gets to second and says to me, 'Gosh, you're swinging the bat great. You're not taking any bad swings, your hands are out front, away from your body—you look great, keep it up.' Now, I'm someone who diagnoses every bit of information. I say to myself, 'That must be it. My hands are out away from my body.' So the next time up the first thing I think about is 'Where are my hands?' I went into a slump."

Gwynn reduces the mystery of hitting to five words: "See the ball and react." However, reacting correctly is the result of constant preparation—and of thought, before the batter comes to the plate and while he is there. Now, it may seem absurd to say that thinking has much to do with an action involving episodes measured in hundredths of seconds. Branch Rickey, who had as full a head as has ever been put in the service of baseball, said: "Full head, empty bat." He had a point. There are limits to how much cerebration can go into hitting. And some entire teams are more free-swinging and less thoughtful than others in their approach to hitting. Lefebvre says that Dave Parker, who spent his glory years in the late 1970s with the Pirates, "had the old Pirates' philosophy of hitting: Anything white and moving, swing at it—that includes paper wrappers blowing across the infield." But over time, and a season is a long time, it pays to pay attention. Bill "Spaceman" Lee, the Red Sox pitcher from 1969 to 1978, once said, "When cerebral processes enter into sports, you start screwing up. It's like the Constitution, which says separate church and state. You have to separate mind and body." In the seventh game of the 1975 World Series, Lee served up an off-speed pitch to Tony Perez, a deadly off-speed hitter. Lee practiced what he preached. Perez's team won the Series.

———◆———

In 1988 Gwynn won his second consecutive batting title and was thoroughly disgusted with himself. His average fell 57 points from the 1987 high. His .313 in 1988 was the lowest average to win the National League title in history, below the .320 of the Giants' Larry Doyle in 1915. In the previous 112 years of the National League, only 9 batting leaders fell below .330. The average winning average over 113 years was .357, and for the 25 years ending in 1988 the average average was .343. But in 1988 Gwynn batted 119 points higher with runners on base (.382) than he did with the bases empty (.263), the largest differential in the National League. His season average was hardly bad and was, of course (we should not lose sight of this just because he does), better than anyone else's in the National League. It was especially impressive, and a tribute to the use he makes of his mind, because in 1988 his body was a problem.

Better men than I have tried and failed, with persistence and wheedling, to wrest from Gwynn an admission that his 1988 injuries hurt his hitting. He is adamant in insisting that they did not, that his problems were bad "mechanics" and, in fact, some sort of moral failure on his part, a failure to just do his job right. I believe that he believes what he says, and that he is mistaken. Even during the last three months of 1987 he had a finger that would lock when he closed his hand around the handle of the bat. It would come open just enough to allow the bat to slide out of his grip. This, remember, was while he was hitting .370. In 1988 his physical problems were much worse.

After Spring Training started he had surgery on his left hand. He was back in the batter's box a week before Spring Training ended but began the season slumping, with (for him) appalling 0-for-9 and 0-for-11 episodes. After 13 games he was hitting .243 and was so beside himself that he once complained so vigorously about a called third strike that he was ejected from a game, his first ejection in 781 games. Next, he tripped rounding first base on the Pittsburgh carpet, severely sprained his thumb and had to sit (well, squirm) on the disabled list for 21 days. On June 13 he was hitting .237. Then the Padres' new manager, Jack McKeon, who had replaced Larry Bowa in May, took Gwynn's mind off his troubles by giving him a new one.

He shifted Gwynn from right field, where he had won two Gold Gloves, to center field. Five minutes after McKeon asked Gwynn to make the shift Gwynn was taking fly balls in center, but he was not a happy camper. Not happy, but well married. His wife, Alicia, gave him a talking-to.

Remember George C. Scott at the beginning of the movie *Patton?* As Patton, Scott tells his troops that you do not win wars by dying for your country, you win by making your enemies die for their country. Alicia suggested that instead of feeling sorry for himself he should concentrate on making pitchers feel sorry for themselves. Good idea. In July he hit .406. He hit .367 in the last 73 games of the season. He tied Pedro Guerrero for the league's highest average with runners in scoring position, .382. In spite of the pain (he had a sign "The finger is fine" in his locker to move the media on to another—any other—subject) and missed games of 1988, his career has been a model of consistency, the virtue he values most. Over the seasons 1984–89 he ranked among the top five hitters in all of baseball in hits, average, on-base percentage and fewest strikeouts.

In this game of fractions of inches and tenths of seconds, it is amazing what players can do while in pain from injuries—or from excesses. One fact is often forgotten: Playing baseball often hurts. In 1964, at age 22, Tim McCarver won a World Series ring. After he retired in 1980 he had a jeweler build a nodule inside the ring, on the bottom, to make the ring, in effect, a few sizes smaller. This was necessary because his hand had shrunk when it stopped taking the constant trauma of stopping major league pitches. And that trauma was just the result of normal playing. Consider some abnormal physical problems.

Gerald Astor of the Hall of Fame library notes that Ty Cobb "one morning had his tonsils removed in a Toledo hotel room (by a doctor who shortly took up residence in an insane asylum) and that afternoon played in an exhibition game, although his throat bled for three weeks." When Mickey Mantle, star running back for Commerce (Oklahoma) High School, was diagnosed with osteomyelitis, a doctor predicted eventual amputation of a leg. Tony Kubek recalls that in 1961 Mantle, who that year hit .317 with 54 home runs and 128 RBIs, frequently had to be pulled from cabs by companions, so stiff were his legs. Once when Johnny Bench sustained a foot injury so serious that even he was willing to notice it, the doctor administering the X-ray discovered three healed bones that had been broken without Bench noticing. He played 1,744 games at catcher. Assume 120 pitches a game, plus warm-ups before each inning plus Spring Training. That is a lot of squatting. His knees became so stiff it would take him 15 minutes to become fully ambulatory after the team plane had landed. He quit after 17 years because "I want to be able to walk when I'm fifty."

Late in Carl Yastrzemski's 23-year career his Achilles tendons became so damaged that he had to tape his calves and ankles so tightly that his feet became numb. At that time he told Tom Boswell, "I actually have to look down to see where my feet are in the batter's box." When Lou Brock was getting up in age for a baseball player— he was 35—he stole 118 bases, the record until Rickey Henderson topped it by 12. Brock says, "You brace your slide—if you slide feet first—with your hand. Pretty soon the pain is terrible. At one point in 1974 I could hardly hold a glass of water." But he could hold a bat well enough to hit .306.

Ed Linn, the sportswriter who helped Sandy Koufax write his autobiography, recalls the condition of the index finger on Koufax's pitching hand in May, 1962. The finger became numb, then white and lifeless, then a deep reddish-blue, and swelled like a grape, with gangrene about to set in. "In the 8 games he pitched with his finger rotting under him, he allowed 4 earned runs in 67⅓ innings for an ERA of 0.53, struck out 77, walked 20." In this wounded condition he beat Warren Spahn, 2–1 (and hit his first home run). He beat Bob Gibson, 1–0, walking no one. He pitched his first no-hitter, with 13 strikeouts. After winning a 16–1 laugher against the Phillies, he faced the Giants. Linn writes, "When he took the mound he found that the formerly lifeless finger had become so sensitive that when he tried to rest the ball against it, in order to throw his curve, it felt as if a knife were cutting into it. With the Giants fully aware that he couldn't throw anything except fastballs, he had a no-hitter until the seventh inning. He still had a three-hit shutout until the ninth inning when the whole hand went so numb that he could no longer hold the ball." Four days later, in New York, he had a three-hit shutout through seven innings when again he lost his ability even to feel the ball, and had to leave the game. Four days later he started in Cincinnati. Linn writes, "Before the first inning was over, the finger split wide open. No blood. Just a deep cleave in the dead meat." Finally, he was sent home.

Players playing well while injured are admirable. Players playing

off-speed stuff. He'd throw you a change-up 0-and-2 or 2-and-0. But because I've been out three weeks they're going to bust me inside to see if I can turn on a fastball inside." That day Gwynn had done 20 "liners" (running on the warning track from one foul line to another). Then he went into the clubhouse "to do my dumbbells," which he uses for curls to strengthen his wrists and forearms. Then he took some fly balls and batting practice. Then he got back to his avocation: worrying. "The pitch Gooden always gets me out on is a straight-over-the-top hard curveball. He'll set it up with a sequence of pitches, fastball in, fastball out, then he'll come back with something hard inside, perhaps a slider." Gwynn was worried that when he got back to swinging at real pitching he would not be able to "stay back," keeping his hands behind his stride. Standing up in the dugout to demonstrate, Gwynn said, "If I take my stride and my hands come with me, I'm not going to hit it, at least not hard. I have nothing left. That's what it means to 'get out in front.' You wind up hitting on your front foot, hitting with your arms. If I take my stride and push my hands back, I'm all right."

He does not often feel he is doing things right. When, early in the 1989 season, Gwynn was among the league leaders in hitting and, in his view, hitting poorly, he said, "The biggest problem I'm having right now is much like the problem I had last year. It's that I'm not staying back. Even though the results are there, I'm not swinging the bat the way I want to swing it. I've hit one ball hard to left field out of the 27 at bats I've had." When was the last time he did not think he had problems? "About the middle of July last year." Early summer 1988, about the time he was at Shea Stadium fidgeting through the last days of idleness, was the low point of Gwynn's major league career. He had been injured. He had had surgery on his hand. He had been on the disabled list, and anyone who had to be around him during this time probably was ready to go on such a list. He does not take to idleness. But, then, he had not really been idle. "I had a lot of time to look at a lot of tapes." What he saw on tape was himself hitting well. But what he was living through was a slump of serious proportions for a hitter of his stature. He says he was so embarrassed that if he had not signed a contract with McDonald's (the Padres are owned by Joan Kroc, widow of Ray Kroc, founder of McDonald's) he would have backed out of his endorsement agreement. "I was hitting .240 and was introducing what they [McDonald's] called a triple play: a big sandwich, a super order of fries and a super Coke. So I'd go up to the on-deck circle and people would yell, 'Hey, Tony, how about a triple play?' " At one point he was hitting .237 and was, he says, going to the plate "thinking like a .230 hitter." By that he means "not having an idea of what I wanted to do." Now, what does thinking and knowing what you want to do have to do with the defensive, reactive task of hitting a baseball?

Steve Carlton was famous for going into a trance before pitching. Some batters do a similar thing. They are in something like a trance while hitting. Actually, "trance" is not quite the right word for the kind of concentration involved in batting; that word suggests mental blankness. That is not what Al Rosen, the San Francisco Giants' general manager, means when he explains why he thinks Will Clark, the Giants' first baseman, is someday going "to shoot the lights out"—have a monster season. "When he's at the plate," Rosen says, "the house could burn down and he would still only see one thing— the pitcher." Red Schoendienst, Stan Musial's roommate on the road, said Musial "started to concentrate when he was tieing his shoelaces in the clubhouse."

"Concentration," said a dugout Spinoza (actually, Ray Knight, 1986 World Series MVP for the Mets), "is the ability to think about absolutely nothing when it is absolutely necessary." Concentration, defined as complete mental blankness, is (to put the point politely) quite easily achieved by some players. Gwynn is not one of them.

When Gwynn was struggling ("struggling" is *the* indispensable word in the baseball players' lexicon) in 1988, and denying all the while that his aches and pains had anything to do with his problems, he said that the problem was "just an attitude." A baseball broadcaster once defended a player accused of having "an attitude problem." The player, said the broadcaster warmly, did not have any attitude. Gwynn's attitude problem was too much self-consciousness. "I was going up there thinking about everything—my mechanics, who was pitching, what he threw, where he liked to pitch. I had never done that before. You should have an idea of what guys try to do to you, but when you get up to the plate, all you are thinking about is seeing the ball come out of his hand and reacting to it. Instead, I was thinking, are my hands right, am I striding too long, are my hips opening up too soon?"

This is a lament as old as baseball. Bobby Murcer of the Yankees once explained what it is like being in a slump: "You decide you'll wait for your pitch. Then, as the ball starts toward the plate, you think about your stance; and then you think about your swing; and then you realize that the ball that went past you for a strike was your pitch." Gwynn knows exactly what Murcer meant. "When you're going good, you don't worry about anything mechanical at the plate. You just go up there and see the ball and react to it. As soon as you start to struggle you start worrying about the mechanical part of it, your hands, your stride." And then, particularly if you are a highly driven person, as Gwynn is, you run the risk of becoming paralyzingly aware of your every movement at the plate. Then, says Gwynn, "instead of just concentrating on seeing the ball out of the pitcher's hand, you go up there and start worrying about am I striding right, are my hands . . . whatever. I've talked to Tim Raines, Keith Hernandez—a lot of hitters—and the guys who are struggling say they're out in front and are trying to stay back. The guys who are swinging the bat good say, 'I'm just seeing the ball right now and putting it in play.' "

When batters are hot they are often peculiar. Gwynn's teammate Tim Flannery once had a hitting streak of 14 games that he was glad to have end: "I'm superstitious. I was eating Chinese food and drinking tequila after every game. The streak had to end or I was going to die." Of course, not all batters are peculiar when they are hot. Henry Aaron was more or less hot for a generation and his pulse never seemed to vary. Nothing else varied either. When Lew Burdette and Warren Spahn were Aaron's teammates on the Milwaukee Braves they once examined a bat he had used for half a season. They found that all the dents were clustered on the "sweet" part of the barrel of the bat. Remember the story about Maris in 1961 worrying because Kubek's rear foot was not in precisely the right spot in the batter's box? Maris understandably wanted nothing to change that might change the groove he was in when he hit 24 home runs in 38 games. Imagine the groove Frank Howard was in when, in a span of just 20 at bats in The Year of the Pitcher, 1968, he hit 10 of his 44 home runs.

When batters are slumping they try to be stoical. Baseball encourages a kind of stoicism that would have caused Marcus Aurelius to say (if he had had Catfish Hunter's flair for colorful summation) that "the sun don't shine on the same dog's ass all the time." But in 1988 Gwynn was not consoled by that philosophy, or by repeated assurances from all sides that he would "come around" because he was "overdue" for a hot spell. Those words seemed to suggest that slumps are things beyond anyone's control, to be endured. That is not Gwynn's attitude toward life. He does not like the optimistic fatalism of the word "overdue," and neither do I.

I grew up in downstate Illinois listening to the Cubs on the radio and listening to my father, a professor of philosophy, across the dinner table. I learned a lot from both. When I first fell for the Cubs, in the early 1950s, they were not much. Only a team named after baby bears would have a shortstop named Smalley. Roy Smalley was a right-handed hitter, if that is the word for a man who in his best year (1953) hit .249. From Smalley I learned the truth about the word "overdue." A portrait of this author as a child would show him with an ear pressed against a radio, listening to an announcer saying: "The Cubs have the bases loaded. If Smalley gets on, the tieing run will be on deck. And Smalley is overdue for a hit." That was the most consoling word in the language: "overdue." It meant: In the long run, everything is going to be all right. No one is really a .222 hitter. We are all good hitters, all winners. It is just that some of us are, well, "overdue" for a hit, or whatever. Unfortunately, my father is a right-handed logician who knows more than it is nice to know about the theory of probability. With a lot of help from Smalley he convinced me that Smalley was not "overdue." Stan Musial batting .249 was overdue for a hot streak. Smalley batting .249 was doing his best. Smalley retired after 11 seasons with a lifetime average of .227. He was still overdue.

By early summer, 1988, the great Gwynn slump had made him tentative and unaggressive. "When you're going bad, you don't want to be fooled. You want to see the ball first and then react, instead of kind of reacting to the ball before it is thrown. I was sitting at the plate waiting for the ball to be released before I even made any movement at all. I was starting my stride after the ball was released, which is too late. Normally I start it right before they release the ball—I pick my hands up and get into a hitting position."

In 1988, "No one was throwing me a change-up early in the count. They worked the count to their favor and then tried to fool me with a change-up or a slow curveball to get me out in front [with his weight shifted to his front leg]. Last year I saw a variety of everything early in the count. This year I'm just seeing fastballs in on my hands, then as the count gets in their favor they start taking a little bit off with the change-up or curve away from me." Why were they pitching him differently? His answer implies that the questioner is dim: "Because they were getting me out." Communication throughout baseball is quick and pervasive, so quick adjustments by batters are vital. "They've got scouts everywhere," says Gwynn, trying not to sound persecuted. He was seeing an unusual number of fastballs. "In the major leagues, when they get you out in a certain way, they stick with it. Everyone has a scout watching, and they said, 'They're getting him out with inside pitches, fastballs in. Get ahead of him, then away. . . .'" He sought help from tapes of the 1984 season because that year, with speedy Alan Wiggins on base so often in front of him, he was seeing a steady diet of fastballs. What he saw in the tapes was that in 1984 he had no trouble hitting inside fastballs to left.

"After about a month and a half I said maybe I'm looking for the ball inside too much. They were trying to bust me inside but were getting me out away. I was looking for the ball in. If you are looking for the ball away, you can still react on the ball in. But if you are looking for the ball in and they throw you away, you can't react to it." Your bat can cover the outside and then come in, but it can not start inside and get back out for a pitch away. By the end of the first six weeks he had struck out, he estimates, 25 times and a dozen of those were on called strikes on the outside corner. "I would just freeze on them. Then one day in early July I came out early and had our left-handed batting practice pitcher throw to me. I had just finished watching tapes from 1984 and I got an idea: Look for the ball away and hit it away. I wanted to work on it against a left-handed pitcher because if you look for the ball away on a right-handed pitcher and it comes in on you, it's easier to react on. But off a left-handed pitcher, if you're looking for the ball away and it comes in, it's more difficult to read. I had him throw for about 25 minutes. After about 10 minutes I started picking the ball up and reacting to it."

That night he was 2-for-4 with two singles to left and two ground balls up the middle, balls that, if the defense had not been playing him up the middle, would have gone through for base hits. The middle infielders might not have been playing him up the middle if the scouts' network had not spread the word that he had been trying to pull the ball more than usual. Next, the Pirates came to San Diego and played him like a left-handed pull hitter because they were going to pitch him inside. They, too, had heard the word. They were to see that the word was out of date. "I had six hits against them and five were to left field." Next came the Cubs, also playing him to pull to right. He got seven hits in that series, five of them straight up the middle. "Then came the All-Star break. I did not go down to the cage and hit. I knew I'd found it." In his first at bat after the break he stroked a clean, sharp single to left.

The slump that ended was a normal baseball phenomenon, the result of a delicate maladjustment in a sport very unforgiving of those. The way Gwynn went about ending it was an unusual combination of sweat and high tech. It involved a form of minute and reiterated scrutiny of baseball's component actions that was not possible until recently.

The biggest difference between Triple-A ball and the big leagues, according to Gwynn, is that big-league pitchers are so consistently "around the plate." Of course they throw harder and their breaking balls have better movement, but the most important difference is that "in Triple-A you didn't know whether they were going to throw a fastball on the black [the edge of the plate] or a fastball behind your back. It was easier to hit up here than in Triple-A because the guys are around the plate and you're playing the same guys over and over. So when I came up I made it a point to *watch*—watch guys throw in the bull pen, on TV, everywhere." Gwynn, perhaps more than any other player, has made a full-time job of baseball's watchfulness.

He has a large, sprawling Southern California–style house. Outside is a satellite dish proportional to the house. What would you like to see? he asks. I answer, the Home Team Sports telecast out of Baltimore of the Orioles-Indians game in Cleveland. Click. Whir. And there is Cal Ripken scooping up a grounder at shortstop on the shore of Lake Erie. Rogers Hornsby (his .424 in 1924 is the highest average of the century) not only refused to go to movies, he would not look out train windows, lest the looking strain his eyes. Gwynn will look at tapes for hours. He has one tape of each team. Each tape has all his at bats against that team in the season. He has a tape that should be called "Tony Gwynn, the Movie," featuring all his at bats in the previous season.

Gwynn is, of course, not the only player making use of such technology. Some players even use it during a game. When Lee Smith, the relief pitcher, was with the Cubs he would watch games from the dugout for a few innings and then go to a videotape room. Drawing upon a file of film, he would study the hitters he might face later that day, checking such things as their tendency to swing at first pitches. But that is information that can be contained in a statistical chart. Video machines are more important for batters who are trying to imprint on their mental retinas a pitcher's motions and the movements of his pitches.

Gwynn records on small videocassettes about the size of audiocassettes. They can be played back in an automatic frame-by-frame staccato sequence. To know if he is swinging correctly, he counts the frames from when the pitcher lets go of the ball until his, Gwynn's, front shoulder "opens up"—turns to the right. Gwynn watches as the Cubs' Rick Sutcliffe releases the ball toward the Gwynn on the screen, and as the tape ticks along from frame to frame, Gwynn counts, "There's one . . . two . . . three . . . four . . . five . . . six . . . seven . . . eight . . . nine . . . ten. . . . There," he says with satisfaction at the high count, "ten frames. That means I'm staying on the ball. I'm keeping my front shoulder in and staying back. If I open it up before then, I'm through, I'm out in front." On the swing he has just watched on tape, he drove the ball for a hit. On the next swing, in the next at bat on the tape, he counts ". . . seven . . . eight . . . nine—I'm gone." At frame nine he was too far forward. "See," he says, "instead of going into the ball, I went like"—here he jumps to his feet to demonstrate how his front shoulder turned too soon toward the right side of the infield. That made it impossible for him to attack the pitch, which was a slider running away from him on the outside of the plate. "That's what I was doing for the first two and a half months, all the time." Could he see the problem on film at that time? Yes, but "I didn't need to see it. I *knew*. Because when you start your swing and your front shoulder goes [opens up—turns out], your plate coverage goes." When he was "opening up" too soon, he was losing coverage of the outside of the plate, which is where he finds his bread and butter—the pitches he can drive to left. "When you open your front shoulder you are telling the pitcher that the only pitch you are going to be able to hit is the inside pitch." The inside pitch, which he does not prefer, became the only pitch he could hit, the only pitch in the zone covered by his swing. Pitchers were then pitching him on the inside edge of the plate until he was behind in the count and had to bat defensively, swinging at anything in or on the edge of the strike zone. Then they were getting him out "away." That is, they were getting him out with pitches on the outside part of the plate where his bat, because of his prematurely turned shoulder, could not reach with authority. His small mechanical flaw had restricted him to the kind of pitches he preferred to let pass. Also, by pulling off the ball, his weight had shifted so his swing had no power to drive the ball. He was hitting too much with his arms. For power he wants to be "closed"—his shoulder not yet turned—at the instant the bat meets the ball.

As the tape ticks along through various Gwynn at bats, he occasionally—*very* occasionally—murmurs to himself, "That's a good swing." Asked how many of his swings are good ones, his laughter wells up and he says, "Not many." He means it. "If you get fooled you're not going to have a good swing. If you swing at a bad pitch you're not going to have a good swing." Such miscalculations happen because—and here we are back to the basic fact of baseball life—the pitcher knows what he is trying to do, and the batter is guessing. Gwynn says that happens to him often. Remember, Mike LaValliere says it happens to Gwynn ten times a season.

Fast-forwarding the tape, he comes to an at bat when there was a runner on first, no outs and a 3–1 count, one of McKeon's favorite hit-and-run counts. The Gwynn on tape looked toward the third-base coach and was pleased to see the hit-and-run sign. "It gives me another hole to shoot at," explains Gwynn watching Gwynn. Yes, but a hit-and-run sign may require him to swing at a pitch he would otherwise let pass. Is it worth the trade-off? "It's a *great* trade-off," he says, "because I want to go the other way. If the second baseman is covering [covering second as the runner breaks from first with the pitch], then that's another matter, because I really don't want to pull the ball unless I have to." But what if the runner starts and the pitch is four inches out of the strike zone? "On which half," he asks, "inner half or outer half? If it's four inches off the outer half, it's still going to work to my advantage—I can still reach out and poke it. On the inside half, it's another matter, it's tough to handle. You can't hit that ball in the hole." During the at bat Gwynn is watching on tape, before he gets a chance to act on the hit-and-run sign, the pitcher balks, the runner on first advances to second. Now Gwynn might be required to do what he does not like to do: pull the ball to the right side (to allow the runner to advance to third). But because Gwynn is hot again, McKeon "is going to let me hack." On the next pitch he is fooled by a split-finger fastball. His weight shifts too soon and his front leg is slightly bent. He beats the ball into the ground, toward a spot to the left of the second baseman. However, he was being pitched inside (remember, the word was out, spread by the scouts), and the opposing team assumed he would pull, so the second baseman was shaded to the right. The badly hit ball made it through the infield for a hit and an RBI.

Wearing a loose-fitting white sport shirt, faded denim slacks and Nike running shoes (he has a contract with Nike; all God's children got shoes but Gwynn's children are particularly well provided for), Gwynn sits on the floor of his den in front of a television set from which pours the unmistakable voice of Harry Caray, who broadcasts Cubs games for WGN, a cable superstation. Gwynn is watching a tape of himself at bat in San Diego, but taped from WGN cable out of Chicago. The Gwynn on screen backs out of the box after each pitch and talks to himself, swings his right arm on a flat plane through an imaginary strike zone. (He should watch what he says when talking to himself. Mel Stottlemyre, once a Yankee pitcher, now the Mets' pitching coach, says he used to read Carl Yastrzemski's lips when Yaz was talking to himself between pitches. "If I saw his lips saying 'Be quick, be quick,' I'd throw him a change-up. If he was saying 'Stay back, weight back,' I'd throw him a fastball.")

Gwynn's slump is ending. As the tape rolls through his VCR, the scene on the screen changes to Wrigley Field. There is a crack of a bat on a ball. "There's another hit for Gwynn," exclaims the husky voice of Harry Caray. "Holy cow. That's his seventh hit of the series." The tape resumes with Gwynn's next at bat. "There's another hit for Gwynn. Holy cow." The tape rolls. Another park, another broadcaster. Another Gwynn hit—an RBI double. "Wow," says the broadcaster. "All I can say is wow." The 1987 batting champion is back in the hunt for the 1988 title.

◆

Major league clubhouses vary in their ambiance. Some are relatively (these things are *very* relative) sedate, others give a visitor the sense of having been swallowed by MTV. San Diego's clubhouse in late July, 1988, was on the lively side, and well it should have been. By then the lark was on the wing, the snail was on the thorn, God was in Heaven and all was right with the world because Tony Gwynn was hitting again. His mood was as bouncy as the beat of the music being pumped through the clubhouse. To be precise his mood was as upbeat as it could be within the circle of self-reproach he had drawn around his performance. He had climbed back to .300, but when asked about the possibility of another batting title, he said: "If I win it, it will be nice, but it isn't going to be worth a hill of beans to me. I pride myself on consistency. You might be consistent for three months and win the title but that is not going to make up for those first three months, for me."

He could pinpoint the hinge of the season. "One at bat turned it around for me. It was against Pittsburgh. Bob Walk was pitching. He threw a running fastball away, I stayed on it, drove it to left field, and from that point on I hit the ball well. After that I hit in nine straight games. Eight of them were multiple-hit games. I went from .237 to .277 in eight games, and I knew my thinking had changed because I was going up to the plate and trying to hit the ball the other way. I had been going to the plate knowing they were going to pitch me inside and I'd try to pull it. Before, I'd know they were going to pitch me inside but I'd just wait a bit and inside-out it." In an 18-game streak he had 15 multihit games, batted .513 (39-for-76) and raised his average more than 60 points to .309. During this period the Padres, too, were recovering—from their horrendous start of the season (16–31)—but they were not really pennant contenders. Was it hard for Gwynn to maintain the intensity necessary to pull himself back into contention for the batting title (that he eventually won at .313)? Gwynn's instant answer indicated distaste for the question.

"No," he said with a quiet emphasis. "Last year, when I was going through bankruptcy and the team was in last place, people used to say, 'How did you do it, hit .370?' I said, playing was easy. That is how I got my relief, where I came to have fun. This year has been in some ways more difficult because I have never swung the bat this poorly before. I mean, I had to grow up, too. You get to the point where you feel like you're better than you really are. You go out and have some success, and then you succeed again and again, and then you start to believe that this is what's 'supposed' to happen."

◆

In society, virtue is supposed to be crowned with success. Hard work should produce accomplishments and accomplishments should bring recognition and respect. It does not always work out that way. A sport is a circumscribed area of controlled striving and, in a limited sense, is a model of a good society, where rules are respected and excellence is rewarded. Part of the pleasure of sport is in savoring this sense of a small, well-ordered universe. Of course, sport includes some young men and some not-so-young men who have never grown up, who are self-absorbed, willful, vain and arrogant, as headlong in satisfying their appetites as in their athletic competition. But precisely because competition at the pinnacle of American sport offers many temptations, and because physical abilities can carry an athlete far without a commensurate portion of good character, the achievements of the genuine grown-ups, of whom Gwynn is one, are all the more to be admired.

Once when Vincent Van Gogh's brother asked him how he painted, Van Gogh answered, "I see things that I have conjured in my imagination and in my memory and mind over a long period of time. Then it all just pours out." As we have seen, that is how Gwynn hits. For him, baseball is (to put the point playfully) a combination of muscle memory and cultural literacy. Until coaxed into elaboration, Gwynn takes a severely minimalist approach to explaining his craft. "I just try to see the ball well and hit it." But what he actually does in preparing to play is strikingly at odds with that downbeat description. And it is a refutation—one would hope that by now it is a redundant refutation—of a myth.

There is a myth of the "natural athlete" whose effortless excellence is a kind of spontaneous blooming. That myth is false and pernicious. It dilutes the emulative value of superior performers. It does so by discounting the extent to which character counts in sport. The myth is especially damaging to blacks. Sport has become an especially important arena of excellence—and a realm of upward mobility—for blacks. However, their successes have sometimes been tainted by a residue of racism, the notion that blacks are somehow especially "suited" to physical endeavors. The problem is not only, or even primarily, ideas as half-baked as Jimmy "The Greek" Snyder's ideas about why blacks have been "bred" for sports. Rather, the primary problem is the idea—itself not necessarily connected with any malevolent theory or motive—that nature has been especially bountiful to particular classes of people. The idea that blacks are "natural" basketball players is akin to the idea, now gathering dust in the museum of antique superstitions, that the Irish are natural fighters. (Actually, the Irish so dominated baseball in the early years of this century that writers of the time speculated on their inbred advantages.) The fundamental fact is this: For an athlete to fulfill his or her potential, particularly in a sport as demanding as baseball, a remarkable degree of mental and moral discipline is required.

A great black player received a lot of semi-disparaging praise as a "natural." Willie Mays had just turned 20 when he made his major league debut. His ebullience—his high-pitched laughter, the post-game stickball games in the streets of Harlem—occasioned frequent references to the "childlike" enthusiasm and "instinctive" play of this "natural." Often the condescension was unconscious, but it was nonetheless corrosive. The truth is that Mays was, from the first, a superb craftsman.

Bill Rigney, whose career as a Giants infielder was ending as Mays's career was beginning, unhesitatingly calls Mays the best player he ever saw. Rigney calls Mays the "complete" player and illustrates Mays's total concentration and mastery of the game with this detail: As a rookie, Mays would reach second base and peer in at the opposing catcher flashing the finger signs to the pitcher for one or two batters. When Mays returned to the dugout he would have decoded the signs, reporting, for example, that the second (or first, or third, or fourth) is the real sign, the others are chaff. Mays received much praise for his baserunning "instincts." But again, such praise often is veiled—and not very well veiled—condescension. Mays's "instincts" were actually the result of meticulous work. For example, almost every day of his career he took "second infield"—that is, he took infield practice before the game, after the starting infielders had practiced. While other players were in the clubhouse changing their shirts and relaxing, he was working out at first base. He did it partly to limber up, but primarily to remind himself of where the infielders play on cutoffs of throws from the outfield. Then when he got a hit he could see out of the corner of his eye whether the other team's infielders were where they should be and whether he could take an extra base.

Mays would have had more doubles if he had had less baseball sense: He would have had more doubles if he had not sometimes stopped at first base rather than advance to second when he could have. By advancing he would have left first base empty and tempted the other team to walk the man batting behind him. (That man often was Willie McCovey, who was pitched to often enough to hit more home runs—521—than any other left-hander in National League history.) Mays was so disciplined and confident that sometimes he would not just take a pitch he wanted to hit, he would swing at and intentionally miss a pitch he could have easily hit. By doing so in an early inning he might cause the pitcher to serve it up again in a later inning when it might be especially needed.

Mays was so intense that he periodically came to the edge of physical collapse. Bill Russell, who revolutionized the role of the center, and hence the nature of basketball, once said of the notion that blacks are "natural" basketball players: Then why did I spend ten hours a day practicing on San Francisco playgrounds? Good question. Gwynn is a "natural" who early on chose a hero because of the hero's work habits.

When Gwynn was a boy in the 1960s he would go to Dodger Stadium. He would go early to get a good look at his hero, Willie Davis. Davis exemplified the difference between 1950s and 1960s baseball. He was an outfielder who got twice as many stolen bases as home runs (398 SB, 182 HR). The 1960 White Sox outfield (Al Smith, Jim Landis, Minnie Minoso) had more stolen bases than home runs (48 to 42). In 1980 five teams' outfields had more stolen bases than home runs. In fact, in 1980 American League outfielders (with the Athletics' trio of Rickey Henderson, Tony Armas and Dwayne Murphy stealing 131 bases and hitting 57 home runs) averaged more stolen bases (13.3) than home runs (13.1).

Davis was Gwynn's hero because Davis was black, left-handed and "aggressive but under control." He admired the way Davis took infield practice. Unlike many established stars whose actions during practices were perfunctory, during infield practice Davis "always went all-out, he'd charge the ball, he'd come straight over the top [with throws], but"—and here comes the key phrase again—"he was always under control. Being aggressive at the plate means attacking the ball. Doing it under control means not going out to get the ball, letting the ball get to you, not trying to hit the ball out in front of the plate." Gwynn admired Davis's work habits. "It was the way he did his business every day." There it is again, the recurring sense of baseball's everydayness, which drives Gwynn in his pursuit of consistency.

There is a fine and sometimes fuzzy line between admirable intensity and disfiguring obsession. Once when the Cincinnati Reds' plane hit severe turbulence Pete Rose turned to a teammate and said, "We're going down. We're going down and I have a .300 lifetime average to take with me. Do you?" No jury would have convicted the teammate if he had strangled Rose, but if he had, the world would have lost a striking specimen of a man utterly defined by his vocation—perhaps too much so. The melancholy example of Rose shows that people with particularly narrow tunnel vision have no peripheral vision for adult responsibilities. However, the grand example of Gwynn is a refreshing reminder that a passion for excellence need not be disfiguring. Gwynn, who had the example of Willie Davis, is in turn an example to his peers, and to the rising generation of players.

In 1989 there were approximately 22 million American boys aged 6 to 18. Approximately 600,000 young Americans played on organized baseball teams. In addition, there were 40,000 college players and 6,000 in the minor leagues. Fewer than 1,000 men played in major league games. Only one-fourth of them had at least five years of major league experience. It has been calculated that the odds of a boy becoming a major league player are more than 100,000 to 1. The odds of the boy becoming an established (five years or more) major league player are about 500,000 to 1. Only about 2 percent of all the players who sign professional contracts ever see the inside of a major league clubhouse.

Only a fortunate few have the gifts necessary to become great athletes. However, no "gift" is sufficient for greatness. Greatness is never given. It must be wrested by athletes from the fleeting days of their physical primes. What nature gives, nurture must refine, hone and tune. We speak of such people as "driven." It would be better to say they are pulled, because what moves them is in front of them. A great athlete has an image graven on his or her imagination, a picture of an approach to perfection.

Stanley Coveleski, who played for the Indians in the 1920s, once said, "The pressure never lets up. Don't matter what you did yesterday. That's history. It's tomorrow that counts. So you worry all the time. It never ends. Lord, baseball is a worrying thing." And Coveleski was a pitcher. Most tomorrows were days off. For Gwynn, the pressure, which comes from within him, is an everyday experience.

Rolling north out of San Diego toward Gwynn's suburban home in a development on a mesa rising above the city, Gwynn inserts the BMW into the flow of freeway traffic and gives himself over to dissecting and deploring his 0-for-4 afternoon against the Astros. "The first couple of times up I opened up too soon. I knew it as soon as I did it. Knepper [the Astros' pitcher] isn't overpowering but he's crafty. He'll throw you a slow breaking ball and then he'll take a little bit off it and throw it again a little bit slower." That is an effective tactic for tantalizing a batter into opening up too soon, turning his shoulders and hips ahead of the arrival of the pitch in the hitting zone. One time up that afternoon, Gwynn bunted. There were runners on first and third, no outs, and the Padres were two runs behind. "Facing Knepper, you can almost bet you're going to get a ground ball. So I figured, why not just bunt the ball, get the run in, move the other runner up, stay out of the double play, and we've still got two cracks to tie it. I thought he'd start me off fastball in, but he started breaking ball in. So when I squared to bunt it, I was trying to bunt it past the pitcher toward second base but I bunted it right to first. All the first baseman had to do was come off the bag and throw to the plate. So I came back to the dugout and Jack McKeon sat me down and said, 'I know you were trying to move up the runners but in that situation go ahead and swing the bat. If you hit into a double play, we get a run in anyway.'"

Oh, well. Tomorrow is another day. Tomorrow Cincinnati will be in town. Gwynn has no tape of the pitcher the Reds will start, but he faced him in Cincinnati and was 1-for-3, a home run. Speaking as though reading a file to himself, Gwynn says, "Right-hander, pretty good fastball, straight over-the-top curveball and straight change—like what I hit out in Cincinnati. Two of the last three home runs I've hit have been on changes." Most of his home runs go to right. "I haven't hit one to left since"—pause—"'eighty-six." He has a good memory but most of what he remembers are problems, such as home runs hit the wrong way.

4

THE DEFENSE

<hr>

Cal Ripken's Information

On the night of July 5, 1989, the Orioles surged to a 5–0 lead midway through the third inning in Toronto. They hung on to win, 5–4. The next morning the box scores in the newspapers included this line in agate type, directly below the inning-by-inning line score: "DP: Baltimore 3, Toronto 1." One of those double plays may have saved the game. It certainly symbolized the Orioles' season.

With Toronto trailing, 5–3, the Blue Jays' Kelly Gruber and George Bell opened the sixth inning with back-to-back singles off the Orioles' starting pitcher, Bob Milacki. Out to the mound went Orioles manager Frank Robinson, out of the game came Milacki, in came relief pitcher Mark Thurmond, up to the plate came Fred McGriff, who, in an earlier at bat, had smashed his nineteenth home run. This time he hit a hard, fast ground ball on the quick new carpet of the Skydome. The ball was headed for right field, far to the first-base side of the infield. Second baseman Billy Ripken, ranging far to his left, fielded the ball, spun counterclockwise and fired the ball to his brother, who arrived at second as the ball and George Bell arrived almost simultaneously. *Almost* simultaneously. The ball beat Bell, shortstop Cal Ripken, Jr., hung in against Bell's hard slide (Bell is big, 6 feet 1 and 202 pounds; Ripken is bigger, nearly 6 feet 5 and 220 pounds) and fired to first to double-up McGriff. Rally killed.

After the third out the two Ripkens ran off the field, same pace, arms held in the same position, forearms cocked slightly above parallel to the ground, eyes straight ahead, looking into the dugout. They ran past their father, the third-base coach. It was just another night on the factory floor for the Ripken men, but it brought the Orioles to the halfway point of the season with a record of 47–34 and a 6½-game lead in the American League East, a lead 4½ games larger than that of any of the three other division leaders.

What else were the Orioles leading in? Not much. Not batting average, not hits, not extra-base hits—not exciting stuff like that. Rather, they were leading in two crucial but, to most fans, boring categories: fewest errors (40), fewest unearned runs allowed. (They also were leading in fewest walks allowed, most intentional walks received, most sacrifice hits, fewest hit batsmen, most triple plays executed [one].) Pat Gillick, general manager of the Blue Jays, said, "Watching the Orioles is like watching a basketball team that's playing well together. Defense is a rhythm, team thing, and everyone's hustling and trying to outdo one another. It's great to watch." No one expected anyone to say anything like that about the 1989 Orioles. The 1988 Orioles had been comprehensively awful in a way that few teams ever have been. The 1989 Orioles were about 400 percent better, and about 80 percent of the difference was defense.

Tom Boswell is right. The 1989 season was baseball's saddest season in seventy years, since 1919, the year of the Black Sox scandal. Wade Boggs was tarnished and Pete Rose was disgraced. Donnie Moore, a relief pitcher, committed suicide, and some friends said he had never gotten over giving up an important home run in the 1986 American League Championship Series. Dave Dravecky of the Giants broke his arm on the mound while trying to make a comeback from cancer—then broke it again in the on-field celebration after the Giants won the pennant. Commissioner Giamatti died. An earthquake shoved the World Series to the periphery of the nation's attention.

However, beginning in the spring, on Opening Day when the Orioles beat Roger Clemens and the Boston Red Sox, and throughout the summer and into the autumn, the Orioles' ups and downs—the unexpected ups, and the downs that never lasted as long as expected—were the sweetest story line in the season. They were in the pennant race entering the last weekend of the season. They were leading the league in not a single major pitching category and their only boasts about their offense were that they were second in walks and third in sacrifice bunts. Yet they finished two games out of first with an offense that outscored their opponents by just 22 runs over 162 games. Why? Defense. The 1989 Orioles made just 87 errors, the fewest in the major leagues. (The 1989 Athletics made 127.) They were the second team in history to make fewer than 90 errors. The Orioles' fielding percentage of .98602 was the highest ever. Good defense—just 38 errors in their first 82 games—propelled the Orioles to the top of their division. Then when the wheels fell off the Orioles' wagon in mid-season, the principal problem was bad defense: 24 errors in 25 games. (The Orioles' slump after the All-Star Game gave rise to one of those What-kind-of-lunatic-thinks-these up? statistics: The Orioles' 5–17 patch tied the 1975 Pirates for the worst streak of 20 or more games by a team in first place the entire time.) Over the last 71 games the Orioles batted an anemic .238 and averaged just 3.8 runs per game. Defense kept them in the race. But over the 162 games it was defense more than anything else that enabled the 1989 Orioles to match the 1967 Cubs for the most victories by a team that lost 100 games the previous year.

On the final day of the 1989 season—the day after the Orioles had been eliminated from the race by Toronto—shortstop Tony Fernandez of the Blue Jays played one inning, then left the game. It was his 140th game, the minimum necessary for him to be credited with the record for fewest errors (6) by a shortstop in a season. (The previous record was 7, set by Eddie Brinkman of the Tigers in 1972.) Fernandez plays all his home games, and thus most of his games, on plastic. In 1989 Ripken played 162 games, most of them on grass and dirt, and made just 8 errors. His final error of the season ended a 47-game errorless streak, the longest of his career. It was only his second throwing error of the season. He led all major league shortstops in putouts (276), assists (531), total chances (815) and double plays (119). In 1989, even more than in his 1983 MVP season, Ripken set the tone of the team, and he did it on defense.

"I was raised to play for the team, not for yourself," Cal Ripken, Jr., says. "When you're not in the race, it makes the last month awful hard." Imagine, then, how hard it is to "play for the team, not for yourself" when the team is like the 1988 Orioles, who were out of the race at the end of the third week of April. No team ever started a season more miserably than the 1988 Orioles. They lost their first 21 games. It is difficult to pick the lowest point in the streak, but it probably came early, in game eight in Kansas City, when the Royals set a club record with seven consecutive hits while scoring nine runs in the first inning. In 1988 the Royals became the first club in 35 years to sweep an entire season series against the Orioles. At the

40-game mark, the Orioles' record was 6–34, the worst record any club ever had that late in a season. The Orioles' record in 1988 was 54–107, the worst record of any major league team in the 1980s. The Orioles had two potential Hall of Famers hitting third and fourth (Cal Ripken and Eddie Murray), and still lost 107 games, the tenth most losses in American League history. The Orioles were 20–61 on the road, the fewest road wins since the 162-game schedule began in 1961. (The 1952 Tigers won just 18 on the road.) The Orioles won fewer games (54) than the Mets won at home (56). The Orioles finished 23½ games out—out of sixth place. By the time the Orioles left the field in Toronto on closing day, 1988, they had compiled progressively worse records for five straight years. Only three other teams have done that, the 1901–1905 Dodgers, the 1932–36 Athletics and the 1938–42 Cubs.

So why, five months later, was that large man skipping—literally skipping, in high bounds—across the Sarasota outfield grass in March, 1989? Because when you have lost 200 games in two years you will try almost anything, even if it makes you look silly. A flexibility and conditioning expert was hired by the Orioles (tell that to an old-time baseball person and stand far back from the explosion) to see if he could help. The skipping person was the shortstop. By Spring Training of 1989, Cal Ripken, Jr., was the only member of the 1983 World Champion Orioles still with the team. By then the Orioles had just two players (both pitchers) over 30 years of age on their 40-man roster and Ripken, then 28, was the team's ranking member in terms of seniority. The 1989 Orioles entered the season with six rookies and twelve players with less than two years' experience. The 1989 Orioles became the first team to get 25 wins and 25 saves from rookie pitchers since saves became an official statistic in 1969. In 1989 the Dodgers had baseball's largest payroll, with a per player average of $850,000. The Orioles had the smallest, averaging about $275,000. (The payroll included Ripken's salary of $2.47 million.) It may have been a bargain basement team, but it was a bargain. Approximately one-third of the way through the 1988 season the Orioles had been 14–42 and 22½ games out of first place. One-third of the way through the 1989 season they were 31–23 and leading the American League East. At that point the Orioles had made just 23 errors, putting them on a pace to break the major league record, set in 1988 by the Twins (playing indoors and on a carpet), for the fewest errors by a team in a season. Orioles infielders had made just 3 errors in May. The catchers and first basemen had made no errors all season. The team had allowed just 6 unearned runs all season. (The Yankees had allowed the Orioles 11 unearned runs in the first three innings of a game the week the season reached the one-third mark.) In 1988 the Orioles were in last place every day of the season. In 1989 they were never in last place and were in first place for 116 days, 98 of them consecutively. By August 1, after 103 games, Orioles pitchers had just 6 complete games. The truth was that the pitching was barely adequate. But the defense made it satisfactory. What made the defense special was the speed of the new players, supplemented by adrenaline. "When you've been around seven or eight years," said Ripken in 1989, his eighth season, "you might think twice about making a diving catch on gravel and sliding into the wall. But at this stage of our young players' development, they don't think about it." Ripken, who will be 29 on Opening Day, 1990, is hardly elderly, even by baseball's standards. But in a sense, he has about 29 years of baseball seniority.

Talk about the fruit not falling far from the tree. Cal Ripken, Jr., was raised in Aberdeen, Maryland, site of the U.S. Army Proving Ground, where tanks and other large things are tested for toughness. But in another sense he was born into baseball, into the Baltimore Orioles' organization.

Cal Ripken, Sr., smokes Lucky Strikes and drinks Schlitz beer. The Luckies are not filtered and the Schlitz is not light. He is a former minor league catcher who looks like something whittled from an old fungo bat. When tanned, his skin is the color of a new baseball glove, but it has the wrinkles and creases of one that's seen a lot of hard use. Any reader of John Tunis's boys' books knows that a short, scrappy former catcher should be "bandy-legged." Cal, Sr., is. He played in Phoenix, Arizona; Wilson, North Carolina; Pensacola, Florida; Amarillo, Texas; Fox Cities, Wisconsin; Little Rock, Arkansas; Leesburg, Virginia; Rochester, New York; Aberdeen, South Dakota. He played in 9 towns in 8 years. He managed in 9 towns in 14 years: Leesburg, Virginia; Appleton, Wisconsin; Aberdeen, South Dakota; Tri-City, Washington; Miami, Florida; Elmira, New York; Rochester, New York; Dallas–Fort Worth, Texas; Asheville, North Carolina.

When Willie Mays was six months old his father taught him to walk by enticing him with a rolling baseball. Cal, Jr.'s, childhood was like that, only more so. He was always around ballparks. Jim Palmer, who at the end of his career was playing with Ripken, remembers the three-year-old Ripken gamboling at the Aberdeen, South Dakota, ballpark in 1964. Ripken remembers, "I had the luxury of taking ground balls with Belanger when I was 14 years old, and asking him all kinds of questions."

"The game," says Tony Kubek, "lends itself to sitting around." Kubek played near the end of the railroad era, when the Yankees still took 30-hour train trips from New York to Kansas City. Thirty hours in close confinement with Casey Stengel was a learning experience. So was learning baseball at the side of the likes of Mark Belanger. Belanger's confidence in his fielding was such that (so says Tony Kubek, a less confident shortstop) he did not wear a protective cup. So the teenaged Ripken was taking tutorials from a master.

Belanger taught him, for example, that on an attempted steal, when you are straddling second base waiting to receive the throw from the catcher, don't reach out for the ball. Let it come to you because you can't pull your glove back to you as fast—say, 80 miles per hour—as the thrown ball is moving. Anyway, says Ripken, because Belanger was so quick with the tag, he got a lot of calls from umpires who could not tell on a bang-bang play whether he actually tagged the runner. "When I was 17, Belanger told me some things I was too young to absorb. For example, when you have a lead, and one out is enough, you can play a deeper double-play depth. Perhaps you will miss a double play you might have had playing at the regular depth, but you will get to some balls you might not have reached at regular double-play depth. And you cut the trailing team from nine down to eight outs remaining. Similarly, when you absolutely must have a double play—say, tie game, eighth inning, one out, runners on first and second, fast runner at the plate—there is a shallower-than-usual double-play depth."

There never has been more of a baseball boyhood than Ripken's. And there are few, if any, better baseball towns than Baltimore. It is a blue-collar town with a tradition of making steel and sausages and baseball teams from scraps. Good teams, too. Several of them. It is arguable that Baltimore deserves to be thought of as America's emblematic baseball city. To begin at the beginning, there is a bit of Baltimore (Francis Scott Key's song) at the beginning of every baseball game. And back at the beginning of big-league baseball, Baltimore was a nursery of greatness.

In the early 1890s the Orioles of John McGraw, Wilbert Robinson and Willie Keeler were one of baseball's best teams. After the 1902 season, $18,000 was enough to cause the Orioles to move to New York and become the Highlanders. In 1906 the name was changed to the Yankees. But the Yankees did not really become the Yankees, the Yankees as they are remembered, until 1920. Then they acquired Baltimore's greatest gift to baseball, by far the largest figure in the history of American sport, George Herman Ruth.

He was the product of a Catholic institution for orphans and other needy children (its second most famous alumnus was a Jewish singer, Al Jolson). He was brought into organized baseball by Jack Dunn, owner of the Orioles franchise in the International League, at a time when the difference in the caliber of baseball played in the major leagues and the high minor leagues was not as great as it is today. (Dunn once built a fence for a West Virginia club as payment for the contract of a young pitcher named Lefty Grove.) In Ruth's first appearance in Baltimore as an Oriole he pitched in an exhibition game against the Brooklyn Dodgers. In his first at bat he hit a long fly that was run down by the Dodgers' right fielder, Casey Stengel. In Ruth's second at bat Stengel played deeper, and Ruth tripled over his head.

Even after Ruth was sold to the Red Sox, the Orioles won seven consecutive International League pennants, from 1919 through 1925. Nearly thirty years later major league baseball came back to Baltimore with the first move of an American League franchise since 1902. The franchise that moved in 1954 was the one that had moved in 1902. Before that season, after just one season in the league, the Milwaukee franchise moved to St. Louis and became the Browns, baseball's most consistently awful team.

Through 52 seasons (1902–53) they finished in the second division 40 times. They were more than 1,000 games under .500 (3,416–4,465, .433). They finished second in their first season in St. Louis, and again in 1922. They did not finish that high again until they won their only pennant, in 1944, when most of America's able-bodied athletes were fighting the Axis. After George Sisler's 12 seasons hitting .344 for the Browns, their most famous players were a one-armed outfielder, Pete Gray, who hit .218 in 77 games in 1945, and a 3-foot-7, 65-pound midget, Eddie Gaedel, who batted once, in 1951.

In Baltimore the franchise that had been a jalopy became a Rolls-Royce. The Orioles' record from 1954 through 1988 was 2,972–

2,557, .538, with winning records against all but three teams (Red Sox, Indians, Yankees). In their first 35 years at Thirty-third Street, through 1988, the Orioles finished first 8 times and won 6 pennants and 3 World Series. They were runners-up 8 times and finished in the first division 21 times. In their first 32 years in Baltimore, until 1986, the Orioles never finished last. From 1960 through 1985 they had only two losing seasons, and were 625 games over .500, an average of 24 games over .500 for 26 seasons. The Orioles' 18 consecutive winning seasons from 1968 through 1985 was the second-longest winning streak in history, surpassed only by the Yankees' 39-year run from 1926 through 1964. (In professional baseball, football and hockey, the franchises with the most consecutive winning seasons are the Yankees, 39 [1926–64]; Canadiens, 32 [1951–83]; Bruins, 22 [1967–89]; Cowboys, 20 [1966–85]; and Orioles, 18 [1968–85].) In the 18 seasons from 1966, when they swept the Dodgers in the World Series, through 1983, when they beat the Phillies in 5 games, the Orioles had a .590 winning percentage and won 6 pennants. It was one of the best long-run performances by any franchise. In the 6 seasons from 1966 through 1971 the Orioles won 4 pennants. In the 9 seasons from 1966 to 1974 they finished first 6 times. In 1969, 1970 and 1971 they became the third major league team in history to win 100 or more games in three consecutive seasons. They won division titles by 19, then 15, then 12 games and swept the first three American League Championship Series (which, at the time, were best-of-5 events) in 3 games each time, twice over the Twins and once over the Athletics.

The Orioles of 1969–71 rank with the best teams in history: with the 1927 Yankees of Ruth and Gehrig; with the 1929–31 Athletics of Jimmie Foxx, Al Simmons, Mickey Cochrane and Lefty Grove; with the 1976 Reds of Johnny Bench, Pete Rose, Tony Perez and Joe Morgan; with the 1952 Dodgers of Roy Campanella, Jackie Robinson, Duke Snider, Gil Hodges and Pee Wee Reese; and the 1961 Yankees of Mickey Mantle, Roger Maris, Elston Howard and Tony Kubek. The Orioles had three Hall of Famers, Frank Robinson and Brooks Robinson, and Jim Palmer. Paul Blair was one of the best defensive center fielders since Tris Speaker. The right side of the infield had Boog Powell and Davey Johnson. The Orioles had three 20-game winners (Palmer, Dave McNally and Mike Cuellar). The 1971 team became the second team in history to have four, with Pat Dobson joining the list.

Over a span of 31 seasons, 1957–87, the Orioles had the best record in the major leagues. In the 24 seasons from 1960 (the year Cal Ripken, Jr., was born into the Orioles organization and the year they almost won their first pennant) through 1983 (Ripken's second season and the year they won their third World Series) the Orioles dominated baseball as it has rarely been dominated. They were 612 games over .500 (2,206–1,594, .581). They had a 99½-game edge over the second-best team during that span, the Yankees. The Orioles won 100 games in 1980 but finished 3 games behind the Yankees. That year 249,605 attended a 5-game series with the Yankees at Memorial Stadium, the largest attendance for a single series in major league history. (In 1935 the Browns drew 80,922 for the whole season.) Even in the 5 years of decline, 1984–88, the Orioles' annual attendance averaged 1.93 million. In 1988, in spite of the stumbling start, in spite of the staggering finish, in spite of a season-long trough between those two troughs, in spite of losing 7 home dates to rain, the most in the major leagues, the Orioles drew 1,660,738, more than 7 other major league clubs. It was the fourth-highest attendance for a team losing 100 games, surpassed only by two early seasons of Mets mania (1965 and 1967) and the Toronto Blue Jays in 1977, the first year of that franchise.

In 1992 the Orioles will begin playing in a new ballpark in downtown Baltimore, hard by the B&O railroad tracks. (A Hall of Famer who went from Baltimore amateur leagues directly to the Tigers—Al Kaline—developed his strong right fielder's arm by throwing rocks at the "O" on the passing B&O freight cars.) Center field in the new park will be located approximately where, from 1906 to 1912, there was a saloon operated by George Ruth. He lived there, on the second floor, with his wife, Katherine, and their son, George Herman. The son probably played ball in the street—in what will be center field. That was one of five locations for the senior Ruth's businesses between 1902 and 1916. After 1912 he ran the Columbia Harness Company at a location where, in 1992, there will be crowds sitting in the new stadium's seats along the third-base line. Father Ruth's partner was listed as "Ruth, George Herman, junior, ball player." That is the first known reference to Babe as a ball player.

Babe Ruth, who was as rambunctious an individualist as ever caroused across America, represented baseball's individualist side. His speciality was baseball's supreme act of solitary achievement, the go-it-alone blow, the home run: Do it quickly, with one swing of the bat. Defense is baseball's collective, team side. The individualism of baseball has been called (by the *Chicago American* in 1906) the source of American military success. The paper editorialized that base ball (the name was two words until well into this century) "is one of the reasons why American soldiers are the best in the world . . . capable of going into action without officers."

It has been said that baseball exemplifies a tension in the American mind, the constant pull between our atomistic individualism and our yearning for community. Baseball is a team game in which the episodic action begins by repeated confrontations between two individuals standing alone, the pitcher and the batter. The spatial separation of the players—every player's action is clearly visible to every spectator—underscores the individualism of baseball. The very fact that there is a "lineup" suggests the one-thing-at-a-time aspect of the game. But baseball is really always a one-against-nine game, and if the batter has one or more teammates on base, there are two (or three, or four) against the nine. Batters and base runners affect and help one another. And to understand defensive play is to recognize that there is no simple batter-against-pitcher confrontation. The batter is working against a pitcher who is thinking and acting with eight other players.

Bart Giamatti characterized baseball as "an individual sport that you play as a team member." It is not a team sport in the sense that football is. In football, 11 men move in an assigned pattern on a prearranged signal. Baseball, however, is most like a team sport on defense, when a full team is on the field. Then it is more of a team sport than most fans realize. If a team on defense is doing its job correctly, all nine men are playing as a team on every pitch. This playing as a team may not involve nine discernible movements. Indeed, it should not. Playing together should not reveal too much. Some, even most, of the playing together can only be inferred. But imagine taut elastic bands connecting every player behind the pitcher. As the pitcher begins his delivery, every player should impart some slight change in the tension of the band, a change that would radiate through the team. Most of the change would be a slight movement, or leaning, denoting the essence of defensive play—anticipation.

There is in baseball an ugly synergism and a lovely synergism and it sometimes seems that there is not much in between. When some aspect of a team's play goes sour, the sourness is contagious, making other aspects sick. And when something goes well it makes ailing things get well. Bad hitting, for example, makes pitchers press, lose concentration and confidence, aim the ball, bollix up their mechanics. All this happens because they go to the mound gloomily convinced that their team will not score many runs so they must pitch nearly perfectly to win. Bad pitching makes the hitters unable to "stay within themselves." They go to the plate thinking they must score a lot of runs just to stay close. On the other hand, good pitching makes good defense—and, as we shall shortly see, vice versa. The Orioles of 1988 and 1989 demonstrated, perhaps in each case more dramatically than ever before, both synergisms, the ugly in 1988 and the lovely in 1989.

The 1988 Orioles hit bottom on Opening Day and stayed there all the way. They were in last place every day. In 1989 the Orioles were the only American League East team that was never in last place for even a day. Still, 1989 was a roller-coaster year. Immediately after the All-Star break the Orioles lost eight in a row, one short of the American League record (held by the 1953 Yankees and 1970 Twins) for consecutive losses by a team in first place. That is the way things go when you have gone as far as defense and adrenaline can carry an otherwise marginal team.

When the Orioles management recognized the extent of the 1988 collapse, they decided to rebuild around defense and pitching. They decided to do so because, as Roland Hemond, their general manager, said, "That's the fastest way to improve." It is fastest because of the particularly powerful synergism between the two. And of the two, defense is primary.

In 1973 Nolan Ryan pitched 326 innings and piled up 383 strikeouts. That means that Ryan himself retired nearly 40 percent of all the batters who made outs while he pitched. If the likes of Ryan were not so rare, sound defense would not be so important. On April 29, 1986, Roger Clemens struck out 20 Mariners. If every pitcher in every game left just 7 outs to be made by the 7 men who play behind the pitcher, a manager could worry almost entirely about what his players do with wood in their hands. It is a mistake to think that the ideal pitching accomplishment would be an 81-pitch game of 27 three-pitch strikeouts. Rather, the ideal would be a 27-pitch game with 27 first pitches put in the strike zone and put in play for outs by the defenders who are paid to make putouts. In 1944 Red Barrett of the Boston Braves pitched a complete game with just 58 pitches— about 2 per out. The people behind him were kept busy. They are supposed to be busy. Ray Miller's credo—"throw strikes, change speeds, work fast"—has, in its unabridged version, seven more words: "Throw strikes, change speeds, work fast *and let everybody else do the work.*"

The pitcher's primary task is to make batters put the ball in play where fielders can reach it. As John Tudor said after he went on a 20–1 tear in 1985, "If I can't throw strikes and let Ozzie [Smith] and Willie [McGee] catch 'em, then I'm beating myself." As Davey Johnson of the Mets says, "We believe *totally* that you pitch in front. Get the first one over. Statistics show that the guys don't hit for much of an average if you are pitching in front. I have told pitchers, I don't care if it is right down the middle. Down the middle for the first two pitches, then move to the corners, and if the count gets even, go back to the middle." Doesn't Johnson worry that the other teams will notice that his teams do that? "Doesn't matter. Your defense is more ready if you're pitching in front. All good staffs are 'strike one, strike two, then go to work.' And if they hit the ball early in the count they haven't had a lot of pitches they could time." That is why Wade Boggs believes he is a better hitter deep in the count. In 1986 the Indians led the American League in errors, in part, Andy Allanson believes, because the pitchers were running so deep in the count with so many hitters that the infielders were losing the edge that a brisk tempo hones. Furthermore, the errors made the pitchers nervous and drained away their aggressiveness, and they began to pitch too carefully. They were afraid to let the batters hit the ball, so they nibbled around the plate, thereby producing more deep counts.

The late Lefty Gomez was making a serious point when he joked that he owed his success to "clean living and a fast outfield." Pitchers, like other players, are paid on the basis of the numbers they put up. The number, other than wins and losses, they care most about is earned run average. It supposedly is the number that comes closest to reflecting the pitcher's pure value—what he does on his own. But a pitcher's ERA is going to rise if, in first-and-third situations with no outs or one out, he gets batters to hit ground balls but his infielders do not turn the double plays. Although Hershiser showed in 1985 that he had special talent (19–3, 2.03 ERA), he was just a .500 pitcher in the two seasons before 1988, splitting 60 decisions (14–14, 3.85 ERA in 1986; and 16–16, 3.06 ERA in 1987). This was in part—in large part—because the Dodger infield was too porous.

In olden times, before the strike zone sagged to the belt, pitchers were praised for being able to throw "the high hard one." A scout once reported to Branch Rickey on an unpromising rookie, "This boy is wild low. He doesn't have enough stuff to be wild high." Today, with the increased emphasis on defense, a sinker-ball pitcher like Hershiser is especially valuable because he pitches down where the strike zone has gone, and in doing so he produces a lot of ground balls. The ideal Hershiser game would closely resemble the 10 major league games in which infielders have made 25 putouts in nine innings. Mike Flanagan, who before going to the Blue Jays pitched for the Orioles when they won two pennants and one World Series, says defense "makes all the difference." The 1979 American League Cy Young Award winner says, "It's the difference between hoping and knowing." When a ball is hit that a good infield would turn into a double play, but the ball gets through for a hit, that "is a momentum-turning play. One or two major plays can make a game. An 11–2 game can come down to one pitch, one play." Or, as Casey Stengel said, "When a fielder gets the pitcher into trouble, the pitcher has to pitch himself out of a slump he isn't in."

Bob Gibson said that the plate's 17 inches includes two dominions: "The middle 12 belong to the hitter. The inside and outside 2½ are mine. If I pitch to spots properly, there's no way the batter is going to hit the ball hard consistently." Listen to Gibson's language carefully. He spoke about pitching the way he practiced it—with precision. So note the words "hard" and "consistently." Gibson was saying that no matter how well you pitch to spots, many pitches are going to be hit, some of them hard. Cal Ripken, Sr., remembers the 1971 Orioles' pitching staff with its four 20-game winners. The pitching was great. The defense was sensational. The four pitchers, Cal, Sr., says, made a lot of mistakes. "If they didn't make mistakes, how did Brooks Robinson get to make all those great plays at third base? They made mistakes that the defense got them out of." From 1968 through 1984 Orioles pitchers had twenty-three 20-win seasons and won six Cy Young awards. It is not a coincidence that the Orioles' pitchers had a lot of Gold Gloves playing behind them. Between 1957, when the Gold Glove awards were begun, and 1988, Orioles won 48, more than any other American League team and second only to the Cardinals' 48½. (How do you win only half an award? By trading a Gold Glove player—in this case, first baseman Keith Hernandez, to the Mets—in the middle of the season.) Brooks Robinson shares with pitcher Jim Kaat the record for the number of Gold Gloves won: 16. Belanger holds the American League record for the highest career fielding average among shortstops who have played 1,000 or more games (.977). Cal Ripken, Jr., considers the truth self-evident: "Defense and pitching go hand in hand. Good defense helps pitching and good pitching helps defense."

Jeff Ballard was emblematic of the Orioles' 1989 season. In 1985 this son of a Montana oil man had left Stanford with a degree in geophysics and a clutch of Stanford baseball records (37 victories, 428 innings, 316 strikeouts). However, he had been only a seventh-round draft choice and his career soon sagged. Bouncing between Rochester and Baltimore his major league record was dismal. It was 2–8 and 6.59 in 1987 and in Baltimore's Plague Year of 1988 his record was 8–12 and 4.40. But in 1989 his record was 18–8 and 3.43, both totals being the best of any Orioles starting pitcher. In fact, his 18 wins were more than any other pitcher in the American League East.

What was the difference? His best fastball was still about 85 miles per hour. In 1989 he came to Spring Training slimmed down and with more stamina, but that was not the difference. The Orioles' new pitching coach, Al Jackson, helped him make two mechanical changes, but they were only part of the difference. Jackson got Ballard, a left-hander, to pitch from the right side of the rubber. That meant that his fastball, which runs away from right-handed hitters, would not run out of the strike zone so often. In 1988 Ballard had been behind in too many counts and had issued too many walks (42 in 153⅓ innings). In 1989 batters would have to hit the ball to get on base. The second mechanical change was to influence where they hit it. Jackson got Ballard to "turn over" his fastball. Now as Ballard released it he turned his wrist, pulling down through the pitch and causing it to stay low in the strike zone. Together, the two changes meant putting the ball where batters would be more apt to hit it, and hit it on the ground. Ballard was a better pitcher in 1989 because he could be more aggressive, coming at the batters, throwing fewer pitches. He was "not afraid of the bat." He was able to let—get, really—the ball be put in play to the Orioles' defense. That was the story of the Orioles' pitching staff in 1989. The staff achieved only 676 strikeouts, the fewest by any major league pitching staff in six years. When you have people who can catch the ball, do not waste pitches and energy on strikeouts. Make the other team put the ball in play.

In June, 1989, sitting in one of the large orange chairs that make the Orioles' clubhouse a strain on the eyes but a testimony to team identity, Cal Ripken, Jr., marveled at the effect the improved Orioles defense was having on Orioles pitching. "It makes them more aggressive. I have been much more busy because of the aggressiveness of the pitching staff. The pitchers say, 'I've got all those people behind me. I'm going to make these guys hit it.' They are not going to think they have to strike out this guy or that guy. It allows the pitcher to focus on the batter's weakness and not worry about defensive weaknesses. Mike Boddicker would try to make the hitter hit a ground ball, or not hit to a certain part of the field because our defense wasn't good in that part. A pitcher shouldn't have to do that."

Ripken says that when Mike Flanagan was traded to Toronto in 1987, he had some mildly embarrassing moments adjusting to life with a good defensive team. "He would give up a line drive or a long fly ball to the gap, and he would run to back up third because he was sure it was a hit. Then he would look up and the ball was being thrown around the horn. Flanagan became much more aggressive, not worrying about where they hit the ball. When he was here [Baltimore], he felt he couldn't make a mistake up [up in the strike zone], because the sluggish Baltimore outfield could not chase down enough fly balls."

Do not try to sell Flanagan or any other pitcher on Bill James's distinction. James says: "Offense is making things happen. Defense is keeping things from happening. People would much rather watch things happen." Actually, James is right, about offense and defense, and, alas, about people. But perhaps people can be convinced that prevention, properly understood, should count as something happening—something interesting, too. Watch Ripken. What's that you say? You would rather watch the pitcher? Watch them both, they are working together.

Every defensive play begins from an act that looks like offense—not to say aggression. It begins when a member of the team playing defense—the pitcher—throws a very hard ball very fast and often close to the batter who is standing not far away. Roger Angell, writing about the pitcher-versus-hitter struggle, says that only boxing has as much hard one-on-one confrontation as baseball. Angell has a point. However, in another sense, it is always nine against the batter. It is commonly said that the pitcher acts and everyone else reacts. That is not quite right. The game does indeed revolve around a 20-foot circle, the pitcher's mound. But Earl Weaver was exaggerating a trifle when he said, "The only thing that matters is what happens on that little lump out in the middle of the field." What is done on that lump depends in large measure on the confidence the pitcher has in his defense, and the reciprocal confidence the defense has in the pitcher's ability to think clearly and execute the correct intentions.

"I like to learn their hitters and our pitchers and cheat a little bit, and cut down the area I have to cover," Ripken says. "I'm not blessed with the kind of range a lot of shortstops have. The way I have success is, I guess, by thinking." Even the quickest player must think ahead because it is too late to think when a hard-hit ball is in play. In 1987 more than 200 players, managers, coaches and general managers were polled on a variety of subjects, including "smartest defensive player." The winner was Ripken. Branch Rickey, the lawyer who was a catcher before he became a savant, was the author of baseball's most elegant aphorism: "Luck is the residue of design." There is design in Ripken's defensive play, and it begins by knowing how his pitchers will try to pitch to particular batters in particular situations.

In La Russa's pithy formulations, defense strategy is "how to pitch them and how to play them." Defense positioning is harder than it used to be. Ray Miller says that as recently as the mid-1960s, 80 percent of all hitters were pull hitters. Today only half a dozen hitters in each league are dead pull hitters. The rest hit the ball to all fields. They may be trying to pull the ball and their bats are slow, but they are so strong they hit into the opposite field. Not all hitters pull the ball, and as the count goes against a hitter, a hitter is less apt to pull. On a 3–1 pitch the hitter can take a full cut. On a 1–2 pitch he has to swing more defensively, protecting the plate.

Tony Kubek says, "You always hear it said, 'Play the hitter.' That's actually about the third thing on the list, or maybe fourth. You play your pitcher, because everyone throws differently. You play the situation in the game. You play the count. For example, 2–0, guys are apt to pull the ball a little more because they're a little more aggressive. The batter gets behind 0–2, he may hit the ball a little late. Every hitter isn't that way. According to [Cardinals manager] Whitey [Herzog], Willie McGee doesn't know if the count is 0–2 or 3–0. Some guys just go up there hacking. You have to know who *they* are."

To illustrate "playing the count," Ripken says that if a runner breaks from first on a 2–0 pitch, the probability is that a hit-and-run has been called, not a steal. Why steal on what may be ball 3? On a 2–0 count the pitcher will be trying hard to be in the strike zone, so the hitter should be able to make contact. Thus when a runner breaks on a 2–0 count the second baseman (if the hitter is left-handed) or the shortstop (if the hitter is right-handed) should not immediately break over to take the throw at second. Instead, he should move in toward the batter so that if the ball is hit he will still be filling what the batter hoped would be an empty hole in the infield. By moving in he will get the ball quicker and still have a chance to force at second the runner who has a running start on the play.

Someday Ripken might not report to work in the middle of the infield. He might go to the corners, to first base or, more likely, to third base, from whence he came to shortstop. On May 30, 1982, Ripken came to Memorial Stadium, got dressed and then glanced at the lineup card to see where he was in the batting order. He noticed a "6" next to his name, indicating his fielding position, shortstop. He thought manager Earl Weaver had made a mistake, had meant to put a "5," third base. But the "6" was no mistake. From that day through 1989 he started every game at shortstop and missed just 31 defensive innings.

Now, there were then, and still are, people—dogmatists impervious to evidence—who say that the "6" was a mistake, that Ripken is too big to be a shortstop. By now they have been shown to be wrong, but they had history on their side.

———◆———

The position of shortstop was an afterthought and an improvisation. It was not created until about 1845. Prior to that baseball was, like the British game "rounders," an eight-man game. Then D. C. Adams of the New York Knickerbockers put himself in the lineup as the ninth man and the innovation was adopted. The name "shortstop" may come from the cricket term "short fielder." In fact, the first shortstops were more outfielders than infielders. They were, among other things, roving cutoff men helping to get the very light (3-ounce) ball back to the infield. When in 1856 the ball was made heavier (5 to 5¼ ounces), most shortstops became infielders. When the heavier ball resulted in an extra infielder, the extra was, more often than not, a light infielder. Until about 1982 the conventional wisdom was that a shortstop should not, could not be constructed along Ripken's lines.

Luis Aparicio is the most recent of those rarities, a shortstop elected to the Hall of Fame. At 5 feet 9 and 160 pounds, Aparicio resembled Pee Wee Reese (5 feet 10, 160), who is in the Hall of Fame, and Phil Rizzuto (5 feet 6, 150), who arguably should be. (The Yankees' Vic Raschi said, "My best pitch is anything the batter grounds, lines or pops in the direction of Rizzuto.") Reese's nickname was "The Little Colonel," Rizzuto's was "Scooter." The prototypical shortstop is Hall of Famer Walter James Vincent Maranville (5 feet 5, 155), known, of course, only as "Rabbit." When great shortstops have not been short they have been skinny, like Marty "Slats" Marion (6 feet 2, 170) and Mark "The Blade" Belanger (6 feet 1, 170). Marion's career batting average was .263 and he hit only 36 home runs in 13 years. Belanger's career batting average was .228 and he hit 20 home runs in 18 seasons. No one built like Ripken has ever played shortstop for long, much less with distinction. Of course the stereotypical shortstop often was not what the stereotype suggested. Rabbit Maranville is regarded as the paradigm of the good fielding, but weak hitting, little shortstop. But he batted clean-up and made 65 errors for the 1914 "Miracle Braves." (Their miracle was winning the pennant after being in last place in July. They won 61 of their last 77 games and then swept the mighty Philadelphia Athletics in the World Series.)

Two changes in the nature of major league shortstops were foreshadowed in the 1950s by two men in Chicago. In 1950 the White Sox gave baseball a glimpse of the future with Chico Carrasquel, a Venezuelan, the first of a long line of Latin shortstops, the greatest of whom was his countryman who followed him to the White Sox— Luis Aparicio. Across town, the Cubs had another kind of shortstop. On Monday, September 21, 1953, the *Chicago Tribune* sports page reported on the previous day's game in St. Louis, which the Cardinals won, 11–6. The second paragraph of the story said: "Ernie Banks, one of several rookies who will challenge Roy Smalley next year for his shaky shortstop job, knocked his first major league homer. The Negro from the Kansas City Monarchs also hit a triple and a single in driving in three runs." He would hit 511 more home runs. There had been many fine-hitting shortstops over the years. One, Honus Wagner, is arguably (Branch Rickey and others have so argued) the finest player ever. (Poor Pittsburgh. Once the home of the greatest-hitting shortstop, in 1988 the Pirates' shortstops got just 16 RBIs, one less than the Pirates' pitchers.) Joe Cronin, Lou Boudreau, Luke Appling and Vern Stephens all were potent offensive shortstops. But until Banks, it had been conventional wisdom that a shortstop, more than any other player, would earn his pay with leather rather than wood. A slugging shortstop like Banks was considered highly unlikely. A slugger would have to be too big to be quick in the field.

However, at 6 feet 1 and 180 pounds, Banks was built like a shortstop, lean and light and nimble. The largest person ever to play shortstop was Parson "Beacon" Nicholson. He was 6 feet 6. But he played only 10 games at short for Washington's 1895 National League team. Before Ripken there were several shortstops who were 6 feet 4, but none played the position regularly. Ripken is the biggest real shortstop baseball has ever seen. However, he rightly insists that he is not slow. Perhaps as a base runner he is on the slow side, but he has baseball quickness. Ripken was an All-State selection in soccer and baseball. His secret love, just behind baseball, is basketball, which he plays all through the winter. "I'm about 6 feet 5, 220 pounds, but sometimes I wind up guarding some of the quickest players on the floor."

He is correct that in the infield it is quickness, not speed, that matters most. Brooks Robinson was painfully slow covering the 90 feet from home to first. But the crucial distance when playing third base is less than 30 feet, and Robinson's catlike quickness made him spectacular at third.

Shortstop is the most important defensive position. (Or, to stop some arguments before they start, let us say it is the most important defensive position in fair territory.) One reason it is so important is that most batters are right-handed and right-handers more often than not hit to the left side of the infield. Another reason is that the shortstop must cover more ground than the second baseman, and must have a stronger arm for throwing to first base from deep in the hole near third. In 1988 the percentage of batted balls put in play to each position was:

catcher	1
pitcher	6

first base	10
second base	13
third base	12
shortstop	15
left field	13
center field	18
right field	12

When baseball people talk about sound defense "up the middle" they mean primarily the middle infielders (shortstop and second basemen) and the center fielder. In 1988 they handled 46 percent of all balls put in play.

Consider the three tables on page 251. The first shows Ripken's defensive numbers for his first six full seasons as shortstop, in all of which he was the starting shortstop in the All-Star Game. The second and third tables give the defensive numbers of the American and National League Gold Glove shortstops in those seasons. The numbers for chances, putouts and assists (his 1984 assist total is the American League record) do not suggest that Ripken has trouble reaching enough balls. What he lacks in range he makes up for in two ways. One is his cannon of an arm that enables him to play deep. On a throw from deep short, Ripken's throws often call to mind Rocky Marciano's knockout punches that traveled about eight inches with devastating effect. Ripken snaps off a throw with a short flick of the arm and the result resembles a line drive. The other way he makes up for having less range than some smaller men might have is by using his head to supplement his legs: anticipation.

Sandy Alderson, the Harvard lawyer who is the Athletics' general manager, says, "The beauty of the game is that there are no absolutes. It's all nuances and anticipation, not like football, which is all about vectors and forces." (You expect that sort of talk from this new breed of baseball executive. Alderson said the Athletics signed the aging veteran Don Baylor because of "the talisman factor." Casey Stengel, call your office. Baseballese isn't what it once was.) Anticipation, to be helpful, requires the predictable execution by pitchers of their intentions.

When Ripken began playing shortstop every day for the Orioles in 1982, Orioles pitchers were so clever and inventive they some-

CAL RIPKEN

	YEAR	G	PO	A	E	DP	PCT.	TC	TC/G	PO/G	A/G	DP/G
Ripken	1983	162	272	534	25	113	.970	831	5.13	1.68	3.30	.70
Ripken	1984	162	297	583	26	122	.971	906	5.59	1.83	3.60	.75
Ripken	1985	161	286	474	26	123	.967	786	4.88	1.78	2.94	.76
Ripken	1986	162	240	482	13	105	.982	735	4.54	1.48	2.98	.65
Ripken	1987	162	240	480	20	103	.973	740	4.57	1.48	2.96	.64
Ripken	1988	161	284	480	21	119	.973	785	4.88	1.76	2.98	.74
		970	1619	3033	131	685	.973	4783	4.93	1.67	3.13	.71

GOLD GLOVE AWARD WINNERS—AMERICAN LEAGUE

	YEAR	G	PO	A	E	DP	PCT.	TC	TC/G	PO/G	A/G	DP/G
Trammell	1983	140	236	367	13	71	.979	616	4.40	1.69	2.62	.51
Trammell	1984	114	180	314	10	71	.980	504	4.42	1.58	2.75	.62
Griffin	1985	162	278	440	30	87	.960	748	4.62	1.72	2.72	.54
Fernandez	1986	163	294	445	13	103	.983	752	4.61	1.80	2.73	.63
Fernandez	1987	146	270	396	14	88	.979	680	4.66	1.85	2.71	.60
Fernandez	1988	154	247	470	14	106	.981	731	4.75	1.60	3.05	.69
		879	1505	2432	94	526	.977	4031	4.59	1.71	2.77	.60

GOLD GLOVE AWARD WINNERS—NATIONAL LEAGUE

	YEAR	G	PO	A	E	DP	PCT.	TC	TC/G	PO/G	A/G	DP/G
Smith	1983	158	304	519	21	100	.975	844	5.34	1.92	3.28	.63
Smith	1984	124	233	437	12	94	.982	682	5.50	1.88	3.52	.76
Smith	1985	158	264	549	14	111	.983	827	5.23	1.67	3.47	.70
Smith	1986	144	229	453	15	96	.978	697	4.84	1.59	3.15	.67
Smith	1987	158	245	516	10	111	.987	771	4.88	1.55	3.27	.70
Smith	1988	150	234	519	22	79	.972	775	5.17	1.56	3.46	.53
		892	1509	2993	94	591	.980	4596	5.15	1.69	3.36	.66

times made playing middle infield a bit difficult. Mike Flanagan developed a "BP [batting practice, meaning slow] fastball," taking a little off his fastball on his own, with no communication with the catcher. Ripken recalls, "Flanagan would play on the hitter's over-aggressiveness. Say it was a 2–0 or 3–1 count. The hitter knows you've got to throw him a strike and assumes it will be a fastball. Flanagan would throw a slightly slower pitch than the batter was looking for. The batter's timing would be off a little bit, which might be the difference between a home run and a pop out. But that made it difficult defensively because you had to put that variable into your thinking. The catcher would put down the fastball [sign] and you would have to decipher from the pattern of pitches—Flanagan did not give anything away in his windup or motion. You could just tell by what he had done in the past."

Ripken had other sorts of problems with many of the pitchers the Orioles had during the grim years before 1989. "Now with young pitchers," said the grizzled 28-year-old at the start of the 1989 season, "they will incorporate the BP fastball into their arsenal before they learn how to pitch. Before they learn how it is useful in the scheme of things, they'll throw it in odd situations, such as with two strikes. That's the worst time to throw it because the batter is more defensive. You're giving him an opportunity to get the bat on the ball when that may be all he's trying to do. You're letting up and he's already defensive. That's the best time to throw your best fastball. But there's no way I can guess with young pitchers. That's when defense is frustrating—when there is a young pitcher with control problems who doesn't know how to pitch."

Kubek remembers the first time he played behind Whitey Ford against the Tigers in Yankee Stadium. "Whitey would turn around and with his eyes would move me toward the center of the diamond when Kaline came up." Ford was going to throw the right-handed Kaline fastballs away and was confident Kaline could not pull those pitches. And Kubek could be sure that the pitch would be put where Ford intended. When Connie Mack had Athletics pitching staffs adorned with the likes of Rube Waddell, Chief Bender, Herb Pennock and Eddie Plank—four Hall of Famers—he became famous for positioning his fielders by waving his scorecard. He knew that his pitchers knew where the ball should be pitched, and that they had the skill to execute their intentions. But there were many seasons when Mack did not bother. Why bother when the pitchers can not execute?

On an evening in May, 1989, the Indians were at Baltimore and had base runners on second and third when there occurred one of those meetings at the mound where cogent thoughts are exchanged and momentous decisions are made. In attendance were pitcher Mark Williamson, manager Frank Robinson, catcher Mickey Tettleton and Ripken. He joined the meeting to learn what was being decided about pitching to the Indians' Pete O'Brien. "I wanted to know if we were going to pitch to him with first base open or try to walk him unintentionally-intentionally. If we were going to throw the ball outside, outside, outside, that would indicate where I would want to play. They said they were going to pitch to him so I asked, 'Going to try to get him out?' [Ripken meant, and was perfectly understood on the mound: Are you going to pitch O'Brien outside but close enough to the outside corner to tempt him to put the ball in play?] That's all I wanted to know." Ripken, remembering his laconic question, laughs. What a difference a year makes. In May, 1988, there was no laughter in the Orioles' clubhouse. And although in 1988 Ripken wanted to know what the Orioles' pitchers were planning, there was such a gap between their intentions and their execution that the information was useless. It was useful in 1989 because the Orioles' pitchers were better. But, again, they were better in part because they had confidence in their defense.

During a game in Baltimore when Oakland had a runner in scoring position, a batter hit a grounder toward Ripken at short. Someone on the Athletics' bench muttered, "Kick it, kick it." Dave Duncan, standing in the dugout, said quietly, "Think what you're saying." It was a nice tribute from a pitching coach to a shortstop who plays in tandem with pitchers.

———◆———

Of course a problem inseparable from intelligent baseball is this: If intelligent behavior on the field is understood by the other team, that behavior becomes valuable information for them. The trick is to behave intelligently but not obviously, or too soon. Roland Hemond became the Orioles' general manager just as I was deciding to write about Ripken. This worried Hemond, for reasons that confirmed the wisdom of the decision. "Cal," Hemond said, "plays the infield like a manager." By that he meant that Ripken is a cerebral player, constantly moving in response to the changing situation, from pitch to pitch, in anticipation of what his pitcher will do, which depends on what the pitcher expects the batter to expect (which depends on what the batter thinks the pitcher expects him to expect). Hemond's worry was that by revealing Ripken's thought processes I would enable opponents to decode Ripken's behavior and make useful inferences about what Orioles pitchers are doing. Before long the book-reading ball clubs (and it is not clear how large that class is) would, in effect, be stealing signals not from the catcher but from the behavior of the large man on the left side of the infield.

Thinking infielders who want to cheat must do so at the last minute, lest they telegraph to the hitter the kind of pitch that is coming. Kubek recalls that Rick Burleson of the Red Sox lacked quickness, so he moved two steps to his right on off-speed pitches to right-handed hitters, and two steps to his left on fastballs—and he moved too soon. He moved as soon as the catcher gave the sign to the pitcher, before the pitcher started his motion. Kubek says that Mickey Mantle feasted on Red Sox pitching during the seasons when Jimmy Piersall was the Red Sox center fielder. Piersall was a fine outfielder but he, too, moved too soon. The Red Sox shortstop would signal with his glove behind his back indicating a fastball (no glove meant a breaking ball). Piersall would move and Mantle would sit on whatever pitch was coming.

Of course an intelligent outfielder can use disinformation against an observant batter. When Tony Gwynn briefly became a center fielder after five seasons (and two Gold Gloves) in right field, he discovered a way to mislead hitters. From center field he could see the catcher's signs, so he would shift "wrong" before the pitcher started his motion, then he would quickly move back to where he really wanted to be. His hope was that the batter would make a mistaken inference from his first move.

Hershiser believes that each player, when his team is at bat, should watch the opponent playing his position—the second baseman watch the second baseman, and so on. "You're the second baseman and you may see that the other second baseman is giving away pitches—maybe he's moving a step on a curveball. Then you let everyone else know. Then the coaching staff doesn't have to do it. Alfredo [Griffin, the Dodgers' shortstop] does this. All of a sudden you'll hear him murmur, 'curveball.' Next pitch, 'slider.' All of a sudden he's got it all right." Gene ("Baseball and malaria keep coming back") Mauch managed the Expos in Montreal's tiny Jarry Park. Mauch stole information by watching the vein in a particular short-stop's neck. Mauch knew that the man used a common, simple signal: Using his glove to shield his mouth so that only his partner playing second could see it, he would either keep his mouth closed, meaning that he would cover second on an attempted steal, or he would open his mouth wide, meaning that the other fellow would cover. If the man's vein stood out, it meant his mouth was open. Tim McCarver played for Mauch there one season and got half a dozen hits by stroking the ball toward the spot that Mauch indicated—always correctly—would be vacated.

The 1920 World Series between Brooklyn and Cleveland is remembered only for the fact that Cleveland's second baseman, Bill Wambsganss, pulled off an unassisted triple play. But something else notable happened involving the other second baseman. Brooklyn's Pete Kilduff scooped up a few too many handfuls of infield dirt. When Burleigh Grimes, the future Hall of Famer, was pitching and the Dodgers' catcher called for Grimes's famous spitball, Kilduff scooped up some dirt to absorb the moisture on the ball that might be hit to him. Eventually the Indians deciphered Kilduff's quirk. Grimes lost games five and seven as the Indians took the Series, 5–2.

The infielders least likely to move in ways that give away valuable information to batters are infielders quick enough to move late. "Quick feet and soft hands." That is Ryne Sandberg's terse summation of the prerequisites for a good infielder. He should know. Sandberg's seventy-second game in 1989 was his one-thousandth game at second base and qualified him to be recorded as the all-time leader in fielding percentage at that position, .989. Through 1989 he had made just 64 errors in 5,889 chances. Between June 10, 1987, and April 29, 1989, he did not make a throwing error, a span of 248 games. He ended the 1989 season on a 90-game errorless streak, having hit 20 home runs since his last error.

Dressing at Wrigley Field prior to playing the Pirates in 1989, while teammates were being put through stretching exercises on the carpeted floor of the clubhouse, Sandberg said something that indicated why he is the standard by which contemporary second basemen are judged. He said he anticipates, but does not begin cheating or even leaning in a particular direction as the pitcher begins his delivery. "I take two steps forward and get into a bent-knees position, balanced on the balls of my feet, ready to go, on every pitch. I believe it's important to anticipate that the ball is going to be hit my way on every pitch." But he leans or moves only after the pitch is on the way to the plate. This is because he has the quickness to wait and watch the flight of the ball to see if it is going where it has been called for. "If I see a fastball and watch the flight of the ball and see that it is high and away to a left-hander, I know he's probably not going to pull the ball." Sandberg often warns the Cubs' first baseman when an off-speed pitch is coming to a left-hander who might pull it. "With Mark Grace playing first, for example, I'll try not to be too obvious, but I'll say, 'Come on, Gracie,' something like that. He will know either a change-up is coming or a slow breaking ball."

Ripken lacks Sandberg's range and has more territory to cover than a second baseman, so he has to be especially careful lest his anticipations become visible, and decipherable. "It's good to get to know a catcher so you can anticipate your movements. If your movements are too extreme, you tell the batter what pitch is coming. Say a pull hitter is up and we're trying to get him out on slow breaking balls, and all of a sudden with two strikes the catcher calls for a fastball away. Suppose there are two strikes on the hitter and we've been giving him a steady diet of off-speed pitches. You know that he's got to wait longer on those pitches, and he's going to look for another off-speed pitch. You know that even a good pull hitter is not going to pull this fastball into the hole [between short and third]. So you want to cheat to your left as far as you can. Now, if you get a good feel for the catcher and you know there's a possibility that he might try to sneak the fastball by on the outside corner, you're not going to be playing as though the hitter is going to pull. But if you've been playing all the way over toward the hole, anticipating the hitter pulling the off-speed pitch, and suddenly you see the catcher call for a fastball on the outside corner, you have to cheat an enormous amount—you have to dead sprint up the middle, and a lot of times you will give away the pitch to the hitter. The farther you have to go, the earlier you have to cheat. If your cheating is not so dramatic, you can go late enough that the hitters can't tell anything from your movement in time to help themselves. A lot of hitters try to look at you but their concentration has to be on the pitcher releasing the ball."

The pace and texture of a baseball game rarely require, and usually will not permit, intense concentration that ties players into knots for two and a half hours. An Orioles coach once said, "In this game it's never going to be third-down-and-one. You don't hit off tackle in baseball and you can't play the game with your teeth gritted. Muscles are fine, but this is a game of relaxation, conditioned reflex and mental alertness." The trick is to be alert while relaxed, or while feigning relaxation, as Ripken does when fraternizing with the enemy.

Ripken is a chatty shortstop, stirring up conversations with runners who arrive in his precinct at second base. But often he is working while chatting. "When they get on base I try to find out what kind of stuff they think our pitcher has. Does it seem to be a hard fork ball, a slow fork ball? Sometimes our pitcher has such a good disguising motion on it, it's difficult for me to tell." Ripken may want to know what the pitches of a particular new Orioles pitcher look like to hitters. "He hasn't pitched enough for me to know whether, with two strikes, batters pull his fork ball or hit it the other way. Right when you start feeling comfortable with a young pitcher he may throw three fork balls to a right-handed hitter and the guy will be out in front of all of them. The hitter misses the first two and fouls off the third and suddenly the catcher calls for a fastball away. You know that this hitter is thinking, 'I've got to wait longer on this fork ball.' So when the catcher calls fastball away, and I know the hitter, I think, 'Okay, I can cheat up the middle.' I know that if he throws a fastball on the outside half of the plate there's no way in the world the batter can pull it. I know he's not going to hit to my right, so I'm going to move to my left." But such anticipation by Ripken is worse than useless, it is injurious if the pitcher can not deliver the particular pitch to the particular spot. "Right when I start thinking this way, and I have confidence that he's going to throw it on the outside half, he'll throw the fastball on the inside part of the plate and the batter will jam it to my right and foil all the plans. Then the next time you just can't cheat."

When base runners arrive at second base Ripken may want to know something other than what the runner thinks about the Orioles' pitcher. "You try to get information, as much as you can. Just to see what they're thinking. If a right-hander hits a ball between first and second, and normally he's a pull hitter, you ask him, 'Did you try to do that?' It gives you an edge if you know he's trying to use the whole field instead of just going up there and seeing the ball and hitting it. If you know he tried to do that, then the next time the situation arises, you remember. Of course you have to decide if you can believe him. A lot of times people won't tell you the truth."

He illustrates this sad commentary on human nature with a story involving White Sox shortstop Ozzie Guillen and Carlton Fisk, the Sox catcher. "Mike Boddicker was pitching and Guillen always pulls

Boddicker. Boddicker was trying to slop him, throwing a lot of off-speed pitches because Ozzie has a lot of movement in his swing. He's a fidgety hitter and sometimes he has a lot of trouble waiting for the ball to get to the plate. He wants to charge out and get it. Now the slower you throw it, the farther he has to go out to get it. So Boddicker has the luxury of throwing his real slow, big breaking ball. When Guillen, a left-hander, gets out so far, the only thing he can do with it is pull it to the first-base side. So I see the breaking ball called and I'm playing him straight up [not to pull] because he hits a lot of balls to left field. I started slowly trying to cheat and right when Boddicker gets into his windup I start running [to my left] up the middle because I'm 100 percent certain that he's going to pull the ball. So what he does is wait and slaps a little weak ground ball to my right and it lazily rolls into left field. You don't feel too good when you get burned. It didn't look good. It made me wonder: Did he try to do that?"

There are ways of finding out. "Players have a way of seeing things and speaking in the dugout. If you can't believe the guy who hit it, you ask someone you can believe. So when Carlton Fisk was at second base I went up and casually said, 'Ozzie really messed me up on that last hook [curve].' Carlton was laughing and chirping. He said Guillen tried to do that, he was watching me all the way and saw me break toward second and he tried to hit it to the left side. It worked and he was so happy he was screaming and singing in the dugout. So the next time Guillen was up I purposely started to cheat toward second early. I ran a couple of steps, then stopped, and he hit the same weak ground ball right to me. If I hadn't talked to Carlton I wouldn't have known that Ozzie was trying to hit behind me, to the side I was cheating away from. I would have been running back up the middle a second time and he would have had two hits."

Why, you may well wonder, would a wise veteran like Fisk give away useful information? "When you play every day," Ripken explains, "and you go through so many at bats and so many situations, it doesn't seem too harmful to tell certain things. I know I tell things to a catcher, for example, and sometimes I think, 'Maybe I shouldn't have said that.' Suppose they're pitching me inside real hard. I just say something like, 'Aren't you tired of pitching me inside?' Then I'll walk away and think that I shouldn't have let them know I was so aware that they are pitching me a particular way."

Besides, Ripken says, "Baseball is not an 'enemy' sport. You do have certain rivals and certain people you do not like. But for the most part it's not a contact sport, it's a pitcher-hitter confrontation more than anything else. The people who come into second base, you have so many things in common with them. It's a friendly sport, I guess." But Ripken rarely stops working. Not long after the incident just described, Guillen arrived at second base in a game against the Orioles. Ripken asked, "Do you know where I'm playing you?" Guillen said no, so Ripken said, "I'm playing you to pull." But the next time Guillen came up Ripken did not play him to pull. As Casey Stengel would have put it, a lot of times people don't always tell the truth.

What is baseball truth? Red Smith knew, and revealed it in a column celebrating the genius of The Genius, Alexander Cartwright, who revealed the truth, or had it revealed to him, in that wonderful epiphany of June 19, 1846, when he, then 25, joined some friends in a meadow beside a Manhattan pond. He had a chart in hand. The dimensions of the baseball field Cartwright laid out that day may have been determined by the size of the meadow, or perhaps Cartwright just stepped off 30 paces and said, "This seems about right." In any case, Red Smith wrote, "Ninety feet between bases represents man's closest approach to absolute truth. The world's fastest man can not run to first base ahead of a sharply hit ball that is cleanly handled by an infielder; he will get there only half a step too late. Let the fielder juggle the ball for one moment or delay his throw an instant and the runner will be safe. Ninety feet demands perfection. It accurately measures the cunning, speed and finesse of the base stealer against the velocity of a thrown ball. It dictates the placement of infielders. That single dimension makes baseball a fine art—and nobody knows for sure how it came to be."

There it is, the basis of the 90-foot-at-a-time game. The aim of the team at bat, as set forth with the admirable simplicity of the rule book, is "to have its batters become runners, and its runners advance." The aim of defense is to prevent that. Bad defensive habits are good news for opponents' base runners.

In Spring Training, 1989, when New York Mets right fielder Darryl Strawberry and first baseman Keith Hernandez got into a scuffle during the taking of the team picture, a wit said that it was the first time in years Strawberry had hit his cutoff man. Some of today's outfielders seem to think that hitting a cutoff man with a throw from the outfield is an unintelligible, trivial and optional ritual. Actually, it is an essential skill. It enables a play to be redirected, away from trying to cut down the lead runner to trying to cut down a trailing runner, or at least prevent him from advancing. He might advance if a throw comes in from the outfield too late to get the lead runner and too high or off-line to be cut off by the appropriate infielders properly positioned. As Tommy Henrich of the Yankees said, "Catching a fly ball is a pleasure, but knowing what to do with it after you catch it is a business."

Done correctly, defense should almost always succeed in frustrating the first-and-third double-steal plays of the sort Tony La Russa likes. Kubek recalls that when Casey Stengel drilled the Yankees on defending against first-and-third double-steal situations, he would put the team's two fastest runners on the bases just to show that if everyone—pitcher, catcher, infielders—did exactly what they were supposed to do, not even the fastest runners could make the double steal work.

The Orioles have three basic defenses for first-and-third steal situations. On one the catcher comes up throwing to third—that is, he does not even consider trying to throw out the runner going from first to second. This is apt to be the option decided upon if the runner on first is fast and the chance of throwing him out is slight. The second play is for the middle infielder, whose job it is to cover second on a steal, to see the runner breaking from third toward home, cut in front of second, take the catcher's throw on the run and fire the ball right back to the catcher. The third is for the middle infielder responsible for covering second to get to second, straddle the bag, ready to receive the throw, and listen for the other middle infielder to shout "tag him" if the runner on third is not going home.

"Most first-and-third baserunning plays," Ripken believes, "rely on a mistake by an infielder in order for the runner on third to score. I think mistakes are at a minimum at this high level of baseball, so these plays are not worth the risk." For example, if the opposing team has runners on first and third and the runner on first does the "stumble start" to get caught in a rundown, there is no way the runner on third can score if the Orioles' infielders do their jobs right. Doing it right means they must make no more than one throw to nail the runner in the rundown between first and second. The first baseman receives the pickoff throw from the pitcher and starts chasing the runner toward second, hard. The object is to get the runner going as fast as he can run as quickly as possible. "I'm inching up," says Ripken, "and when I see him at full speed I take off toward second and yell 'Now!' " Once the runner is in high gear, Ripken charges directly at him. No runner in baseball—"I can chase down Rickey Henderson at that speed"—is fast enough to come to a screeching halt, reverse direction and force Ripken to make a second throw, back to first—the second throw on which the runner from third could score.

———◆———

The Orioles have three bunt defenses for situations with a runner on second. On one play the first baseman charges. He or the pitcher must field the ball. The second baseman and shortstop rotate to their left—the second baseman covering first, the shortstop covering second. The third baseman stays at third in the hope that it is a bad bunt, meaning one pushed hard enough that either the pitcher or first baseman can pounce on the ball and get it to third before the runner gets there.

On the second play the first baseman stays back, the pitcher covers the first base side, the third baseman charges the ball, the second baseman covers second and the shortstop covers third. It is sometimes said, mistakenly, that the shortstop "races the runner to third." Actually, it is a timing play, with the shortstop breaking for third well before the hitter puts his bat on the ball, and thus well before the runner breaks full speed for third. The timing works this way: The Orioles' pitcher looks back toward the runner, and when the pitcher turns his head back to the plate, Ripken runs toward third. The pitcher must deliver the ball as soon as he turns back to the plate or the batter might have time to adjust to what he sees and hit the ball through the huge hole vacated at short. "In recent years," Ripken says, "people have become more aggressive. They will square around to bunt and if there is no place to bunt it, they will pull back and try to hit the ball through."

The third play is exactly the opposite. It is a pickoff play. It begins like the second play: The pitcher looks back at the runner, then turns back to the plate. As he turns his head, the third baseman charges in and Ripken runs toward third. But when the catcher gives a hand sign—say, opening his hand between his thighs—the pitcher turns and throws to the second baseman who has sprinted to second base, behind the runner who has focused his attention on the problem of beating Ripken to third.

"There is so much information out there," Ripken says, "you ought to use it." Information in the form of knowledge of an opposing manager once enabled Ripken to make a 6–3 assist on a bunt. It was a two-out squeeze play. Ripken was playing alongside one of the many immobile third basemen the Orioles used in the 1980s. The runner broke from third, Ripken knew it would be safe for him to spring in toward the middle of the diamond because the batter would not be swinging with the runner coming. Ripken fielded the ball and nipped the batter at first. The play was made by anticipation, which meant guessing right about the opposing manager. Ripken thinks (he is not sure) it was Billy Martin, who liked first-pitch squeeze plays.

Martin was "tendency-prone," but he had so many tendencies it was hard to predict what he would do next. The proliferation of plays on a Martin-managed team showed how well he understood that the key to offense is multiplying scoring opportunities. The key to that is multiplying base runners. Good defense reduces base runners three ways: by reducing hits, reducing errors and increasing double plays. Today there are about 60 percent more double plays per base runner than there were in the dead-ball era. This is the result of quicker fielders and quicker movement of the live ball on smooth (and often carpeted) infields. And there is another difference: gloves.

In the 1880s about half the runs scored were unearned. In the 1980s about one-ninth were unearned. True, for a few years in the 1880s an error was charged to the pitcher for a walk, balk, wild pitch or hit batter. Still, the decline in the number of errors, and the improvement of defense generally, constituted as radical a change in the game as the increase in the number of long hits. And by far the most important reason for the change—more important than the improvement of playing fields—was the introduction of, and then the revolutionary improvement of, gloves.

The first gloves were flesh-colored because the wearers were embarrassed by the unmanliness of seeking protection from stinging hits and throws. But catching the ball in a glove was more artistic than catching balls in caps, a practice that faded out as fielders' gloves came in. They came in quickly. The path of progress was blazed by a pioneer who weighed physical pain against moral opprobrium and chose to endure the latter. In 1875 Charles Waite, a Boston (or perhaps St. Louis—this is ancient history) first baseman,

braved a wave of derision from fans and competitors when he wore
a small glove. It looked almost like one of today's batters' gloves,
minus the fingers. The trail up the mountain of improvement is
steep and strewn with scoffers, but Waite was the wave of the future.
He began the transformation of defensive baseball from a two-
handed to an essentially one-handed skill. All fielders have worn
gloves since the retirement in 1894 of Jerry Denny of Louisville.
(Bill James calls Denny "the last real man.") The tiny padded gloves
of the 1890–1920 era, which weighed about 10 ounces, were large
enough to be the main reason why errors per game declined from
6.66 to 2.83. The year 1920 is a notable demarcation because it saw
the introduction of the Bill Doak glove featuring webbing between
the thumb and fingers. By the end of the 1950s, improvement of
gloves was not over but innovations had done about as much as
could be done to cut the rate of errors. Then artificial turf helped
a little, but only a little because by then groundskeeping of dirt and
real grass was good almost everywhere. The improvement in defense is the main reason scoring has declined an average of .14 run
per decade for 11 decades (even though scoring has increased since
The Revolution Against the Pitcher after the 1968 season, and the
introduction of the DH in 1973).

Until 1954 players were not even required to take their gloves
back to the bench with them when they came to bat. They would
just toss their gloves on the grass, which gives you a good idea of how
little regard the players had for this tool. And in fact, as late as the
early 1950s many gloves still were remarkably small and premod-
ern. Charlie Gehringer, who played second base for the Tigers from
1924 through 1942, lived to see the difference modern gloves could
make. "In our day you didn't see the plays you do today. I can't
remember anyone catching one like jumping over the fence and it
would stick in the big glove, 'cause it wouldn't. Maybe I dove for a
ball once or twice, but you'd only hurt yourself probably and still
wouldn't do more than knock it down. Today [balls] stick and you
can get up and throw them out if they're hit hard. Nobody seemed
to think fielding was that important . . . hitting made all the difference."

Technologies do indeed condition crafts. In the 1960s Randy
Hundley abandoned the traditional stiff catcher's mitt in favor of a
flexible hinged model. This made it possible for him to squeeze the
ball without using his unprotected right hand. Soon two young fu-

ture Hall of Famers, Johnny Bench and Carlton Fisk (Bench is in the Hall, Fisk is heading there), perfected one-handed catching. But what is fine for geniuses like those two is less than fine for lesser talents. Some old-time catchers such as Birdie Tebbetts, and the not-at-all-old Tim McCarver, believe one-handed catching has led to laziness and a decline of the catcher's craft. "Too much reaching," says Tebbetts. "Too much blocking of balls with their gloves instead of shifting their bodies. Too much backhanding." Tebbetts also believes that base stealers are benefiting from the catchers' practice of keeping their throwing hands away from their gloves. This, he says, adds to the time it takes to wing the ball on its way toward second base. McCarver is equally disapproving: "The fundamental purpose of a catcher never gets taught to most kids. If a catcher can't block a tough pitch in the dirt with a runner on third in a one-run game, the pitcher can't let his best curveball or split-finger go for fear it will end up at the screen. You'd be surprised how many times during the season a pitcher gets blamed for hanging a curveball or split-finger, and the reason he hung it is because he's afraid his catcher won't catch the tough one."

It takes Ripken about two weeks to break in a glove and he usually uses two a year. He changes gloves during the year because he wants a glove that is still somewhat stiff, because he does not want it to close too easily. "At third base you catch more balls one-handed. You have to lunge more to your left and right so you break your glove in 'longer,' more like a lacrosse stick. At shortstop your glove is flatter because a lot of the balls you catch are not actually *caught*. You do not squeeze the ball, you *almost* catch it, with a flat hand. The ball almost ricochets into your [throwing] hand. Some Latin players actually do deflect the ball to show how quick their hands are. It looks good but it's too risky for me." Some middle infielders want gloves with tight "basket weave" webbing between the thumb and fingers because they are afraid they may get a finger caught in the hole of an "H-weave" web while trying to grab the ball and turn a double play. Ripken, who prefers the H-weave, says that if you catch the ball properly it is not in the webbing. Furthermore, the holes in the H-weave are useful when you are trying to catch pop-ups in day games when the sun is blinding—in Oakland, for example. You can shield your eyes by holding the glove high, but you can follow the flight of the ball by looking through the webbing. Needless to say, the Japanese have seen a commercial possibility in this.

They have put tinted plastic—in effect, sunglasses—in the webbing of some gloves.

The dramatic improvement in baseball defense—the skills, information and equipment—is one reason why it has become riskier for a team to rely heavily on winning by having big innings. Such innings are harder to come by when good defense cuts down on base runners, increases double plays and reduces the number of "four-out innings." The big-inning approach to baseball in the 1950s produced a predictable response from pitchers; it produced a generation of pitchers skilled at throwing hard sliders at the bottom of the lowered strike zone. Then along came artificial turf and teams tailored to it. Such teams were stocked with swift hitters who liked low, hard pitches. Those pitches were perfect to drive down onto the hard, fast surfaces. While baseball was frozen in the Fifties' big-inning frame of mind, baseball architecture was changing in a way that would, in time, change minds. It has been said that we make our buildings and then they make us. That has been true in baseball. Architecture has been called frozen music. The new music of baseball has often been monotonous. Richie Hebner, who played for the Pirates, Phillies, Mets, Tigers and Cubs, blurted out the melancholy truth: "I stand at the plate in Philadelphia and I don't honestly know whether I'm in Pittsburgh, Cincinnati, St. Louis or Philly. They all look alike." Fourteen of the parks currently in use were opened between 1953 and 1971. Eleven of them are congenial to pitchers. In a remarkably few years baseball abandoned such hitters' havens as Ebbets Field in Brooklyn, the Polo Grounds in Manhattan, Sportsman's Park in St. Louis, Crosley Field in Cincinnati (Robin Roberts, the Phillies' Hall of Fame pitcher, on his great thrill in All-Star competition: "When Mickey Mantle bunted with the wind blowing out at Crosley Field"), Forbes Field in Pittsburgh and Connie Mack Stadium in Philadelphia.

The second wave of material changes that altered baseball thinking began in the late 1960s. In 1968 there were only two fields—one and a half actually—with artificial turf. They were the Astrodome and the Comiskey Park infield. Today there are ten. (Comiskey Park has since gone back to grass.) It is easier for artificial turf teams to adapt to playing on grass than for grass teams to adapt to turf. This is the fielders' version of the hitters' axiom, "Look for the fastball and adjust to everything else." Fielders get used to fast surfaces and adjust to those that are less fast. And other adjustments are required.

Ray Miller says that on turf, when one person shifts, everyone shifts, because if you leave a big gap you are risking a triple. One statistic suggests that artificial turf is probably more favorable to hitters (the ball scoots through the infield faster) than to infielders (the ball gets deep quicker so infielders with strong arms can play deeper and sweep more territory). The statistic is this: Artificial turf stadiums tend to reduce double plays and grass fields tend to increase them. An Elias Bureau study of double-play groundouts indicates that some teams have a significant difference in the number of double plays they make at home and on the road. This suggests a new "park factor." The crucial variables affecting double plays include the amount of foul territory for pop fouls to be caught in, the size and contours of the outfield, and the likelihood that teams will play for big innings. If they play for big innings, and disdain plays such as sacrifice bunts and stolen bases, that will increase the number of double plays (more runners loitering on first).

As a catcher, Tim McCarver liked artificial turf because throws from the outfield to home plate got there quicker on a bounce on the hard surface. The fraction-of-a-second difference could be enough to enable him to tag the runner with the ball in his hand rather than in his glove. A catcher, says McCarver, will die before dropping a ball held in his hand. Ray Miller believes that improved defense has done more than artificial turf has done to take away the bunt. Good bunters can kill the ball on artificial grass, but today's better athletes play more shallow in the infield and spring to the ball more quickly. Plastic has made defense easier in many ways. Ripken thinks lights have, too. He prefers to play at night because defense is more difficult during day games, especially in high summer, and particularly in older parks. Then it is harder for infielders to see the ball coming off the bat because fans are apt to be wearing white or other light colors, and in most older parks the seats come down to field level.

Players serious about defense pay attention to their surroundings. When Keith Hernandez was with the Mets he played 81 games a year in a stadium located beneath the flight paths into La Guardia Airport. He studied takeoff and landing patterns as indicators of wind direction because, he said, the fluttering of flags and pennants was not an accurate indicator. In Fenway Park Ripken generally prepares to back up the left fielder in case the left fielder, having failed in an attempt to catch a ball up against The Wall, is not in a position to play the carom.

"As a third baseman," says Ripken, "every time you go to a new park you should roll a ball down the line to see if it rolls foul or fair." If the groundskeeper is earning his keep, the ball will roll one way or the other. A determined groundskeeper for a bunting team should be able to build an inward slope on the foul lines, a decline of as much as two inches in the two feet from the foul line to the infield grass. Such a slope radically improves the odds on a bunt staying fair. The groundskeeper at Comiskey Park provided such a slope in the late 1950s for the benefit of Luis Aparicio and Nellie Fox. The swift, spray-hitting Dodgers of the early 1960s were helped by a huge roller that was used not only to compress the hard infield but also to mash the outfield grass, making it a faster surface on which more balls could zip past outfielders to the fence. A groundskeeper is the servant of the manager, who may use him the way a president uses the CIA: stealthily. When the Cincinnati Reds had Frank Robinson, Gus Bell and other sluggers, the groundskeeper dug a hole in the front of the mound where some visiting pitchers would plant their feet when delivering the ball to the plate. This increased the odds on some pitches floating high in the strike zone. Ripken says, gratefully, that for years—before the Orioles discovered the joy of running—the Memorial Stadium groundskeeper "would doctor the infield when Rickey Henderson came in, watering down the baselines from first to second. Make it muddy, a slow track. We didn't have anyone who stole bases."

The 1962 pennant race may have been decided by a groundskeeper. In August the Dodgers, leading the league and the Giants by 5½ games, were coming to Candlestick Park for a three-game series. That was the year Maury Wills stole 104 bases and won the MVP Award. Alvin Dark, the Giants' manager, directed his groundskeeper, Matty Schwab, to do something about Wills and other Dodgers base runners. Schwab did, with a vengeance. Many years later Noel Hynd, author of *The Giants of the Polo Grounds*, told, in *Sports Illustrated*, the story of the creation of "Lake Candlestick." At dawn on the day of the first game of the series Schwab was at work building what he jovially called a "speed trap." He and his partners in crime dug up topsoil from an area 5 feet by 15 feet that covered the area where Wills would stand when poised to spring toward second. Where the topsoil had been, Schwab put a spongy mixture of peat moss and sand, and watered it well. Then he covered it—barely—with an inch of topsoil. Umpire Tom Gorman, noticing Dodgers first baseman Ron Fairly building a sand castle near the bag, ordered the grounds crew to correct the mess. The crew saluted smartly and went to work. They carted away wheelbarrows full of Schwab's concoction. Then they replaced it with wheelbarrows full of the same stuff. The Dodgers lost the first game, 11–2, stealing no bases. They lost the next two, 5–4 and 5–1. The season ended with the Giants and Dodgers tied for first. The first game of the three-game play-off was at Candlestick. Umpire Jocko Conlan dashed to San Francisco to prevent any secret mischief, so Schwab did it openly, sanding and watering the base paths into a swampy mess and blaming the mess on a mistake by "a new man." The Giants won game one, 8–0. Down in Los Angeles the Dodgers won the second game, 8–7, thanks in part to Wills's four stolen bases. The wildness of the Dodgers' pitchers cost them the third game and the pennant, 6–4. The Giants lost the World Series to the Yankees in seven games but they did not lose their sense of justice. They voted Schwab a full Series share.

Maury Wills did not forget that groundskeepers can be lethal weapons. In April, 1981, Wills, then the Seattle Mariners' manager, had his groundskeeper lengthen the batter's box, extending the front a foot toward the mound to allow Seattle hitters to move up and swing at the curveballs of Oakland's Rick Langford before they curved. Alas, the Oakland manager, Billy Martin, was no fool—and he was just the sort to try such a thing himself. He demanded that the umpires measure the box.

Most of what a good groundskeeper can do to serve the home team is well within the range of permissible modifications. The most common ploy—one obviously not available to a team playing on artificial turf—is to let the grass grow high. "It slows the ball down," says Ripken. "With the faster hitters you know the ball is not going to get to you so fast. Consequently you have to move in a little bit." He prefers to play back in order to get a better angle for cutting off a wider range of ground balls. That is one reason why he likes playing on artificial turf. "Turf is quick but the ball bounces high enough that more of the ball's quick movement is up and down rather than toward the outfield." On the other hand, hitters run faster on turf because the traction is better. "You don't slip as much getting out of the batter's box, you don't have uneven baselines." However, a hard surface in front of home plate means that many batted balls will head toward, and perhaps past, infielders more quickly. It also means that they will bounce higher, consuming more fractions of a second getting to infielders and perhaps enabling fast hitters to beat the ball to first.

The beauty of a ballpark is in the eye of the beholder, and a future Hall of Fame pitcher and a future Hall of Fame shortstop may see the same park quite differently. Musing about the people who made Tiger Stadium, Jim Palmer says, "It is almost as though they asked themselves, 'What can we do to make it as hard as possible on pitchers?' " It is, Ripken says, the kind of park "where good pitches are hit for home runs.

"In Detroit," says Ripken, "you know Sparky is going to make the infield as slow as he can, for pitching and defense. If you have a club of singles hitters, a club suited to artificial turf, you will emphasize speed. You want your infield hard and the ground in front of home plate like corduroy so your hitters can chop down and make the ball bounce in odd directions. But if you've built your team like our team [Ripken was speaking in 1988, before the transformation of the Orioles] or Earl's [Earl Weaver's] teams of the past—pitching, defense and three-run homers—you don't have a high-average-hitting ball club. You hit home runs. Sparky's teams have always been that way. When the Kansas City Royals, a team tailored to a spacious park with artificial turf, come to Baltimore they have to play Orioles baseball. In Detroit they make sure they dig a quicksand pit in front of home plate. If you hit it right down it doesn't bounce at all. And they have great infielders [shortstop Alan Trammell, second baseman Lou Whitaker] with a lot of range, and good pitching. Is Walt Terrell's record better at home than on the road? He's a good sinkerball pitcher, keeps the ball down and away. If you hit the ball on the ground in Detroit, you have little chance for a hit. In Texas they made the infield extremely fast. The grass is about this fast"—he holds two fingers about half an inch apart—"like a putting green. And it's very true and always hard because the weather is so hot." The infield at Arlington Stadium has peculiar properties, and not just because the sun bakes the ground so hard and the grass is cut so short. There is something about the way the grass is mowed, according to many baseball people. They say it causes ground balls to "snake" across the infield. Jim Lefebvre says he has seen some infielders, who are not used to the Texas grass, shift their gaze to check a runner and look back just in time to see the ball weave through their legs. Ripken says Anaheim Stadium's grass is similar. Ryne Sandberg says the way the grass is mowed in San Diego and

San Francisco causes grounders to snake. Sandberg says the Shea Stadium infield is cut shallow (that is, the outfield grass is closer to the infield grass than in most other parks) so he can not play as deep as he prefers. If he did, the "lip" of the outfield grass would be in front of him, a potential cause of bad bounces.

Clearly there is some home-field advantage in baseball. In only five seasons in this century has a league recorded more road wins than home wins. The norm is for the home team to win between .535 and .555, which means more than 5 out of 10 but fewer than 6 out of 10. And when the pressure is on, the advantage does not change. Through 1989 home teams won only 54 percent of all World Series games and 47 percent of all Series have been clinched on the road. Only once—in 1987, when four games were played in Minnesota's high-decibel Metrodome—has there been a Series in which every game was won by the home team. The home-field advantage is remarkably small considering that the home team is enjoying home cooking and other comforts, has the services of a compliant groundskeeper, is used to the hitting background, and knows how to play the fences and the caroms in the corners and foul territory.

Such details about different parks are known to watchful players on visiting teams. "I watch different shortstops in their home ballparks," Ripken says. "For example, Tony Fernandez in Toronto because their turf [Ripken was referring to Toronto's old stadium] is bad. They have an underground drainage system. Water got in it during the off-season, froze and pushed the concrete up. They never corrected it. They laid the carpet right over the bumps. If you are walking normally you can trip over them. So Tony, who likes to play deep, played shallower at home, to play in front of the bumps. His angles on his backhands were a lot different. He would be going straight across instead of back. So I played in and gave up some range but didn't have to worry about the bumps as a variable." Ripken pauses, then adds, "I talked to Tony and he said he does play deeper with a runner on second if the run means a lot." This sharing of information is the socialism of shortstops.

Perhaps middle infielders feel—they certainly should feel—class solidarity. They have a unifying grievance. Their speciality is not properly appreciated. One reason for this is, of course, that the prevention of offense is not usually considered glamorous. Until Ozzie Smith began earning a salary with two commas in the number—$2 million—defense was not well remunerated. To paraphrase Ralph Kiner's celebrated aphorism, defense is not where the Cadillacs are. (Today Kiner would say Mercedes. Much has changed in America since the late 1940s.) Another reason defense is not properly appreciated is that defensive excellence is difficult to express in the language baseball aficionados like to speak: statistics.

———◆———

Baseball may be in some ways a product of nineteenth-century sensibilities, but baseball's fascination with quantification makes it very much attuned to the twentieth century. The development of certain familiar technologies (adding machines, calculators, computers), and the related development of research skills and data-gathering agencies and bureaucracies, have produced in this century a surge in the quantity of social information available. This has led, in turn, to the growth of the social sciences, and to the growth of hubris, even intellectual triumphalism. The ability to measure and quantify patterns of behavior has produced misplaced confidence in the diagnostic, predictive, evaluative and therapeutic capabilities of the "behavioral" sciences. Baseball analysts (players, managers, writers, fans) often have a similarly misplaced confidence in their ability to reduce reality to numerical expression.

Baseball has many statistics, all of which can be interesting. However, one category matters more than all the rest: runs. Every other statistic is subordinate. All other statistics, from walks to assists, concern categories of actions that are important as contributions to the creation or prevention of runs. The art, and increasingly the science, of run-prevention is elusive in a way that is frustrating to typical baseball fans. They want achievements quantified in ways that will enable a cool appraisal to result in definitive discriminations between players.

Baseball is a game of visible, discrete actions. Much can be seen and counted. Much, but not everything. Because baseball lends itself to quantification, it is an amazingly, relentlessly, even obsessively and oppressively self-conscious activity. And baseball breeds its own kinds of statistical confusions. Statistics must be read with an eye out for factors that skew numbers.

Many such factors are obvious. A pitcher who wins 20 games for a good team might be pressed to win 12 for a weak team. Indeed, a different bull pen can make almost that much difference. A hitter batting .300 in Wrigley Field might hit .270 in Montreal's poor visibility. A batter who hits 15 home runs in St. Louis might hit 30 in Tiger Stadium. A player who steals 40 bases on the kind of teams Whitey Herzog has built for the Kansas City and St. Louis stadiums might steal just 15 for a team playing the stand-around-and-wait-for-a-three-run-home-run style of baseball. Any pitcher's ERA is subject to four "biases" (Bill James's word): the caliber of the league he is in, the park in which he pitches half his games, the bull pen that tries to stop whatever trouble he gets into, and the defense arrayed around him. Some of the influences that must be inferred behind the statistics are less obvious, and this is especially true with fielding statistics. Consider the matter of double plays.

The more double plays a team makes, the better its middle infielders, right? Not necessarily. A high number of double plays may be mostly evidence of a shaky pitching staff that is putting too many runners on base. In 1948 the Browns had a miserable 59–94 season but turned a major league record number of double plays. The reason was suggested by their team ERA: a horrendous 5.01. So many runners were getting on that there were abundant opportunities for double plays. In 1949 the Athletics had a mediocre 81–73 year but broke the Browns' short-lived double-play record. Again, shaky pitching (a 4.23 ERA) provided the prerequisite for double plays: base runners. In dismal 1988 Cal and brother Bill at second base led all other American League combinations in double plays and total chances. Only 17 middle-infield combinations in American League history have made more double plays in a season than Ripken and Ripken made in 1988, an achievement that testifies about equally to the good gloves of the Ripkens and the bad pitching that put so many runners on base. Only seven teams in the last 40 years have led the league in ERA and double plays.

When a player goes through a nine-inning game and gets no assists, his defensive statistics change, if only slightly, in a way that might at first blush suggest that he is not doing his job on defense as well as he should. His ratio of assists to innings played goes down. But that may not mean anything important. Consider how an entire team can have its defensive statistics shifted slightly in that direction by a quite successful evening. On June 25, 1989, for only the second time in history, a team played a nine-inning game and got no assists. Here is a list of the putouts by the Mets as they beat the Phillies, 5–1, at Shea Stadium:

HOW PUTOUTS WERE ACHIEVED

METS VS. PHILLIES
June 25, 1989
at Shea Stadium

Left fielder Kevin McReynolds	1	Fly out
Right fielder Mark Carreon	3	Fly outs
Center fielder Mookie Wilson	2	Fly outs
First baseman Dave Magadan	2	Grounders
Second baseman Gregg Jefferies	1	Pop-up
Shortstop Kevin Elster	2	Pop-ups
Third baseman Howard Johnson	0	
Catcher Barry Lyons	13	Strikeouts
	3	Pop-ups
Pitcher Sid Fernandez	0	
Pitcher Rick Aguilera	0	

Some formulas for measuring a defensive player's "range factor" are attempts to put an artificial precision into a subject that will not hold still for such precision. It is an attempt to attach a numerical value to an activity in which the explanatory value of the number is largely vitiated by the number of variables involved. Determining range factor involves measuring a player's chances (putouts plus assists plus errors) per game. But an infielder playing behind, say, a sinker-ball pitcher such as Hershiser, may field many more ground balls than a better infielder playing behind a pitcher who throws a lot of fly outs. A staff full of ground-ball pitchers could produce a pretty nifty range factor for an infielder not much more mobile than a stump. An infielder playing behind a power pitcher like Roger Clemens or Nolan Ryan may have the range of a cheetah but that virtue will not be statistically apparent because the catcher will be getting so many putouts from the pitcher's strikeouts. A second baseman on a team loaded with left-handed pitchers is apt to generate statistics that "prove" that he has less range than a second baseman on a team that relies on right-handed pitchers and therefore is a team that fields more balls off the bats of left-handed hitters. There are kinds of preoccupations with defensive statistics that can produce bad baseball as well as bogus achievements. Kubek says there are outfielders who, in order to run up their number of assists, will play 30 feet too shallow early in games. Playing that way allows some unnecessary doubles and triples to go over their heads but at the end of the year they do have a lot of assists and a lot of people are saying they must have great arms, and they may even win Gold Gloves.

"Because of salary structures and incentive clauses," Kubek says, "we are so locked in on offensive statistics. That is what arbitration is about—offensive statistics. Defense is hard to measure." Hard, indeed. That is one reason why defense does not get its due from the people who parcel out baseball's laurels.

◆

In 1987 Ozzie Smith batted .303, scored 104 runs and drove in 75, an astonishing total considering he did not hit a single home run. He did hit 40 doubles and 4 triples. He walked 89 times and, to pass the time while waiting to get back to shortstop, he stole 43 bases. At shortstop he did about what you would expect from the most elegant shortstop of his era, and perhaps the finest fielder ever. He led the league in assists and fielding average. So he prevented no one knows how many runs that would have been scored if a lesser shortstop had been out there. His team won the pennant. And who was the National League MVP? Andre Dawson of the last-place Cubs. Why? Power. Dawson hit 49 home runs. The Cardinals could not have finished first without Smith. The Cubs could have finished last without Dawson. Defense got slighted yet again.

Defense, says Tom Boswell, is "the cognoscenti corner of baseball, the poorly lighted room in the gallery." It is that, and it is also the virtually vacant room at the Hall of Fame. Now, in a sense a Hall of Famer is any player of the type elected to the Hall of Fame. But the correct question is: Does the composition of the Hall of Fame reflect reasonable criteria? The answer is: Not yet. Defensive skills have not yet been given their due recognition. This is apparent in the underrepresentation of middle infielders. Of the 157 persons elected to the Hall of Fame through 1989 (counting those elected primarily for their playing as opposed to managerial, umpiring or other abilities, and not counting players whose careers were in the Negro leagues), only 10 were second basemen, and they included hitting giants such as Napoleon Lajoie and Rogers Hornsby. Joe Morgan is the 11th second baseman voted into the Hall. He, too, was an offensive star with 2,518 hits, 268 home runs and 689 stolen bases. Only 6 shortstops who entered the major leagues since the 1920s are in the Hall of Fame (Luis Aparicio, Luke Appling, Ernie Banks, Lou Boudreau, Pee Wee Reese, Arky Vaughan).

Respect for defense got a boost in 1982 with the election of Aparicio. He had a career batting average of only .262 and hit only 83 home runs in 18 seasons. But he holds the major league record for the most games played at the most demanding defensive position. Aparicio also holds the major league record for career assists (8,016), consecutive years leading a league in assists (6), most chances accepted (12,564), most years leading a league in chances accepted (7), most double plays (1,553). He holds the American League record for career putouts (4,548). He shares the major league record for most years leading a league in fielding (8) and the American League record for most years leading the league in putouts (4). While the election of Aparicio was welcome, it hardly balanced the books. Consider the case of two men who have not yet been admitted. Their cases indicate the continuing underestimation of the importance of defense.

There are two reasons—each of them sufficient—why Bill Mazeroski should be in the Hall of Fame. One reason is that as he was leaving the church on his wedding day, with his bride on his arm, he put a plug of tobacco in his cheek. The other sufficient reason is his defensive play. Many men are in the Hall only because of their hitting. This group includes some players who were at best mediocre on defense and were far from being among baseball's best batters (another Pirate, Ralph Kiner, comes to mind). But Mazeroski was no slouch as a hitter. His career average was .260 over 17 seasons. And he hit the most dramatic home run in World Series history, the ninth-inning shot over the left-field wall in Forbes Field that beat the Yankees in the seventh game of the 1960 World Series. It is the only home run that ended a Series.

Jim Kaplan, author of *Playing the Field* and poet laureate of the defensive dimension of baseball, thinks that the glitter of that moment has distracted people from Mazeroski's true greatness. Kaplan believes it is demonstrable that Mazeroski was the greatest defensive second baseman ever and that it is arguable that he was the greatest defensive player of *any* position. Kaplan notes that when Mazeroski took infield practice at the 1958 All-Star Game, "stars from both leagues stopped to watch him—the fielding equivalent of watching Ted Williams hit." Mazeroski led National League second basemen in putouts 5 times, total chances 8 times, assists 9 times (a record) and range factor (putouts and assists divided by games) 10 times. His major league records include double plays by a second baseman in a season (161), in a career (1,706) and the number of years leading the league in double plays (8). His lifetime fielding average of .983 was achieved in spite of the notoriously bad infield at Forbes Field.

The exclusion of Mazeroski from Cooperstown is a case of simple discrimination against defensive skills. The exclusion of Richie Ashburn is harder to fathom. Ashburn was much more than merely adequate at bat. He had a .308 lifetime average, with two batting titles. He batted over .300 in 9 of his 15 seasons. Mays and Mantle batted better than .300 ten times each, in 22 and 18 seasons, respectively. Mantle's career on-base average was .422, Mays's was .384, Ashburn's was .394. Doubles? Mays averaged 24 a year, Ashburn 21, Mantle 19. Mays scored an average of 94 runs, Mantle 93, Ashburn 88 while hitting just 29 home runs in his career—an average of fewer than two a year. That is a big part of his problem: He did too much without home runs. Another part of his problem is that he did it 90 miles too far west. If he had put up most of his numbers in New York City, under the media microscope, he would already be enshrined at Cooperstown.

Now we come to what should be the clincher, the fact that Ashburn holds six of the ten most important records for single-season putouts in the outfield, five of the top nine for total chances.

Ashburn retired after the 1962 season, which he played with the Mets. It was the Mets' slapstick (40 wins, 120 losses) first season. He was named the Mets' MVP, and said, "Most valuable player on the worst team ever? Just how did they mean that?" He is fifth in career putouts and chances behind four Hall of Famers (Mays, Tris Speaker, Max Carey, Ty Cobb), all of whom played at least 288 more games than Ashburn played. Many balls he caught, which less swift and less intelligent outfielders would not have, were snared at the end of long sprints. He caught them because the play started with him well positioned and intelligently anticipating. A substantial number of those balls were doubles denied. Why is a double denied on defense so much less admirable than a double delivered on offense?

"The typical American male," wrote James Thurber, "strikes out the Yankees side before going to sleep at night." But there are many red-blooded Americans (of both sexes; this is the Nineties, for Pete's

ALL-TIME SINGLE-SEASON LEADERS: PUTOUTS BY AN OUTFIELDER

Taylor Douthit	1928	547
Richie Ashburn	1951	538
Richie Ashburn	1949	514
Chet Lemon	1977	512
Dwayne Murphy	1980	507
Richie Ashburn	1956	503
Dom DiMaggio	1948	503
Richie Ashburn	1957	502
Richie Ashburn	1953	496
Richie Ashburn	1958	495

ALL-TIME SINGLE-SEASON LEADERS: CHANCES BY AN OUTFIELDER

Taylor Douthit	1928	566
Richie Ashburn	1951	560
Richie Ashburn	1949	538
Chet Lemon	1977	536
Richie Ashburn	1957	527
Dom DiMaggio	1948	526
Dwayne Murphy	1980	525
Richie Ashburn	1956	523
Richie Ashburn	1953	519
Lloyd Waner	1931	515

sake) who, when on the edge of sleep, dash deep into the hole between short and third to spear a hot grounder and then throw Rickey Henderson out at first. These sensitive, caring, learned Americans demand that the Hall of Fame shape up and fill out its ranks with the likes of Mazeroski and Ashburn. Those two may not rank with Dreyfus on the list of history's great victims, but the undervaluing of defense does say much about the standard measures of baseball excellence. And it says much about the misunderstanding of how games are won.

Games are won by a combination of informed aggression and prudence based on information. La Russa says, "Be aggressive offensively—when in doubt, push. But defensively, it's the opposite. Be very basic, take the outs that are there, don't gamble in a way that will open up a big inning for the other team." There are sometimes more outs within reach than seem possible. One night in 1987 the Giants, playing at home, had hit 5 home runs and were still losing, 6–5. Then they tied the score in the ninth and had the bases loaded with one out. The Reds brought their outfield in. The Giants' Will Clark singled sharply up the middle. The Giants won, right? Right, but they might not have. The Reds' center fielder, Eric Davis, charged the ball, scooped it up and sprinted across second base for a force-out on the runner coming from first. It was such a bang-bang play he still would have had time to throw on to first and get the batter for an inning-ending, and perhaps game-saving, double play. He had time, but there was no first baseman to throw to. When the Reds' first baseman, Dave Parker, saw Clark's hit go past the infield, he decided the game was over and left the base. The moral of the story is: It isn't over until it's over. As has been said.

But it is over when one team, the one with the fewest runs, runs out of outs. You can win a game even if you have terrible pitching that gives up runs in bunches. Just be sure to score one more run than the sum of the bunches. (On August 25, 1922, the Cubs were pounded by the Phillies for 23 runs. The Cubs won, 26–23. As Bob Prince, the Pirates' broadcaster, used to say at the end of a cliff-hanger victory, "Had 'em all the way!") You can score only one run and win. Happens all the time. You can win getting only one hit. It is possible to win getting no hits. But to win a nine-inning game you must get 27 outs.

It is exceedingly rare that a team wins even a division title while leading the league in errors. The porous Dodgers of 1985 led the major leagues with 166 errors. Before that, the last time a team led the league in errors and won the division was 1971. The Giants of that year had stone hands but they had large muscles. If you are going to be sloppy in the field you had better be able to bring Bobby Bonds, Willie Mays and Willie McCovey to the plate.

Casey Stengel was right: "I don't like them fellas who drive in two runs and let in three." "You can't win," says La Russa, "unless you catch the ball behind good pitching and don't give the other team extra outs." "That was Earl's philosophy," says Ripken. "Let's not give them any more outs than they're entitled to." For six months—Spring Training and the first five months of the season—baseball conversation, even among baseball people, is about pitching and hitting, and especially power hitters. In the seventh month, September, the question is always Who is going to win? And invariably the answer, at least the answer given by baseball people, is "the team that gets the best pitching *and defense.*" One of the elements in Earl Weaver's equation for winning a pennant was to make fewer than 100 errors in a season. Think of 100 errors as 100 times in which the other teams enjoyed four-out innings. Bill Rigney says that when he is asked to evaluate a team, the first question he wants answered is, How well do they catch the ball? Add up all the hits, bases on balls and stolen bases you get on offense, Rigney says. In how many games does the total top 27? That is how many outs your defense must produce.

To understand the primacy of defense, try this. Imagine that the rules of baseball were amended to require four outs to retire a side. What would happen? Scores would soar, games would go on and on and on. A 33 percent increase in the number of outs almost certainly would result in much more than a 33 percent increase in runs. But mediocre defense does just that: It gives the other team four-out innings. A ground ball just beyond the reach of an infielder who was improperly positioned, a double play just missed because a flawed flip from the shortstop caused the second baseman to deliver the ball to first a fraction of a second too late—such lapses do not show up in a box score. But when an excellent defensive team plays a mediocre defensive team, the two teams might as well be playing under different rules. The team playing against the mediocre defensive team is, in effect, getting four or more outs in, perhaps, four or more innings.

"Positioning the defense," says Whitey Herzog, "can be worth five or ten games a year." A pitcher worth ten games a year may have a million-dollar salary. So why do some clubs not bother with defensive charts? Sloth. "The premium," says La Russa, "is on getting guys out. The stuff we do offensively, talking about how to hit the guy, talking about how we are going to do things in particular situations—bunts, whatever—all that is well and good. There's a place for it. But the premium is on the stuff you do to get guys out—positioning, and how you are going to pitch particular players. I want to be able to have a comfortable feeling, sitting in the dugout, that whoever comes to bat, I have a general idea where the ball is supposed to go, and a pretty specific idea of how you're going to go after him. So when you're watching the game you can compare what you think going in with what you are seeing. A lot of times the key at bats come late in the game. You want to be able to adjust if a hitter has been doing things you have not anticipated."

The wonder is that, given how much information there is floating around, there are not more unusual adjustments made. Tom Trebelhorn, manager of the Brewers, says, "When we play Sparky and the Tigers, I love to do goofy stuff." Then he tells a story that demonstrates that the stuff is not so goofy. In 1987 he used a six-man infield with one outfielder. With a Tiger runner on third and no one out, Trebelhorn played a five-man infield. He brought in his center fielder, Robin Yount, a former shortstop, to play slightly to the right of second base. The pitcher was responsible for any ball hit up the middle and there were three infielders between second and third. The Tiger batter was Chet Lemon, a right-handed pull hitter. The Brewers' pitcher threw Lemon off-speed pitches down, he pulled a ground ball into the packed left side of the infield for the first out. Immediately there was a rain delay. In the clubhouse Trebelhorn told his team that when they went back out on the field they would play a six-man infield. The next Tiger batter was to be Pat Sheridan, a left-hander. In 24 at bats against the Brewers he had hit 17 ground balls. The only balls he had hit in the air had all gone to a certain small area of right-center field, where Trebelhorn planned to play his single outfielder. Trebelhorn told his pitcher to go to the mound, pick up the resin bag and throw it down as a signal for two outfielders to run into the infield. Trebelhorn told the pitcher to keep the ball down. Alas, the best laid plans . . . The pitcher got the ball up in the strike zone and Sheridan hit it to the one outfielder, but deep enough for a sacrifice fly, scoring the runner from third. "In this particular game," Trebelhorn says, "we were down about 5–0; we were dying on the vine. I got my guys excited. We ended up losing about 8–5, but the maneuver took the focus off the negative and put it on something positive. And there was some commonsense statistical information to back it up."

Information is everywhere. Late one afternoon before a night game in Boston, Tony La Russa was standing behind the batting cage watching Doug Jennings take batting practice. La Russa said, "Watch. You'll see why I had to bunt yesterday in Baltimore." In Baltimore Jennings was up and Luis Polonia was at second with no one out. As La Russa watched from behind the Fenway cage, Jennings, a left-hander, hit one BP fastball—about 58 miles per hour—after another toward short. "That's his stroke," La Russa said. "There is no way he is going to advance the runner by pulling an 85-mile-per-hour fastball to the right side." That is the sort of information the big man on the left side—the shortstop—likes to know. He can get it from advance scouts who facilitate anticipation.

William Ashley Sunday, who later became famous as just plain Billy, the evangelist, was playing center field for the White Stockings, as they were then known, when a Detroit batter belted a long fly. Sunday dashed after it with, he later said, a prayer on his lips. Perhaps he would have run faster and made the catch with less fuss if he had not been praying, but never mind. He made the catch and came to a momentous conclusion: "I am sure the Lord helped me to catch that ball and it was my first experience in prayer." Gosh. A career of saving souls might not have happened if back then the White Stockings had used advance scouts to tell Sunday where to play, thereby making his long run, and Divine Intervention, unnecessary.

An advance scout's reports, other than those about players new to the league, are less important for information on the player's general tendencies than on how he is hitting *right now*, meaning in the last three or four games. Ripken says this was important, for example, when trying to decide how to play defense against Reggie Jackson, a left-hander. "When Reggie was hitting the ball well, he waited a long time and hit the ball to my right. But when he was struggling, he would swing harder and get out earlier and he would pull more balls. He would get over the top of balls—'top' them. So if I knew Reggie was struggling I could play him more to pull. When he was hot he hit a lot of homers to left-center field. He would hit hard ground balls—rockets—to my right. When everyone's hitting the ball well, they see the ball longer and they wait to see what it's going to do. When they're hot they're quick."

Quickness is the quality most rewarded in baseball. Quick moves by the pitcher to the plate, by the catcher to second. Remember Ted Williams on hitting: "Wait-wait-wait and then quick-quick-quick." Defensive quickness decides games because the difference between baseball success and failure is measured in tenths, sometimes hundredths, of seconds. Quickness has constant synergism on defense. Around the infield, and the outfield, too, it radiates. Keith Hernandez has, by the aggressive mobility and artistry of his play, made more of a change in the playing of first base than anyone since Charles Comiskey, who was the first first baseman to play off the bag with no runners on base. No one any longer thinks of first base as a safe place to park an arthritic and immobile elder. In his prime Hernandez showed the baseball world the ripple effect of an infielder's range. Because he could move so well to his right, all the holes in the Mets' infield were squeezed just a bit narrower than they otherwise would have been as the rest of the infield edged to its right. No one can say for sure how many potential hits were thereby turned into outs in the course of a season, but it is certain that the ERA of the Mets' pitching staff reflected the Hernandez Factor.

Such a ripple effect can originate anywhere in the infield, and dramatically from center field. Tris Speaker played such a shallow center field that several times—once in the 1912 World Series—he completed an unassisted double play at second base. Shortstop Mark Belanger had such range going back on pop-ups that he was virtually a fourth outfielder, enabling the left fielder and center fielder to play a bit deeper than they otherwise would have. When first and third basemen have good range, shortstops and second basemen are able to squeeze the biggest hole on the diamond, the one exploited by Wade Boggs and others who hit back up the middle. The better a third baseman is at going to his left, especially on slow grounders, the deeper the shortstop can play. The concept of third-base play was altered suddenly in five games in October, 1970. The World Series that year between the Orioles and Reds was the first Series involving a park (Cincinnati's Riverfront Stadium) with artificial turf. The Reds had four right-handed power hitters (Johnny Bench, Tony Perez, Lee May, Hal McRae). They spent five days pulling the ball at the best glove ever stationed at third base, Brooks Robinson, and they spent the winter regretting it.

In October, 1987, almost four years to the day after he made the final putout of the World Series (catching a soft semi-line drive off the bat of the Phillies' Gary Maddox), Ripken was watching the Cardinals-Twins Series at home on television and marveling at something he saw, something that proved the importance of a third baseman with good range. "A left-hander was pitching for the Cardinals with a runner on first and a 2-and-0 count on Gary Gaetti, a strong right-handed pull hitter. And Ozzie [Smith] is playing him up the middle. [Terry] Pendleton has tremendous range for a third baseman, but no one can throw hard enough to throw the ball by Gaetti. [By "throw the ball by" Ripken means *almost* by—preventing Gaetti from pulling the pitch.] So I think: 'Maybe the situation dictates that the pitcher will pitch around Gaetti, not give him a pitch to hit.' But the pitcher throws the ball inside and Gaetti hits a sharp one-hopper to straightaway short, where Ozzie isn't. Pendleton is playing so far off the line that he almost catches it. Ozzie dives for it and catches it at straightaway short and forces the runner at second. I am sitting there thinking, 'How in the world can Ozzie think he can play that far up the middle?' The answer was in the fact that Pendleton nearly caught the ball and he had no business even being close to it."

Ripken's house suffers from no shortage of television sets of all shapes and sizes. He takes busman's holidays, watching the competition. And he has lodged in his capacious memory another episode involving Gaetti, another that proves the point about the advantage of a third baseman with good range to his left. The Tigers were playing the Twins. Alan Trammell was the Tigers' shortstop, as he has been since he was 19 in 1977. Tom Brookens was playing third. Frank Tanana, a left-hander, was pitching for the Tigers. Gaetti was up and Trammell was not playing him to pull, "because Brookens has good range," explains Ripken, with the wistfulness of someone who has played next to 28 third basemen (and 16 second basemen) since 1982. "Outfield range is just as important. If you have a center fielder like Gary Pettis [of the Rangers] or Devon White [of the Angels] who can catch the ball from bull pen to bull pen, it wouldn't make a lot of sense, if you were the right fielder or left fielder, to play in the area where he can catch the ball." A swift center fielder takes away some of the other team's extra-base speed because he allows his fellow outfielders to play close to the foul lines, where doubles often fall. This, says Ripken, is especially important in an outfield configured like that of Baltimore's Memorial Stadium. The left- and right-field foul lines are 309 feet. But the fence curves quickly out to 360 feet and is 385 in the power alleys. Most teams visiting Memorial Stadium squeeze those alleys—that is, they play their left and right fielders a lot more toward center than they do in other parks, assuming that hits down the line will be doubles and that squeezing the alleys can prevent triples. "But," says Ripken, "teams that have great center fielders put their right and left fielders on the lines and the center fielder runs rampant and they cover all the territory and catch everything."

Watch outfielders in the outfield when their team is taking pregame batting and infield practice. Most do not do what Tony Gwynn does. He, like Ripken, believes that the way to prepare to play baseball is to play baseball. So during Padres pregame sessions, when Gwynn's group is not hitting, he will be in the outfield taking fly balls "off the bat," meaning flies hit off batting practice pitches rather than off fungo bats. He will play one ball as though there is a man on second base, another as though there is nobody on, a third he will play "do-or-die"—a potential winning run on second. He will even practice climbing the fence on batting practice home runs that barely make it over the fence. Tony La Russa requires the Athletics' outfielders to take balls off the bats of hitters taking batting practice 20 minutes a day in Spring Training, 5 minutes before each game during the season. "You can take 1,000 fungoes a day and it won't be as good as 10 minutes pretending you are in a game, taking balls off the bat during batting practice." "Pete Rose says that everyone practices their strengths," says Ripken. "You like to do what you are good at. But Pete also said he practiced what he believed to be his weaknesses. That is what I do. That is why you may see me practicing my backhand." There is another reason for practicing his backhand, particularly on the road. The visiting team takes infield practice after the home team has practiced. When an infield has been chewed up—or when an infield is simply bad, as Cleveland's was when Ripken first came to the major leagues—practicing your backhand is safer than fielding balls coming directly at you. If they take bad bounces they are apt to bounce off you. Ripken has not missed infield practice before even one game while in the major leagues. There is, he says, a big difference between being in shape and being "in baseball shape." The latter means, for example, being able to throw repeatedly across an infield.

Repetition is inseparable from craftsmanship, but it also is the source of the strain of baseball's everydayness. It takes a special toll on infielders who are especially in the grip of the game's one-pitch-at-a-time rhythm. At one point in his career, Mickey Mantle was moved from center field to first base to rest his constantly aching legs for a few games. Soon he wanted to return to the outfield, where he could relax. When Rod Carew moved from second to first he discovered that a first baseman, far from being immobile, must always be doing something. Watch an excellent first baseman such as Don Mattingly, hold runners on first base. The instant the pitcher is committed to deliver the ball to the plate, the first baseman should make a strenuous move, one comparable to that made by a base runner when stealing or participating in a hit-and-run play. "It's like stealing a base," says Keith Hernandez. "Take two explosive steps at the last possible moment. The point is to get into position to cover the hole. You get hurt more in the hole than down the line. Nowadays there are so few dead-pull left-handed hitters. There used to be Willie McCovey or John Milner. But there aren't any more. Still, you'll see so many first basemen sitting on the line. Because they're lazy. It gets boring over the season to come off the bag. You're tired and don't feel like getting out there." That is a true test of professionalism, this ability to do the small and boring and cumulatively stressful and draining things that must be done during the half of the game when you are at your defensive position.

Mark Belanger used to say there is no such thing as a fielding slump. Ripken disagrees. "There are slumps in fielding as well as in hitting. In hitting your timing gets off, and you get out front of pitches—too soon, or behind. Similarly, you become anxious as shortstop, you are leaning too far—so far ahead of the pitch that it is impossible to correct" if the ball is pitched somewhere it is not supposed to go and is hit in an unanticipated direction. Assuming an average of 130 pitches per game over a 162-game season, Ripken tenses, rocks forward on the balls of his feet and begins to lean or move in toward the infield grass, or to one side or the other, 21,000 times each season. Ripken has rocked forward on the balls of his feet more often than any other player since May 30, 1982—the day his consecutive-game streak began. Barring injury, in June, 1990, he will move into second place on the consecutive-games list, passing Everett Scott's 1,307. And if Ripken's career goes as it has gone since 1982, the eyes of the baseball world will be on him in June, 1995. One day that month he will, if playing at home, trot out to take his position in the infield prior to the top of the first inning. Or if playing on the road he may come to bat, perhaps still hitting third, in the top of the first inning. When he does, another of baseball's "unbreakable" records will be broken. Ripken will have surpassed Lou Gehrig's streak of 2,130 consecutive games played.

The authors of *The Elias Baseball Analyst* are sparkling diamonds in the diadem of American letters. But on one subject they are grumps, and are mistaken. They dismiss a streak such as Ripken's as "a record of will, not skill." But that misses a subtle and profoundly important point about the relationship of baseball skill to intense discipline of will. The Elias authors said in their 1988 edition that there is one baseball question they can not answer: "Lou Gehrig played in 2,130 consecutive games. Why?" They can not answer it because their distinction between records that reflect skill and records that "merely" reflect will is too stark. Natural gifts, however great, and skills, however sharply honed, still must be summoned to application by strength of will. The summoning is not easy on a muggy August mid-week night in Cleveland when neither team is in the hunt for a pennant. Skills must be willed into action by an intensity that does not well up spontaneously. Such intensity must be cultivated. For some players, such as Ripken, playing every day is part of an ongoing mental preparation not only for the long season and a long career, but also for tonight's game.

To the argument that "everyone needs a day off," Ripken says, placidly, that he gets lots of days off, between October and April. He insists, reasonably, that his is not a 1,000-game streak, it is a series of 162-game streaks. Were anyone to ask, Is 162 consecutive games too many for a large, young, healthy, well-conditioned athlete?, the obvious answer would be, of course not. Also, there is that positive argument for continuing the streak. Ripken's streak is his way of maintaining the mixture of relaxation and intensity necessary for high performance over a long season. Barring injury, Ripken will break Lou Gehrig's record when he is 35, in the 71st game of the 1995 season. And he will play in the 72nd game, and the 73rd, and . . .

Playing every day is something Ripken learned by osmosis, early. The boy is indeed father to the man, and Ripken's baseball boyhood bred in him a respect for the game's relentlessness. When Ripken was younger his game face was not always, as it is now, calm and almost blank. "I used to throw bats and things until I saw myself do it on TV." He has a soft, almost high voice and shy half-smile that seems a halfway measure to prevent unseemly mirth from making it to the surface. He is a difficult man to see depths in, but they are there. His passions are submerged beneath his public self, which is steadiness personified. But with Ripken it is possible, as Duncan (not

Dave the pitching coach, but the fellow in *Macbeth,* Act I, Scene IV) said, "to find the mind's construction in the face." His is a deceptively bland countenance. The blandness is actually a quiet force, a kind of confidence that comes only to athletes and other performers, and only to a few of them. It is confidence in *being able to do it.*

Ripken is one of 14 players who have won both Rookie of the Year and MVP awards, and he is the only player to have won them in consecutive years. (Fred Lynn won both in the same year, 1975.) He is the only shortstop other than Ernie Banks to hit 20 or more home runs in 8 consecutive seasons. Through 1989 Ripken had led all major league shortstops in home runs and RBIs for 6 of the last 7 seasons. He had hit 196 home runs as a shortstop, third behind Ernie Banks (293) and Vern Stephens (213). He was one of only 4 major leaguers with 20 or more home runs in each of the last 8 seasons. His total of 204 home runs ranked him eighth in the major leagues during those 8 years. Through the 1989 season Ripken was the only active American League player who had hit 20 or more home runs in each of his first 8 seasons. Dale Murphy was the only other player to hit 20 or more in those 8 seasons. Entering 1990 Ripken was second only to Boston's Dwight Evans in the number of extra-base hits by an American Leaguer over the previous 8 seasons. (Ripken had 494, Evans 500. Dale Murphy led the major leagues over that span with 508.) Through 1989 his career slugging average was .461, comparable to the averages of such Hall of Fame shortstops as Honus Wagner (.469), Joe Cronin (.468) and Arky Vaughan (.453). But when asked which gives him greatest satisfaction, hitting or defense, Ripken does not hesitate:

"When you do things right defensively you feel the greatest gratification. When I had all those chances [906, while setting an American League record for assists, 583] in 1984 and the pitching was tremendous, you could rely on them, there was no better feeling than to know that the guy was going to throw *this* pitch, he was going to throw it where he said he was going to throw it, and the hitter was going to hit it—if he hit it—at *this* place. Having guessed—no, having figured it out—and done it, and moved the right way, and taken a ball up the middle, and having somebody scream in the dugout back at you, 'How can you play me there?' Say he's a right-handed pull hitter and so the shortstop normally would play a right-handed pull hitter in the hole. But then the sequence of the count, and the pitcher on the mound who has a 90-mile-per-hour fastball, and the fact that he's got two strikes on him, *told* me that I can actually *know* that *this* guy's not going to pull *this* pitch, so I can run up the middle and he'll hit a line drive or a one-hopper right by the pitcher's glove and I can catch it up the middle and make the play. Then you hear somebody screaming in the dugout 'How can you play me there?'—to me, that's more gratifying than getting a bases-loaded hit. That's the game within the game."

◆

The game within the game, in the mind, is elegant. But the game itself, on the field, has a rough side. It is sometimes said that baseball is not a contact sport. This idea is encouraged by baseball's gentle terminology of "touching" a base or "tagging" a runner. But baseball has a constant undercurrent of dust-raising episodes—episodes that certainly seem to the participants to amount to contact. For example, try telling Tim McCarver that there was not serious contact involved on the two occasions when runners slid into him at home plate hard enough to lodge their spikes in his shin guards. Professional baseball is, as Heywood Broun wrote, "agreeably free of chivalry." No chivalry, but there is a code of acceptable behavior. At home plate the code is, as we have seen, a subject of constant and semi-violent negotiations among batters, pitchers and umpires. The code is clearer at second base, where the first outs of most double plays are made while arriving runners are trying to prevent the ball from being fired to first in time to make the second out.

"Everybody understands the extent of the contact and even if you get hit hard, if it's within certain guidelines, you think it's all right," says Ripken. Middle infielders making double plays usually receive the ball from the other middle infielder who has fielded it. He touches second and flings the ball on its way to first base while avoiding, or absorbing the impact of, the runner who is sliding, or even rolling, in from first. Many middle infielders, when receiving the throw as pivotman in a double play, throw the relay to first sidearm because the low trajectory of the throw forces the incoming runner to get down into his slide a stride or so earlier. This gives the pivotman some protection from collision. One reason for this practice is that middle infielders generally have been smaller than many of the base runners who come barreling into second. Ripken often sidearms the ball to first even when not turning the double play, even from fairly deep short, because the release is quicker that way than it is when throwing fully overhand. His arm is so powerful he can gun the ball without the whipping motion of an overhand throw. Furthermore, when making the pivot, Ripken has a big man's confidence about collisions. He remembers Darrell Miller, a 200-pounder playing for the Angels, attempting to take him out with a hard slide at second and then lying on the ground holding his side and gasping up at Ripken, "Are . . . you . . . all . . . right?"

Fear of collisions is the principal reason for the "phantom tag," whereby the pivotman glides past the bag a split second before getting the ball. But Ripken wants to earn the reputation with umpires of always touching second base, so that in a situation in which he may have to miss the bag—for example, when a flip from the second baseman pulls him away from the bag—the umpire may give him the benefit of the doubt. Commenting on the way Walt Weiss of the Athletics turns a double play—rocketing right across the bag, directly at the on-charging runner, while throwing to first—Ripken explains, "You want to catch the ball and continue your momentum toward first without regard for the guy coming in. Your luxury, as a shortstop, is that you can see where he is. You can be the aggressor."

When asked if he was glad that Kirk Gibson, the former tight end from Michigan State University, had left the American League, going from the Tigers to the Dodgers, Ripken replies with a flash of the competitiveness that sleeps, when it sleeps, lightly within him: "He never got me." And he adds, "I always thought I had the advantage because he was in front of me. If I was a second baseman I'd be a little more concerned, because you can't see him, you don't know when he's going to hit you. Don Baylor, who had the speed and power combined, used to slide in and say, 'I could have really got you.' I'd say, 'I bet you could've.'" Ripken laughs. "Baylor ended someone's career in a collision at second. He always said—I've known him since I was eleven—'I'm not going to get you. But I'll let you know when I could've.'"

Bo Jackson of the Royals is one of the biggest men in baseball and may be the fastest in a 90-foot sprint. His blend of hard bulk and explosive speed has brought to baseball a kind of kinetic energy not seen before, not even in the man to whom he is frequently compared, Mickey Mantle. Tony Kubek, broadcasting for the Blue Jays, saw Jackson early in 1989 and knew he had seen something so remarkable it might rewrite whole chapters of "The Book," that compilation of baseball's received wisdom. In the Royals' opening game against the Blue Jays, Jackson hit a solid single up the middle, directly across the carpet to Toronto's center fielder, Lloyd Moseby, who fielded the ball cleanly and fired it back to the infield—but not before Jackson had slid into second. In another game in that series Jackson went from second to third on a grounder hit to the Blue Jays' shortstop, Tony Fernandez. "The Book" decrees that you do not try to advance on a ball hit to the left side, least of all when your team is behind, as the Royals were at the time. But Jackson was almost at third by the time the ball got to Fernandez. Then, with Jackson on third, Frank White bunted. The ball trickled foul. But before the Blue Jays' catcher, Ernie Whitt, had fully risen from his crouch to pounce on the ball, Jackson ran across the plate. "There are," says Kubek, "different kinds of fears. I know darn well there was fear when Jackson was running the bases yesterday. Tony Fernandez taking the throw from Moseby, knowing that Bo's coming, missed the ball. There was fear on Ernie Whitt's part when Frank White bunted."

Many baseball players saw—and those who didn't see it have heard about it—the NFL game in which the Seattle Seahawks' linebacker, Brian Bosworth, was the only obstacle between Bo Jackson and the end zone. Bosworth was not, it turned out, much of an obstacle. Jackson ran right over him. Most baseball players have seen the tape of Jackson smashing into Rick Dempsey, then the Indians' catcher, hitting him so hard that Dempsey was knocked far from the plate and all the way on to the disabled list. Tony Gwynn certainly remembers it: "Jackson just jumped up. Didn't faze him." Ripken has seen many strong, fast players. And standing at shortstop he has seen Jackson taking a lead off first. Ripken knows Jackson and likes him, but Ripken will worry more about him when he has learned more about baseball.

When asked how big a problem Jackson is when he is on first base, Ripken replies with the pure baseball man's sense of superiority to someone who is less than completely committed to his craft: "Oh, Bo has many fundamental strengths. He could be just like Rickey [Henderson], but it seems that when some people have that much speed they don't take the trouble to get a good jump. Their speed takes care of their jump. But think how fast they could get to second base if they did all the little things everybody else has to do. Bo's not yet a great base stealer, as great as he can be, because he has not learned the fundamentals—how to get a good jump, how to time the pitchers. He hasn't stolen that many bases and he's faster than Willie Wilson in a dead sprint. But I'll bet he's not as fast as Willie first-to-home because he [Bo] doesn't 'cut' the bases as well." (Through 1989 Wilson had stolen 588 bases, placing him eighth on the all-time list.) "Because Bo's physical tools are superior to those of everyone else, he can run faster, throw harder, hit the ball farther than anyone else. But he doesn't yet get up well with the pitch. He doesn't read the ball off the bat as well as he could if he had had more baseball experience." (By "getting up with the pitch" Ripken means that a runner on first, while facing the catcher, should begin to glide sideways toward second and then be able to turn smoothly and sprint off the glide if the ball is put in play. A runner on first "reads the ball off the bat" well if he instantly knows whether it will be a ground ball, a routine fly or a long drive.)

Now the baseball purist in Ripken is speaking with undisguised disapproval: "The same is true on the double play. Bo doesn't get there [to second] as fast as some other people, even though he is faster than everybody. I'm not as worried about Bo as I someday will be. Don Baylor used to be fast and he got so he could get there quicker than anybody because he did things the right way." In those words—"the right way"—the Ripken blood, and that of baseball, speaks.

CONCLUSION

———◆———

"Maybe the Players Are Livelier."

A baseball elder gazed upon the game and was not pleased by what he saw:

> Baseball today is not what it should be. The players do not try to learn all the fine points of the game as in the days of old, but simply try to get by . . . [sic] It makes me weep to think of the men of the old days who played the game and the boys of today. It's positively a shame, and they are getting big money for it, too.

So wrote a former player and manager years after retiring. He wrote it for the *Spalding Base Ball Guide* of 1916.

It is an old baseball tradition, complaining about the character and quality of contemporary players. However, baseball is both intensely traditional and interestingly progressive. By progressive I mean steadily improving. The traditional side is obvious in baseball's absorption with its past and its continuities. Charles Finley, who as owner of the Oakland Athletics fielded some of the finest teams of the 1970s, suffered from incurable fidgets and tried to inflict upon baseball various innovations, such as designated runners and orange baseballs. But he did acknowledge the game's remarkable continuity. He liked to say, "The day Custer lost at Little Bighorn, the Chicago White Sox beat the Cincinnati Red Legs, 3–2. Both teams wore knickers. And they are still wearing them today." There is an aura of changelessness to sport. There is the flux of competition, but it occurs within the ordering confinement of clear rules. Yet like any human contrivance, sport is an organic institution, evolving with changes in the forces that play upon it. Baseball's seasons, coming one after another and comprising a nearly seamless web, are deeply satisfying to one's sense of social transmission. It is the sense of society always changing somewhat but having as its primary business the passing along of slowly accumulated customs, mores and techniques. Memory, says Tom Boswell of the *Washington Post,* is baseball's fourth dimension. For the fan, freezing and savoring images is an important part of the pleasure. No sport matches baseball's passion for its past. And there is a second sense in which memory is always central to baseball's present. Many of those who play and manage have ravenous appetites for remembrance. It is how they, and their craft, become better.

Baseball, it is said, is only a game. True. And the Grand Canyon is only a hole in Arizona. Not all holes, or games, are created equal. The Grand Canyon is the work of the Colorado River. Where did baseball come from? Lots of places, including (it seems so natural) Valley Forge. Baseball was evolving from lower forms of activity at about the time the colonies were evolving into a nation, and baseball became a mode of work—as distinct from a mere pastime— remarkably soon after the nation got going.

This is a nation that knows precisely when it got going. Unlike most nations, this one had a clear founding moment, in Philadelphia, presided over by the Founding Fathers. It is, therefore, natural, and tolerable as amiable nonsense, that the national pastime claims to have had a founding moment and a Founding Father. Part of the agreeable nonsense about baseball being an echo of our pastoral past is the myth that Abner Doubleday invented the sport one fine day in 1839 in the farmer Phinney's pasture at Cooperstown. Actually, the thing Doubleday helped begin was the Civil War. (He was stationed at Fort Sumter when the first shots were fired.) *The New York Times* obituary of Doubleday did not even mention baseball. The untidy truth is that the sport evolved from two similar, but interestingly different, games based in two cities, New York and Boston.

The New York version won the evolutionary contest, partly because New York had one of the essential ingredients of social success, a great lawgiver. The United States had a population of about 20 million and New York City about 700,000 the day (June 19, 1846)

Alexander Joy (his parents certainly knew how to name baseball's constitutionalist) Cartwright went to a meadow on the slopes of Murray Hill near Third Avenue in Manhattan and laid out a diamond-shaped playing area with bases 90 feet apart. Puritan values made many early American communities inhospitable to play. Play is, after all, a "pastime," and to some stern Americans back then it seemed impious to think of the Creator's precious gift of time as something to be whiled away. Play was then considered a form of idleness, and an idle brain was the Devil's playground. But baseball, which began as play, quickly became a form of work. As pure play it was a spontaneous, improvised adaptation of games with English roots. The diary of George Ewing, a soldier in the Continental Army thawing out at Valley Forge in 1778, records that on April 17 there was a game of "base." It was, no doubt, a cousin of the game of "baste ball" that a Princeton student described in 1786.

Baseball's adolescence was the era between 1876, the founding of the National League, and 1902, the formalization of relations between the National and American leagues. In 1876 the nation celebrated its centennial, puffed out its chest, and went rollicking toward industrialism and urbanization. By 1902 America was a world power, as full of energy and confidence as the Rough Rider in the White House. Between 1876 and 1902 there were five or six (it is a matter of opinion) major leagues. This was an era of healing wounds from the Civil War (visored baseball caps were inspired by soldiers' caps worn during the Civil War—and perhaps partly by jockeys' caps) and creating the commonalities that would build a nation of immigrants. Baseball was part of that healing and building. This rambunctious age saw the democratization of literacy, and that brought the dawn of the age of newspapers. The price of a ton of newsprint plummeted from $40 in 1860 to $2 in the 1890s and editors, eager for a regular supply of noncontroversial news, launched sports sections where advertisers could sell to male readers.

Today baseball is big business, part of the vast entertainment industry that has grown in response to the growth of leisure time and disposable income. In 1989, 55,174,603 spectators, a number equal to approximately one-fifth of the combined populations of the United States and Canada, paid to get into the 26 major league ballparks. What spectators pay to see is a realm of excellence, in which character, work habits and intelligence—mind—make the difference between mere adequacy and excellence. The work is long, hard, exacting and sometimes dangerous. The work is a game that men play but they do not play at it. That is why they, and their craft, are becoming better.

Baseball has been called the greatest conversation piece ever invented in America. No topic of baseball conversation is more interesting and instructive than this question: Is the caliber of play as good as it used to be? I believe it is better. Sandy Alderson, the Athletics' general manager, says that judging a baseball team is a lot like surfing in the sense that waves come in, break and go back out, but you can not tell from one or two or even a dozen whether the tide is coming in or going out. Telling that takes more time. Gauging the trajectory of a baseball team takes more than a few games. Judging the trajectory of baseball itself is inherently problematic. But baseball has a trajectory; nothing stands still. John Thorn, a baseball historian and analyst, may be right that baseball "has changed less than any other American institution of comparable antiquity." Thirty years ago historian Bruce Catton wrote that if someone from President McKinley's era were brought back to earth and seated in a baseball park "he would see nothing that was not completely familiar." "Dugout to dugout," said Bill Veeck, "the game happily remains unchanged in our changing world." Well, as we say in Washington, yes and no. Yes, the structure of the game is essentially what it has been since the turn of the century. But for many reasons noted earlier, hitting and pitching and fielding and managing have changed enough over the years that it is not easy to make comparisons between the achievements of today and yesterday.

For many reasons, including dumb luck and other mysteries, extraordinary constellations of talent can come together in one short era, in any field of endeavor. Consider that thirteen thinly populated colonies produced the fifty-five men who went to Philadelphia to the Constitutional Convention in 1787. There are similar clusters of extraordinary talents and achievements in baseball. Ten of baseball's thirteen .400 batting averages occurred in a 15-year period, 1911 through 1925, when baseball was an adolescent and, after 1920, the lively ball era was in its infancy. Twenty-eight times American League hitters have had 150 or more RBIs in a season. But all 28 occurred in the 29 seasons between 1921 and 1949. And 19 of the 28 seasons were by 4 sluggers: 7 by Gehrig, 5 by Ruth, 4 by Jimmie

Foxx, 3 by Hank Greenberg. Note that 14 of those were by first basemen who were contemporaries. In 1935 Greenberg had 100 RBIs *before the All-Star break*. And he did not make the All-Star team, even as a backup. His misfortune was to be playing first base at the same time as Lou Gehrig and Jimmie Foxx. As if putting an exclamation point to punctuate an era, two men from the same team, Ted Williams and Vern Stephens of the Red Sox, both got 159 RBIs in 1949. In the National League there have been only 7 seasons of 150 or more RBIs. Six of the 7 were within 16 years (1922–37). (The seventh was by the Dodgers' Tommy Davis in 1962.) Only 7 players have compiled 100 or more extra-base hits in a season. Consider the list of the 9 times it has been done:

100 OR MORE EXTRA-BASE HITS IN ONE SEASON

YEAR	PLAYER	2B	3B	HR	TOTAL
1921	Babe Ruth	44	16	59	119
1927	Lou Gehrig	52	18	47	117
1930	Chuck Klein	59	8	40	107
1932	Chuck Klein	50	15	38	103
1937	Hank Greenberg	49	14	40	103
1948	Stan Musial	46	18	39	103
1922	Rogers Hornsby	46	14	42	102
1930	Lou Gehrig	42	17	41	100
1932	Jimmie Foxx	33	9	58	100

It has been 4 decades since anyone has done it and 4 of these achievements were in a 3-year span, 1930–32. Only 6 players have had seasons in which they hit at least .350, had at least 150 RBIs and hit 40 or more home runs.

PLAYER	YEAR	HR	RBI	AVG
Babe Ruth	1921	59	171	.378
Babe Ruth	1927	60	164	.356
Babe Ruth	1930	49	153	.359
Babe Ruth	1931	46	163	.373
Lou Gehrig	1927	47	175	.373

PLAYER	YEAR	HR	RBI	AVG
Lou Gehrig	1930	41	174	.379
Lou Gehrig	1934	49	165	.363
Lou Gehrig	1936	49	152	.354
Jimmie Foxx	1932	58	169	.364
Jimmie Foxx	1933	48	163	.356
Rogers Hornsby	1922	42	152	.401
Hack Wilson	1930	56	190	.356
Chuck Klein	1930	40	170	.386

Note that this has been done 13 times, all in a span of 16 seasons (1921–36). More than half of these super seasons occurred in a 4-year burst (1930–33).

There are almost as many ways to play with baseball numbers as there are ways to play with a baseball. Taken together, the many meanings that can be given to, or extracted from, the numbers compel this conclusion: There is an irreducible indeterminacy in baseball judgments. This is so in spite of, or perhaps because of, the abundance of data. About pitching, the records are clear but their meanings are not. Cy Young once told a reporter, "I won more games than you ever saw." He won 511. John Thorn and John B. Holway note that although Bob Feller won only 266 games, he lost 4 years to World War II. He had won 107 before Pearl Harbor and had just turned 23. At 23 Walter Johnson had 57 wins; Cy Young and Grover Cleveland Alexander had none. Alexander finished with 373, tied with Christy Mathewson. But Alexander did not get to the major leagues until he was 24 and lost most of a season to World War I. But for the war he probably would have won 400 games, something no one is apt to do again. The 5 best pitchers of the postwar period have been (I will brook no argument) Warren Spahn, Sandy Koufax, Bob Gibson, Jim Palmer and Tom Seaver. Seaver won 311 and lost 205 in a 20-year career, often with weak teams. His winning percentage of .603 is almost identical to that of Walter Johnson (.599), who toiled most of the time for weak teams. Seaver's career ERA was 2.86. But Walter Johnson won 416 games, the second-highest total, even though his Senators were shut out in 65 of his starts and got only one run in 38 others. True, Johnson played in baseball's truest "pitcher's park," Washington's Griffith Stadium. (When Johnson was pitching there the left-field line was 407 feet, center 421, right 328.) Johnson could (in a hoary old baseball saying) "throw a blueberry through a battleship." Someone has calculated that if Christy Mathewson had played for the Senators when Johnson did, when the Senators were often weak, instead of for the Giants when they were usually a powerhouse, Mathewson would have won 276 games instead of 373, and if Johnson had played for those Giants he would have won 567 rather than "only" 416. Such calculations have a spurious precision. Still, they can make points by pointing to broad general conclusions, one of which is that Johnson was the best pitcher, ever. Period. (By the way, he hit .433 in 1925, a record for a pitcher, and in 1913 fielded 1.000 with 103 chances, another record.)

Christy Mathewson pitched 3 shutouts in the 1905 World Series. Walter Johnson pitched 11 shutouts in one season. Carl Hubbell won 24 consecutive regular-season games (16 at the end of 1936 and 8 at the beginning of 1937). Seven times in the modern dead-ball era (1900 to 1919) pitchers pitched 300 innings without yielding a single home run. Detroit's Ed Killian pitched 1,001 innings from 1903 through 1907 without a home run. Pitchers used to pitch more—more innings, more games, more complete games, more shutouts. But, then, as has been noted, they often threw fewer pitches per inning than are thrown today. The nature of the ball, the role of the relief pitcher, the five-man rotation, the need today to pitch warily through lineups well stocked with power hitters—all these and other differences make it difficult to make definitive comparisons. Furthermore, modern-day strikeout records are more impressive than those of the first six decades of the century. In 1988 Roger Clemens struck out 291 batters in 264 innings for an average of 9.92 strikeouts per 9 innings. That tied him for fourteenth on the list (fifteenth after 1989) of best single-season strikeout ratios. The year before, Nolan Ryan, then 40, recorded the best ratio ever. Here is a list of the top 20 seasons:

PITCHERS WITH MOST STRIKEOUTS
PER 9 INNINGS, ONE SEASON
(Since 1900, Minimum Innings: 175)

	PITCHER	CLUB	YEAR	IP	SO	SO PER 9 INN.
1.	Nolan Ryan	Astros	1987	211.2	270	11.48
2.	Dwight Gooden	Mets	1984	218	276	11.39
3.	Nolan Ryan	Rangers	1989	239.1	301	11.32

(Continued)

	PITCHER	CLUB	YEAR	IP	SO	SO PER 9 INN.
4.	Sam McDowell	Indians	1965	273	325	10.71
5.	Nolan Ryan	Angels	1973	326	383	10.57
6.	Sandy Koufax	Dodgers	1962	184.1	216	10.55
7.	Nolan Ryan	Angels	1972	284	329	10.43
8.	Sam McDowell	Indians	1966	194.1	225	10.42
9.	Nolan Ryan	Angels	1976	284	327	10.36
10.	Nolan Ryan	Angels	1977	299	341	10.26
11.	Sandy Koufax	Dodgers	1965	335.2	382	10.24
12.	Sandy Koufax	Dodgers	1960	175	197	10.13
13.	Mike Scott	Astros	1986	275.1	306	10.01
14.	Nolan Ryan	Angels	1978	235	260	9.96
15.	Roger Clemens	Red Sox	1988	264	291	9.920
16.	Nolan Ryan	Angels	1974	333	367	9.918
17.	J. R. Richard	Astros	1978	275	303	9.916
18.	Nolan Ryan	Astros	1986	178	194	9.81
19.	Herb Score	Indians	1955	227.1	245	9.70
20.	Nolan Ryan	Astros	1984	183.2	197	9.65

Of those 20 seasons, one is from the 1950s, 5 are from the 1960s, and the other 14 are from the 1970s and 1980s.

The lesson to be learned here is that any baseball numbers must be considered in a complex baseball context. Nolan Ryan's career strikeout record, which rose to 5,076 in 1989, is not to be sneezed at, but he is pitching in an era when striking out has lost its stigma for batters. It is an era in which free swingers hold the bat at the knob and hack, not caring very much if they often do not make contact. When Ryan joined the Rangers in 1989 he had as a team-mate Pete Incaviglia, who went directly from college to the major leagues. As was noted earlier, whatever else he learned at Oklahoma State, he did not learn the strike zone or the iniquity of striking out. Incaviglia is an egregious case, but an instructive one. In 1986 he led the league in strikeouts with 185. He tied for the lead in 1988 with 153. His total from those two seasons was 338, just 19 short of Ty

Cobb's total strikeouts (357) over 24 seasons. Bo Jackson, another man who took a fast track to the major leagues, struck out 318 times in the 1988–89 seasons. In the magic year of 1941 (it was my bad luck to have been born on May 4 of that year, so I missed a full month of the season), Ted Williams struck out just 27 times while hitting .406 and belting 37 home runs. That year DiMaggio hit in 56 consecutive games and struck out just 13 times. Bo Jackson accumulates more strikeouts in two months than those *two* hitters accumulated—40—in a full season.

The modern power pitcher whose strikeout numbers most resemble those of Ryan is Steve Carlton. In 1971 Carlton was 20–9 with the Cardinals. Before the 1972 season he was traded from the Cardinals to the Phillies. In 1972 the Phillies finished last and had a team batting average 24 points worse than the Cardinals. Yet Carlton won 27 games. It makes you wonder how many he might have won if he had not been traded.

Some baseball people believe that pitching is especially subject to wide fluctuations in quality because the talent pool is always shallow and expansion of the number of teams can drain it to the muddy bottom. In 1960 one American Leaguer (Mickey Mantle) hit 40 or more home runs. In 1961 two new teams were added—only about 20 new pitchers—and the American League suddenly had 6 hitters with 40 or more home runs. Some people say expansion is the reason Roger Maris broke Ruth's record in 1961. However, Kubek notes that since 1961 the American League has gone from 10 to 14 teams and the National League has expanded from 8 to 12 teams and no one has come close to Maris's record. Anyway, in 1927 Ruth hit 7 of his 60 home runs off rookie pitchers.

Craig Wright says, "This is the first time in baseball history that speed and power have flourished at the same time." This is partly because the prevalence of power hitters makes pitchers want to put maximum body force into more pitches, even when they are throwing from a stretch position. That makes them somewhat slower to the plate, and thus makes speed on the base paths more valuable. Today, says Tom Trebelhorn, "there are people you can not throw out unless they make a mistake. It's physics—it's time and motion. By the time you can get the ball from here to here, they can run from there to there." One reason games are longer is that players are quicker. As base stealing has become more important, pitchers have had to throw to first more frequently. A good base runner takes a lead long enough to require him to dive to get safely back to first on a good throw-over, so then he must dust himself off. It takes time. The baseball consensus is that catching is not as good as it once was. The scarcity of talented catchers makes the quality worse. "Since the shortest way to the big leagues is as a catcher," observes Jack McKeon, "it means that in the position where a kid needs the most experience he is getting the least." Baseball people who think the work ethic is weakening point to the paucity of good catchers. Catching, it seems, is déclassé and, more to the point, difficult. This is an era when good catchers are scarce and several of the best are methuselahn (Bob Boone and Carlton Fisk will both be 42 on Opening Day, 1990). But help is on the way in a familiar form. It is an American tradition that immigrants do the hard work, the dirty work, the heavy lifting. Two of the best young catchers are the Padres' Benito Santiago and the Indians' Sandy Alomar, Jr., both from Puerto Rico.

"Absolutely true," says La Russa about the notion that more and more players are getting to the major leagues before they know the fine points of the game. Or the not-really-terribly-fine points, such as how to hit a cutoff man on a throw from the outfield. In the decade 1979 through 1988, 47 percent of baseball's 6,476 draft picks came from college programs. Seven of the top ten picks in 1988 were from colleges. College programs must do the work done not so long ago by the minor leagues. Tim McCarver remembers that when he signed with the Cardinals in 1959 they had 5 Class-D teams and 7 in higher classifications. Today the Cardinals have just 8 minor league teams. Some clubs have only 5. Is three years in a serious college baseball program—at, say, Southern California or Miami or Arizona State—comparable to three years in the minor leagues? "Absolutely not," insists Al Rosen. He says the inculcation of the basics of baseball is stronger and the competition is tougher in the minor leagues. As proof, Rosen cites the number of players who have outstanding college careers but who struggle and even fail in the professional rookie leagues.

Jim Lefebvre says that because young players are "force-fed" so quickly into the major leagues, it is common to see mistakes of a sort that once were rare. For example, in a 1988 game against Texas the Athletics had runners on first and third with one out when a ground ball was hit right over third base. The third baseman fielded the ball and, hoping to start a double play, looked at the runner on third to freeze him, then threw to second. When he threw, the runner on third made a mistake: He broke for home. He would have been out by 20 feet if the Rangers had not obligingly made their own mistake. The second baseman did his job: He fired the ball toward home. But the pitcher inexplicably—reflexively, but where did he get *that* reflex?—cut off the throw. In fact, the throw was gunned so hard it knocked his glove off. "There are," says Lefebvre, "a lot of instinctive-type things young players don't do right. When I came up the Dodgers had 16 farm teams—3 Triple-A teams. The players that made it to the majors were *survivors*. They knew their trade. They played, they played, they played."

Doug Melvin, director of the Orioles' farm system, says professional experience is bound to be more intense than any college program: "Look at the number of games they play. In three seasons a good college team may play 140 games. A kid would get perhaps 400 games with us." Immersion in baseball is more complete in a professional setting. The best way to study "situation baseball" is to be in the situations, often. For a second baseman, for example, there are 20 or so possible permutations of his duties, as cutoff man or in some other role, depending on where the ball is hit (fly ball? down the line? between the right fielder and center fielder?), whether there are runners on base (runner on third? first and third? second and third?) and what the score is.

Coaches' salaries are going up because more teaching must be done at the major league level. In 1988 Mark Grant, the large and slightly wacky Padres relief pitcher, was 24 and in his second full season. One morning at Wrigley Field he was lolling around the clubhouse listening to the wisdom of Pat Dobson, the Padres' pitching coach, about the importance of making a quality pitch to a particular spot with a runner on first and a left-handed hitter up. Keep the ball away, said Dobson, so the batter can not pull it. If he gets a hit to left, at least the fielder has a shorter throw to third from left field than from right, so there is a better chance of having runners at first and second rather than first and third. So a right-hander like Grant should throw a left-hander something like a slider, hard and away, rather than a curve that would come in on the left-hander and would have the effect of speeding up his bat. Grant was fascinated by, and grateful for, this lesson. It was the sort of lesson that a young pitcher should learn long before he breaks into the big leagues.

I can give a personal example of a well-coached young player. During the seventh game of the 1987 World Series between the Twins and the Cardinals, Geoffrey Will, then 13, was sprawled on a sofa, in the invertebrate way of an adolescent, watching the telecast. In the sixth inning the Twins' pitcher threw over to first baseman Kent Hrbek just as the Cardinals' base runner, Tommy Herr, broke for second. Getting Herr out in a two-toss (*at most* two-toss) rundown should have been as close to automatic as anything in baseball can be. But Hrbek turned, fired the ball to second—and then stood where he was, in the baseline. Laconically, but instantly, the 13-year-old on the sofa said: "Interference." He had seen in a flash what Hrbek was doing wrong and anticipated what Herr would do right. Hrbek should have gotten out of the baseline, either retreating quickly to first base or trusting the pitcher to get over and cover first. Standing in the baseline he was an invitation to Herr, who took it. Herr reversed himself and ran smack into Hrbek in an awful tangle of limbs as Hrbek belatedly tried to get back to first. The umpire should have called interference on Hrbek and awarded Herr second base. Instead, the umpire blew the call twice, first by not calling interference and second by calling Herr out (television clearly showed that he was safe). However, Geoffrey had demonstrated the result of good coaching at the junior high school level, coaching of a caliber that remarkably few players get even at much higher levels of baseball.

Mayo Smith, who managed the Phillies, Reds and Tigers until 1970, once said, "Open up a ball player's head and you know what you'd find? A lot of little broads and a jazz band." Not true. Maybe once upon a time, but I doubt even that. Obviously baseball, like banking and medicine and journalism, has its share of lowlifes and scatterbrains, but there are remarkably few. They can not last. The competition is too intense. Baseball's modern-day drug problems have never been as serious as the old problem with alcohol. (When Clyde Sukeforth was managing the Dodgers' Triple-A club in Montreal in the 1930s he once called a club meeting to say, "We're going to play a baseball game today. I want nine sober volunteers.") Today's athletes, looking for long careers with lucrative final years, are better educated than players used to be about healthy living. They use less alcohol than earlier generations of players. La Russa says that ten years ago, when he started managing, he would try to build team cohesion by occasionally having parties on road trips. But the success of such parties generally depended on moderate use of alcohol. He estimates that half his current team does not drink—at all. He does not drink. Before the 1989 World Series resumed after the earthquake there was some sensible worrying about how the eventual winner should behave. Would popping champagne corks be appropriate? "I don't care anything about champagne," said La Russa. "I tasted some once because Dave Parker wanted me to know what Dom Pérignon tasted like. I'm not even comfortable with Budweiser being advertised in our ballpark."

Today's players are physically more impressive than players were even in the early postwar era. Al Rosen remembers that when he was Cleveland's third baseman in the 1950s (in 1953 he hit 43 home runs and drove in 145 runs) he was considered a physically imposing slugger. He was 5 feet 10½ and 180 pounds. In 1989 the average height of major league players was a shade under 6 feet 3. But what about refinement, the essence of craftsmanship? Tony Kubek, whose father and three uncles played professional baseball, believes that "the greatest teacher is visualization—seeing others do it and aspiring to their level." Before he died in 1988, Carl Hubbell mentioned the advantages young players have today just because they are able to watch major league players on television: "I was raised on a cotton farm in Meeker, Oklahoma. Didn't even get a newspaper. Never saw so much as a picture of a real major league pitcher in his windup."

There is less rawness in today's baseball than there was long ago. I am not thinking about peccadillos. Yogi Berra was not the first and may not have been the last catcher to toss pebbles into batters' shoes. But no one plays the game with the high-spikes savagery of Ty Cobb. And although Cobb may have set the major league record for concentrated meanness, he was hardly the only player for whom viciousness was a normal part of the game. John McGraw merrily recalled the time when

the other team had a runner on first who started to steal second, but . . . spiked our first baseman on the foot. Our man retaliated by trying to trip him. He got away, but at second Heinie Reitz tried to block him off while Hughie . . . covered the bag to take the throw and tag him. The runner evaded Reitz and jumped feet first at Jennings to drive him away from the bag. Jennings dodged the flying spikes and threw himself bodily at the runner, knocking him flat. In the meantime the batter hit our catcher over the hands with his bat so he couldn't throw, and our catcher trod on the umpire's feet with his spikes and shoved his big mitt in his face so he couldn't see the play.

As a manager McGraw was a cauldron of hectoring fury. According to a Chicago sportswriter, McGraw was "the incarnation of rowdyism, the personification of meanness and howling blatancy." But his was meanness with a purpose. He reckoned that relentless bullying of umpires could get his team 50 extra runs a season, or one every three days. Bill James says the coaches' box was invented to confine the vituperative energies of the great St. Louis teams of the 1880s, which were managed by Charles Comiskey. Until the box was invented, players acting as coaches ran up and down the foul lines spouting obscenities at opposing pitchers. There are today no rivalries comparable to the last fierce rivalry, that between the New York Giants and the Brooklyn Dodgers. Bill Rigney remembers a day in 1951 when the Dodgers completed a sweep of a three-game series with the Giants at Ebbets Field, enlarging their big lead over the Giants. The two clubhouses were separated by a thin, locked door. In the minutes after the final out, Jackie Robinson was pounding on the door with a bat, taunting Giants' (and former Dodgers') manager Leo Durocher, "Leo, I can smell Laraine's perfume," referring to Durocher's wife, actress Laraine Day. Eddie Stanky, the Giants' fiercely combative second baseman from Alabama, shouted through the door a blistering racial insult. Hank Thompson, the Giants' third baseman, a black man, was seated near Stanky, who is white. Thompson told Stanky he approved of Stanky's words. As Cal Ripken says, baseball is not an "enemy sport." But that was not always true.

There is not only less unruly behavior on the field, there is less mischief with the field and other elements of the game. Baseball is more rigorously policed by the leagues than it used to be, so groundskeepers are less likely to try such chicanery as moving second base slightly (as much as a foot, which is a lot in the race between the runner and the ball) toward or away from first. Some teams may still make the pitcher's mound in the visiting team's bull pen higher or lower and with a different slope than the mound on the field in the hope that this will cause a relief pitcher (or the starting pitcher in the first inning) to have trouble controlling his first pitches. But no one today will do what Bill Veeck reportedly did. It is said that

Veeck's Cleveland Indians used to move the outfield fences as much as 20 feet, depending on the opponent of the day. Eddie Stanky, who lacked Lord Chesterfield's interest in gentlemanliness, tampered with the balls. When he managed the light-hitting 1967 White Sox he would store game balls for a week or more in a room with a humidifier running full blast. This made the air, and the balls, soggy with moisture. Removed from the room a few hours before a game, the surface of the balls would be dry but there would be two ounces of moisture inside, enough to take a dozen feet off the flight of a fly ball.

It has been said that baseball in the pre–Civil War era taught a puritanical America the virtues of play. But industrialists of the Gilded Age would approve of the way baseball has become a big business. Fifty years ago baseball was a comparatively mom-and-pop operation. Sunday play was not permitted in Pittsburgh and Philadelphia until 1934. In 1922 the U.S. Supreme Court held, for purposes of antitrust regulations, that baseball is not a business. Today sports columnist Jim Murray says, "If it isn't, General Motors is a sport." General Motors would like to have baseball's recent rate of revenue growth.

To gauge baseball's current popularity, consider the way things were not so very long ago. One of the most exciting games ever played was the exclamation mark at the end of one of the most exciting seasons baseball has known. It was the third game of the three-game play-off between the New York Giants and Brooklyn Dodgers in 1951. The game, which was won by the Giants on Bobby Thomson's three-run home run in the bottom of the ninth, capped "The Miracle of Coogan's Bluff" in which the Giants stormed back into the pennant race by erasing a huge Dodger lead after August 11. The game was played at the Polo Grounds, which had a capacity of more than 55,000. The attendance that day was only 34,320.

The 1989 season demonstrated a dynamic of success: The better things get, the more they get better. In 1989 major league baseball drew 55,174,603 fans, breaking by 2,175,699 the record set in 1988. It was the fifth year in which a new record was set. The Toronto Blue Jays drew 3,375,573, an American League record. Eight other teams also set attendance records: the Cardinals (3,082,000), Athletics (2,667,225), Orioles (2,534,875), Red Sox (2,510,014), Cubs (2,491,-942), Royals (2,477,700), Giants (2,059,829) and Rangers (2,043,993).

One reason so many people went to see baseball played is that it has never been played so well. And because so many people want to see it, in ballparks and in their living rooms, the caliber of play should continue to rise. Money matters; money attracts talent. After the 1988 season baseball struck a bonanza. As a result, the level of the game should be even higher in the 1990s and beyond. This is so even if there is expansion of up to six more teams, which there probably will, and should, be. Indeed, expansion, which means more careers open to talents, should in time make baseball even better.

Peter Ueberroth's final services to baseball were two new television contracts. CBS will pay $1.08 billion for exclusive over-the-air (noncable) coverage of major league baseball in the four seasons 1990 through 1993. In 1989 NBC and ABC were paying about $100 million apiece for baseball. CBS will pay $270 million a season. This will buy 16 regular-season games, the All-Star Game, both League Championship Series and the World Series. Even if both LCSs and the Series go to 7 games, CBS would be televising just 38 games, paying $7.1 million per game, or $790,000 per inning, $132,000 per out. That is a lot of six packs of beer. Also, ESPN made a four-season $400 million deal to telecast 6 games a week, 175 per season. In 1990 each team will get about $14 million—$10.38 million from CBS and $3.8 million from ESPN. In 1989 twelve teams had payrolls of less than $14 million. Then there are revenues from network radio. Ticket sales bring about $7.17 per ticket—more than $350 million annually. There also are substantial revenues from local radio, television, food and souvenir concessions and parking. (Of course all this must go to support the crushing costs of wood bats.)

Baseball's general health is served by making baseball a more lucrative life. It is a matter of supply and demand. The more dollar demand there is for talent, the more talent is apt to be supplied. The pool of money is growing. When, in the mid-1990s, expansion comes, the number of jobs will grow, too. When the relative longevity of baseball careers is considered, the balance tips increasingly toward baseball in the competition with other sports for the services of young athletes. For those who become established major league players (playing at least two years), the average career now lasts about ten years. That may not seem long to you and me, but remember what Robert Frost said: "Happiness makes up in height for what it lacks in length."

Ray Miller, moralist and social scientist, says "baseball is losing top athletes because baseball is not the easy way." A young football or basketball star can go into a college program, get an education and go straight to the top professional level. A college baseball player goes out to play in minor league parks, most of which are a lot less spiffy than the ones he played in as an undergraduate. Furthermore, baseball is not the easy way because its skills are harder to master than those of other sports. Consider, says Al Rosen, football. A wide receiver or defensive end needs serious skills. The receiver has to learn his routes, the defensive end his zones, or man-to-man coverage. But these skills do not compare in difficulty with the skills required to hit a baseball. Rosen notes that two superb athletes who are NFL quarterbacks, John Elway of the Broncos and Jay Schroeder of the Raiders, both played college baseball and both had major league teams interested in them—but not very interested. Both, says Rosen, would have risen at most to Single-A ball. The highest degree of difficulty is in hitting. It is the reason why baseball is a business in which most beginners, even those destined for the top, begin in the mail room—deep in the minors. And most will not make it to the top.

Baseball demands extraordinary talent, and baseball talent is difficult to judge. Ron Fraser, baseball coach of the University of Miami Hurricanes, says that only 5 percent of all drafted players make it to the major leagues. Of the 258 *first-round* picks in the ten years through 1986, just 55 percent made it to the major leagues. The picks most likely to be well-picked were pitchers, because their talents can be more reliably judged than those of batters using aluminum bats. (However, when the young Sandy Koufax was given a tryout by the Giants at the Polo Grounds the catcher told him, "Make sure you get a good college education, kid, because you won't make it in the majors.")

Today there are choruses of people lamenting the large salaries earned by players. This moralizing makes no economic sense. The salaries are earned: The players make more for the owners than the owners pay in salaries. But the belief that large amounts of money must be bad for players is nothing new. A 1914 editorial in a baseball magazine advised players to ponder the terrible swiftness with which players become men in the crowd: "It is, as a rule, a man's own business how he spends his money. But nevertheless we wish to call attention to the fact that many men do so in a very unwise manner. A very glaring instance of this among baseball players is the recent evil tendency to purchase and maintain automobiles. Put the money away, boys, where it will be safe. You don't need these automobiles. The money will look mighty good later on in life. Think it over, boys."

Baseball has come a long way since the days when, on road trips, players slept two to a bed. (Rube Waddell's roommate made manager Connie Mack put a clause in Waddell's contract to prevent him from eating crackers in bed.) In 1988 a Honus Wagner baseball card issued in 1910 sold for $110,000. It was issued by a cigarette company and Wagner, a passionate foe of smoking, demanded that the company stop issuing it, and thus few of the cards ever existed. The 1988 value of $110,000, adjusted for inflation, was approximately equal in value to the $10,000 Wagner earned in 1910. In 1929 Lefty O'Doul hit .398 with 254 hits—a National League record never surpassed. It earned him a $500 raise. In 1932 he hit "only" .368 and his salary was cut $1,000. A player in the Pacific Coast League in the late 1940s was summoned to the St. Louis Browns but refused to report because his salary in the major leagues would have been less than half of what he was making in the minors. In 1976 the average salary was $52,380. In 1989 the major league minimum salary was $68,000, more than 100 players earned at least $1 million, 20 earned at least $2 million and the average salary was about $513,730. In 1990 several will earn more than $3 million. Hershiser worries that today's stratospheric salaries will have the effect of making it harder than it used to be to keep players around baseball after their playing days. "Baseball will lose a lot of knowledge because players will make enough money that they will not have to stay in baseball. In the past a lot of players stayed in baseball because it was their only asset." Maybe, but many of them would have stayed in the game anyway because the game was in their blood, as it is in Hershiser's. He was baseball's best-paid player in 1989 and I will wager that he will be in baseball, perhaps as a general manager, long after he retires.

Many Cassandras said that money, combined with the sudden arrival of a substantially free market in talent, was going to make a shambles of competitive balance. There still are grounds for anxiety. The fresh infusions of broadcasting money could become important to baseball's competitive balance because of the inherent inequalities among teams regarding the value of local broadcasting rights. Around the time Ueberroth was finalizing the national agreements, the Yankees were finalizing a local cable agreement giving them $41 million a year for 12 years. The Milwaukee Brewers, who compete against the Yankees in the American League East, will get about $3 million a year from local television revenues. The $38 million differential is worrisome. But as the Yankees (and Atlanta Braves) have recently shown, the absence of baseball acumen in the front office can be a great leveler, regardless of financial assets.

So far, the Cassandras have been wrong. The end of the reserve clause did not bring on an era of *Sturm und Drang* and ruinous imbalance. All the talent did not wind up on the two coasts, in the New York and Los Angeles markets, leaving a wasteland of mediocrity in the middle. A few crazed owners, like Ted Turner of the Braves, did not ruin competitive balance by building checkbook dynasties. There was some *Sturm und Drang;* there was no competitive imbalance. In fact, the coming of free agency coincided with the demise of the last of the dynasties, the Oakland Athletics and Cincinnati Reds of the early and mid-1970s. In the first decade of free agency, all 12 National League teams and 11 of the 14 American League teams (all except Cleveland, Seattle and Texas) won division championships.

Pennant races are more riveting than ever because there are so many fresh faces in the races in any five-year span. In the great National League pennant race of 1964, when in late September the front-running Phillies lost 10 in a row and the pennant, the Giants were not eliminated until the next to last day of the season—and finished fourth. But that was before divisional play, so six teams finished below the Giants. Today it is possible to have four races for first places. Those races are remarkably open these days. We live in an era of baseball equality. Not perfect equality, of course, but the thrill of victory has been spread around.

Of the original 16 major league franchises, the Phillies were the last to win a World Series. That was in 1980, by which time there were 26 franchises. The St. Louis Browns only got to the World Series by dashing through the yawning gaps that World War II had made in baseball by 1944. The Browns lost the Series. The Browns had gone to Baltimore and become the Orioles when the franchise won its first Series, in 1966. In 1988 the Cubs broke the St. Louis Browns' record of 43 consecutive seasons without winning a league championship. (After 1989 their record was 44.) But nowadays any team can hope to win, if not right now, then soon. Through 1989 there have been 221 division or league champions in modern major league history. Only 30 of them won after a losing season the year before. But nowadays the mighty are not mighty for long and the losers can reasonably expect to rise through the falling debris of one-shot winners.

On an August afternoon in 1984, when the Cubs were sweeping a doubleheader against the Mets in Wrigley Field en route to their first divisional championship, Salty Saltwell of the Cubs' front office was asked why the Cubs were doing so well. He replied, without hesitation, with the explanation that comes naturally to baseball people: "We're playing way over our heads." Indeed they were. The 1984 Cubs were 96–65. The 1983 Cubs had been 71–91, finishing fifth. The 1985 Cubs finished fourth, 77–84. Saltwell's assessment was as much a deduction as an inference; it was as much the application of a general principle as a judgment of the particular players. It is axiomatic nowadays that teams win division titles, pennants and World Series because a number of their key players have what are called "career years."

It was not always that way. For many years a few teams dominated baseball year in and year out. From 1926 through 1964 the Yankees had 39 consecutive winning seasons, including 26 first-place finishes. The closest any clubs have come to that achievement is not even close. The 1968–85 Orioles had 18 consecutive winning seasons. The 1951–67 White Sox had 17. Through 1989 the team with the longest such streak was the Toronto Blue Jays with 7 seasons. Between 1903 and 1964 there were 61 World Series and a team from New York appeared in 39 of them. In 13 of those Series both teams were from New York. In 1951 all three New York teams finished first. (That year the city had six 20-game winners.) From 1949 through 1953 the Yankees won 5 consecutive pennants. If the Dodgers had won two particular games—the last game of the 1950 season against the Phillies and the third and final game of the 1951 play-off (the game won by the Giants' Bobby Thomson's home run)—the Dodgers, too, would have won 5 pennants in those 5 years, and for half a decade all World Series games would have been played in New York. The Dodgers and Yankees also won pennants in 1947, 1955 and 1956. In the decade 1947–56 the Yankees won 8 pennants, the Dodgers 6. In the 11 seasons from 1946 through 1956 the Yankees won 90 games 10 times, the Dodgers 9 times. The Yankees won 1,061 games, the Dodgers won just 20 fewer. The Yankees finished second in 1954 although they won 103 games. (The Indians set an American League record that year with 111 wins.) If 103 wins had sufficed, as it usually does, to win the pennant, the Yankees would have been in 10 consecutive World Series.

More recently there has been wholesome turmoil. The 1977–78 Yankees were the last World Series winners to repeat. From the 1979 Yankees through the 1989 Dodgers (and excluding the 1981 strike season) defending champions have averaged 12.7 fewer wins the next season. For most teams in major league history, life has been a mild roller-coaster ride. Most teams that improve their record from one season to the next suffer, in the third season, a decline of about one-third of what they gained in the second season. Only one team in history, the 1937–42 Dodgers, has increased its winning percentage in 6 consecutive seasons—an achievement that almost presupposes starting from a deep hole. (The 1937 Dodgers were 62–91.) Today, when there are no dominating teams, everyone is riding the roller coaster. Since the Yankees and Dodgers met in the 1977 and 1978 World Series, only La Russa's Athletics of 1988 and 1989 have played in two consecutive Series. In 1987 the Twins became the tenth team in 10 years to win the World Series. In the 1970s the Reds and Pirates each won 6 division titles. But the Reds and Pirates were the only National League teams *not to* win division titles in the 1980s. In the 11 seasons from 1979 through 1989, 4 divisional championship teams won 100 or more games in a season and then failed to repeat as division winners the next year. In the 1980s only 3 of 40 division winners (8 percent) have won their division the next year. (They were all in the American League: the 1980–81 Yankees, the 1984–85 Royals, the 1988–89 Athletics.) Forty-two percent of the division winners had losing records the next year. On the other hand, 13 teams in the 1980s won division titles a year after finishing in the second division or below .500. The participants in the 1982 World Series, the Cardinals and the Brewers, each finished 11 games behind in 1983. In 1986 the teams that were in the 1985 World Series (the Royals and the Cardinals) finished a total of 44½ games out of first. Three of the 1986 division winners tumbled in 1987 to below .500. These days a world champion one year can win more games the next year and do worse. Because of the 1988 Athletics, the Twins became the first team in history to win the World Series (1987), then win more games the next year but not finish first. By the end of the 1988 season the Mets, who did not even make it to the World Series, were the closest any team could come to claiming to be a "dynasty." They had won 90 or more games 5 seasons in a row. No other team had won 90 games in both 1987 and 1988. But in 1989 they won just 87 and finished 6 games behind. So much for the Mets' dynastic pretensions. The Athletics won 203 times in the 1988 and 1989 seasons. By the time the dust had settled from the Athletics' 1989 post-season perform-ance—the dismantling of the Blue Jays, 4-1, in the LCS and the sweep of the Giants in the World Series—it was arguable that the Athletics were just one more World Series season away from being rightly denoted a dynasty. La Russa said flatly that neither the 1927 Yankees nor the Big Red Machines of 1975 and 1976 were better than the 1989 Athletics. Two retired Reds, Johnny Bench and Joe Morgan, thought their teams were better. For the record, here are some of the offensive records:

	1975 Reds	1976 Reds	1989 Athletics
Runs	840	857	712
Home Runs	124	141	127
Extra-Base Hits	439	475	372
Stolen Bases	168	210	157
Errors	102	102	127
Run Differential	+254 (840−586)	+224 (857−633)	+136 (712−576)
	1.57 per game	1.38 per game	.84 per game

The 1989 Athletics had much better pitching, starters and relievers, than those Reds teams had. At least regarding the 1989 Athletics and the 1975–76 Reds, I think La Russa is right.

However good today's best teams are, there are no really awful teams today. The original Mets of 1962 were awful. They won 40 while losing 120, finishing tenth, 18 games out of ninth. But they were a lot better off than the 1916 Athletics. Victimized by Connie Mack's fire sale of talent after the team lost the 1914 World Series to the manifestly inferior Braves, the 1916 team sagged to eighth, 54½ games out of first, with a 36–117 record. But the 1916 Athletics were better than those 1899 Cleveland Spiders, who were 20–134. If the season had not ended when it did, there is no telling to what depths of sorrow the Spiders could have sunk. They lost 40 of their last 41 games. Through 1989 only the Seattle Mariners had failed to reach .500 for a season in the 1980s. But they are special: By 1990 they were two short of the record of 15 consecutive losing seasons set by the 1919–33 Red Sox (right after they sold you-know-who) and the 1953–67 Philadelphia and Kansas City Athletics. But if there are no terrible teams, neither are there any great teams. The Elias Bureau has produced a table that expresses today's volatility numerically. In the 1980s division winners had winning percentages of just .529. Furthermore, in the seasons immediately before those in which they won their division titles, these teams finished, on average, nearly 8.7 games out of first. This is not the way it used to be. This Elias table lists, by decades, the average winning percentages of division and league champions, and the average number of games they finished out of first place in the seasons immediately prior to winning their titles.

YEARS	PCT.	MARGIN
1900–09	.624	+1.81
1910–19	.580	−8.30
1920–29	.584	−4.05
1930–39	.593	−3.17
1940–49	.583	−6.15
1950–59	.595	−2.68
1960–69	.548	−8.14
1970–79	.575	+0.55
1980–89	.529	−8.69

The "0.55" for 1970–79 reflects the existence of that vanished species, the dynasty, which roamed the land then in the form of the Oakland Athletics and then Cincinnati's "Big Red Machine."

There has not been so much volatility since the 1940s, when a world war siphoned off most of the talent. The fact that there is no dominant team today causes some people to conclude that baseball has less talent. But equality does not mean mediocrity. The fact that there is no great team does not prove that baseball is not as good as it was when there was a dynasty such as the Yankees once were. On the contrary, the volatility is evidence of the wide dispersal of excellence.

Most track and field records have been improving rapidly for decades. The size and balletic skills of players have made today's basketball a game that would be virtually unrecognizable to a Rip Van Winkle who fell asleep 40 years ago watching a basketball game in the late 1940s. (Falling asleep was easy to do at a 1940s basketball game.) The best college teams of the 1940s would not survive—or even get to—the first round of today's NCAA basketball tournament. Football, too, has been transformed. In fact, the kinetic energy involved in 6-foot-8 linemen who have a sprinter's speed in 20-yard bursts has made football too dangerous for creatures constructed with human knees and necks. Given the general improvement, often constituting radical change, in so many sports, it does seem reasonable to conclude that baseball, too, must be much better than ever.

However, the fact that extraordinary improvement has characterized sport generally does not itself compel us to conclude that the same *must* be true of baseball. The difference is that baseball is more difficult. Or, to put the point in a way perhaps slightly less annoying to partisans of other sports, baseball is difficult in peculiarly demanding ways. Baseball involves so many situations that must be mastered mentally, and so many skills involving that mental mastery, and so much anticipation, and so much execution within extraordinarily fine tolerances. Thus the fact that there is abundant and obvious improvement in the performances in other sports does not demonstrate that baseball, too, is better.

It is better. However, many fans are reluctant to receive this good news. Baseball fans are generally a cheerful lot, at least between late February and late October. (Literary critic Jonathan Yardley says there are only two seasons: baseball season and The Void.) However, human beings seem to take morose pleasure from believing that once there was a Golden Age, some lost Eden or Camelot or superior ancient civilization, peopled by heroes and demigods, an age of greatness long lost and irrecoverable. Piffle. Things are better than ever, at least in baseball, which is what matters most. And the reason for the improvement says something heartening about life. Stephen Jay Gould teaches biology, geology and the history of science at Harvard. His special interest is evolutionary processes. As a student of life's long-term trends, he has pondered the extinction of the .400 hitter (none since 1941) and he concludes that the cause is not, as you had feared, "entropic homogeneity." Rather, the reason is that systems equilibrate as they improve. While the highest averages have declined, the average batting average has remained remarkably stable over time. It was around .260 in the 1870s and is about that today. (It was .255 in 1989.) But the highest averages have declined because narrowing variation is a general property of systems undergoing refinement. Variations in batting averages—the gap between the highest averages and the leagues' averages—shrink as improvements in play eliminate many inadequacies of the majority of pitchers and fielders. Today's "just average" player is better than yesterday's. Gould says major league players meet today in competition "too finely honed toward perfection to permit the extremes of achievement that characterized a more casual age." As baseball has been sharpened—every pitch, swing and hit is charted—its range of tolerance has narrowed, its boundaries have been drawn in and its rough edges smoothed. As Gould says, Wee Willie Keeler could "hit 'em where they ain't" (to the tune of .432 in 1897) partly because "they"—the fielders—were not where they should have been. They did not know better. Today's players play as hard as the old-timers did, and know much more. Try the following experiment in filling up nine positions. A team assembled just from players who entered baseball since 1945 (which would exclude, for example, Williams, DiMaggio and Musial) would not be demonstrably inferior to a team drawn from all the players who played during the first half of the century.

Catcher	Johnny Bench, Yogi Berra
First base	Willie McCovey, Willie Stargell
Second base	Rod Carew, Joe Morgan
Third base	Mike Schmidt, Brooks Robinson
Shortstop	Ernie Banks, Ozzie Smith
Outfield	Willie Mays, Mickey Mantle, Henry Aaron, Frank Robinson, Roberto Clemente, Carl Yastrzemski
Left-handed pitcher	Sandy Koufax
Right-handed pitcher	Bob Gibson

Furthermore, although the first black players did not make it to the major leagues until 1947 and baseball was not really fully open to blacks until the mid-1950s, it is possible to select an all-black team that could hold its own with a team drawn from all the other players during the first nine decades of this century.

Catcher	Roy Campanella
First base	Willie McCovey
Second base	Rod Carew

Third base	Jackie Robinson (he played 256 games at third)
Shortstop	Ernie Banks
Outfield	Willie Mays, Henry Aaron, Frank Robinson
Pitcher	Bob Gibson

Tony Gwynn hit "only" .332 in the 1980s because average play has improved so much that there are fewer opportunities for geniuses like Gwynn to exploit (in Gould's phrase) "suboptimality in others." The "play" in playing professional baseball is, Gould says, gone. Baseball has become a science in the sense that it emphasizes repetitious precision in the execution of its component actions. That is why variation decreases at both ends, with the highest and lowest averages edging toward the league average. Standard deviations (take a deep breath: the square root of the sum of the squares of all individual averages minus the major league average divided by the total number of players) are narrowed by progress. The extinction of the .400 hitter, like the rareness of the dynastic team, is evidence of progress, not regression.

It is inconceivable that a protean figure like Babe Ruth could burst upon baseball today. Remember how disproportionate his achievements were to those of his contemporaries. In 1919 the Yankees led the major leagues in home runs with 45. But up in Boston, Ruth hit 29. And in 1920, as a Yankee, he hit 54. The American League's second-best slugger in 1920 was George Sisler. He hit only 19. The National League champion had 15. Only one American League team other than the Yankees had more than 44. Ruth's biographer, Robert W. Creamer, notes that when Ruth was sold to the Yankees after the 1919 season he was already recognized as the greatest home-run hitter in baseball history—and he had hit just 49 (the number Mark McGwire hit in his 1987 rookie season). The career leader at the time was Roger Connor with 136. Ruth became baseball's career home-run hitter in 1921, which was just his third season as a full-time (nonpitching) player. He proceeded to break his own record 577 times. When in 1934 he hit his 700th home run, only two other players had more than 300. When he retired his total of 714 was nearly twice the total of the man in second place (Gehrig, then at 378). Over a 6-season span (1926–31) Ruth averaged 50 home runs, 154 RBIs, 147 runs and a .354 average.

Suppose Ruth had more frequently gone to bed early and with Mrs. Ruth. Suppose he had not downed a couple of hot dogs (and a glass of bicarbonate soda) before most games. Suppose he had not had the habits that caused him to balloon one winter to a gargantuan 49¾-inch waist—larger than his chest. (Perhaps the Yankees would not be wearing pinstripes today, an innovation ordered by their owner, the elegant Jacob Ruppert, who hoped the stripes would make Ruth look less obese.) If Ruth had lived sensibly and trained as we now know how to train, he would loom even larger over his era, like an Everest in Kansas.

But he could not so loom today. Once when Mickey Mantle was weary of hearing the batting achievements of his era dismissively discussed as mere products of a livelier ball, he said, "Maybe the players are livelier now." Certainly they are generally bigger and stronger and faster, and they know more about a game that rewards *knowing*. Baseball is an intensely emulative industry. What works gets noticed almost immediately and is communicated quickly among baseball people, who are great talkers. As the Elias people write, "There are no copyrights on strategy." That is why baseball is a game of watchfulness. Success goes to those who are paying attention, day by day, from April to October.

A baseball season is a surefire quality detector. By late October one team is certified the best. Five months later 26 teams start all over again. And nowadays, more often than not, the team that proved itself to be the best the previous year goes on to be proven, over the next six months, to be no longer the best. Competition has intensified, not just because talent has been emancipated and become mobile, but also, and even more, because of the progressive nature of the game. Knowledge matters, knowledge is cumulative, knowledge travels. The margin between baseball success and failure has been shrinking. It never has been large.

A team that plays only .500 ball is considered barely respectable. But a team that wins 11 of every 20 games wins 89 games and probably is a pennant contender. The best five-year team record is that of the 1906–10 Cubs: .693. So baseball's best sustained performance still did not quite amount to winning seven out of ten, consistently. In recent decades it has become increasingly rare for a team (the 1961 Yankees, 1969–70 Orioles, 1975 Reds, 1986 Mets) to win twice as many games as it loses. Since divisional play began in 1969, 60 percent of the titles have been won by six or fewer games, 50 percent by five or fewer. More than a fifth (22.5 percent) have been won by two or fewer games. Many games turn on a single play, a single pitch, so championships can be—and frequently are—decided by a half dozen plays or pitches.

"Don't you know how hard this all is?" said Ted Williams, talking about baseball. Actually, very few people, even among the most attentive fans, know. But Henry Heitmann knew. *The Baseball Encyclopedia* contains this entry, surely one of the most melancholy career totals:

	W	L	PCT	ERA	G	GS	CG	IP	H	BB	SO	ShO	Relief Pitching W L SV			BATTING AB H HR			BA
Henry Heitmann				HEITMANN, HARRY ANTON B. Oct. 6, 1896, Albany, N. Y.						D. Dec. 15, 1958, Brooklyn, N. Y.						BR TR 6'			175 lbs.
1918 BKN N	0	1	.000	108.00	1	1	0	.1	4	0	0	0	0	0	0	0	0	0	–

On July 27, 1918, the Dodgers gave the ball to pitcher Heitmann and sent him out to cope with the Cardinals. This he did not do. He gave up four hits and four runs. He got one Cardinal out. That was the beginning of his major league career, and the end of it. (Hence his career ERA of 108.) His career is a complete contrast with that of Warren Spahn. Spahn was not only the winningest left-hander, he also came within six losses of being the losingest. That is what longevity means in baseball: a lot of both winning and losing. Spahn won more games after turning 35 than Sandy Koufax won in his career, which ended when Koufax was 30. Careers in sports have different spans and paces, but they all have one thing in common. They end, going downhill. The photographer Margaret Bourke-White once described her work as "a trusted friend, who never deserts you." Every baseball player is deserted. The natural attrition of skills spares no one. So there is an inevitable poignancy inherent in the careers of even the best professional athletes. They compress the natural trajectory of human experience—striving, attaining, declining—into such a short span. Their hopes for fulfillment are hostage to their bodies, to attributes that are short-lived and subject to decay. The decay occurs in public, in front of large audiences. The decay is chronicled and monitored by millions of people who study the unsparing statistics that are the mathematics of baseball accomplishment. But poignancy is not the same thing as sadness. Baseball is a remarkably cheerful business.

Baseball is, of course, hardly immune to the ills of the society of which it is an expression. Thus, being a fan is not unalloyed fun. For one famous fan, baseball was heartbreaking. One of the costs of the 1919 Black Sox gambling scandal was that baseball lost one of its best writers, Ring Lardner, whose disillusionment drove him away from the game. Shortly after Lardner died in 1933, his friend F. Scott Fitzgerald wrote a summation of Lardner's life. It was affectionate and generally approving, but it contained Fitzgerald's conclusion that Lardner had invested too much of his talent in writing about something that Fitzgerald considered unworthy of such attention: baseball. "A boy's game," wrote Fitzgerald, "with no more possibilities in it than a boy could master, a game bounded by walls which kept out novelty or danger, change or adventure. This material, the observation of it under such circumstances, was the text of Ring's schooling, during the most formative period of the mind. . . . However deeply Ring might cut into it, his cake had the diameter of Frank Chance's diamond." Actually, the diamond of the mind can be larger than Fitzgerald thought.

There is, of course, a sense in which sport is the toy department of life. But professional sport, and especially baseball, has serious resonances in society. A nation's preferred forms of recreation are not of trivial importance. They are tone-setting facets of the nation's life. Scores of millions of Americans spend billions of hours a year watching baseball, listening to broadcasts of it, talking and reading and thinking about it. This pleasurable preoccupation is, at its best, an appreciation of grace, self-control and the steady application of an elegant craft.

"Knowin' all about baseball," said humorist Kin Hubbard, "is just about as profitable as bein' a good whittler." Wrong. Knowing a lot (no one knows all) about baseball confers not only the profit of an elevating pleasure, but also that of instruction. It teaches a general truth about excellence. However, if we must talk about profits, permit me this concluding unscientific postscript.

I am a layman who has spent some time trespassing—respectfully—on the turf of specialists, the men and women who write about baseball full time. I am by vocation a commentator on social events, trends and problems. People who do what I do in periodic journalism often seem to be professional scolds. My interest in writing this book has been to have fun exploring the spirit and practice and ethic of something fun, a sport. But I can not forbear from drawing a lesson.

The national pastime is better than ever in almost every way and is getting even better every year. The same can not be said about the nation. America consumes too much and saves too little. Indeed the nation's savings rate, the worst among industrial nations, is a scandal because it is a choice: Public policies contribute to it. Small savings and huge government deficits cause underinvestment, which causes slow growth of productivity, which produces economic anemia and uncompetitiveness. Increasingly we are being outperformed by—and even owned by—our competitors. We should be chagrined, but not surprised. They are studying harder and longer, and working harder and longer and better than we are. From a population approximately one-half the size of ours, Japan is producing an equal number of engineers. In 1985, 55 percent of U.S. doctoral degrees in engineering were awarded to foreign nationals, many of whom went home. In the late 1980s about half the Ph.D.s being hired in the high-tech electronics industry were foreign born. We produce 35,000 lawyers a year. Japan muddles through with only a fraction of that depressing total. American children spend 180 days in school, Japanese children spend 240 days and the school days are longer. Japanese students outperform American students in math, science and engineering. American children outperform Japanese in English. For now.

Such facts have given rise to a spate of analyses, the theme of which is that America's problems are the result of "imperial overstretch," a national impulse to try to do too much abroad. I believe America's real problem is individual understretch, a tendency of Americans to demand too little of themselves, at their lathes, their desks, their computer terminals. The baseball men I have spent time with while preparing this book demonstrate an admirable seriousness about their capabilities. They also demonstrate the compatibility of seriousness and fun. In fact, what makes baseball especially fun is seeing the way its best players apply their seriousness.

A generation ago a wit said that Americans most wanted to read books about animals or the Civil War, so the ideal book would be *I Was Lincoln's Vet.* Nowadays it sometimes seems that Americans are most interested in "how-to" books, especially those that teach one how to attain thin thighs quickly or sexual ecstasy slowly. Today the shelves in bookstores groan beneath the weight of books purporting to explain how to attain excellence in business, and especially how to beat the Japanese in commercial competition. I will not belabor the point but I do assert it: If Americans made goods and services the way Ripken makes double plays, Gwynn makes hits, Hershiser makes pitches and La Russa makes decisions, you would hear no more about the nation's trajectory having passed its apogee.

America, the first modern nation, has led the world in what historian Daniel Boorstin calls "mass producing the moment." We do this with photographs, movies, tapes, records, compact disks and copying machines. Modern manufacturing is the mass production of identical products. In merchandising, the development of franchising (McDonald's, Holiday Inns) has made it possible to go from coast to coast having identical experiences eating and sleeping. You can go all the way on the interstate highway system and never really see the particularities of a town. A sport like baseball, although a small universe of rule-regulated behavior, is actually a refreshing realm of diversity. The games are like snowflakes. They are perishable and no one is exactly like any other. But to see the diversities of snowflakes you must look closely and carefully. Baseball, more than any other sport, is enjoyed by the knowledgeable. The pleasures it gives to fans are proportional to the fans' sense of history. Its beauties are visible to the trained eye, which is the result of a long apprenticeship in appreciation. The more such apprenticeships we have, the more we will be able to drive away one of the retrograde features of today's baseball experience, the multiplication of irrelevant sights and sounds in ballparks.

When Roger Angell of *The New Yorker* first decorously expressed his disapproval of Houston's Astrodome, he said that the most common complaint about the place is valid but incidental. The most common complaint is that going to a game there amounts to exchanging your living room for a larger one. But what matters most, Angell said, is the violence done by the entire ambiance of the Astrodome. It is violence done to "the quality of baseball time." A person absorbed in a baseball game should be "in a green place of removal" where tension is intensified slowly, pitch by pitch. The contest has its own continuum and that continuum is degraded by attempts to "use up" time with planned distractions such as entertaining scoreboards, dancing ball girls, costumed mascots and the like. The attempt to attract fans by planned distractions is worse than gilding the lily. It attacks the lily by disregarding its virtue. Baseball's foremost virtue as a spectator sport is that, as Angell says, it "is perhaps the most perfectly visible sport ever devised." That is why it is the sport that most rewards the fan's attention to details and nuances. Nuances should matter to the observer because they matter so much to the participants—managers and players—who determine who wins.

Bart Giamatti, speaking with Roger Angell, deplored "the NFL-ization of baseball." He meant the infestation of ballparks by clown-ish mascots (the bastard children of the San Diego Chicken) and the pollution of the parks' atmospheres by "dot races," rock music trivia quizzes and other distractions. Some franchises, said Giamatti, "are like theatrical companies who only want to do Shakespeare in mo-torcycle boots and leather jackets. They've given up on the beautiful language." The language should suffice. Perhaps NFL-ization is a concession to the "television babies," those Americans under 40 who find rock videos pleasurable and even, in some sense, intelligi-ble. Baseball is a sport for the literate, and not merely in the sense that it involves, for the aficionado, a lot of reading and has frequently been the subject of literature. It is also a mode of expression more suited to a literary than a pictorial culture. A baseball game is an orderly experience—perhaps too orderly for the episodic mentali-ties of television babies. A baseball game is, like a sentence, a linear sequence; like a paragraph, it proceeds sequentially. But to enjoy it you have to be able to read it. Baseball requires baseball literacy.

"This ain't a football game," said Orioles manager Earl Weaver. "We do this every day." That is why baseball is a game you can not play with your teeth clenched. But neither can you play it with your mind idling in neutral. Baseball is a game where you have to do more than one thing very well, but one thing at a time. The best baseball people are (although you do not hear this description ban-died about in dugouts) Cartesians. That is, they apply Descartes's methods to their craft, breaking it down into bite-size components, mastering them and then building the craft up, bit by bit. Descartes, whose vocation was to think about thinking, said (I am paraphrasing somewhat): The problem is that we make mistakes. The solution is to strip our thought processes down to basics and begin with a rock-solid foundation, some certainty from which we can reason carefully to other certainties. His bedrock certainty was *Cogito ergo sum*—"I think, therefore I am." His theory was that by assembling small certainties, one could build an unassailable edifice of truths. As any infielder could have told Descartes, errors will happen, no mat-ter how careful you are. But Descartes's method is not a bad model of how best to get on with things in life: Master enough little prob-lems and you will have few big problems.

Dizzy Dean once said after a 1–0 game, "The game was closer than the score indicated." In a sense it may well have been. Games are often decided by marginal moves and episodes less stark and noticeable than a run. They are won, and championship seasons are achieved, by the attention to small matters, and the law of cumulation. In the 1952 musical *Pajama Game* there is a song about a wage increase:

> Seven and a half cents doesn't mean a hell of a lot,
> Seven and a half cents doesn't mean a thing,
> But give it to me every hour, forty hours every week,
> And that's enough for me to be living like a king,
> I figured it out.

Ray Kroc, the founder of McDonald's, figured it out. Sell enough 15-cent hamburgers (which is what they cost in the 1950s) and you are a billionaire. Do enough 15-cent things right in baseball—"It breaks down to its smallest parts," Rick Dempsey said—and you may win. Let those parts slide and try to rely on $100 achievements—spectacular events—and you will lose. The best players pay the most attention to baseball's parts. Frank Crosetti, a Yankee coach, saw every game DiMaggio played and never saw him thrown out going from first to third. When DiMaggio was asked why he placed such a high value on excellence he said, "There is always some kid who may be seeing me for the first or last time. I owe him my best."

DiMaggio's dignity was bound up with his brand of excellence. "People said, 'You're so relaxed on the ball field.' I'd say, 'But I knew what I was doing.'" There is also dignity in honest mediocrity, even in the unforgiving meritocracy of professional sports. And there is our obligation for special discipline on the part of the especially gifted. This was the theme of one of the spate of baseball movies in the late 1980s, *Bull Durham*.

In olden days, most baseball movies went like this. Boy meets baseball and falls in love. Then boy meets girl and inexplicably (one grand passion should suffice) falls in love again. The girl's role is to sit in the bleachers beneath a broad-brimmed hat and look anxious in his adversity and adoring in his inevitable triumph over it. *Bull Durham* is different in two particulars, one of which is the girl, who is decidedly no girl. The other is the ball player, who is no Lou Gehrig. He is not the Pride of the Yankees, or even of the Durham Bulls.

Annie is more than 30 summers old but is a fetching sight wearing a short off-the-shoulder dress and, as exquisite accessories, batting gloves. She pitches Whitman and Blake to students of English at a community college and also at one ball player each season. "A guy will listen to anything if he thinks it's foreplay," she says from considerable experience. Annie, the thinking person's theist ("I believe in the church of Baseball"), takes one player as her lover each season but is not, by her lights, promiscuous: "I am, within the framework of a baseball season, monogamous." Furthermore, "I'd never sleep with a player hitting under .250 unless he had a lot of RBIs or was a great glove man up the middle. A woman's got to have standards."

But when it comes to keeping standards, which is the movie's moral theme, the hero is Crash Davis, a journeyman catcher. He once made it to the major leagues, but only for a cup of coffee. Now in his twelfth minor league season, he is brought to Durham to teach baseball's craftsmanship to a promising but unpolished pitcher, Ebby Calvin "Nuke" LaLoosh. When Annie asks Crash, in effect, to compete with Nuke for the privilege of being her lover for a season, he walks away, saying: "I'm not interested in a woman who is interested in that boy." In terms of physical skills, Crash is not much. But in terms of character, he is the real keeper of the flame of craftsmanship. While Annie teaches Nuke about, well, life, Crash teaches him that his million-dollar arm does not mean he can get by with a five-cent brain. In baseball, concentration is required of everyone. Alas, Nuke is a male bimbo, an airhead who has to be tutored by Crash even about the clichés that comprise the basic interview. ("We gotta play 'em one day at a time. . . . I just wanna give it my best shot.") When Nuke asks why Crash dislikes him, Crash goes to the heart of the matter: " 'Cause you don't respect yourself, which is your problem, but you don't respect the game—and that's my problem."

Nuke has no idea how much hard work is required to achieve excellence, even when nature has given great talent. It has been said that the difference between the major and minor leagues is just a matter of "inches and consistency." That is essentially true of the difference between excellence and mere adequacy in poetry or surgery or anything else.

When Nuke bounces into the dugout after one good inning, there's this exchange:

Nuke: "I was good, eh?"

Crash: "Your fastball was up and your curveball was hanging. In the Show [major leagues], they woulda ripped you."

NUKE: "Can't you let me enjoy the moment?"
CRASH: "The moment's over."

Crash has learned the essential lesson of life. Nothing lasts. The past is past. Everything must be achieved anew—on the next pitch, the next at bat, in the next game, the next season.

Past performance gives rise to averages, on which managers calculate probabilities about performances to come. The more you study, the less surprised you are. But no matter how hard you study, you are still surprised agreeably often. And the surprises that come to the studious are especially delicious. One reason for surprises is that no one puts batteries in the players: They are not robots. They are people whose personalities and characters vary under pressure, including the most important pressure, that which they put on themselves. William James knew what baseball people know: "There is very little difference between one man and another; but what little there is is very important." All players who make it to the major leagues are superior athletes. The different degrees of superiority in terms of natural physical skills are less marked and less important than another difference. It is the difference in the intensity of the application to the craftsmanship of baseball. Some people work harder than others, a lot harder.

Standing in the manager's office in Baltimore's Memorial Stadium late on a Sunday afternoon in the middle of June, 1989, and in the dishevelment of a man eager to get out of uniform and out of town, Tony La Russa, manager of the Oakland Athletics, was being asked why the Orioles, recently such lowly wretches, were playing so well. They had just beaten the Athletics three times in three days. What was the secret? Was it pitching? Defense? Neither, said La Russa, his natural curtness now compounded with impatience at journalistic obtuseness. The secret, he said, clipping every word like a fuse, is no secret. It is at the core of all baseball success. It is intensity: "They are playing hard."

Intensity in athletics has many manifestations. As a youngster, Pete Maravich dribbled a basketball wherever he walked, and sometimes while sitting. At movies he selected aisle seats so he could bounce the ball during the show. The young Ted Williams walked around San Diego squeezing a rubber ball to develop his forearms. After the Yankees lost the 1960 World Series on Bill Mazeroski's ninth-inning home run over the left-field wall in Forbes Field, Mickey Mantle wept during the entire flight back to New York. It

sometimes seems odd, or even perverse, that intensity—the engagement of the passions—should matter in professional athletics. To
some people this seems inexplicable now that players are pulling
down such princely sums. Tommy Lasorda, manager of the Los
Angeles Dodgers, is known as a good baseball mind and an extraordinary motivator. He is often asked if it is really necessary to motivate
someone making a million dollars. Damn right, says Lasorda. To
most people, the word "motivate," when used in an athletic context,
means to inflame players the way Knute Rockne is said to have
aroused his teams at Notre Dame. Lasorda is quite capable of that.
He can be an exquisitely profane Pericles (if that is not too oxymo-
ronic). But that is not the heart of the matter. In a baseball context,
to motivate is to maintain the cool concentration and discipline
necessary for maximum performance during six months of competition in a game especially unforgiving of minor mistakes.

It is the everydayness of baseball that demands of the player a
peculiar equilibrium, a balance of relaxation and concentration.
One afternoon, during Andre Dawson's 1987 MVP season, he was
in right field in Wrigley Field and the Cubs were clobbering the
Astros, 11-1. In the top of the sixth inning Dawson ran down a foul
fly, banging into the brick wall that is right next to the foul line. In
the seventh inning he charged and made a sliding catch on a low line
drive that otherwise would have been an unimportant single. When
asked after the game why he would risk injuries in those situations
when the outcome of the game was not in doubt, Dawson replied
laconically, "Because the ball was in play." Dawson probably found
the question unintelligible. The words and syntax were clear enough
but the questioner obviously was oblivious to the mental (and moral)
world of a competitor like Dawson. At the beginning of this book I
said that baseball heroism is not a matter of flashes of brilliance;
rather, it is the quality of (in John Updike's words) "the players who
always *care,*" about themselves and their craft.

This book is a study of that sort of heroism. It is not an exercise
in hero worship. Rather, more soberly, it is an act of hero appreciation. I use the word "hero" advisedly, cognizant of the derision it
invites. We live in a relentlessly antiheroic age. Perhaps in a demo-
cratic culture there always is a leveling impulse, a desire to cut down
those who rise. Today, however, there also seems to be a small-
minded, mean-spirited resentment of those who rise, a reluctance
to give credit where it is due, a flinching from unstinting admiration,

a desire to disbelieve in the rewarded virtue of the few. We have a swamp of journalism suited to such an age, a journalism infused with a corrosive, leveling spirit.

Yet it has been said that no man is a hero to his valet, not because no man is a hero but because all valets are valets. It requires a certain largeness of spirit to give generous appreciation to large achievements. A society with a crabbed spirit and a cynical urge to discount and devalue will find that one day, when it needs to draw upon the reservoirs of excellence, the reservoirs have run dry. A society in which the capacity for warm appreciation of excellence atrophies will find that its capacity for excellence diminishes. Happiness, too, diminishes as the appreciation of excellence diminishes. That is no small loss, least of all to a nation in which the pursuit of happiness was endorsed in the founding moment.

America has been called the only nation founded on a good idea. That idea has been given many and elaborate explanations, but the most concise and familiar formulation is the pursuit of happiness. For a fortunate few people, happiness is the pursuit of excellence in a vocation. The vocation can be a profession or a craft, elite or common, poetry or carpentry. What matters most is an idea of excellence against which to measure achievement. The men whose careers are considered here exemplify the pursuit of happiness through excellence in a vocation. Fortunate people have a talent for happiness. Possession of any talent can help a person toward happiness. As Aristotle said, happiness is not a condition that is produced or stands on its own; rather, it is a frame of mind that accompanies an activity. But another frame of mind comes first. It is a steely determination to do well.

When Ted Williams, the last .400 hitter, arrived in Boston for his first season he said, with the openness of a Westerner and the innocence of a 20-year-old, "All I want out of life is that when I walk down the street folks will say, 'There goes the greatest hitter who ever lived.' " Today, if you see Williams walking down the street and you say, "There goes the greatest hitter who ever lived," you may get an argument but you will not get derision. He won 6 batting titles and lost another by one hit. (In 1949 George Kell batted .3429, Williams .3427.) He batted .406 in 1941 and .388 in 1957, when his 38-year-old legs surely cost him at least the 5 hits that would have given him his second .400 season.

The hard blue glow from people like Williams lights the path of progress in any field. I said at the outset that this was to be an antiromantic look at baseball. I meant that baseball is work. Baseball is hard and demands much drudgery. But it is neither romantic nor sentimental to say that those who pay the price of excellence in any demanding discipline are heroes. Cool realism recognizes that they are necessary. As a character says in Bernard Malamud's baseball novel *The Natural,* when we are without heroes we "don't know how far we can go."

ACKNOWLEDGMENTS

Bill Rosen of Macmillan is a splendid rarity, an editor who knows more than the writer does about the writer's subject but who is too gracious to prove it too often.

Michael Erlinger and Russ Jaeger are currently students at Georgetown University and tomorrow can be anything they want to be if they apply to their vocations the diligence that they applied to checking the numbers in this volume. Their diligence was supplemented by David Hallstrom's. Not since Tinker, Evers and Chance has such an awesome trio teamed up to stamp out errors. Mary Moschler fields line drives all day long in my office with the aplomb of a Cal Ripken, thereby making it possible for me to pay attention to him. Again, as always, I owe much (time, for example, and efficiency) to my assistant, Dusa Gyllensvard. She organized the complicated itineraries and many interviews that made this book possible. I believe that if today I said, "Dusa, I must speak with Honus Wagner," she would say "You shall," and I would. Come to think of it . . .

Gail Thorin was the closer on this project, coming in from the bull pen and getting a save. As her reward, she learned the meaning of "closer" and "save." She already knew the meaning of "bull pen," I think.

Seymour Siwoff and the other encyclopedic minds at the Elias Bureau answered every question I threw at them. Any errors remaining in this book are evidence that I did not throw enough. Concerning three subjects—the designated hitter rule, the mysterious matter of a ball player being "overdue" and the movie *Bull Durham*—I have drawn upon a few paragraphs of my writings that have appeared elsewhere.

Finally, thanks to all the baseball people—players, managers, front office personnel, writers and broadcasters—who were so generous with their time and teaching. They gave me a wide window on their world. I thank them all for admission to their society, for the benefit of their instruction and, most of all, for the pleasure of their company.

INDEX

333